# ACCA

# SBR

# Strategic Business Reporting

# Study Text

**British Library Cataloguing-in-Publication Data**

A catalogue record for this book is available from the British Library.

Published by:
Kaplan Publishing UK
Unit 2 The Business Centre
Molly Millar's Lane
Wokingham
Berkshire
RG41 2QZ

ISBN: 978-1-78740-599-8

*Acknowledgements*

These materials are reviewed by the ACCA examining team. The objective of the review is to ensure that the material properly covers the syllabus and study guide outcomes, used by the examining team in setting the exams, in the appropriate breadth and depth. The review does not ensure that every eventuality, combination or application of examinable topics is addressed by the ACCA Approved Content. Nor does the review comprise a detailed technical check of the content as the Approved Content Provider has its own quality assurance processes in place in this respect.

The IFRS Foundation logo, the IASB logo, the IFRS for SMEs logo, the "Hexagon Device", "IFRS Foundation", "eIFRS", "IAS", "IASB", "IFRS for SMEs", "IFRS", "IASs", "IFRSs", "International Accounting Standards" and "International Financial Reporting Standards", "IFRIC" and "IFRS Taxonomy" are **Trade Marks** of the IFRS Foundation.

*Trade Marks*

The IFRS Foundation logo, the IASB logo, the IFRS for SMEs logo, the "Hexagon Device", "IFRS Foundation", "eIFRS", "IAS", "IASB", "IFRS for SMEs", "NIIF IASs" "IFRS", "IFRSs", "International Accounting Standards", "International Financial Reporting Standards", "IFRIC", "SIC" and "IFRS Taxonomy".

Further details of the Trade Marks including details of countries where the Trade Marks are registered or applied for are available from the Foundation on request.

# Contents

# Introduction

This document references IFRS® Standards and IAS® Standards, which are authored by the International Accounting Standards Board (the Board), and published in the 2019 IFRS Standards Red Book.

# How to use the Materials

Strategic Business Reporting is an exam at the Strategic Professional level of the ACCA qualification. It assumes knowledge acquired at the Fundamentals level including the core technical capabilities to prepare and analyse financial reports for single and combined entities

These Kaplan Publishing learning materials have been carefully designed to make your learning experience as easy as possible and to give you the best chances of success in your examinations.

The product range contains a number of features to help you in the study process. They include:

1    Detailed study guide and syllabus objectives

2    Description of the examination

3    Study skills and revision guidance

4    Study text

5    Question practice

The sections on the study guide, the syllabus objectives, the examination and study skills should all be read before you commence your studies. They are designed to familiarise you with the nature and content of the examination and give you tips on how to best to approach your learning.

The **Study Text** comprises the main learning materials and gives guidance as to the importance of topics and where other related resources can be found. Each chapter includes:

- The **learning objectives** contained in each chapter, which have been carefully mapped to the examining body's own syllabus learning objectives or outcomes. You should use these to check you have a clear understanding of all the topics on which you might be assessed in the examination.

- The **chapter diagram** provides a visual reference for the content in the chapter, giving an overview of the topics and how they link together.

- The **content** for each topic area commences with a brief explanation or definition to put the topic into context before covering the topic in detail. You should follow your studying of the content with a review of the illustration/s. These are worked examples which will help you to understand better how to apply the content for the topic.

- **Test your understanding** sections provide an opportunity to assess your understanding of the key topics by applying what you have learned to short questions. Answers can be found at the back of each chapter.

- **Summary diagrams** complete each chapter to show the important links between topics and the overall content of the paper. These diagrams should be used to check that you have covered and understood the core topics before moving on.

- **Question practice** is provided through this text.

Quality and accuracy are of the utmost importance to us so if you spot an error in any of our products, please send an email to mykaplanreporting@kaplan.com with full details, or follow the link to the feedback form in MyKaplan.

Our Quality Coordinator will work with our technical team to verify the error and take action to ensure it is corrected in future editions.

## Icon Explanations

 **Definition** – Key definitions that you will need to learn from the core content.

 **Key point** – Identifies topics that are key to success and are often examined.

 **Supplementary reading** – These sections will help to provide a deeper understanding of core areas. The supplementary reading is **NOT** optional reading. It is vital to provide you with the breadth of knowledge you will need to address the wide range of topics within your syllabus that could feature in an exam question. **Reference to this text is vital when self studying.**

 **Test your understanding** – Exercises for you to complete to ensure that you have understood the topics just learned.

 **Illustration** – Worked examples help you understand the core content better.

 **Tutorial note** – Included to explain some of the technical points in more detail.

 **Footsteps** – Helpful tutor tips.

**Links to other syllabus areas** – This symbol refers to areas of interaction with other parts of your syllabus, either in terms of other ACCA papers that you have studied, or may go on to study, or even further professional qualifications that you may decide to pursue on completion of ACCA.

### On-line subscribers

Our on-line resources are designed to increase the flexibility of your learning materials and provide you with immediate feedback on how your studies are progressing.

If you are subscribed to our on-line resources you will find:

1    On-line referenceware: reproduces your Study Text on-line, giving you anytime, anywhere access.

2    On-line testing: provides you with additional on-line objective testing so you can practice what you have learned further.

3    On-line performance management: immediate access to your on-line testing results. Review your performance by key topics and chart your achievement through the course relative to your peer group.

Ask your local customer services staff if you are not already a subscriber and wish to join.

## Paper introduction

### Paper background

The Strategic Business Reporting (SBR) syllabus requires students to examine corporate reporting from a number of perspectives, not only from the point of view of the preparer of corporate reports, but also from the perspective of a variety of different stakeholders such as finance providers. The syllabus further requires the assessment and evaluation of the reporting decisions made by management and their implications for a range of stakeholders and entities. It also explores the professional and ethical responsibilities of the accountant to these stakeholders.

### Objectives of the syllabus

Candidates should be able to:

*    Apply fundamental ethical and professional principles to ethical dilemmas and discuss the consequences of unethical behaviour

*    Evaluate the appropriateness of the financial reporting framework and critically discuss changes in accounting regulation

*    Apply professional judgement in the reporting of the financial performance of a range of entities

*    Prepare the financial statements of groups of entities

*    Interpret financial statements for different stakeholders

*    Communicate the impact of changes and potential changes in accounting regulation on financial reporting.

KAPLAN PUBLISHING

## Syllabus

### Core areas of the syllabus

- Fundamental ethical and professional principles

- The financial reporting framework

- Reporting the financial performance of a range of entities

- Financial statements of groups of entities

- Interpret financial statements for different stakeholders

- The impact of changes and potential changes in accounting regulation

### Approach to INT and UK syllabus elements

The international syllabus has been used as the basis of this Study Text. The additional content required for those sitting the UK paper is in Chapter 24.

The UK exam primarily tests International Financial Reporting Standards. The Examiner has indicated that part of one of the Section B questions in the UK paper will be adapted to assess UK specific content. This question may be based on either a single entity or a group and will be worth 15-20 marks. It may have discursive and/or numerical content and requirements, and could cover the following syllabus areas:

- The financial reporting requirements for UK and Republic of Ireland entities (UK GAAP) and their interaction with the Companies Act requirements

- The reasons why an entity might choose to adopt FRS 101 or FRS 102

- The scope and basis of preparation of financial statements under UK GAAP

- The concepts and pervasive principles set out in FRS 102

- The principal differences between UK GAAP and International Financial Reporting Standards.

## ACCA Performance Objectives

In order to become a member of the ACCA, as a trainee accountant you will need to demonstrate that you have achieved nine performance objectives. Performance objectives are indicators of effective performance and set the minimum standard of work that trainees are expected to achieve and demonstrate in the workplace. They are divided into key areas of knowledge which are closely linked to the exam syllabus.

There are five Essential performance objectives and a choice of fifteen Technical performance objectives which are divided into five areas.

The performance objectives which link to this exam are:

1    Ethics and professionalism (Essential)

2    Stakeholder relationship management (Essential)

3    Record and process transactions and events (Technical)

4    Prepare external financial reports (Technical)

5    Analyse and interpret financial reports (Technical)

The following link provides an in depth insight into all of the performance objectives:

https://www.accaglobal.com/content/dam/ACCA_Global/Students/per/PER-Performance-objectives-achieve.pdf

KAPLAN PUBLISHING

## Progression

There are two elements of progression that we can measure: first how quickly students move through individual topics within a subject; and second how quickly they move from one course to the next. We know that there is an optimum for both, but it can vary from subject to subject and from student to student. However, using data and our experience of student performance over many years, we can make some generalisations.

A fixed period of study set out at the start of a course with key milestones is important. This can be within a subject, for example 'I will finish this topic by 30 June', or for overall achievement, such as 'I want to be qualified by the end of next year'.

Your qualification is cumulative, as earlier papers provide a foundation for your subsequent studies, so do not allow there to be too big a gap between one subject and another. We know that exams encourage techniques that lead to some degree of short term retention, the result being that you will simply forget much of what you have already learned unless it is refreshed (look up Ebbinghaus Forgetting Curve for more details on this). This makes it more difficult as you move from one subject to another: not only will you have to learn the new subject, you will also have to relearn all the underpinning knowledge as well. This is very inefficient and slows down your overall progression which makes it more likely you may not succeed at all.

In addition, delaying your studies slows your path to qualification which can have negative impacts on your career, postponing the opportunity to apply for higher level positions and therefore higher pay.

You can use the following diagram showing the whole structure of your qualification to help you keep track of your progress.

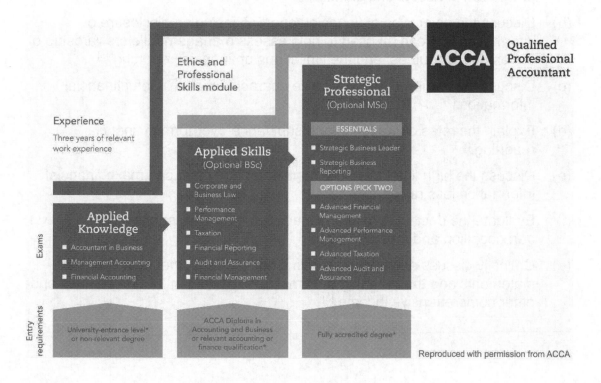

Reproduced with permission from ACCA

## Syllabus objectives

We have reproduced the ACCA's syllabus below:

## A    FUNDAMENTAL ETHICAL AND PROFESSIONAL PRINCIPLES

### 1    Professional behaviour and compliance with accounting standards

(a)    Appraise and discuss the ethical and professional issues in advising on corporate reporting.[3]

(b)    Assess the relevance and importance of ethical and professional issues in complying with accounting standards.[3]

### 2    Ethical requirements of corporate reporting and the consequences of unethical behaviour

(a)    Appraise the potential ethical implications of professional and managerial decisions in the preparation of corporate reports.[3]

(b)    Assess the consequences of not upholding ethical principles in the preparation of corporate reports.[3]

(c)    Identify related parties and assess the implications of related party relationships in the preparation of corporate reports.[3]

## B    THE FINANCIAL REPORTING FRAMEWORK

### 1    The applications, strengths and weaknesses of an accounting framework

(a)    Discuss the importance of a conceptual framework in underpinning the production of accounting standards.[3]

(b)    Discuss the objectives of financial reporting including disclosure of information that can be used to help assess management's stewardship of the entity's resources, and the limitations of financial reporting.[3]

(c)    Discuss the nature of the qualitative characteristics of useful financial information.[3]

(d)    Explain the roles of prudence and substance over form in financial reporting.[3]

(e)    Discuss the high level measurement uncertainty that can make financial information less relevant.[3]

(f)    Evaluate the decisions made by management on recognition, derecognition and measurement.[3]

(g)    Critically discuss and apply the definitions of the elements of financial statements and the reporting of items in the statement of profit or loss and other comprehensive income.[3]

## C REPORTING THE FINANCIAL PERFORMANCE OF A RANGE OF ENTITIES

### 1 Revenue

(a) Discuss and apply the criteria that must be met before an entity can apply the revenue recognition model to a contract.[3]

(b) Discuss and apply the five step model which relates to revenue earned from a contract with a customer.[3]

(c) Apply the criteria for recognition of contract costs as an asset.[3]

(d) Discuss and apply the recognition and measurement of revenue including performance obligations satisfied over time, sale with a right of return, warranties, variable consideration, principal versus agent considerations and non-refundable up-front fees.[3]

### 2 Non-current assets

(a) Discuss and apply the timing of the recognition of non-current assets and the determination of their carrying amounts including impairment and revaluations.[3]

(b) Discuss and apply the accounting requirements for the classification and measurement of non-current assets held for sale.[3]

(c) Discuss and apply the accounting treatment of investment properties including classification, recognition, measurement and change of use.[3]

(d) Discuss and apply the accounting treatment of intangible assets including the criteria for recognition and measurement subsequent to acquisition.[3]

(e) Discuss and apply the accounting treatment for borrowing costs.[3]

### 3 Financial instruments

(a) Discuss and apply the initial recognition and measurement of financial instruments.[2]

(b) Discuss and apply the subsequent measurement of financial assets and financial liabilities.[2]

(c) Discuss and apply the derecognition of financial assets and financial liabilities.[2]

(d) Discuss and apply the reclassification of financial assets.[2]

(e) Account for derivative financial instruments, and simple embedded derivatives.[2]

(f) Outline and apply the qualifying criteria for hedge accounting and account for fair value hedges and cash flow hedges including hedge effectiveness.[2]

(g) Discuss and apply the general approach to impairment of financial instruments including the basis for estimating expected credit losses.[2]

(h) Discuss the implications of a significant increase in credit risk.[2]

(i) Discuss and apply the treatment of purchased or originated credit impaired financial assets.[2]

## 4 Leases

(a) Discuss and apply the lessee accounting requirements for leases including the identification of a lease and the measurement of the right of use asset and liability.[3]

(b) Discuss and apply the accounting for leases by lessors.[3]

(c) Discuss and apply the circumstances where there may be re-measurement of the lease liability.[3]

(d) Discuss and apply the reasons behind the separation of the components of a lease contract into lease and non-lease elements.[3]

(e) Discuss the recognition exemptions under the current leasing standard.[3]

(f) Discuss and apply the principles behind accounting for sale and leaseback transactions.[3]

## 5 Employee benefits

(a) Discuss and apply the accounting treatment of short term and long term employee benefits and defined contribution and defined benefit plans.[3]

(b) Account for gains and losses on settlements and curtailments.[2]

(c) Account for the 'Asset Ceiling' test and the reporting of actuarial gains and losses.[2]

## 6 Income taxes

(a) Discuss and apply the recognition and measurement of deferred tax liabilities and deferred tax assets.[3]

(b) Discuss and apply the recognition of current and deferred tax as income or expense.[3]

(c) Discuss and apply the treatment of deferred taxation on a business combination.[2]

## 7 Provisions, contingencies, events after the reporting date

(a) Discuss and apply the recognition, de-recognition and measurement of provisions, contingent liabilities and contingent assets including environmental provisions and restructuring provisions.[3]

(b) Discuss and apply the accounting for events after the reporting period.[3]

## 8 Share-based payment

(a) Discuss and apply the recognition and measurement of share-based payment transactions.[3]

(b) Account for modifications, cancellations and settlements of share-based payment transactions.[2]

## 9 Fair value measurement

(a) Discuss and apply the definitions of 'fair value' measurement and 'active market'.[3]

(b) Discuss and apply the 'fair value hierarchy'.[3]

(c) Discuss and apply the principles of highest and best use, most advantageous and principal market.[3]

(d) Explain the circumstances where an entity may use a valuation technique.[3]

## 10 Reporting requirements of small and medium-sized entities (SMEs)

(a) Discuss the key differences in accounting treatment between full IFRS Standards and the IFRS for SMEs Standard.[3]

(b) Discuss and apply the simplifications introduced by the IFRS for SMEs Standard.[3]

## 11 Other reporting issues

(a) Discuss and apply the accounting for, and disclosure of, government grants and other forms of government assistance.[2]

(b) Discuss and apply the principles behind the initial recognition and subsequent measurement of a biological asset or agricultural produce.[2]

(c) Outline the principles behind the application of accounting policies and measurement in interim reports.[2]

(d) Discuss and apply the judgements required in selecting and applying accounting policies, accounting for changes in estimates and reflecting corrections of prior period errors.[3]

## D FINANCIAL STATEMENTS OF GROUPS OF ENTITIES

## 1 Group accounting including statements of cash flow

(a) Discuss and apply the principles behind determining whether a business combination has occurred.[2]

(b) Discuss and apply the method of accounting for a business combination including identifying an acquirer and the principles in determining the cost of a business combination.[2]

(c) Apply the recognition and measurement criteria for identifiable acquired assets and liabilities including contingent amounts and intangible assets.[3]

(d) Discuss and apply the accounting for goodwill and non-controlling interest.[3]

(e) Apply the accounting principles relating to a business combination achieved in stages.[3]

(f) Discuss and apply the application of the control principle.[3]

(g) Determine and apply appropriate procedures to be used in preparing consolidated financial statements.[3]

(h) Discuss and apply the implications of changes in ownership interest and loss of control.[3]

(i) Prepare group financial statements where activities have been discontinued, or have been acquired or disposed of in the period.[3]

(j) Discuss and apply the treatment of a subsidiary which has been acquired exclusively with a view to subsequent disposal.[2]

(k) Identify and outline the circumstances in which a group is required to prepare consolidated financial statements; the circumstances when a group may claim an exemption from the preparation of consolidated financial statements, and why directors may not wish to consolidate a subsidiary and where this is permitted.[2]

(l) Prepare and discuss group statements of cash flows.[3]

## 2 Associates and joint arrangement

(a) Identify associate entities.[3]

(b) Discuss and apply the equity method of accounting for associates.[3]

(c) Apply the method of accounting for associates.[3]

(d) Discuss and apply the application of the joint control principle.

(e) Discuss and apply the classification of joint arrangements.[3]

(f) Prepare the financial statements of parties to the joint arrangement.[3]

## 3 Changes in group structures

(a) Discuss and apply accounting for group companies in the separate financial statements of the parent company.[2]

(b) Apply the accounting principles where the parent reorganises the structure of the group by establishing a new entity or changing the parent.[2]

## 4 Foreign transactions and entities

(a) Outline and apply the translation of foreign currency amounts and transactions into the functional currency and the presentational currency.[3]

(b) Account for the consolidation of foreign operations and their disposal.[2]

## E INTERPRET FINANCIAL STATEMENTS FOR DIFFERENT STAKEHOLDERS

## 1 Analysis and interpretation of financial information and measurement of performance

(a) Discuss and apply relevant indicators of financial and non-financial performance including earnings per share and additional performance measures.[3]

(b) Discuss the increased demand for transparency in corporate reports, and the emergence of non-financial reporting standards.[3]

(c) Appraise the impact of environmental, social, and ethical factors on performance measurement.[3]

(d) Discuss the current framework for integrated reporting (IR) including the objectives, concepts, guiding principles and content of an Integrated Report.[3]

(e) Determine the nature and extent of reportable segments.[3]

(f) Discuss the nature of segment information to be disclosed and how segmental information enhances the quality and sustainability of performance.[3]

## F THE IMPACT OF CHANGES AND POTENTIAL CHANGES IN ACCOUNTING REGULATION

### 1 Discussion of solutions to current issues in financial reporting

(a) Discuss and apply the accounting implications of the first time adoption of new accounting standards.[2]

(b) Identify issues and deficiencies which have led to proposed changes to an accounting standard.[3]

(c) Discuss the impact of current issues in corporate reporting. This learning outcome may be tested by requiring the application of one or several existing standards to an accounting issue. It is also likely to require an explanation of the resulting accounting implications (for example, accounting for cryptocurrency in the Digital Age or accounting for the effects of a natural disaster and the resulting environmental liabilities).

The following examples are relevant to the current syllabus:[3]

– accounting policy changes

– materiality in the context of financial reporting

– defined benefit plan amendments, curtailment or settlement

– management commentary

– sustainability reporting

(d) Discuss developments in devising a structure for corporate reporting that addresses the needs of stakeholders.[3]

The superscript numbers in square brackets indicate the intellectual depth at which the subject area could be assessed within the examination. Level 1 (knowledge and comprehension) broadly equates with the Knowledge module, Level 2 (application and analysis) with the Skills module and Level 3 (synthesis and evaluation) to the Professional level. However, lower level skills can continue to be assessed as you progress through each module and level.

## The examination

### Examination format

The syllabus is assessed by a three-hour fifteen minute examination. It examines professional competences within the business reporting environment.

Students will be examined on concepts, theories, and principles, and on their ability to question and comment on proposed accounting treatments.

Students should be capable of relating professional issues to relevant concepts and practical situations. The evaluation of alternative accounting practices and the identification and prioritisation of issues will be a key element of the exam. Professional and ethical judgement will need to be exercised, together with the integration of technical knowledge when addressing business reporting issues in a business context.

Students will be required to adopt either a stakeholder or an external focus in answering questions and to demonstrate personal skills such as problem solving, dealing with information and decision making. Students will have to demonstrate communication skills appropriate to the scenario.

The paper also deals with specific professional knowledge appropriate to the preparation and presentation of consolidated and other financial statements from accounting data, to conform with accounting standards.

The paper will comprise two sections:

**Section A** consists of two scenario based questions that will total 50 marks. The first question will be based on the financial statements of group entities, or extracts thereof, and is also likely to require consideration of some financial reporting issues. Candidates should understand that in addition to the consideration of the numerical aspects of group accounting (max 25 marks), a discussion and explanation of these numbers will also be required. The second question in Section A will require candidates to consider (i) the reporting implications and (ii) the ethical implications of specific events in a given scenario.

Two professional marks will be awarded in the ethical issues question in Section A

**Section B** consists of two questions, which may be scenario or case-study or essay based and will contain both discursive and computational elements. Section B could deal with any aspect of the syllabus but will always include either a full question, or part of a question, that requires the appraisal of financial and/or non-financial information from either the preparer's or another stakeholder's perspective.

Two professional marks will be awarded in the Section B question that requires analysis.

**UK syllabus students** sit an exam that is identical in format to the International syllabus exam. ACCA has indicated that parts of Section B questions in the UK paper will be adapted to assess UK specific content for between 15-20 marks.

|  | Number of marks |
|---|---|
| Section A | |
| Two compulsory questions | 50 |
| Section B | |
| Two compulsory questions of 25 marks each | 50 |
|  | ——— |
| Total time allowed: 3 hours and 15 minutes | 100 |

## Strategic Professional CBE

From March 2020, ACCA introduced Strategic Professional computer based examinations (CBE) in selected locations. Strategic Professional CBE will be extended to other locations over time, across subsequent examination sessions. Once CBE are offered in a location, the paper-based exam will no longer be available. For more information regarding when Strategic Professional CBE will be introduced in your market, please refer to the ACCA Global website.

This Study Text is appropriate for both CBE and paper-based exams. It is essential that students who will be sitting the CBE become familiar with the CBE environment as part of their exam preparation. For additional support please refer to the ACCA Global website.

## Study skills and revision guidance

This section aims to give guidance on how to study for your ACCA exams and to give ideas on how to improve your existing study techniques.

### Preparing to study

### Set your objectives

Before starting to study decide what you want to achieve – the type of pass you wish to obtain. This will decide the level of commitment and time you need to dedicate to your studies.

### Devise a study plan

Determine which times of the week you will study.

Split these times into sessions of at least one hour for study of new material. Any shorter periods could be used for revision or practice.

Put the times you plan to study onto a study plan for the weeks from now until the exam and set yourself targets for each period of study – in your sessions make sure you cover the course, course assignments and revision.

If you are studying for more than one paper at a time, try to vary your subjects as this can help you to keep interested and see subjects as part of wider knowledge.

When working through your course, compare your progress with your plan and, if necessary, re-plan your work (perhaps including extra sessions) or, if you are ahead, do some extra revision/practice questions.

**Effective studying**

**Active reading**

You are not expected to learn the text by rote, rather, you must understand what you are reading and be able to use it to pass the exam and develop good practice. A good technique to use is SQ3Rs – Survey, Question, Read, Recall, Review:

(1)  **Survey the chapter** – look at the headings and read the introduction, summary and objectives, so as to get an overview of what the chapter deals with.

(2)  **Question** – whilst undertaking the survey, ask yourself the questions that you hope the chapter will answer for you.

(3)  **Read** through the chapter thoroughly, answering the questions and making sure you can meet the objectives. Attempt the exercises and activities in the text, and work through all the examples.

(4)  **Recall** – at the end of each section and at the end of the chapter, try to recall the main ideas of the section/chapter without referring to the text. This is best done after a short break of a couple of minutes after the reading stage.

(5)  **Review** – check that your recall notes are correct.

You may also find it helpful to re-read the chapter to try to see the topic(s) it deals with as a whole.

**Note-taking**

Taking notes is a useful way of learning, but do not simply copy out the text. The notes must:

- be in your own words
- be concise
- cover the key points
- be well-organised
- be modified as you study further chapters in this text or in related ones.

Trying to summarise a chapter without referring to the text can be a useful way of determining which areas you know and which you don't.

KAPLAN PUBLISHING

**Three ways of taking notes:**

**Summarise the key points of a chapter.**

**Make linear notes** – a list of headings, divided up with subheadings listing the key points. If you use linear notes, you can use different colours to highlight key points and keep topic areas together. Use plenty of space to make your notes easy to use.

**Try a diagrammatic form** – the most common of which is a mind-map. To make a mind-map, put the main heading in the centre of the paper and put a circle around it. Then draw short lines radiating from this to the main sub-headings, which again have circles around them. Then continue the process from the sub-headings to sub-sub-headings, advantages, disadvantages, etc.

**Highlighting and underlining** – you may find it useful to underline or highlight key points in your study text, but do be selective. You may also wish to make notes in the margins.

## Revision

The best approach to revision is to revise the course as you work through it. Also try to leave four to six weeks before the exam for final revision. Make sure you cover the whole syllabus and pay special attention to those areas where your knowledge is weak. Here are some recommendations:

Read through the text and your notes again and condense your notes into key phrases. It may help to put key revision points onto index cards to look at when you have a few minutes to spare.

Review any assignments you have completed and look at where you lost marks – put more work into those areas where you were weak. The SBR examining team produce detailed marking guides at the end of the solutions to past exam questions. These are available in the Exam Kit.

Practise exam standard questions under timed conditions. If you are short of time, list the points that you would cover in your answer and then read the model answer, but do try to complete at least a few questions under exam conditions.

Make sure that you read the ACCA article, 'What is the Examiner Asking?' This will help you to ensure that you fully understand what is required of you in the exam. It can be found here:

https://www.accaglobal.com/uk/en/student/sa/study-skills/questions.html

Also practise producing answer plans and comparing them to the model answer.

If you are stuck on a topic find somebody (a tutor) to explain it to you.

Read good newspapers and professional journals, especially ACCA's Student Accountant – this can give you an advantage in the exam.

Ensure you know the structure of the exam – how many questions there are, what types of question you will be expected to answer, and the time you will spend on each question. During your revision attempt all the different styles of questions you may be asked.

**Further reading**

The examining team have stated the need for students to read widely.

Technical articles relevant to SBR can be found on the ACCA website at the following address:

https://www.accaglobal.com/uk/en/student/exam-support-resources/professional-exams-study-resources/strategic-business-reporting/technical-articles.html

Please be aware that ACCA update their list of examinable documents annually. You should refer to this before undertaking any further reading.

# Frameworks

## Chapter learning objectives

Upon completion of this chapter you will be able to:

- Discuss the importance of a conceptual framework in underpinning the production of accounting standards

- Discuss the objectives of financial reporting including disclosure of information that can be used to help assess management's stewardship of the entity's resources and the limitations of financial reporting

- Discuss the nature of the qualitative characteristics of useful financial information

- Explain the roles of prudence and substance over form in financial reporting

- Discuss the high level measurement uncertainty that can make financial information less relevant

- Evaluate the decisions made by management on recognition, derecognition and measurement

- Critically discuss and apply the definitions of the elements of financial statements

- Discuss and apply the definitions of 'fair value' measurement and 'active market'

- Discuss and apply the 'fair value hierarchy'

- Discuss and apply the principles of highest and best use, most advantageous and principal market

- Explain the circumstances where an entity may use a valuation technique.

**PER**

One of the PER performance objectives (PO7) is to prepare external financial reports. You take part in preparing and reviewing financial statements – and all accompanying information – and you do it in accordance with legal and regulatory requirements. Working through this chapter should help you understand how to demonstrate that objective.

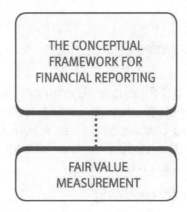

## 1 Introduction

This chapter considers two documents issued by the International Accounting Standards Board (the Board) that underpin a range of IFRS and IAS Standards:

- The *Conceptual Framework for Financial Reporting* – used by the Board when developing or revising an IFRS or IAS Standard, and by preparers of financial statements when no relevant IFRS or IAS Standard exists, and

- IFRS 13 *Fair Value Measurement* – used by preparers of financial statements when an IFRS or IAS Standard requires or allows the use of a fair value measurement (with some exceptions).

 **Progression**

You will have seen the content of this chapter in your prior studies. However, the ACCA SBR exam will test it at a much higher level.

## 2 *Conceptual Framework for Financial Reporting*

### Introduction

### The importance of a conceptual framework

A conceptual framework is a set of theoretical principles and concepts that underlie the preparation and presentation of financial statements.

If no conceptual framework existed, then accounting standards would be produced on a haphazard basis as particular issues and circumstances arose. These accounting standards might be inconsistent with one another, or perhaps even contradictory.

A strong conceptual framework means that there are principles in place from which all future accounting standards draw. It also acts as a reference point for the preparers of financial statements if no accounting standard governs a particular transaction (although this will be extremely rare).

This section of the text considers the contents of the *Conceptual Framework for Financial Reporting* (*Conceptual Framework*) in more detail.

## Background

The *Framework for the Presentation and Preparation of Financial Statements* was issued in 1989.

In 2004 the Board and the US Financial Accounting Standards Board (FASB) started a joint project to revise their respective frameworks. As a result of this project the Board issued the *Conceptual Framework for Financial Reporting* in 2010. Most of the text from the 1989 *Framework* was simply rolled over but two chapters were revised. These covered:

- The objective of financial reporting

- The qualitative characteristics of useful financial information.

The Board and the FASB subsequently suspended work on this joint project.

Several criticisms emerged of the 2010 *Conceptual Framework*

- It did not cover certain areas, such as derecognition, and presentation and disclosure

- Guidance in some areas was unclear, such as with regards to measurement uncertainty

- Some aspects were out of date, such as recognition criteria for assets and liabilities.

As a result of criticism, the *Conceptual Framework* was identified as a priority project so, in 2012, the Board restarted this project without the FASB.
A Discussion Paper outlining the Board's thinking was published in 2013 and an Exposure Draft of the proposed amendments was published in 2015. Feedback from these documents informed the revised *Conceptual Framework*, which was published in 2018.

## The purpose of the *Conceptual Framework*

The purpose of the *Conceptual Framework* is to assist:

(a)  **the Board** when developing new IFRS Standards, helping to ensure that these are based on consistent concepts

(b)  **preparers of financial statements** when no IFRS Standard applies to a particular transaction, or when an IFRS Standard offers a choice of accounting policy

(c)  **all parties** when understanding and interpreting IFRS Standards.

The *Conceptual Framework* is not an accounting standard. It does not override the requirements in a particular IFRS Standard.

## The objective of financial reporting

The *Conceptual Framework* states that the purpose of financial reporting is to provide information to current and potential investors, lenders and other creditors that will enable them to make decisions about providing economic resources to an entity.

If investors, lenders and creditors are going to make these decisions then they require information that will help them to assess:

- an entity's potential future cash flows, and

- management's stewardship of the entity's economic resources.

To assess an entity's future cash flows, users need information about:

- economic resources of the entity e.g. assets

- economic claims against the entity e.g. liabilities and equity

- changes in economic resources and claims e.g. income and expenses.

**Summary of the content of the Conceptual Framework**

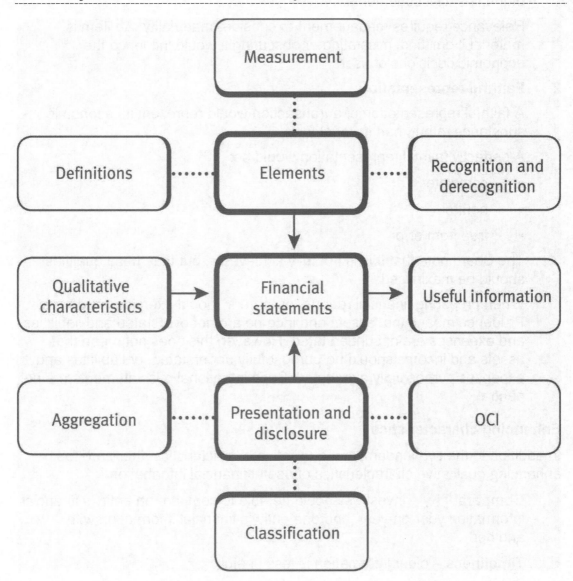

## Qualitative characteristics of useful financial information

### Fundamental characteristics

The *Conceptual Framework* states that financial information is only useful if it is:

- relevant
- a faithful representation of an entity's transactions.

Relevance and faithful representation are the **fundamental characteristics** of useful financial information.

**1 Relevance**

Relevant information will make an impact on the decisions made by users of the financial statements.

Relevance requires management to consider materiality. An item is material if omitting, misstating or obscuring it would influence the economic decisions of users.

**2 Faithful representation**

A faithful representation of a transaction would represent its economic substance rather than its legal form.

A perfectly faithful representation would be:

- complete
- neutral
- free from error.

The Board note that this is not fully achievable, but that these qualities should be maximised.

When preparing financial reports, preparers should exercise **prudence**. Prudence means that assets and income are not overstated and liabilities and expenses are not understated. However, this does not mean that assets and income should be purposefully understated, or liabilities and expenses purposefully overstated. Such intentional misstatements are not neutral.

### Enhancing characteristics

In addition to the two fundamental qualitative characteristics, there are four enhancing qualitative characteristics of useful financial information:

- **Comparability** – investors should be able to compare an entity's financial information year-on-year, and one entity's financial information with another.

- **Timeliness** – older information is less useful.

- **Verifiability** – knowledgeable users should be able to agree that a particular depiction of a transaction offers a faithful representation.

- **Understandability** – information should be presented as clearly and concisely as possible.

## Cost constraint

Producing financial reports takes time and costs money.

When developing IFRS Standards, the Board assesses whether the benefits of reporting particular information outweigh the costs involved in providing it.

### Cost constraint – an example

IFRS 16 *Leases,* which replaced IAS 17 *Leases,* radically changed lessee accounting by requiring all lessees to recognise an asset and liability at the inception of a lease (unless the lease is short-term or of minimal value). However, IFRS 16 did not change the accounting treatment of leases by lessors. This was because most stakeholders did not believe that the requirements relating to lessors in IAS 17 were 'broken'. The perceived time and costs involved in implementing substantial changes to lessor accounting was therefore believed to outweigh any benefits.

## Financial statements and the reporting entity

### Financial statements

The *Conceptual Framework* notes that financial statements are a particular type of financial report.

The purpose of financial statements is to provide information to users about an entity's:

*   assets
*   liabilities
*   equity
*   income
*   expenses.

This information is provided in:

*   a statement of financial position
*   statements of financial performance
*   other statements, such as statements of cash flows and notes.

Financial statements are prepared on the assumption that the entity is a **going concern**. This means that it will continue to operate for the foreseeable future. If this assumption is not accurate, then the financial statements should be prepared on a different basis.

## The reporting entity

A reporting entity is one that prepares financial statements (either through choice, or as a result of legal requirements).

Financial statements produced for two or more entities that are not parent/subsidiaries are called 'combined financial statements'. It can be difficult in these circumstances to determine the boundary of the reporting entity. Note that the *Conceptual Framework* does not stipulate how or when to prepare combined financial statements, although the Board may develop a standard on this issue in the future.

Financial statements produced for a reporting entity that comprises a parent company and its subsidiaries are called 'consolidated financial statements'. These financial statements show the parent and its subsidiaries as a single economic entity. This information is important for investors in the parent because their economic returns are dependent on distributions from the subsidiary to the parent.

Unconsolidated financial statements also provide useful information to investors in a parent company (for example, about the level of distributable reserves) but they are not a substitute for information provided in consolidated financial statements.

## The elements of financial statements

The elements are the building blocks of financial statements:

- statements of financial position report assets, liabilities and equity

- statements of financial performance report income and expenses.

| Economic resource | Asset | **'A present economic resource controlled by an entity as a result of a past event'** (para 4.3). |
|---|---|---|
| Economic claim | Liability | **'A present obligation of the entity to transfer an economic resource as a result of a past event'** (para 4.26). |
| | Equity | The residual interest in the net assets of an entity. |

| Changes in economic resources and claims as a result of financial performance | Income | Increases in assets or decreases in liabilities that result in an increase to equity (excluding contributions from equity holders). |
|---|---|---|
| | Expenses | Decreases in assets or increases in liabilities that result in decreases to equity (excluding distributions to equity holders). |
| Other changes in economic resources and claims | | Contributions from, and distributions to, equity holders. Exchanges of assets and liabilities that do not increase or decrease equity. |

An economic resource is a '**right that has the potential to produce economic benefits**' (para 4.4).

## Recognition and derecognition

### Recognition

Items are only recognised in the financial statements if they meet the definition of one of the elements. However, not all items meeting these definitions are recognised.

Elements are recognised if recognition provides users with useful financial information. In other words recognition must provide:

- relevant information
- a faithful representation of the asset or liability, and resulting income, expenses or equity movements.

Recognition might not provide relevant information if there is uncertainty over the existence of the element or if there is a low probability of an inflow or outflow of economic resources.

**Recognition – an example**

IAS 37 *Provisions, Contingent Liabilities and Contingent Assets* prohibits recognition of contingent liabilities and assets because it is not probable that resources will flow from or to the reporting entity.

Recognition of an element might not provide a faithful representation if there is a very high degree of measurement uncertainty.

Judgement is required in deciding if recognition of an element is appropriate. This is why specific recognition criteria vary from one IFRS Standard to another.

If an asset or liability is not recognised, disclosures may be required to ensure users fully understand the reporting entity's economic transactions and the implications that these may have on future earnings and future cash flows.

> ### Test your understanding 1 – Bottle
>
> Bottle operates in the publishing industry. The Bottle brand is highly respected and, as a result, the books published by Bottle receive extensive coverage both online and in national and international press. The brand is internally generated and, in accordance with IAS 38 *Intangible Assets*, is not recognised in Bottle's financial statements.
>
> **Required:**
>
> **Discuss the extent to which the accounting treatment of the Bottle brand is consistent with the *Conceptual Framework*.**

### Derecognition

Derecognition is the removal of some or all of an asset or liability from the statement of financial position. This normally occurs when the entity:

- loses control of the asset, or

- has no present obligation for the liability.

Accounting for derecognition should faithfully represent the changes in an entity's net assets, as well as any assets or liabilities retained.

This is achieved by:

- derecognising any transferred, expired or consumed component

- recognising a gain or loss on the above, and

- recognising any retained component.

Sometimes an entity might appear to have transferred an asset or liability. However, derecognition would not be appropriate if exposure to variations in the element's economic benefits is retained.

**Derecognition – an example**

An entity sells a building for $2 million and retains the right to buy it back for $3 million in five years' time. At the date of sale, the building had a fair value of $7 million. Property prices are expected to rise.

The entity does not derecognise the building from its statement of financial position. The entity has not lost control over the building because its ability to buy the building back for substantially less than fair value enables it to benefit from future price rises.

The cash received would be recognised as a loan liability.

## Measurement

When recognised in the financial statements, elements must be quantified in monetary terms.

The *Conceptual Framework* outlines two broad measurement bases:

- Historical cost
- Current value (this includes fair value, value-in-use, and current cost).

### Selecting a measurement base

The information provided to users by the measurement base must be useful. In other words it must be relevant and offer a faithful representation of the transactions that have occurred.

When selecting a measurement basis, the *Conceptual Framework* states that relevance is maximised if the following are considered:

- The characteristics of the asset and/or liability
- The ways in which the asset and/or liability contribute to future cash flows.

This applies to the Board when developing or revising an IFRS Standard. It also applies to preparers of financial statements when applying an IFRS Standard that permits a choice of measurement bases.

**Selecting a measurement basis – an example**

Mist purchases an investment property in a prime location. Property prices are increasing in this area. As such, the value of the property is susceptible to market factors, and could substantially differ from the initial purchase price paid by Mist.

> IAS 40 *Investment Property* offers a choice of accounting policy. Mist might choose:
>
> - The fair value model if they intend to sell the asset because this most faithfully represents the future cash flows they will receive from its eventual disposal
>
> - The cost model if they have no intention of selling the property because this best matches the rental income generated with the cost of the asset.
>
> Note that Mist might have no intention of selling the asset but still conclude that the fair value model provides the most relevant information about the building to financial statement users. This might be because increases in property prices will enable Mist to charge higher rents to its tenants, thus contributing to greater net cash inflows.

## Presentation and disclosure

### Effective presentation and disclosure

Effective presentation and disclosure is a balance between allowing entities to flexibly report relevant information about their financial performance and position, and requiring information that enables comparisons to be drawn year-on-year and with other entities.

The Board believes that:

- entity specific information is more useful than standardised descriptions

- duplication makes financial information less understandable.

### Classification

Classification of an asset or liability into separate components may provide relevant information if the components have different characteristics.

**Classification – an example**

At the reporting date, Bottled owed $10 million to a bank.

$1 million of this loan is due for repayment within 12 months and is presented as a current liability.

The remaining $9 million is presented as a non-current liability.

Classifying the liability in this way provides additional information to users, which helps them to assess Bottled's future cash flows, as well as its solvency.

Offsetting classifies dissimilar items together and is therefore generally not appropriate.

## Classification – an example

Ellipsis has $3 million in an account held with Animal Bank. This money earns 1% interest per year. The balance is presented in Ellipsis' statement of financial position as a current asset.

Ellipsis also has a $1 million overdraft in an account held with Sotoro Bank. This incurs an interest charge of 10% a year. This overdraft is presented in Ellipsis' statement of financial position as a current liability.

Ellipsis must not offset its $3 million cash balance with its $1 million overdraft e.g. it cannot show a net $2 million current asset. The cash balance and the overdraft have different characteristics and risks, and offsetting would obscure these differences. Separate classification provides relevant information to the users of the financial statements.

## Aggregation

Aggregation refers to the adding together of items that have shared characteristics.

Aggregation is useful because it summarises information that would otherwise be too detailed. However, too much aggregation obscures relevant information.

Different levels of aggregation will be required throughout the financial statements. For example, the statement of profit or loss may be heavily aggregated, but accompanying disclosure notes will disaggregate the information.

## Profit or loss and other comprehensive income

The *Conceptual Framework* states that the statement of profit or loss is the primary source of information about an entity's financial performance. As such, income and expenses should normally be recognised in this statement.

When developing or revising standards, the Board notes that it might require an income or expense to be presented in other comprehensive income if it results from remeasuring an item to current value and if this means that:

- profit or loss provides more relevant information, or
- a more faithful representation is provided of an entity's performance.

Income and expenditure included in other comprehensive income should be reclassified to profit or loss when doing so results in profit or loss providing more relevant information. However, the Board may decide that reclassification is not appropriate if there is no clear basis for identifying the amount or timing of the reclassification.

**Other comprehensive income – an example**

Entity A owns land and buildings that are accounted for using the revaluation model in IAS 16 *Property, Plant and Equipment*. At the reporting date, Entity A revalued these assets from $250 million to $300 million. IAS 16 stipulates that the $50 million gain must be recognised in other comprehensive income.

Property, plant and equipment is not held for trading, but is instead used over more than one period to produce, supply, store and distribute goods. Including this $50 million gain in profit or loss would not offer a faithful representation of Entity A's financial performance during the period.

**Test your understanding 2 – Cryptocurrencies**

Cryptocurrencies are digital currencies that operate independently of a central bank. Some businesses now accept cryptocurrencies in place of traditional currencies.

The market price of cryptocurrency is highly volatile. Investors can earn large returns by buying cryptocurrency on an exchange when the quoted price is low and selling on an exchange when the quoted price rises.

Cryptocurrencies have proved problematic with regards to financial reporting because they do not seem to fall within the scope of an issued IFRS or IAS Standard. As such, preparers of financial statements must use the *Conceptual Framework* to devise an accounting treatment that provides useful information to financial statement users.

**Required:**

**Using the *Conceptual Framework*, discuss how an entity might account for an investment in cryptocurrency that it holds to trade.**

## Criticisms of financial reporting

The *Conceptual Framework* provides a principles-based approach to financial reporting. However, users are increasingly critical of the very nature of financial reporting. As a result, new forms of non-financial reporting have emerged, which are discussed later in this text.

Some of the criticisms of financial reporting are discussed below.

### Historical information

The statement of profit or loss shows the performance of the entity over the past reporting period. However, investors are more interested in future profits. Moreover by the time financial statements are published, the information presented will be several months out of date.

KAPLAN PUBLISHING

### Unrecognised assets and liabilities

Some assets and liabilities are not recognised in financial statements prepared using IFRS Standards, such as internally generated goodwill. A company's reputation and its employee's skills play a pivotal role in its success but these are unrepresented on the statement of financial position.

### Clutter

Financial reports have been criticised in recent years for becoming increasingly cluttered as a result of extensive disclosure requirements. These disclosures can be very generic and they make it harder for the users to find relevant information.

### Financial/non-financial information

Current and past profits and cash flows are not the only determinate of future success. Long-term success is also dependent on how an entity is governed, the risks to which it is exposed and how well these are managed, and whether its business activities are sustainable into the medium and long-term. Financial statements prepared in accordance with IFRS Standards say little about these areas.

### Estimates

Financial reporting uses many estimates (e.g. depreciation rates). Estimates are subjective and could be manipulated in order to achieve particular profit targets. The subjective nature of estimates reduces comparability between companies.

The statement of cash flows somewhat compensates for the impact of accounting estimates. However, the cash position of an entity can also be window-dressed (such as by delaying payments to suppliers).

### Professional judgement

Financial reporting requires judgement. For example, judgement is required by lessors when classifying a lease as a finance lease or an operating lease. Subjective decisions reduce comparability and increase the risk of bias.

### Use of historical cost

Some accounting standards, such as IAS 16 *Property, Plant and Equipment*, permit assets to be measured at historical cost. In times of rising prices, the statement of profit or loss will not show a sustainable level of profit.

### Policy choices

Some standards, such as IAS 16 *Property, Plant and Equipment* and IAS 40 *Investment Properties*, allow entities to choose between cost and fair value models. This makes it harder to investors to compare financial statements on a like-for-like basis.

## 3 IFRS 13 *Fair Value Measurement*

### Introduction

The objective of IFRS 13 is to provide a single source of guidance for fair value measurement where it is required by a reporting standard, rather than it being spread throughout several reporting standards.

Many accounting standards require or allow items to be measured at fair value. Some examples from your prior studies include:

- IAS 16 *Property, Plant and Equipment*, which allows entities to measure property, plant and equipment at fair value

- IFRS 3 *Business Combinations*, which requires the identifiable net assets of a subsidiary to be measured at fair value at the acquisition date.

### Scope

IFRS 13 does not apply to:

- share-based payment transactions (IFRS 2 *Share-based Payments*)

- leases (IFRS 16 *Leases*).

 **The definition of fair value**

Fair value is defined as **'the price that would be received to sell an asset or paid to transfer a liability in an orderly transaction between market participants at the measurement** date' (IFRS 13, para 9).

Market participants are knowledgeable, third parties. When pricing an asset or a liability, they would take into account:

- Condition

- Location

- Restrictions on use.

It should be assumed that market participants are not forced into transactions (i.e. they are not suffering from cash flow shortages).

IFRS 13 notes that there are various approaches to determining the fair value of an asset or liability:

- Market approaches (valuations based on recent sales prices)

- Cost approaches (valuations based on replacement cost)

- Income approaches (valuations based on financial forecasts).

Whatever approach is taken, the aim is always the same – to estimate the price that would be transferred in a transaction with a market participant.

## The price

Fair value is a market-based measurement, not one that is entity specific. As such, when determining the price at which an asset would be sold (or the price paid to transfer a liability), observable data from active markets should be used where possible.

An **active market** is a market where transactions for the asset or liability occur frequently.

IFRS 13 classifies inputs into valuation techniques into three levels.

- **Level 1** inputs are quoted prices for identical assets in active markets.

- **Level 2** inputs are observable prices that are not level 1 inputs. This may include:

    - Quoted prices for similar assets in active markets

    - Quoted prices for identical assets in less active markets

    - Observable inputs that are not prices (such as interest rates).

- **Level 3** inputs are unobservable. This could include cash or profit forecasts using an entity's own data.

    A significant adjustment to a level 2 input would lead to it being categorised as a level 3 input.

Priority is given to level 1 inputs. The lowest priority is given to level 3 inputs.

 **Inputs to determine fair value**

IFRS 13 gives the following examples of inputs used to determine fair value:

|  | Asset | Example |
|---|---|---|
| **Level 1** | Equity shares in a listed entity | Unadjusted quoted prices in an active market. |
| **Level 2** | Building held and used | Price per square metre for the building from observable market data, such as observed transactions for similar buildings in similar locations. |
| **Level 3** | Cash-generating unit | Profit or cash flow forecast using own data. |

## Test your understanding 3 – Baklava

Baklava has an investment property that is measured at fair value. This property is rented out on short-term leases.

The directors wish to fair value the property by estimating the present value of the net cash flows that the property will generate for Baklava. They argue that this best reflects the way in which the building will generate economic benefits for Baklava.

The building is unique, although there have been many sales of similar buildings in the local area.

**Required:**

**Discuss whether the valuation technique suggested by the directors complies with International Financial Reporting Standards.**

## Markets

The price received when an asset is sold (or paid when a liability is transferred) may differ depending on the specific market where the transaction occurs.

### Principal market

IFRS 13 says that fair value should be measured by reference to the **principal market**.

The principal market is the market with the greatest activity for the asset or liability being measured.

The entity must be able to access the principal market at the measurement date. This means that the principal market for the same asset can differ between entities.

### Most advantageous market

If there is no principal market, then fair value is measured by reference to prices in the most advantageous market.

The most advantageous market is the one that maximises the net amount received from selling an asset (or minimises the amount paid to transfer a liability).

Transaction costs (such as legal and broker fees) will play a role in deciding which market is most advantageous. However, fair value is not adjusted for transaction costs because they are a characteristic of the market, rather than the asset.

**Test your understanding 4 – Markets**

An asset is sold in two different active markets at different prices. An entity enters into transactions in both markets and can access the price in those markets for the asset at the measurement date as follows:

|  | Market 1 $ | Market 2 $ |
| --- | --- | --- |
| Price | 26 | 25 |
| Transaction costs | (3) | (1) |
| Transport costs | (2) | (2) |
| Net price received | 21 | 22 |

**What is the fair value of the asset if:**

**(a)    market 1 is the principal market for the asset?**

**(b)    no principal market can be determined?**

## Non-financial assets

### What is a non-financial asset?

The difference between financial and non-financial assets is covered in detail in Chapter 12. Financial assets include:

- Contractual rights to receive cash (such as receivables)

- Investments in equity shares.

Non-financial assets include:

- Property, plant and equipment

- Intangible assets.

### The fair value of a non-financial asset

IFRS 13 says that the fair value of a non-financial asset should be based on its **highest and best use**.

The highest and best use of an asset is the use that a market participant would adopt in order to maximise its value.

The current use of a non-financial asset can be assumed to be the highest and best use, unless evidence exists to the contrary.

The highest and best use should take into account uses that are:

- physically possible

- legally permissible

- financially feasible.

IFRS 13 says a use can be legally permissible even if it is not legally approved.

## Test your understanding 5 – Five Quarters

Five Quarters has purchased 100% of the ordinary shares of Three Halves and is trying to determine the fair value of the net assets at the acquisition date.

Three Halves owns land that is currently developed for industrial use. The fair value of the land if used in a manufacturing operation is $5 million.

Many nearby plots of land have been developed for residential use (as high-rise apartment buildings). The land owned by Three Halves does not have planning permission for residential use, although permission has been granted for similar plots of land. The fair value of Three Halves' land as a vacant site for residential development is $6 million. However, transformation costs of $0.3 million would need to be incurred to get the land into this condition.

**Required:**

**How should the fair value of the land be determined?**

## Investor perspective

Below is an extract from a disclosure note about the fair value of an entity's financial assets and liabilities:

**Fair value of financial instruments**

|  | Level 1 $m | Level 2 $m | Level 3 $m |
|---|---|---|---|
| Financial asset – traded equities | 110 | – | – |
| Financial liability – contingent consideration | – | – | 33 |

*The fair values of the traded equities have been determined by reference to market price quotations.*

*The fair value of contingent consideration is estimated based on the forecast future performance of the acquired business over a timeframe determined as part of the acquisition agreement, discounted as appropriate. Key assumptions include growth rates, expected selling volumes and prices and direct costs during the period.*

This disclosure informs investors that the fair value of investments in equities has been derived using level 1 inputs (quoted prices for identical assets in active markets). This measurement required no judgement, eliminating the risk of bias, and can be verified by knowledgeable third parties.

In contrast, the disclosure informs investors that the fair value of the contingent liability has been derived using level 3 inputs. This measurement therefore involved a high level of judgement, increasing the risk of management bias. There is also a risk that the amount the entity eventually pays will differ materially from the year-end carrying amount. For this reason, the disclosure provides additional information about how management have estimated the fair value of the liability, so that the investors can assess the adequacy of the methodology used and reach a conclusion as to whether the level of measurement uncertainty is acceptable to them.

Due to the level of risk, some investors may decide to sell their shares in an entity if its fair value measurements are overly reliant on level 3 inputs.

**Test your understanding 6 – IFRS 13 and the *Conceptual Framework***

The *Conceptual Framework* says that the purpose of financial reporting is to provide useful financial information to users of the financial statements.

**Required:**

**Discuss how the application of IFRS 13 enhances the usefulness of financial information. Your answer should refer to the qualitative characteristics of useful financial information.**

## 4 Chapter summary

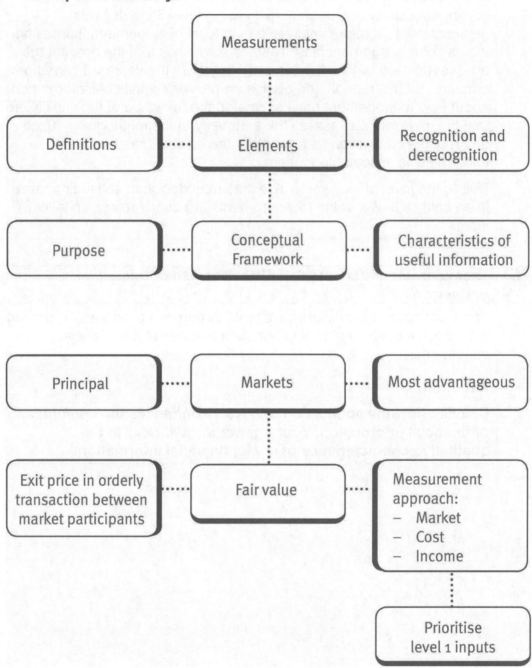

## Test your understanding answers

### Test your understanding 1 – Bottle

The brand is an economic resource controlled by Bottle. It has the potential to bring economic benefits because of the exposure that Bottle-branded books receive.

Despite meeting the definition of an element, the brand is not recognised in the financial statements. However, the *Conceptual Framework* states that elements should only be recognised if this provides relevant information, or a faithful representation of the asset or liability. If there is a high degree of measurement uncertainty then recognition may not provide a faithful representation.

The cost of an internally generated brand cannot be reliably measured. This is because the costs of setting up and developing the brand cannot be separated from the operating costs of the business. The fair value of a brand is also very difficult to determine because brands are unique.

Thus, it would seem that the accounting treatment of the brand, per IAS 38 *Intangible Assets*, is consistent with the *Conceptual Framework*.

### Test your understanding 2 – Cryptocurrencies

One of the purposes of the *Conceptual Framework* is to assist preparers of financial statements when no IFRS Standard applies to a particular transaction.

The definition of an asset in the *Conceptual Framework* is an economic resource controlled by an entity from a past event. Cryptocurrency meets this definition because it can be traded or used to buy goods and therefore have the potential of producing economic benefits.

Items should be recognised in the financial statements if they meet the definition of an element and if recognition provides relevant information and a faithful representation of the underlying item. If cryptocurrency is traded then information about such investments will help users when assessing an entity's future cash flows. As such, recognition is appropriate.

When measuring elements, the *Conceptual Framework* outlines two broad measurement bases:

- historical cost, and

- current value.

When selecting a measurement basis, the *Conceptual Framework* states that relevance is maximised if the following are considered:

- The characteristics of the asset and/or liability

- The ways in which the asset and/or liability contribute to future cash flows.

In terms of future cash flows, many entities sell investments in cryptocurrency in order to benefit from fair value gains. However, the historical cost of cryptocurrency may differ significantly from its current value. As such, the shareholders of an entity that trades in cryptocurrency are likely to be interested in the current value of the investment because the eventual sale will have a significant impact on future net cash flows. Moreover, under historical cost, information about value changes is not normally reported until disposal. Therefore it would seem that a measurement based on current value – such as fair value – will provide relevant and timely information to shareholders.

The *Conceptual Framework* notes that profit or loss is the primary source of information about an entity's economic performance. However, income and expense might be reported in other comprehensive income if it results from remeasuring an item to current value and if this means that:

- profit or loss provides more relevant information, or

- a more faithful representation is provided of an entity's performance.

Whilst the value of cryptocurrency is highly volatile, that value is likely to be extracted from a short-term sale. As such, it would seem that reporting gains and losses in profit or loss would provide the most relevant information about economic performance in the period.

In conclusion, by applying the *Conceptual Framework*, an appropriate accounting treatment for an investment in cryptocurrency would be to remeasure the investment to fair value at the reporting date and to present the resulting income or expense in the statement of profit or loss.

### Test your understanding 3 – Baklava

The directors' estimate of the future net cash flows that the building will generate is a level 3 input. IFRS 13 gives lowest priority to level 3 inputs. These should not be used if level 1 or level 2 inputs exist.

Observable data about the recent sales prices of similar properties is a level 2 input. The fair value of the building should therefore be based on these prices, with adjustments made as necessary to reflect the specific location and condition of Baklava's building.

## Test your understanding 4 – Markets

(a)  If Market 1 is the principal market then the fair value would be measured using the price that would be received in that market less transport costs. The fair value would therefore be $24 ($26 – $2). Transaction costs are ignored as they are not a characteristic of the asset.

(b)  If neither market is the principal market for the asset then the fair value would be measured in the most advantageous market. The most advantageous market is the market that maximises the net amount received from the sale.

   The net amount received in Market 2 ($22) is higher than the net amount received in Market 1 ($21). Market 2 is therefore the most advantageous market. This results in a fair value measurement of $23 ($25 – $2). IFRS 13 specifies that transaction costs play a role when determining which market is most advantageous but that they are not factored into the fair value measurement itself.

## Test your understanding 5 – Five Quarters

Land is a non-financial asset. IFRS 13 says that the fair value of a non-financial asset should be based on its highest and best use. This is presumed to be its current use, unless evidence exists to the contrary.

The current use of the asset would suggest a fair value of $5 million.

However, there is evidence that market participants would be interested in developing the land for residential use.

Residential use of the land is not legally prohibited. Similar plots of land have been granted planning permission, so it is likely that this particular plot of land will also be granted planning permission.

If used for residential purposes, the fair value of the land would be $5.7 million ($6m – $0.3m).

It would seem that the land's highest and best use is for residential development. Its fair value is therefore $5.7 million.

**Test your understanding 6 – IFRS 13 and the *Conceptual Framework***

To be useful, financial information must be relevant and provide a faithful representation of the transaction that an entity has entered into. A completely faithful representation is complete, neutral and free from error.

Measuring items at fair value is often argued to provide relevant information to an entity's stakeholders. However, IFRS 13 does not specify when assets or liabilities should be measured at fair value – this is governed by other IFRS and IAS Standards.

When measuring fair value, IFRS 13 requires entities to use a level 1 input when available – quoted prices for identical assets in active markets. These inputs require no judgement and so the resulting measurement should be neutral.

The prioritisation of observable inputs in IFRS 13 – both level 1 and level 2 – mean that the resulting valuations are verifiable.

IFRS 13 enhances comparability between entities. For example, management estimates – level 3 inputs – should only be used if no other inputs are available. Similarly, IFRS 13 requires entities to measure fair value from the perspective of a market participant, rather than an individual entity, which will aid investors when comparing one entity with another. Requirements to measure fair value using the principal market, and to base the fair value of non-financial assets using the highest and best use, reduce the scope for management bias and ensure that entities are determining fair value consistently.

Requirements to disclose estimation methods when a fair value is determined using level 3 inputs help ensure that financial statements are understandable.

# The professional and ethical duty of the accountant

## Chapter learning objectives

Upon completion of this chapter you will be able to:

- Appraise and discuss the ethical and professional issues in advising on corporate reporting

- Assess the relevance and importance of ethical and professional issues in complying with accounting standards

- Appraise the potential ethical implications of professional and managerial decisions in the preparation of corporate reports

- Assess the consequences of not upholding ethical principles in the preparation of corporate reports.

**PER**

One of the PER performance objectives (PO2) is ethics and professionalism. You need to take into account all relevant information and use professional judgement, your personal values and scepticism to evaluate data and make decisions. You should identify right from wrong and escalate anything of concern. You also need to make sure that your skills, knowledge and behaviour are up-to-date and allow you to be effective in your role. Working through this chapter should help you understand how to demonstrate that objective.

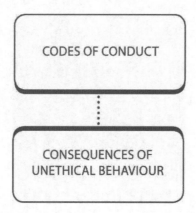

## 1 Introduction

A number of user groups rely on the financial statements to make economic decisions. It is important that these users are not misled.

The ethical beliefs of individual accountants may be too simplistic when dealing with real-life, complex ethical dilemmas. Accountants must study ethics in order to develop skills that help them to decide on the right course of action.

> **Progression**
>
> Ethics was a fundamental component of the Audit and Assurance syllabus. It is also central to Strategic Business Leader and Advanced Audit and Assurance.

## 2 Approaches to accounting and ethics

### Rules

Some national accounting standards are primarily **rules based**. In other words, they provide extensive and detailed guidance about the accounting treatment of particular transactions.

This approach is sometimes criticised for nurturing a 'rule-book mentality'. Complying with the letter of the law rather than the spirit of the accounting standard may actually prevent transactions from being faithfully represented.

### Principles

IFRS Standards are often **principles based**, albeit with some detailed rules in place to eliminate uncertainties and to increase comparability.

Principles-based approaches to accounting create ethical challenges because of the professional judgement that accountants are required to exercise. An understanding of ethical principles, such as those contained in the ACCA *Code of Ethics and Conduct*, is essential.

## 3 Ethical codes

### The code of ethics and conduct

The ACCA requires its members to adhere to a code of professional ethics. This provides a set of moral guidelines for professional accountants.

The fundamental principles of this code are:

(a) **Integrity** – to be straightforward and honest in all professional and business relationships.

(b) **Objectivity** – to not allow bias, conflict of interest or undue influence of others to override professional or business judgments.

(c) **Professional Competence and Due Care** – to maintain professional knowledge and skill at the level required to ensure that a client or employer receives competent professional services based on current developments in practice, legislation and techniques and act diligently and in accordance with applicable technical and professional standards.

(d) **Confidentiality** – to respect the confidentiality of information acquired as a result of professional and business relationships and, therefore, not disclose any such information to third parties without proper and specific authority, unless there is a legal or professional right or duty to disclose, nor use the information for the personal advantage of the professional accountant or third parties.

(e) **Professional behaviour** – to comply with relevant laws and regulations and avoid any action that discredits the profession.

### Integrity and objectivity

There are times when an accountant may have an incentive to misrepresent the performance or position of an entity:

- **Profit related bonuses:** An accountant might be motivated to maximise profit in the current period in order to achieve their bonus. Alternatively, if current period targets have been met, an accountant might be motivated to shift profits into the next reporting period.

- **Financing:** An entity is more likely to be given a loan if it has valuable assets on which the loan can be secured. An incentive may therefore exist for the accountants to over-state assets on the statement of financial position.

- **Achieving a listing:** A company that is being listed on a stock exchange will want to maximise the amount that it receives from investors. This creates an incentive for the accountants to over-state the assets and profits of a company before it lists.

The *Code of Ethics and Conduct* encourages accountants to act in straight-forward and honest ways, and to not let bias impact their judgements.

## Professional competence and due care

New accounting standards are frequently issued and older standards are often updated or withdrawn. Accounting knowledge becomes out-of-date very quickly.

In order to comply with the code of ethics, accountants have a responsibility to ensure that they are aware of changes to accounting standards. This is often referred to as CPD (Continuing Professional Development).

CPD involves:

- Reading technical articles

- Attending seminars or presentations

- Attending training courses.

Without up-to-date technical knowledge, it is unlikely that an accountant can produce financial statements that comply with IFRS Standards. Material errors within financial statements will mislead the users.

### Conceptual Framework

The *Conceptual Framework* states that financial information is only useful if it is relevant and if it offers a faithful representation of an entity's transactions.

A perfectly faithful representation of an entity's transactions would be complete, neutral, and free from error. Without adherence to the ACCA *Code of Ethics and Conduct*, it is likely that an entity's financial statements will fall short of the standard required by user groups.

## 4 Ethics in the digital age

### Contemporary challenges

Accountants use and interact with a plethora of new digital technologies. This increases the range of ethical issues that they may face.

### Professional competence

Accountants must ensure that they have the knowledge to perform their role adequately. They may be required to become proficient with new software relatively quickly, and to deal with situations, transactions or data that they have not dealt with before.

The increasing use of distributed ledger technology (ledgers with no central data store, where transactions are recorded in multiple places at the same time) demands technical competence. Errors could have serious economic consequences. Professional accountants must be honest about whether they are capable of dealing with such large volumes of sensitive information.

## Confidentiality

Accountants have access to lots of data. This data may be internal (employee-related) or external (customer or supplier-related). Data theft can cause financial loss or reputational damage. There may also be legal consequences. Professional accountants must understand local and international laws and regulations around data security and design controls to ensure legal compliance.

## Ethics and AI

The accounting profession is making more use of artificial intelligence (AI). For example, AI can:

- extract data from pdfs and spreadsheets and populate reports

- identify anomalies in spending, which may detect or prevent fraud

- detect non-compliance issues (such as errors in expense claims, purchases orders, and sales invoices), which will limit financial loss.

The use of AI allows accounting professionals to allocate more of their time to developing strategy and problem-solving but it also raises ethical issues:

- What will happen to accounting data if AI fails?

- Will AI be a threat to employment?

- Is there a risk of bias in the AI system (e.g. reviewing the expense claims of certain employees)?

## 5 The impact of ethical and unethical behaviour

### Consequences

The journals and magazines of professional institutes regularly include details of professional disciplinary proceedings brought against individual members who were believed to have fallen short of the ethical standards expected of them.

The consequences of unethical behaviour in deliberately presenting incorrect financial information are severe. Many accountants have been fined or jailed for not fulfilling their professional duties.

The consequences for individuals include:

- Fines

- The loss of professional reputation

- Being prevented from acting as a director or officer of a public company in the future

- The possibility of being expelled by a professional accountancy body

- A prison sentence.

## Ethics and profits

It is commonly argued that the primary objective of a company is to maximise the wealth of its shareholders. Acting ethically might be seen to contradict this objective. For example, whilst it may be ethical to incur costs associated with looking after the environment, such costs reduce profits.

However, in modern society, companies are considered to be corporate citizens within society. Corporate social responsibility is increasingly important to investors and other stakeholders. It can attract 'green' investors, ethical consumers and employees and so in turn have a positive impact on financial results. Thus, it could be argued that the performance and sustainability of a company may not be maximised unless it behaves in an ethical manner.

## 6 Exam focus

The examining team have specified that the exam will test ethical issues around non-compliance with IAS 1 *Presentation of Financial Statements* (Chapter 3) and the disclosure of related party transactions (Chapter 15).

Remember that two professional marks will be allocated in the SBR exam for the application of ethical principles to the question scenario and for a recommendation of how the ethical dilemma might be resolved.

### Test your understanding 1 – Cookie

The directors of Cookie are very confident about the quality of the products that the company sells. Historically, the level of complaints received about product quality has been low. However, when calculating their warranty provision, they have over-estimated the number of items that will be returned as faulty. The directors believe that this is acceptable because it is important for financial statements to exhibit prudence.

**Required:**

**Discuss the ethical issues raised by the treatment of the warranty provision.**

## Test your understanding 2 – Totorus

Totorus has a number of investments in listed shares that are designated to be measured at fair value through other comprehensive income. A new ACCA qualified accountant has started work at Totorus and she has discovered that the finance director measures the fair value of these investments as the present value of the expected future dividend receipts. This calculation gives a higher fair value figure than the quoted share price. The finance director has justified this fair value measurement to the accountant on the grounds that Totorus does not trade shares in the short-term and so quoted share prices understate the value that Totorus will realise over the lifetime of these investments.

**Required:**

**Discuss why the finance director's fair value measurement is not in line with International Financial Reporting Standards, and discuss the ethical issues that arise.**

## 7 Chapter summary

Codes of ethics

The principles in the ACCA Code of Ethics and Conduct are:
- Integrity
- Objectivity
- Professional competence and due care
- Confidentiality
- Professional behaviour

Consequences of unethical behaviour

The consequences of failing to act ethically are many and can be severe. They include:
- Prison sentence
- Fines or repayments of amounts taken fraudulently
- Loss of professional reputation
- Being prevented from acting in the same capacity in the future
- Investigation by professional accountancy body

## Test your understanding answers

### Test your understanding 1 – Cookie

Financial statements are important to a range of user groups, such as shareholders, banks, employees and suppliers. Prudence is important because over-stated assets or under-stated liabilities could mislead potential or current investors. However, excessive cautiousness means that the financial performance and position of an entity is not faithfully represented.

A faithful representation is often presumed to have been provided if accounting standards have been complied with. It would appear that the directors are not calculating the provision in line with the requirements of IAS 37, which requires provisions to be recognised at the 'best estimate' of the expenditure to be incurred. This may mean that profit is understated in the current period and then over-stated in subsequent periods.

Professional ethics is a vital part of the accountancy profession and ACCA members are bound by its *Code of Ethics and Conduct*. This sets out the importance of the fundamental principles of confidentiality, objectivity, professional behaviour, integrity, and professional competence and due care.

Integrity is defined as being honest and straight-forward. Over-estimating a provision in order to shift profits from one period to another demonstrates a lack of integrity.

If the provision is being over-stated in order to achieve bonus targets or profit expectations in the next financial period, then this demonstrates a lack of objectivity.

If the directors are unaware of the requirements of IAS 37, then they may not be sufficiently competent. The finance director may need to attend training courses to improve their knowledge.

Financial statements should faithfully represent the transactions that have occurred. Compliance with the ethical code thus encourages accountants to ensure that they are technically capable and sufficiently independent to comply with the requirements of IFRS Standards.

**Test your understanding 2 – Totorus**

Totorus is using an estimation technique to measure fair value. This is unobservable and so, according to IFRS 13 *Fair Value Measurement*, is a level 3 input. Totorus' intention to hold the asset is not relevant. IFRS 13 states that fair value is a market-based measurement, and not an entity-specific measurement. Totorus should be measuring fair value using the quoted share price. This is a level 1 input, which IFRS 13 prioritises.

Financial statements are important to a range of user groups, such as shareholders, banks, employees and suppliers. These groups require the financial statements to faithfully represent the performance and position of the company so that they can make adequate investment decisions. The public trusts accountants as a result of their professional status and it is vital that this trust is not broken. Professional ethics are therefore a vital part of the accountancy profession and ACCA members are bound by its *Code of Ethics and Conduct*. By following the code of ethics, it is more likely that a faithful representation of the company will be offered because the needs of the users will be prioritised.

If the sole purpose of using the level 3 input is to increase the carrying amount of the investment, then the principles of integrity and objectivity have been compromised.

If the director is unaware of the requirements of IFRS 13, then it could be argued that they are not complying with the ethical principle of professional competence.

Stakeholders are becoming increasingly reactive to the ethical stance of a company. Deliberate falsification of the financial statements could harm the reputation of Totorus. It could also harm the reputation of the accountancy profession as a whole.

The accountant should approach the finance director and remind them of the basic ethical principles and try to persuade them of the need to amend the fair value measurement used. This accountant should document this discussion. Should the finance director remain unmoved, the accountant may wish to contact the ACCA ethical helpline and take legal advice before undertaking any further action.

# Performance reporting

## Chapter learning objectives

Upon completion of this chapter you will be able to:

- Critically discuss and apply the reporting of items in the statement of profit or loss and other comprehensive income

- Discuss and apply the judgements required in selecting and applying accounting policies, accounting for changes in estimates and reflecting corrections of prior period errors

- Outline the principles behind the application of accounting policies and measurement in interim reports.

**PER**

One of the PER performance objectives (PO7) is to prepare external financial reports. You take part in preparing and reviewing financial statements – and all accompanying information – and you do it in accordance with legal and regulatory requirements. Working through this chapter should help you understand how to demonstrate that objective.

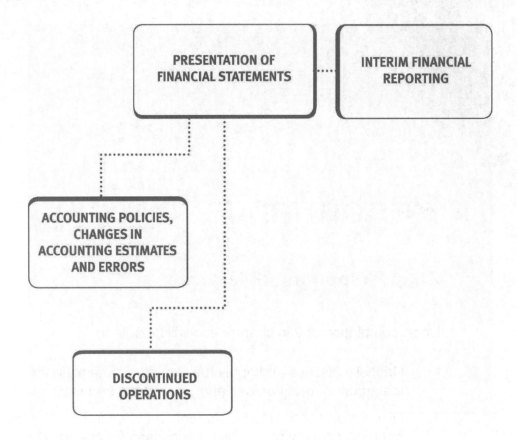

## 1 Performance reporting

### Introduction

This chapter considers four IFRS and IAS Standards that help investors assess the financial performance of an entity:

- IAS 1 *Presentation of Financial Statements* – this outlines recommended formats and minimum content for an entity's financial statements.

- IFRS 5 *Non-current Assets Held for Sale and Discontinued Operations* – this outlines presentation requirements in the statement of profit or loss when an activity is discontinued during the period.

- IAS 8 *Accounting Policies, Changes in Accounting Estimates, and Errors* – this ensures that entities select accounting policies that provide useful information about financial performance and position. Moreover, it provides accounting requirements that enable investors to be able to draw adequate conclusions about financial performance after an entity changes its accounting policies or estimates, or corrects a prior period error.

- IAS 34 *Interim Financial Statements* – this provides the principles to be followed if an entity produces financial statements for a period that is shorter than a full financial year.

**Progression**

With the exception of IAS 34, you will have seen the content of this chapter in your prior studies. However, the ACCA SBR exam will test it at a much higher level.

## 2 IAS 1 *Presentation of Financial Statements*

### Components of financial statements

According to IAS 1 *Presentation of Financial Statements*, a complete set of financial statements has the following components:

- a statement of financial position

- a statement of profit or loss and other comprehensive income (or statement of profit or loss with a separate statement of other comprehensive income)

- a statement of changes in equity

- a statement of cash flows (discussed in a later chapter)

- accounting policies note and other explanatory notes.

Other reports and statements in the annual report (such as a financial review, or an environmental report) are outside the scope of IAS 1.

### The statement of financial position

#### Assets

IAS 1 says that an entity must classify an asset as current on the statement of financial position if it:

- is realised or consumed during the entity's normal trading cycle, or

- is held for trading, or

- will be realised within 12 months of the reporting date.

All other assets are classified as non-current.

#### Liabilities

IAS 1 says that an entity must classify a liability as current on the statement of financial position if it:

- is settled during the entity's normal trading cycle, or

- is held for trading, or

- will be settled within 12 months of the reporting date.

All other liabilities are classified as non-current.

**Test your understanding 1 – Mouse**

Mouse is a company that manufactures and sells cheese. It has recently developed a new range of cheese that, at the year end, requires a further 15 months to fully mature. Once matured, the cheese will be sold to retailers.

The directors of Mouse believe that this new cheese should be classified as a non-current asset on the statement of financial position.

**Required:**

**Discuss whether the directors of Mouse are correct.**

## The statement of profit or loss and other comprehensive income

IAS 1 provides the following definitions:

**Other comprehensive income** (OCI) are income and expenses recognised outside of profit or loss, as required by particular IFRS Standards.

**Total comprehensive income** (TCI) is the total of the entity's profit or loss and other comprehensive income for the period.

**The *Conceptual Framework***

The *Conceptual Framework* states that the statement of profit or loss is the primary source of information about an entity's financial performance. Income and expenses should normally be recognised in this statement.

When developing standards, the Board notes that it might decide that certain income or expenses should be presented in other comprehensive if they result from remeasuring an item to current value and if this means that:

- profit or loss provides more relevant information, or
- it provides a more faithful representation of an entity's performance.

IAS 1 requires that OCI is classified into two groups as follows:

- items that might be reclassified (or recycled) to profit or loss in subsequent accounting periods:
    - foreign exchange gains and losses arising on translation of a foreign operation (IAS 21)
    - effective parts of cash flow hedging arrangements (IFRS 9)
    - Remeasurement of investments in debt instruments that are classified as fair value through OCI (IFRS 9)

- items that will not be reclassified (or recycled) to profit or loss in subsequent accounting periods:
  - changes in revaluation surplus (IAS 16 & IAS 38)
  - remeasurement components on defined benefit plans (IAS 19)
  - remeasurement of investments in equity instruments that are classified as fair value through OCI (IFRS 9).

**The *Conceptual Framework***

According to the *Conceptual Framework*, income and expenditure included in other comprehensive income should be reclassified to profit or loss when doing so results in profit or loss providing more relevant information. However, when developing or amending an IFRS Standard, the Board may decide that reclassification is not appropriate if there is no clear basis for identifying the amount or timing of the reclassification.

IAS 1 requires an entity to disclose income tax relating to each component of OCI. This may be achieved by either:

- disclosing each component of OCI net of any related tax effect, or
- disclosing OCI before related tax effects with one amount shown for tax.

Entities can prepare one combined statement showing profit or loss for the year and OCI. Alternatively, an entity can prepare a statement of profit or loss and a separate statement of OCI.

**The statement of profit or loss and OCI**

For illustration, one of the recommended formats from the implementation guidance in IAS 1 is provided below:

**XYZ Group – Statement of profit or loss and other comprehensive income for the year ended 31 December 20X3**

|  | $000 |
|---|---|
| Revenue | X |
| Cost of sales | (X) |
|  |  |
| Gross profit | X |
| Other operating income | X |
| Distribution costs | (X) |
| Administrative expenses | (X) |
| Other operating expenses | (X) |
| Finance costs | (X) |
| Share of profit of associates | X |
|  |  |
| Profit before tax | X |
| Income tax expense | (X) |
|  |  |
| Profit for the period | X |

| | |
|---|---|
| Other comprehensive income | |
| Items that will not be reclassified to profit or loss: | |
| Changes in revaluation surplus | X |
| Remeasurement gain on defined benefit pension plans | X |
| Remeasurement of equity investments designated to be accounted for through OCI | X |
| Income tax relating to items that will not be reclassified | (X) |
| | ─── |
| | X |
| | ─── |
| Items that may be reclassified subsequently to profit or loss: | |
| Cash flow hedges | X |
| Exchange differences on translating foreign operations | X |
| Income tax relating to items that may be reclassified | (X) |
| | ─── |
| | X |
| | ─── |
| Total other comprehensive income net of tax for the year | X |
| | ─── |
| Total comprehensive income for the year | X |
| | ─── |
| Profit attributable to: | |
| Owners of the parent | X |
| Non-controlling interest | X |
| | ─── |
| | X |
| | ─── |
| Total comprehensive income attributable to: | |
| Owners of the parent | X |
| Non-controlling interest | X |
| | ─── |
| | X |
| | ─── |

### Statement of changes in equity

IAS 1 requires all changes in equity arising from transactions with owners in their capacity as owners to be presented separately from non-owner changes in equity. This would include:

- issues of shares

- dividends.

A comparative statement for the prior period must also be published.

## XYZ Group – Statement of changes in equity for the year ended 31 December 20X3

| | Equity capt'l | Ret'd earng's | Transl'n of for'gn operations | Financial assets thru' OCI | Cash flow hdg's | Reval'n surplus | Total |
|---|---|---|---|---|---|---|---|
| | $000 | $000 | $000 | $000 | $000 | $000 | $000 |
| Balance at 1 Jan 20X3 | X | X | (X) | X | X | – | X |
| Changes in accounting policy | – | X | – | – | – | – | X |
| Restated balance | X | X | X | X | X | X | X |
| **Changes in equity for 20X3** | | | | | | | |
| Dividends | – | (X) | – | – | – | – | (X) |
| Issue of equity capital | X | – | – | – | – | – | X |
| Total comprehensive income for year | – | X | X | X | X | X | X |
| Transfer to retained earnings | – | X | – | – | – | (X) | – |
| Balance at 31 December 20X3 | X | X | X | X | X | X | X |

In addition to these columns, there should be columns headed:

(a)　Non-controlling interest

(b)　Total equity

## General features of financial statements

### Going concern

The *Conceptual Framework* states that financial statements are normally prepared on the assumption that the reporting entity will continue for the foreseeable future. In other words, it is assumed the entity will not enter liquidation, or cease to trade.

IAS 1 states that management should assess whether the going concern assumption is appropriate. Management should take into account all available information about events within at least twelve months of the end of the reporting period.

The following are indicators of a going concern uncertainty:

- A lack of cash and cash equivalents

- Increased levels of overdrafts and other forms of short-term borrowings

- Major debt repayments due in the next 12 months

- A rise in payables days

- Increased levels of gearing

- Negative cash flows, particularly in relation to operating activities

- Disclosures or provisions relating to material legal claims

- Large impairment losses.

Where there is uncertainty, management should consider all available information about the future, including current and expected profitability, debt repayment finance and potential sources of alternative finance. If there is greater doubt or uncertainty, then more work will be required to evaluate whether or not the entity can be regarded as a going concern.

Once management have assessed that there are no material uncertainties as to the ability of an entity to continue for the foreseeable future, the financial statements should be prepared on the assumption that the entity will in fact continue. In other words, the financial statements will be prepared on a going concern basis.

### Accruals basis of accounting

The accruals basis of accounting means that transactions and events are recognised when they occur, not when cash is received or paid for them.

### Consistency of presentation

The presentation and classification of items in the financial statements should be retained from one period to the next unless:

- it is clear that a change will result in a more appropriate presentation, or

- a change is required by an IFRS or IAS Standard.

### Materiality and aggregation

An item is material if its omission or misstatement could influence the economic decisions of users taken on the basis of the financial statements. This could be based on the size or nature of an omission or misstatement.

When assessing materiality, entities should consider the characteristics of the users of its financial statements. It can be assumed that these users have knowledge of business and accounting.

To aid user understanding, financial statements should show material classes of items separately.

Immaterial items may be aggregated with amounts of a similar nature, as long as this does not reduce understandability.

**Offsetting**

IAS 1 says that assets and liabilities, and income and expenses, should only be offset when required or permitted by an IFRS standard.

**Comparative information**

Comparative information for the previous period should be disclosed.

**Disclosures**

**Disclosure note presentation**

IAS 1 says that entities must present their disclosure notes in a systematic order. This might mean:

- Giving prominence to the most relevant areas
- Grouping items measured in similar ways, such as assets held at fair value
- Following the order in which items are presented in the statement of profit or loss and the statement of financial position.

**Compliance with IFRS Standards**

Entities should make an explicit and unreserved statement that their financial statements comply with IFRS Standards.

**Accounting policies**

Entities must produce an accounting policies disclosure note that details:

- the measurement basis (or bases) used in preparing the financial statements (e.g. historical cost, fair value, etc)
- each significant accounting policy.

> **Investor perspective**
>
> This is an extract from an accounting policies note on intangible assets.
>
> *'Impairment: Given the subjectivity involved, actual outcomes could vary significantly from these estimates.*
>
> *Amortisation: Amortisation is recorded to write down intangible assets to their residual values over their estimated useful lives. The selection and review of these residual values and estimated useful lives requires the exercise of management judgement.'*
>
> The disclosure note highlights the key estimates and uncertainties that impact the carrying amount of the reporting entity's intangible assets balance. This reminds investors that measuring and reporting these assets relies on estimation techniques. Although management should be professionally competent and objective, there is always a risk that their estimates may be inaccurate (whether intentional or not).

### Sources of uncertainty

An entity should disclose information about the key sources of estimation uncertainty that may cause a material adjustment to assets and liabilities within the next year, e.g. key assumptions about the future.

### Reclassification adjustments

Reclassification adjustments are amounts 'recycled' from other comprehensive income to profit or loss.

IAS 1 requires that reclassification adjustments are disclosed, either on the face of the statement of profit or loss and other comprehensive income or in the notes.

### Criticisms of the use of other comprehensive income

The accounting treatment and guidance with respect to other comprehensive income (OCI) has been criticised in recent years. Some of these criticisms are as follows:

- Many users ignore OCI, since the gains and losses reported there are not related to an entity's trading cash flows. As a result, material expenses presented in OCI may not be given the attention that they require.

- Reclassification from OCI to profit or loss results in profits or losses being recorded in a different period from the change in the related asset or liability. This contradicts the definitions of income and expenses in the *Conceptual Framework*.

## 3 IFRS 5 *Non-current Assets Held for Sale and Discontinued Operations*

### Definitions

IFRS 5 *Non-current Assets Held for Sale and Discontinued Operations* says that a discontinued operation is a component of an entity that has been sold, or which is classified as held for sale, and which is:

- a separate line of business (either in terms of operations or location)
- part of a plan to dispose of a separate line of business, or
- a subsidiary acquired solely for the purpose of resale.

An operation is held for sale if its carrying amount will not be recovered principally by continuing use. To be classified as held for sale (and therefore to be a discontinued operation) at the reporting date, it must meet the following criteria.

- The operation is available for sale immediately in its current condition.
- The sale is highly probable and is expected to be completed within one year.
- Management is committed to the sale.
- The operation is being actively marketed.
- The operation is being offered for sale at a reasonable price in relation to its current fair value.
- It is unlikely that the plan will change or be withdrawn.

### Presentation

IFRS 5 requires information about discontinued operations to be presented in the financial statements.

- A single amount should be presented on the face of the statement of profit or loss and other comprehensive income that is comprised of:
  - the total of the post-tax profit or loss of discontinued operations
  - the post-tax gain or loss on the measurement to fair value less costs to sell or on the disposal of the discontinued operation.
- An analysis of the single amount described above should be provided on the face of the statement of profit or loss and other comprehensive income or in the notes to the financial statements.
- If a decision to sell an operation is taken after the year-end but before the accounts are approved, this is a non-adjusting event after the reporting date and disclosed in the notes. The operation does not qualify as a discontinued operation at the reporting date and separate presentation is not appropriate.
- In the comparative figures the operations are also shown as discontinued (even though they were not classified as such at the end of the previous year).

**Example presentation**

**Statement of profit or loss (showing discontinued operations as a single amount, with analysis in the notes)**

|  | 20X2 $m | 20X1 $m |
|---|---|---|
| Revenue | 100 | 90 |
| Operating expenses | (60) | (65) |
| Profit from operations | 40 | 25 |
| Finance cost | (20) | (10) |
| Profit before tax | 20 | 15 |
| Income tax expense | (6) | (7) |
| Profit from continuing operations | 14 | 8 |
| **Discontinued operations** | | |
| **Loss from discontinued operations\*** | (25) | (1) |
| Profit/(loss) for the year | (11) | 7 |

\* Analysis of this loss would be given in a disclosure note.

**Investor perspective**

The *Conceptual Framework* notes that the purpose of financial reporting is to provide information to current and potential investors, lenders and other creditors that will enable them to make decisions about providing economic resources to an entity. To make these decisions, users require information that will help them to assess an entity's future cash flows.

This means that financial statement users are more concerned with future profits than past profits. They will be able to make a better assessment of future profits if they are clearly informed about operations that have been discontinued during the period.

### Test your understanding 2 – Discontinued operations

The Portugal group of companies has a financial year-end of 30 June 20X4. The financial statements were authorised three months later. The group is disposing of many of its subsidiaries, each of which is a separate major line of business or geographical area.

- A subsidiary, England, was sold on 1 January 20X4.

- On 1 January 20X4, an announcement was made that there were advanced negotiations to sell subsidiary Switzerland and that, subject to regulatory approval, this was expected to be completed by 31 October 20X4.

- The board has also decided to sell a subsidiary called France. Agents have been appointed to find a suitable buyer but none have yet emerged. The agent's advice is that potential buyers are deterred by the expected price that Portugal hopes to achieve.

- On 10 July 20X4, an announcement was made that another subsidiary, Croatia, was for sale. It was sold on 10 September 20X4.

**Required:**

**Explain whether each of these subsidiaries meets the definition of a 'discontinued operation' as defined by IFRS 5.**

## 4 IAS 8 *Accounting Policies, Changes in Accounting Estimates and Errors*

### Accounting policies

Accounting policies are the principles and rules applied by an entity which specify how transactions are reflected in the financial statements.

Where a standard exists in respect of a transaction, the accounting policy is determined by applying that standard.

Where there is no applicable standard or interpretation, management must use its judgement to develop and apply an accounting policy. The accounting policy selected must result in information that is relevant and reliable. Management should refer to

- standards dealing with similar and related issues

- the *Conceptual Framework*.

Provided they do not conflict with the sources above, management may also consider:

- pronouncements from other standard-setting bodies, as long as they use a similar conceptual framework

- other accepted industry practices.

## Changes in accounting policies

An entity should only change its accounting policies if required by a standard, or if it results in more reliable and relevant information.

New accounting standards normally include transitional arrangements on how to deal with any resulting changes in accounting policy.

If there are no transitional arrangements, changes in accounting policy should be applied **retrospectively.** The entity adjusts the opening balance of each affected component of equity, and the comparative figures are presented as if the new policy had always been applied.

### The *Conceptual Framework*

One of the enhancing qualitative characteristics of useful financial information is comparability. The requirement in IAS 8 to adjust changes in accounting policy retrospectively prevents such changes from distorting users' assessments of an entity's financial position and performance year-on-year. This will help when performing trend analysis, thus informing their investment decisions.

## Changes in accounting estimates

Making estimates is an essential part of the preparation of financial statements. For example, preparers have to estimate allowances for financial assets, inventory obsolescence and the useful lives of property, plant and equipment.

A change in an accounting estimate is **not** a change in accounting policy.

According to IAS 8, a change in accounting estimate must be recognised **prospectively** by including it in the statement of profit or loss and other comprehensive income for the current period and any future periods that are also affected.

## Prior period errors

Prior period errors are misstatements and omissions in the financial statements of prior periods as a result of not using reliable information that should have been available.

IAS 8 says that material prior period errors should be corrected **retrospectively** in the first set of financial statements authorised for issue after their discovery. Opening balances of equity, and the comparative figures, should be adjusted to correct the error.

## Problems with IAS 8

It has been argued that the requirements of IAS 8 to adjust prior period errors retrospectively may lead to earnings management. By adjusting prior period errors through opening reserves, the impact is never shown within a current period statement of profit or loss.

The Board are considering amending some aspects of IAS 8. These proposed amendments are a current issue, and detailed in Chapter 23 of this Study Text.

### Test your understanding 3 – Geranium

Geranium's production machinery has always been depreciated on a straight line basis. At the start of the current reporting period, Geranium decides that a depreciation method based on units of production would more accurately represent the resources consumed. At this date, the carrying amount of the production machinery was $2 million. However, if the machinery had been depreciated using a units of production method since the purchase date, it would instead have a carrying amount of $1.5 million. The directors wish to charge $0.5 million additional depreciation to correct this discrepancy.

**Required:**

**Discuss whether the directors of Geranium are correct.**

## 5 IAS 34 *Interim Financial Reporting*

Interim financial reports are prepared for a period shorter than a full financial year. Entities may be required to prepare interim financial reports under local law or listing regulations.

IAS 34 does not require the preparation of interim reports, but sets out the principles that should be followed if they are prepared and specifies their minimum content.

### The *Conceptual Framework*

Financial information is more useful to primary user groups if it is published on a timely basis. Interim financial reports provide up-to-date information on the performance, position and cash flows of an entity for the period-to-date. This information helps users react more quickly to positive or negative changes during the financial year.

## Components of interim reports

An interim financial report should include, as a minimum, the following components:

- condensed statement of financial position as at the end of the current interim period, with a comparative statement of financial position as at the end of the previous financial year

- condensed statement of profit or loss and other comprehensive income for the current interim period and cumulatively for the current financial year to date (if, for example the entity reports quarterly), with comparatives for the interim periods (current and year to date) of the preceding financial year

- condensed statement showing changes in equity. This statement should show changes in equity cumulatively for the current year with comparatives for the corresponding period of the preceding financial year

- condensed statement of cash flows cumulatively for the year to date, with a comparative statement to the same date in the previous year

- selected explanatory notes

- basic and diluted EPS should be presented on the face of interim statements of profit or loss and other comprehensive income for those entities within the scope of IAS 33 *Earnings per Share*.

## Accounting policies

The same accounting policies should be applied in an entity's interim financial statements as are applied in its annual financial statements.

# 6 Chapter summary

```
┌─────────────────────────────────────────┐      ┌───────────────────────────┐
│ Presentation of financial statements     │      │ Interim financial         │
│ • Statement of financial position        │      │ statements                │
│ • Statement of profit or loss and other  │······│ • Definition              │
│   comprehensive income                   │      │ • Components              │
│ • Statement of changes in equity         │      └───────────────────────────┘
└─────────────────────────────────────────┘

        ┌──────────────────────────────┐
        │ Accounting policies,         │
        │ changes in accounting        │
        │ estimates and errors         │
        │ • Selection                  │
        │ • Changing policies          │
        │   and estimates              │
        │ • Prior period errors        │
        └──────────────────────────────┘

                ┌──────────────────────────────┐
                │ Discontinued operations      │
                │ • Definition                 │
                │ • Presentation               │
                └──────────────────────────────┘
```

Test your understanding answers

### Test your understanding 1 – Mouse

IAS 1 *Presentation of Financial Statements* says that an asset should be classified as a current asset if it is sold in the ordinary course of business. Mouse's business model is to manufacture and sell cheese. As such, even though the asset will not be realised within 12 months of the reporting date, the cheese should be classified as inventories and presented as a current asset on the statement of financial position.

### Test your understanding 2 – Discontinued operations

England has been sold during the year. It is a discontinued operation per IFRS 5.

Switzerland is a discontinued operation per IFRS 5. There is clear intention to sell, and the sale is highly probable within 12 months.

France is not a discontinued operation per IFRS 5. It does not seem that France is being offered for sale at a reasonable price in relation to its current fair value. The sale does not seem to be highly probable within 12 months.

Croatia is not a discontinued operation per IFRS 5. The conditions for classification as held for sale were not met until after the year end.

### Test your understanding 3 – Geranium

According to IAS 8 *Accounting Policies, Changes in Accounting Estimates and Errors*, the choice of depreciation method is an accounting estimate. Changes in accounting estimates are dealt with prospectively.

The directors' proposal is incorrect – Geranium is not permitted to post a 'catch up' adjustment of $0.5 million. Instead, the remaining carrying amount of $2 million will be depreciated in the current and future periods using the new depreciation method.

# Revenue

## Chapter learning objectives

Upon completion of this chapter you will be able to:

- Discuss and apply the criteria that must be met before an entity can apply the revenue recognition model

- Discuss and apply the five step model relating to revenue earned from a contract with a customer

- Apply the criteria for recognition of contract costs as an asset

- Discuss and apply the recognition and measurement of revenue including performance obligations satisfied over time, sale with a right of return, warranties, variable consideration, principal versus agent considerations and non-refundable up-front fees.

**PER**

One of the PER performance objectives (PO6) is to record and process transactions and events. You need to use the right accounting treatments for transactions and events. These should be both historical and prospective – and include non-routine transactions. Working through this chapter should help you understand how to demonstrate that objective.

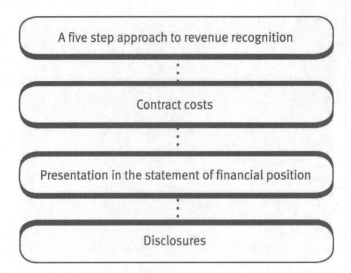

A five step approach to revenue recognition

Contract costs

Presentation in the statement of financial position

Disclosures

# 1 IFRS 15 Revenue from Contracts with Customers

 **Revenue** is income arising in the course of an entity's normal trading or operating activities.

'Revenue' presented in the statement of profit or loss should not include proceeds from the sale of non-current assets or sales tax.

 **Investor perspective**

An entity's revenue figure is arguably the most important factor to consider when assessing its financial performance. As a performance metric, revenue is generally well understood by users of the financial statements. Revenue is used when assessing market share, and also forms the basis for many key financial statement ratios (such as gross profit margin).

The old revenue recognition standard (IAS 18 *Revenue*) was heavily criticised for containing principles that were difficult to apply to all but the most simple of transactions, and for lacking guidance in many key areas. This problem was exacerbated as entities entered into increasingly complex transactions. Many accounting scandals involved the manipulation of revenue, highlighting the fact that IAS 18 was not up to scratch.

For this reason, the Board viewed the development of IFRS 15 *Revenue from Contracts with Customers* as an extremely important project. IFRS 15, which was issued in 2014, provides a comprehensive and robust revenue recognition model. This should improve the comparability of revenue recognition across entities, enabling investors to make better and more informed decisions.

**Progression**

You will have studied revenue in your prior studies but SBR will examine much more complicated scenarios. Remember that revenue recognition is a key audit risk and so may feature in Advanced Audit and Assurance.

 **2 Revenue recognition**

## A five step process

IFRS 15 *Revenue from Contracts with Customers* (para IN7) says that an entity recognises revenue by applying the following five steps:

1 'Identify the contract

2 Identify the separate performance obligations within a contract

3 Determine the transaction price

4 Allocate the transaction price to the performance obligations in the contract

5 Recognise revenue when (or as) a performance obligation is satisfied.'

The following illustration will help you to gain an understanding of the basic principles of the IFRS 15 revenue recognition model.

**Illustration 1 – The five steps**

On 1 December 20X1, Wade receives an order from a customer for a computer as well as 12 months' of technical support. Wade delivers the computer (and transfers its legal title) to the customer on the same day.

The customer paid $420 upfront. If sold individually, the selling price of the computer is $300 and the selling price of the technical support is $120.

**Required:**

**Apply the 5 stages of revenue recognition, per IFRS 15, to determine how much revenue Wade should recognise in the year ended 31 December 20X1.**

## Solution

### Step 1 – Identify the contract

There is an agreement between Wade and its customer for the provision of goods and services.

### Step 2 – Identify the separate performance obligations within a contract

There are two performance obligations (promises) within the contract:

- The supply of a computer

- The supply of technical support.

### Step 3 – Determine the transaction price

The total transaction price is $420.

### Step 4 – Allocate the transaction price to the performance obligations in the contract

Based on standalone selling prices, $300 should be allocated to the sale of the computer and $120 should be allocated to the technical support.

### Step 5 – Recognise revenue when (or as) a performance obligation is satisfied

Control over the computer has been passed to the customer so the full revenue of $300 allocated to the supply of the computer should be recognised on 1 December 20X1.

The technical support is provided over time, so the revenue allocated to this should be recognised over time. In the year ended 31 December 20X1, revenue of $10 (1/12 × $120) should be recognised from the provision of technical support.

**Note**: the SBR exam is unlikely to require you to apply all five steps to a transaction. Exam questions will most likely focus on one or two of these steps. Few marks are awarded for knowledge regurgitation. Marks will instead be awarded for knowledge and application of the **relevant** steps.

The five steps of revenue recognition will now be considered in more detail.

### Step 1: Identify the contract

IFRS 15 says that a contract is an agreement between two parties that creates rights and obligations. A contract does not need to be written.

An entity can only account for revenue from a contract if it meets the following criteria:

*   the parties have approved the contract and each party's rights can be identified

*   payment terms can be identified

*   the contract has commercial substance

*   it is probable that the entity will be paid.

> **The contract**
>
> Aluna has a year end of 31 December 20X1.
>
> On 30 September 20X1, Aluna signed a contract with a customer to provide them with an asset on 31 December 20X1. Control over the asset passed to the customer on 31 December 20X1. The customer will pay $1 million on 30 June 20X2.
>
> By 31 December 20X1, as a result of changes in the economic climate, Aluna did not believe it was probable that it would collect the consideration that it was entitled to. Therefore, the contract cannot be accounted for and no revenue should be recognised.

### Step 2: Identifying the separate performance obligations within a contract

### Performance obligations

Performance obligations are promises to transfer distinct goods or services to a customer.

Some contracts contain more than one performance obligation. For example:

*   An entity may enter into a contract with a customer to sell a car, which includes one year's free servicing and maintenance.

*   An entity might enter into a contract with a customer to provide 5 lectures, as well as to provide a textbook on the first day of the course.

Distinct performance obligations within a contract must be identified. A promised good or service is distinct if:

*   the customer can benefit from the good or service on its own or by using resources that are readily available, and

*   the promise to provide the good or service is separately identifiable from other contractual promises.

**Identifying performance obligations – construction of a school**

Starling entered into a contract to build a school for one of its customers. To fulfil the contract, Starling must provide various services, such as clearing the site, laying foundations, procuring the materials, construction, wiring of the building, installation of equipment, and decoration.

The customer can benefit from each of these services individually, evidenced by the fact that these services could be purchased separately from a range of entities. However the services are not separately identifiable because Starling is being contracted to significantly integrate them into an identified output (a school).

As such, Starling accounts for all of the promised services as a single performance obligation.

### Principals and agents

An entity must decide the nature of each performance obligation. IFRS 15 (para B34) says this might be:

- **'to provide the specified goods or service itself (i.e. it is the principal), or**

- **to arrange for another party to provide the goods or service (i.e. it is an agent)'.**

An entity is the principal if it controls the good or service before it is transferred to the buyer.

If an entity is an agent, revenue is recognised based on the fee it is entitled to.

### Warranties

Most of the time, a warranty is assurance that a product will function as intended. If this is the case, then the warranty will be accounted for in accordance with IAS 37 *Provisions, Contingent Liabilities and Contingent Assets*.

If the customer has the option to purchase the warranty separately, then it should be treated as a distinct performance obligation. This means that a portion of the transaction price must be allocated to it (see step 4).

### Step 3: Determining the transaction price

IFRS 15 defines the transaction price as the amount of consideration the entity expects in exchange for satisfying a performance obligation. Sales tax is excluded.

When determining the transaction price, the following must be considered:

- variable consideration
- significant financing components
- non-cash consideration
- consideration payable to a customer.

**Variable consideration**

If a contract includes variable consideration then an entity must estimate the amount it will be entitled to.

IFRS 15 says that this estimate **'can only be included in the transaction price if it is highly probable that a significant reversal in the amount of cumulative revenue recognised will not occur when the uncertainty is resolved'** (IFRS 15, para 56).

> **Test your understanding 1 – Bristow**
>
> On 1 December 20X1, Bristow provides a service to a customer for the next 12 months. The consideration is $12 million. Bristow is entitled to an extra $3 million if, after twelve months, the number of mistakes made falls below a certain threshold.
>
> **Required:**
>
> **Discuss the accounting treatment of the above in Bristow's financial statements for the year ended 31 December 20X1 if:**
>
> (a) **Bristow has experience of providing identical services in the past and it is highly probable that the number of mistakes made will fall below the acceptable threshold.**
>
> (b) **Bristow has no experience of providing this service and is unsure if the number of mistakes made will fall below the threshold.**

Note that if a product is sold with a right to return it then the consideration is variable. The entity must estimate the variable consideration and decide whether or not to include it in the transaction price.

The refund liability should equal the consideration received (or receivable) that the entity does not expect to be entitled to.

## Test your understanding 2 – Nardone

Nardone enters into 50 contracts with customers. Each contract includes the sale of one product for $1,000. The cost to Nardone of each product is $400. Cash is received upfront and control of the product transfers on delivery. Customers can return the product within 30 days to receive a full refund. Nardone can sell the returned products at a profit.

Nardone has significant experience in estimating returns for this product. It estimates that 48 products will not be returned.

**Required:**

**How should the above transaction be accounted for?**

### Financing

In determining the transaction price, an entity must consider if the timing of payments provides the customer or the entity with a financing benefit.

IFRS 15 provides the following indications of a significant financing component:

- the difference between the amount of promised consideration and the cash selling price of the promised goods or services

- the length of time between the transfer of the promised goods or services to the customer and the payment date.

If there is a financing component, then the consideration receivable needs to be discounted to present value using the rate at which the customer borrows money.

## Test your understanding 3 – Rudd

Rudd enters into a contract with a customer to sell equipment on 31 December 20X1. Control of the equipment transfers to the customer on that date. The price stated in the contract is $1 million and is due on 31 December 20X3.

Market rates of interest available to this particular customer are 10%.

**Required:**

**Explain how this transaction should be accounted for in the financial statements of Rudd for the year ended 31 December 20X1.**

### Non-cash consideration

Any non-cash consideration is measured at fair value.

If the fair value of non-cash consideration cannot be estimated reliably then the transaction is measured using the stand-alone selling price of the good or services promised to the customer.

## Test your understanding 4 – Dan and Stan

Dan sold a good to Stan. Control over the good was transferred on 1 January 20X1. The consideration received by Dan was 1,000 shares in Stan with a fair value of $4 each. By 31 December 20X1, the shares in Stan had a fair value of $5 each.

**Required:**

**How much revenue should be recognised from this transaction in the financial statements of Dan for the year ended 31 December 20X1?**

### Consideration payable to a customer

If consideration is paid to a customer in exchange for a distinct good or service, then it should be accounted for as a purchase transaction.

Assuming that the consideration paid to a customer is not in exchange for a distinct good or service, an entity should account for it as a reduction of the transaction price.

## Test your understanding 5 – Golden Gate

Golden Gate enters into a contract with a major chain of retail stores. The customer commits to buy at least $20 million of products over the next 12 months. The terms of the contract require Golden Gate to make a payment of $1 million to compensate the customer for changes that it will need to make to its retail stores to accommodate the products.

By the 31 December 20X1, Golden Gate has transferred products with a sales value of $4 million to the customer.

**Required**

**How much revenue should be recognised by Golden Gate in the year ended 31 December 20X1?**

### Step 4: Allocate the transaction price

The total transaction price should be allocated to each performance obligation in proportion to stand-alone selling prices.

The best evidence of a stand-alone selling price is the observable price when the good or service is sold separately.

If a stand-alone selling price is not directly observable then it must be estimated. Observable inputs should be maximised whenever possible.

If a customer is offered a discount for purchasing a bundle of goods and services, then the discount should be allocated across all performance obligations within the contract in proportion to their stand-alone selling prices (unless observable evidence suggests that this would be inaccurate).

**Test your understanding 6 – Shred**

Shred sells a machine and one year's free technical support for $100,000. The sale of the machine and the provision of technical support have been identified as separate performance obligations. Shred usually sells the machine for $95,000 but it has not yet started selling technical support for this machine as a stand-alone product. Other support services offered by Shred attract a mark-up of 50%. It is expected that the technical support will cost Shred $20,000.

**Required:**

**How much of the transaction price should be allocated to the machine and how much should be allocated to the technical support?**

## Step 5: Recognise revenue

Revenue is recognised when (or as) the entity satisfies a performance obligation by transferring a promised good or service to a customer.

An entity must determine at contract inception whether it satisfies the performance obligation over time or satisfies the performance obligation at a point in time.

IFRS 15 (para 35) states that an entity satisfies a performance obligation over time if **one** of the following criteria is met:

(a)  **'the customer simultaneously receives and consumes the benefits provided by the entity's performance as the entity performs**

(b)  **the entity's performance creates or enhances an asset (for example, work in progress) that the customer controls as the asset is created or enhanced, or**

(c)  **the entity's performance does not create an asset with an alternative use to the entity and the entity has an enforceable right to payment for performance completed to date'.**

If a performance obligation is satisfied over time, then revenue is recognised over time based on progress towards the satisfaction of that performance obligation.

**Test your understanding 7 – Evans**

On 1 January 20X1, Evans enters into a contract with a customer to provide monthly payroll services. Evans charges $120,000 per year.

**Required:**

**What is the accounting treatment of the above in the financial statements of Evans for the year ended 30 June 20X1?**

**Test your understanding 8 – Crawford**

On 31 March 20X1, Crawford enters into a contract to construct a specialised factory for a customer. The customer paid an upfront deposit which is only refundable if Crawford fails to complete construction in line with the contract. The remainder of the price is payable when the customer takes possession of the factory. If the customer defaults on the contract before completion of the factory, Crawford only has the right to retain the deposit.

**Required:**

**Should Crawford recognise revenue from the above transaction over time or at a point in time?**

Methods of measuring progress towards satisfaction of a performance obligation include:

- output methods (such as surveys of performance, or time elapsed)
- input methods (such as costs incurred as a proportion of total expected costs).

If progress cannot be reliably measured then revenue can only be recognised up to the recoverable costs incurred.

**Test your understanding 9 – Baker**

On 1 January 20X1, Baker enters into a contract with a customer to construct a specialised building for consideration of $2 million plus a bonus of $0.4 million if the building is completed within 18 months. Estimated costs to construct the building are $1.5 million. If the contract is terminated by the customer, Baker can demand payment for the costs incurred to date plus a mark-up of 30%. On 1 January 20X1, as a result of factors outside of its control, such as the weather and regulatory approval, Baker is not sure whether the bonus will be achieved.

At 31 December 20X1, Baker is still unsure whether the bonus target will be met. Baker decides to measure progress towards completion based on costs incurred. Costs incurred on the contract to date are $1.0 million.

**Required:**

**How should Baker account for this transaction in the year ended 31 December 20X1?**

If a performance obligation is not satisfied over time then it is satisfied at a point in time. The entity must determine the point in time at which a customer obtains control of a promised asset.

An entity controls an asset if it can direct its use and obtain most of its remaining benefits. Control also includes the ability to prevent other entities from obtaining benefits from an asset.

IFRS 15 (para 38) provides the following indicators of the transfer of control:

- **'The entity has a present right to payment for the asset**

- **The customer has legal title to the asset**

- **The entity has transferred physical possession of the asset**

- **The customer has the significant risks and rewards of ownership of the asset**

- **The customer has accepted the asset'.**

> **Test your understanding  10 – Clarence**
>
> On 31 December 20X1, Clarence delivered the January edition of a magazine (with a total sales value of $100,000) to a supermarket chain. Legal title remains with Clarence until the supermarket sells a magazine to the end consumer. The supermarket will start selling the magazines to its customers on 1 January 20X2. Any magazines that remain unsold by the supermarket on 31 January 20X2 are returned to Clarence.
>
> The supermarket will be invoiced by Clarence in February 20X2 based on the difference between the number of issues they received and the number of issues that they return.
>
> **Required:**
>
> **Should Clarence recognise revenue from the above transaction in the year ended 31 December 20X1?**

## 3 Contract modifications

A contract modification is a change in the scope or price of a contract.

The modification is accounted for as a **separate contract** if:

- The scope of the contract increases because of the addition of distinct goods or services, and

- The price increases by an amount that reflects the stand-alone selling prices of the additional goods or services.

If not accounted for as a separate contract, the modification will be accounted for as:

- **the termination of the existing contract and the creation of a new contract** if the remaining goods are distinct from those transferred before the modification. The transaction price for this new contract is the total of

  - the original consideration unrecognised, and

  - the additional consideration promised from the modification.

- **part of the original contract**, if the remaining goods and services are not distinct from those transferred before the modification and so form part of a single performance obligation. This modification will impact the contract price and the stage of contract completion. It is dealt with by adjusting the amount of cumulative revenue recognised at the modification date.

**Modifications – remaining goods and services not distinct**

The reporting entity, a construction company, enters into a contract to construct a commercial building for another company. One year later, both companies agree to modify the contract by changing the floor plan of the building. This results in an increase to the contract price.

The remaining goods and services to be provided under the modified contract are not distinct from the services transferred before the date of contract modification. This is because the contract still contains one performance obligation (i.e. to construct a commercial building).

Consequently, the reporting entity accounts for the contract modification as if it was part of the original contract. A cumulative catch-up adjustment will be required.

**Test your understanding 11 – Salty**

Salty enters into a contract to supply 1,000 products to Sweet for $60 each. The products are transferred over an eight month period, and control passes on delivery. After Salty has transferred 700 products the contract is modified to require an additional 200 products to be transferred (i.e. 1,200 in total). The price for the additional 200 products is $57, which is the standalone selling price at the date of the contract modification.

By the reporting date, Salty has transferred 900 products in total to Sweet.

**Required:**

(a) **Discuss, with calculations, how much revenue should be recognised in relation to the above by the reporting date.**

(b) **Discuss, with calculations, how much revenue should be recognised in relation to the above by the reporting date if the contract specified a price of $40 for the additional 200 products. Assume the normal standalone selling price at the modification date is $57.**

## 4 Contract costs

IFRS 15 says that the following costs must be recognised as an asset (i.e. capitalised):

- The costs of obtaining a contract. This must exclude costs that would have been incurred regardless of whether the contract was obtained or not (such as some legal fees, or the costs of travelling to a tender).

- The costs of fulfilling a contract if they do not fall within the scope of another standard (such as IAS 2 *Inventories*) and the entity expects them to be recovered.

The capitalised costs of obtaining and fulfilling a contract will be amortised to the statement of profit or loss as revenue is recognised.

General costs, and costs of wasted labour and materials, are expensed to profit or loss as incurred.

| **Test your understanding 12 – Strangers** |
|---|
| Strangers offers consultancy services. It incurred the following costs on a successful contract bid: |

|  | $ |
|---|---|
| External fees incurred researching potential customer | 30,000 |
| Travel costs to deliver proposal | 20,000 |
| Commission to sales staff for winning the bid | 15,000 |

**Required:**

**Discuss which of the above costs can be capitalised in accordance with IFRS 15.**

## 5 Presentation on the statement of financial position

When an entity has recognised revenue before it has received consideration, then it should recognise either:

- a receivable if the right to the consideration is unconditional, or

- a contract asset.

An entity has an unconditional right to receive consideration if only the passage of time is required before payment is due.

A contract liability should be recognised if the entity has received consideration (or has an unconditional right to receive consideration) before the related revenue has been recognised.

## 6 Disclosures

IFRS 15 requires an entity to disclose

- revenue recognised from contracts with customers

- contract balances and assets recognised from costs incurred obtaining or fulfilling contracts

- significant judgements used, and any changes in judgements.

## 7 Judgement

Management judgement is required throughout the revenue recognition process. For example:

- Contracts with customers do not need to be in writing but may arise through customary business practice. An entity must therefore ascertain whether it has a constructive obligation to deliver a good or service to a customer.

- A contract can only be accounted for if it is probable that the entity will collect the consideration that it is entitled to. Whether benefits are probable is, ultimately, a judgement.

- The entity must identify distinct performance obligations in a contract. However, past performance may give rise to expectations in a customer that goods or services not specified in the contract will be transferred. The identification of distinct performance obligations thus relies on management judgement about both contract terms, and the impact of the entity's past behaviour on customer expectations.

- Variable consideration should be included in the transaction price if it is highly probable that a significant reversal in the amount of cumulative revenue recognised to date will not occur. This may involve making judgements about whether performance related targets will be met.

- The transaction price must be allocated to distinct performance obligations, based on observable, standalone selling prices. However, estimation techniques must be used if observable prices are not available.

- If a performance obligation is satisfied over time, revenue is recognised based on progress towards the completion of the performance obligation. There are various ways to measure completion, using either input or output methods, and the entity must determine which one most faithfully represents the transaction.

- If a performance obligation is satisfied at a point in time, the entity must use judgement to ascertain the date at which control of the asset passes to the customer.

These judgements increase the risk that the management of an entity could manipulate its profits. Adherence to the ACCA ethical code is, therefore, vital.

## 8 Chapter summary

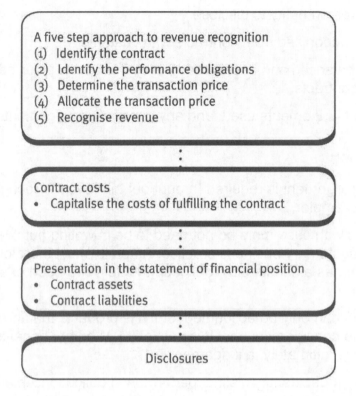

A five step approach to revenue recognition
(1) Identify the contract
(2) Identify the performance obligations
(3) Determine the transaction price
(4) Allocate the transaction price
(5) Recognise revenue

Contract costs
- Capitalise the costs of fulfilling the contract

Presentation in the statement of financial position
- Contract assets
- Contract liabilities

Disclosures

# Test your understanding answers

## Test your understanding 1 – Bristow

The $12 million consideration is fixed. The $3 million consideration that is dependent on the number of mistakes made is variable.

Bristow must estimate the variable consideration. It could use an expected value or a most likely amount. Since there are only two outcomes, $0 or $3 million, then a most likely amount would better predict the entitled consideration.

(a) Bristow expects to hit the target. Using a most likely amount, the variable consideration would be valued at $3 million.

Bristow must then decide whether to include the estimate of variable consideration in the transaction price.

Based on past experience, it seems highly probable that a significant reversal in revenue recognised would not occur. This means that the transaction price is $15 million ($12m + $3m).

As a service, it is likely that the performance obligation would be satisfied over time. The revenue recognised in the year ended 31 December 20X1 would therefore be $1.25 million ($15m × 1/12).

(b) Depending on the estimated likelihood of hitting the target, the variable consideration would either be estimated to be $0 or $3 million.

Whatever the amount, the estimated variable consideration cannot be included in the transaction price because it is not highly probable that a significant reversal in revenue would not occur. This is because Bristow has no experience of providing this service. Therefore, the transaction price is $12 million.

As a service, it is likely that the performance obligation would be satisfied over time. The revenue recognised in the year ended 31 December 20X1 would be $1 million ($12m × 1/12).

### Test your understanding 2 – Nardone

The fact that the customer can return the product means that the consideration is variable.

Using an expected value method, the estimated variable consideration is $48,000 (48 products × $1,000). The variable consideration should be included in the transaction price because, based on Nardone's experience, it is highly probable that a significant reversal in the cumulative amount of revenue recognised ($48,000) will not occur.

Therefore, revenue of $48,000 and a refund liability of $2,000 ($1,000 × 2 products expected to be returned) should be recognised.

Nardone will derecognise the inventory transferred to its customers. However, it should recognise an asset of $800 (2 products × $400), as well as a corresponding credit to cost of sales, for its right to recover products from customers on settling the refund liability.

### Test your understanding 3 – Rudd

Due to the length of time between the transfer of control of the asset and the payment date, this contract includes a significant financing component.

The consideration must be adjusted for the impact of the financing transaction. A discount rate should be used that reflects the characteristics of the customer i.e. 10%.

Revenue should be recognised when the performance obligation is satisfied.

As such revenue, and a corresponding receivable, should be recognised at $826,446 ($1m × $1/1.10^2$) on 31 December 20X1.

The receivable is subsequently accounted for in accordance with IFRS 9 *Financial Instruments*.

### Test your understanding 4 – Dan and Stan

The contract contains a single performance obligation.

Consideration for the transaction is non-cash. Non-cash consideration is measured at fair value.

Revenue should be recognised at $4,000 (1,000 shares × $4) on 1 January 20X1.

Any subsequent change in the fair value of the shares received is not recognised within revenue but instead accounted for in accordance with IFRS 9 *Financial Instruments*.

## Test your understanding 5 – Golden Gate

The payment made to the customer is not in exchange for a distinct good or service. Therefore, the $1 million paid to the customer must be treated as a reduction in the transaction price.

The total transaction price is essentially being reduced by 5% ($1m/$20m). Therefore, Golden Gate reduces the price allocated to each good by 5% as it is transferred.

By 31 December 20X1, Golden Gate should have recognised revenue of $3.8 million ($4m × 95%).

## Test your understanding 6 – Shred

The selling price of the machine is $95,000 based on observable evidence.

There is no observable selling price for the technical support. Therefore, the stand-alone selling price needs to be estimated.

A residual approach would attribute $5,000 ($100,000 – $95,000) to the technical support. However, this does not approximate the stand-alone selling price of similar services (which normally make a profit).

A better approach for estimating the selling price of the support would be an expected cost plus a margin (or mark-up) approach. Based on this, the selling price of the service would be $30,000 ($20,000 × 150%).

The total of standalone selling prices of the machine and support is $125,000 ($95,000 + $30,000). However, total consideration receivable is only $100,000. This means that the customer is receiving a discount for purchasing a bundle of goods and services of 20% ($25,000/$125,000).

IFRS 15 assumes that discounts relate to all performance obligations within a contract, unless evidence exists to the contrary.

The transaction price allocated to the machine is $76,000 ($95,000 × 80%).

The transaction price allocated to the technical support is $24,000 ($30,000 × 80%).

The revenue will be recognised when (or as) the performance obligations are satisfied.

**Test your understanding 7 – Evans**

The payroll services are a single performance obligation.

This performance obligation is satisfied over time because the customer simultaneously receives and consumes the benefits of the payroll processing. This is evidenced by the fact that the payroll services would not need to be re-performed if the customer changed its payroll service provider.

Evans must therefore recognise revenue from the service over time. In the year ended 30 June 20X1, they would recognise revenue of $60,000 (6/12 × $120,000).

**Test your understanding 8 – Crawford**

In assessing whether revenue is recorded over time, it is important to note that the factory under construction is specialised. Therefore, the asset being created has no alternative use to the entity.

However, Crawford only has an enforceable right to the deposit received and therefore does not have a right to payment for work completed to date.

Consequently, Crawford must account for the sale of the unit as a performance obligation satisfied at a point in time, rather than over time. Revenue will most likely be recognised when the customer takes possession of the factory (although a detailed assessment should be made of the date when the customer assumes control).

## Test your understanding 9 – Baker

Constructing the building is a single performance obligation.

The bonus is variable consideration. Whatever the estimated value, it must be excluded from the transaction price because it is not highly probable that a significant reversal in the amount of cumulative revenue recognised will not occur.

The construction of the building should be accounted for as an obligation settled over time. This is because the building has no alternative uses for Baker, and because payment can be enforced for the work completed to date.

Baker should recognise revenue based on progress towards satisfaction of the construction of the building. Using costs incurred, the performance obligation is 2/3 ($1.0m/$1.5m) complete. Accordingly, the revenue and costs recognised at the end of the year are as follows:

|  | $m |
|---|---|
| Revenue ($2m × 2/3) | 1.3 |
| Costs ($1.5m × 2/3) | (1.0) |
| Gross profit | 0.3 |

## Test your understanding 10 – Clarence

The performance obligation is not satisfied over time because the supermarket does not simultaneously receive and benefit from the asset. Clarence therefore satisfies the performance obligation at a point in time and will recognise revenue when it transfers control over the assets to the supermarket.

The fact that the supermarket has physical possession of the magazines at 31 December 20X1 is an indicator that control has passed. Also, Clarence will invoice the supermarket for any issues that are stolen and so the supermarket does bear some of the risks of ownership.

However, as at 31 December 20X1, legal title of the magazines has not passed to the supermarket. Moreover, Clarence has no right to receive payment until the supermarket sells the magazines to the end consumer. Finally, Clarence will be sent any unsold issues and so bears significant risks of ownership (such as the risk of obsolescence).

All things considered, it would seem that control of the magazines has not passed from Clarence to the supermarket chain. Therefore, Clarence should not recognise revenue from this contract in its financial statements for the year ended 31 December 20X1.

**Test your understanding 11 – Salty**

(a) The contract modification is accounted for as a separate contract because the products are distinct, and the price increase reflects the products' standalone selling prices.

By the reporting date, control over 900 of the products under the original contract has transferred. Revenue of $54,000 should be recognised (900 × $60).

(b) The contract price increase does not reflect the standalone selling price of the goods, so the modification is not accounted for as a separate contract. Because the goods are distinct, it should be accounted for as a termination of the existing contract and the creation of a new contract.

By the contract modification, 700 goods had been transferred so revenue of $42,000 (700 × $60) should have been recognised on these.

Now that the original contract is deemed to be cancelled, a transaction price should be determined for the new contract. This is the unrecognised consideration from the original contract (300 × $60) plus the additional consideration promised from the modification (200 × $40) i.e. $26,000. This amounts to a price per product of $52 ($26,000/500).

After the modification, a further 200 products were transferred to Sweet. Revenue of $10,400 (200 × $52) should be recognised on these.

The total revenue recognised in the year is therefore $52,400 ($42,000 + $10,400).

**Test your understanding 12 – Strangers**

Strangers recognises an asset for $15,000 spent on sales commissions. These costs were only incurred because the bid was successful, and they will be recovered through the fees earned from the new contract.

The external research fees and travel costs would have been incurred regardless of whether the contract bid was successful. As such, these costs must be expensed to profit or loss as incurred.

# Non-current assets

## Chapter learning objectives

Upon completion of this chapter you will be able to:

- Discuss and apply the recognition, derecognition and measurement of non-current assets including impairments and revaluations

- Discuss and apply the accounting requirements for the classification and measurement of non-current assets held for sale

- Discuss and apply the accounting treatment of investment properties including classification, recognition, measurement and change of use

- Discuss and apply the accounting treatment of intangible assets including the criteria for recognition and measurement subsequent to acquisition

- Discuss and apply the accounting treatment for borrowing costs

- Discuss and apply the accounting for, and disclosure of, government grants and other forms of government assistance.

**PER**

One of the PER performance objectives (PO6) is to record and process transactions and events. You need to use the right accounting treatments for transactions and events. These should be both historical and prospective – and include non-routine transactions. Working through this chapter should help you understand how to demonstrate that objective.

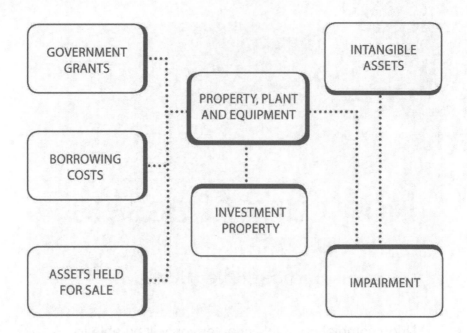

 **Progression**

The IFRS Standards in this chapter were also examined in Financial Reporting. The SBR exam will feature more open-ended questions and real-life scenarios.

# 1 IAS 16 *Property, Plant and Equipment*

### Definition

IAS 16 defines property, plant and equipment as tangible items that:

- **'are held for use in the production or supply of goods or services, for rental to others, or for administrative purposes**

- **are expected to be used during more than one period'** (IAS 16, para 6).

Tangible items have physical substance.

### Initial recognition

An item of property, plant and equipment should be recognised as an asset when:

- it is probable that the asset's future economic benefits will flow to the entity

- the cost of the asset can be measured reliably.

**The *Conceptual Framework***

The revised *Conceptual Framework* says that elements are recognised if recognition results in:

- relevant information

- a faithful representation of the asset or liability, and resulting income, expenses or equity movements.

The recognition criteria in IAS 16, and most other IFRS and IAS Standards, differ from the above because they were based on previous versions of the *Conceptual Framework* and were not updated when the *Conceptual Framework* was reissued.

The *Conceptual Framework* does not override the requirements of individual IFRS and IAS Standards. The recognition of property, plant and equipment is therefore determined by reference to the criteria in IAS 16.

Property, plant and equipment should initially be measured at its cost. According to IAS 16, this comprises:

- the purchase price

- costs that are directly attributable to bringing the asset to the necessary location and condition

- the estimated costs of dismantling and removing the asset, including any site restoration costs. This might apply where, for example, an entity has to recognise a provision for the cost of decommissioning an oil rig or a nuclear power station.

IAS 16 says that the following costs should **never** be capitalised:

- administration and general overheads

- abnormal costs (repairs, wastage, idle time)

- costs incurred after the asset is physically ready for use (unless these costs increase the economic benefits the asset brings)

- costs incurred in the initial operating period (such as initial operating losses and any further costs incurred before a machine is used at its full capacity)

- costs of opening a new facility, introducing a new product (including advertising and promotional costs) and conducting business in a new location or with a new class of customer (including training costs)

- costs of relocating/reorganising an entity's operations.

**Measurement models**

IAS 16 allows a choice between:

- the cost model

- the revaluation model.

**The *Conceptual Framework***

The *Conceptual Framework* outlines two measurement bases:

* historical cost

* current value (such as fair value).

If an accounting standard permits a choice of measurement base, such as is the case with IAS 16, the *Conceptual Framework* notes that preparers of the financial statements must aim to maximise relevance. To do this, they should consider:

* the characteristics of the asset and/or liability

* the ways in which the asset and/or liability contribute to future cash flows.

Many items of property, plant and machinery generate cash flows indirectly, by being used in combination with other assets to produce goods for customers. As such, the *Conceptual Framework* notes that historical cost is likely to provide the most relevant information.

However, some items of property, plant and equipment – such as land and buildings – are highly sensitive to market factors. Over time, particularly when prices rise, the fair value of land and buildings may materially differ from the purchase price. As such, it may be that a measurement based on current value provides more relevant information about the financial position of the reporting entity.

Such decisions are judgemental. Preparers must ensure that the qualitative characteristics of useful information are maximised as far as possible.

### Cost model

Under the **cost model**, property, plant and equipment is held at cost less any accumulated depreciation and impairment losses.

### Revaluation model

Under the **revaluation model**, property, plant and equipment is carried at fair value less any subsequent accumulated depreciation and impairment losses.

If the revaluation model is adopted, then IAS 16 provides the following rules:

* Revaluations must be made with 'sufficient regularity' to ensure that the carrying amount does not differ materially from the fair value at each reporting date.

* If an item is revalued, the entire class of assets to which the item belongs must be revalued.

- If a revaluation increases the value of an asset, the increase is presented as other comprehensive income (and disclosed as an item that will not be recycled to profit or loss in subsequent periods) and held in a 'revaluation surplus' within other components of equity.

- If a revaluation decreases the value of the asset, the decrease should be recognised immediately in profit or loss, unless there is a revaluation reserve representing a surplus on the same asset.

## Depreciation

The key principles with regards to depreciation are as follows:

- All property, plant and equipment with a finite useful life must be depreciated. The depreciable amount of an asset is its cost less its residual value.

- Residual value is an estimate of the net selling proceeds received if the asset was at the end of its useful life and was disposed of today.

- Depreciation is charged to the statement of profit or loss, unless it is included in the carrying amount of another asset.

- Depreciation begins when the asset is available for use and continues until the asset is derecognised, even if it is idle.

- Depreciation must be allocated on a systematic basis, reflecting the pattern in which the asset's future economic benefits are expected to be consumed. In practice, many entities depreciate property, plant and equipment on a straight line basis over its estimated useful life.

- Depreciation methods based on the revenue generated by an activity are not appropriate. This is because revenue reflects many factors, such as inflation, sales prices and sales volumes, rather than the economic consumption of an asset.

- The depreciation method, residual value and the useful life of an asset should be reviewed annually and revised if necessary. Any adjustments are accounted for as a change in accounting estimate.

## Componentisation

Some parts of an asset may require regular replacement (e.g. the seats in an aircraft.) The replacement parts should be capitalised and the carrying amount of the part being replaced (e.g. the old seats) should be derecognised. If the carrying amount of the replaced part is not known then the cost of the new replacement part can be used to estimate the cost of the replaced part when it was originally acquired.

Some assets, such as aircrafts, can only be operated if regular inspections for faults are carried out. The cost of these inspections can be capitalised. Any remaining carrying amount relating to the previous inspection should be derecognised.

Depreciation should be charged separately on each significant component part of an item of PPE. Parts which have the same useful life can be grouped together.

## Derecognition

IAS 16 says that an asset should be derecognised when disposal occurs, or if no further economic benefits are expected from the asset's use or disposal.

- The gain or loss on derecognition of an asset is the difference between the net disposal proceeds, if any, and the carrying amount of the item.

- When a revalued asset is disposed of, any revaluation surplus may be transferred directly to retained earnings, or it may be left in the revaluation surplus within other components of equity.

## Disclosures

IAS 16 requires entities to disclose:

- measurement bases used

- useful lives and depreciation rates

- a reconciliation of carrying amounts at the beginning and end of the period.

If items of property, plant and equipment are stated at revalued amounts, information about the revaluation should also be disclosed.

### Test your understanding 1 – Cap

Cap bought a building on 1 January 20X1. The purchase price was $2.9m, associated legal fees were $0.1m and general administrative costs allocated to the purchase were $0.2m. Cap also paid sales tax of $0.5m, which was recovered from the tax authorities. The building was attributed a useful life of 50 years. It was revalued to $4.6m on 31 December 20X4 and was sold for $5m on 31 December 20X5.

Cap purchased a machine on 1 January 20X3 for $100,000 and attributed it with a useful life of 10 years. On 1 January 20X5, Cap reduced the estimated remaining useful life to 4 years.

**Required:**

**Explain how the above items of property, plant and equipment would have been accounted for in all relevant reporting periods up until 31 December 20X5.**

## 2 Government grants

### Definitions

IAS 20 *Accounting for Government Grants and Disclosure of Government Assistance* defines the following terms:

**Government grants** are transfers of resources to an entity in return for past or future compliance with certain conditions. They exclude assistance that cannot be valued and normal trade with governments.

**Government assistance** is government action designed to provide an economic benefit to a specific entity. It does not include indirect help such as infrastructure development.

### Recognition

IAS 20 says that government grants should not be recognised until the conditions for receipt have been complied with and there is reasonable assurance that the grant will be received.

Grants should be matched with the expenditure towards which they are intended to contribute in the statement of profit or loss:

- Income grants given to subsidise expenditure should be matched to the related costs.

- Income grants given to help achieve a non-financial goal (such as job creation) should be matched to the costs incurred to meet that goal.

### Grants related to assets

Grants for purchases of non-current assets should be recognised over the expected useful lives of the related assets. IAS 20 provides two acceptable accounting policies for this:

- deduct the grant from the cost of the asset and depreciate the net cost

- treat the grant as deferred income and release to profit or loss over the life of the asset.

### Repayments

A government grant that becomes repayable is accounted for as a revision of an accounting estimate.

(a) **Income-based grants**

Firstly, debit the repayment to any liability for deferred income. Any excess repayment must be charged to profits immediately.

(b) **Capital-based grants deducted from cost**

Increase the cost of the asset with the repayment. This will also increase the amount of depreciation that should have been charged in the past. This should be recognised and charged immediately.

(c) **Capital-based grants treated as deferred income**

Firstly, debit the repayment to any liability for deferred income. Any excess repayment must be charged against profits immediately.

## Government assistance

As implied in the definitions set out earlier, government assistance helps businesses through advice, procurement policies and similar methods. It is not possible to place reliable values on these forms of assistance, so they are not recognised in the financial statements.

## Disclosures

IAS 20 requires the following disclosures:

- the accounting policy and presentation methods adopted

- the nature of government grants recognised in the financial statements

- unfulfilled conditions relating to government grants that have been recognised.

> **Test your understanding 2 – Clock**
>
> On 1 June 20X1, Clock received written confirmation from a local government agency that it would receive a $1 million grant towards the purchase price of a new office building. The grant becomes receivable on the date that Clock transfers the $10 million purchase price to the vendor.
>
> On 1 October 20X1 Clock paid $10 million in cash for its new office building, which is estimated to have a useful life of 50 years. By 1 December 20X1, the building was ready for use. Clock received the government grant on 1 January 20X2.
>
> **Required:**
>
> **Discuss the possible accounting treatments of the above in the financial statements of Clock for the year ended 31 December 20X1.**

## 3 IAS 23 *Borrowing Costs*

### Definition

Borrowing costs are defined as **'interest and other costs that an entity incurs in connection with the borrowing of funds'** (IAS 23, para 5).

### Recognition

Borrowing costs should be capitalised if they relate to the acquisition, construction or production of a **qualifying asset**.

IAS 23 defines a qualifying asset as one that takes a substantial period of time to get ready for its intended use or sale.

### Capitalisation period

Borrowing costs should only be capitalised while construction is in progress.

IAS 23 stipulates that:

- Capitalisation of borrowing costs should commence when all of the following apply:
  - expenditure for the asset is being incurred
  - borrowing costs are being incurred
  - activities that are necessary to get the asset ready for use are in progress.

- Capitalisation of borrowing costs should cease when substantially all the activities that are necessary to get the asset ready for use are complete.

- Capitalisation of borrowing costs should be suspended during extended periods in which active development is interrupted.

### Specific and general borrowings

Where a loan is taken out specifically to finance the construction of an asset, IAS 23 says that the amount to be capitalised is the interest payable on that loan less income earned on the temporary investment of the borrowings.

If construction of a qualifying asset is financed from an entity's general borrowings, the borrowing costs eligible to be capitalised are determined by applying the weighted average general borrowings rate to the expenditure incurred on the asset.

### Disclosures

IAS 23 requires the following disclosures:

- the value of borrowing costs capitalised during the period
- the capitalisation rate.

> ### Test your understanding 3 – Hi-Rise
>
> On 1 January 20X1, Hi-Rise obtained planning permission to build a new office building. Construction commenced on 1 March 20X1. To help fund the cost of this building, a loan for $5 million was taken out from the bank on 1 April 20X1. The interest rate on the loan was 10% per annum.
>
> Construction of the building ceased during the month of July due to an unexpected shortage of labour and materials.
>
> By 31 December 20X1, the building was not complete. Costs incurred to date were $12 million (excluding interest on the loan).
>
> **Required:**
>
> **Discuss the accounting treatment of the above in the financial statements of Hi-Rise for the year ended 31 December 20X1.**

## 4 Investment property

### Definitions

IAS 40 *Investment Property* relates to **'property (land or buildings) held (by the owner or by the lessee as a right-of-use asset) to earn rentals or for capital appreciation or both'** (IAS 40, para 5).

Examples of investment property are:

- land held for capital appreciation
- land held for undecided future use
- buildings leased out under an operating lease
- vacant buildings held to be leased out under an operating lease.

The following are **not** investment property:

- property held for use in the production or supply of goods or services or for administrative purposes (IAS 16 *Property, Plant and Equipment* applies)
- property held for sale in the ordinary course of business or in the process of construction of development for such sale (IAS 2 *Inventories* applies)
- property being constructed or developed on behalf of third parties (IFRS 15 *Revenue from Contracts with Customers* applies)
- owner-occupied property (IAS 16 applies)
- property that is being constructed or developed for use as an investment property (IAS 16 currently applies until the property is ready for use, at which time IAS 40 starts to apply)
- property leased to another entity under a finance lease (IFRS 16 *Leases* applies).

## Measurement

On recognition, investment property is recognised at cost.

After recognition an entity may choose either:

- the cost model
- the fair value model.

The policy chosen must be applied to all investment properties.

### Cost model

If the cost model is chosen, investment properties are held at cost less accumulated depreciation. No revaluations are permitted.

### Fair value model

Under the fair value model, the entity remeasures its investment properties to fair value each year. No depreciation is charged.

All gains and losses on revaluation are reported in the statement of profit or loss.

If, in exceptional circumstances, it is impossible to measure the fair value of an individual investment property reliably then the cost model should be adopted.

## Transfers

Transfers to or from investment property can only be made if there is a change of use. There are several possible situations in which this might occur and the accounting treatment for each is set out below:

### Transfer from investment property to owner-occupied property

Use the fair value at the date of the change for subsequent accounting under IAS 16.

### Transfer from investment property to inventory

Use the fair value at the date of the change for subsequent accounting under IAS 2 *Inventories*.

### Transfer from owner-occupied property to investment property to be carried at fair value

Normal accounting under IAS 16 (cost less depreciation) will have been applied up to the date of the change. On adopting fair value, there is normally an increase in value. This is recognised as other comprehensive income and credited to the revaluation surplus in equity in accordance with IAS 16. If the fair valuation causes a decrease in value, then it should be charged to profits.

### Transfer from inventories to investment property to be carried at fair value

Any change in the carrying amount caused by the transfer should be recognised in profit or loss.

## Illustration 1 – Investment property

Lavender owns a property, which it rents out to some of its employees. The property was purchased for $30 million on 1 January 20X2 and had a useful life of 30 years at that date. On 1 January 20X7 it had a market value of $50 million and its remaining useful life remained unchanged. Management wish to measure properties at fair value where this is allowed by accounting standards.

**Required:**

**How should the property be treated in the financial statements of Lavender for the year ended 31 December 20X7.**

## Solution

Property that is rented out to employees is deemed to be owner-occupied and therefore cannot be classified as investment property.

Management wish to measure the property at fair value, so Lavender adopts the fair value model in IAS 16 Property, Plant and Equipment, depreciating the asset over its useful life and recognising the revaluation gain in other comprehensive income.

Before the revaluation, the building had a carrying amount of $25m ($30m × 25/30). The building would have been revalued to $50m on 1 January 20X7, with a gain of $25m ($50m – $25m) recognised in other comprehensive income.

The building would then be depreciated over its remaining useful life of 25 years (30 – 5), giving a depreciation charge of $2m ($50m/25) in the year ended 31 December 20X7. The carrying amount of the asset as at 31 December 20X7 is $48m ($50m – $2m).

## Illustration 2 – ABC

ABC owns a building that it used as its head office. On 1 January 20X1, the building, which was measured under the cost model, had a carrying amount of $500,000. On this date, when the fair value of the building was $600,000, ABC vacated the premises. However, the directors decided to keep the building in order to rent it out to tenants and to potentially benefit from increases in property prices. ABC measures investment properties at fair value. On 31 December 20X1, the property has a fair value of $625,000.

**Required:**

**Discuss the accounting treatment of the building in the financial statements of ABC for the year ended 31 December 20X1.**

**Solution**

When the building was owner-occupied, it was an item of property plant and equipment. From 1 January 20X1, the property was held to earn rental income and for capital appreciation so it should be reclassified as investment property.

Per IAS 40, if owner occupied property becomes investment property that will be carried at fair value, then a revaluation needs to occur under IAS 16 at the date of the change in use.

The building must be revalued from $500,000 to $600,000 under IAS 16. This means that the gain of $100,000 ($600,000 – $500,000) will be recorded in other comprehensive income and held in a revaluation reserve within equity.

Investment properties measured at fair value must be revalued each year end, with the gain or loss recorded in profit or loss. At year end, the building will therefore be revalued to $625,000 with a gain of $25,000 ($625,000 – $600,000) recorded in profit or loss.

Investment properties held at fair value are not depreciated.

## Disclosures

In respect of investment properties, IAS 40 says that an entity must disclose:

- whether the cost or fair value model is used
- amounts recognised in profit or loss for the period
- a reconciliation between the carrying amounts of investment property at
- the beginning and end of the period
- the fair value of investment property if the entity uses the cost model.

Investor perspective

The International Accounting Standards Board believes that information about the fair value of investment properties is highly relevant. However, to reduce the cost and burden of producing financial statements, entities are permitted a choice between a cost model and a fair value.

IAS 40 requires entities to reconcile the carrying amount of investment properties year-on-year. However, if an entity uses the cost model, IAS 40 requires that the aggregate fair value of investment property is disclosed.

An example of this reconciliation is provided below:

|  | $m |
|---|---|
| Cost: |  |
| At beginning of year | 150 |
| Additions | 20 |
| Reclassification | (10) |
| Disposals | (7) |
|  | ____ |
| End of year | 153 |
|  | ____ |

|  | $m |
|---|---|
| Accumulated depreciation and impairment: |  |
| At beginning of year: | 75 |
| Depreciation charge | 2 |
| Impairment charge | 1 |
| Reclassification | (2) |
| Disposals | (5) |
|  | ____ |
| End of year | 71 |
|  | ____ |
| Net carrying amount at end of year | 82 |
|  | ____ |

*The estimated fair value of the Group's investment property is $210 million (20X6: $240 million). This fair value has been determined by applying an appropriate rental yield to the rentals earned by the investment property. A valuation has not been performed by an independent surveyor.*

From this disclosure, investors can determine that the carrying amount of investment properties is below their fair value. In other words, the financial statements of this entity understate its value.

Disclosure of the fair value of investment properties enhances the ability of investors to compare this entity with entities that use the fair value model. The disclosure also informs investors that the fair value of its investment properties has been estimated using a judgemental methodology and without the use of an independent expert – this may mean that the valuation is more susceptible to bias and manipulation.

## 5    IAS 38 *Intangible Assets*

 **Definition**

An **intangible asset** is defined as **'an identifiable non-monetary asset without physical substance'** (IAS 38, para 8).

### Examples of intangible assets

Intangible assets include:

*   goodwill acquired in a business combination
*   computer software
*   patents
*   copyrights
*   motion picture films
*   customer list
*   mortgage servicing rights
*   licences
*   import quotas
*   franchises
*   customer and supplier relationships
*   marketing rights.

### Recognition criteria

An entity should recognise an intangible asset if all the following criteria are met.

*   The asset is identifiable
*   The asset is controlled by the entity
*   The asset will generate future economic benefits for the entity
*   The cost of the asset can be measured reliably.

An intangible asset is identifiable if it:

*   **'is separable (capable of being separated and sold, transferred, licensed, rented, or exchanged, either individually or as part of a package), or**
*   **it arises from contractual or other legal rights, regardless of whether those rights are transferable or separable from the entity or from other rights and obligations'** (IAS 38, para 12).

If an intangible asset does not meet the recognition criteria, expenditure should be charged to the statement of profit or loss as it is incurred. Once the expenditure has been so charged, it cannot be capitalised at a later date.

Note that the accounting treatment of goodwill arising on a business combination is dealt with in IFRS 3 *Business Combinations* rather than IAS 38 *Intangible Assets*.

### Initial recognition

When an intangible asset is initially recognised, it is measured at cost.

### Subsequent recognition

After recognition, an entity must choose either the cost model or the revaluation model for each class of intangible asset.

### Cost model

The cost model measures the asset at cost less accumulated amortisation and impairment.

### Revaluation model

The revaluation model measures the asset at fair value less accumulated amortisation and impairment.

The revaluation model can only be adopted if fair value can be determined by reference to an active market. An **active market** is one where the products are homogenous, there are willing buyers and sellers to be found at all times, and prices are available to the public.

Active markets for intangible assets are rare. They may exist for assets such as:

- milk quotas
- stock exchange seats.

Active markets are unlikely to exist for brands, newspaper mastheads, music and film publishing rights, patents or trademarks.

Revaluations should be made with sufficient regularity such that the carrying amount does not differ materially from actual fair value at the reporting date.

Revaluation gains and losses are accounted for in the same way as revaluation gains and losses of tangible assets held in accordance with IAS 16 *Property, Plant and Equipment*.

## Amortisation

An entity must assess whether the useful life of an intangible asset is finite or indefinite.

- An asset with a finite useful life must be amortised on a systematic basis over that life. Normally the straight-line method with a zero residual value should be used. Amortisation starts when the asset is available for use.

- An asset has an indefinite useful life when there is no foreseeable limit to the period over which the asset is expected to generate net cash inflows. It should not be amortised, but be subject to an annual impairment review.

### Test your understanding 4 – Innovate

Ten years ago, Innovate developed a video game called 'Our Sports'. This game sold over 10 million copies around the world and was extremely profitable. Due to its popularity, Innovate release a new game in the Our Sports series every year. The games continue to be best-sellers.

The directors have produced cash flow projections for the Our Sports series over the next five years. Based on these projections, they have prudently valued the Our Sports brand at $20 million and wish to recognise this in the statement of financial position as at 30 September 20X3.

On 30 September 20X3, Innovate also paid $1 million for the rights to the 'Pets & Me' videogame series after the original developer went into administration.

**Required:**

**Discuss the accounting treatment of the above in the financial statements of Innovate for the year ended 30 September 20X3.**

## Research and development expenditure

**Research** is defined as **'original and planned investigation undertaken with the prospect of gaining new scientific or technical knowledge and understanding'** (IAS 38, para 8).

Research expenditure cannot be recognised as an intangible asset (although tangible assets used in research should be recognised as property, plant and equipment).

**Development** is defined as **'the application of research findings or other knowledge to a plan or design for the production of new or substantially improved materials, devices, products, processes, systems or services before the start of commercial production or use'** (IAS 38, para 8).

IAS 38 says that development expenditure must be recognised as an intangible asset if the entity can demonstrate that:

- the project is technically feasible

- the entity intends to complete the intangible asset, and then use it or sell it

- the intangible asset will generate future economic benefits

- it has adequate resources to complete the project

- it can reliably measure the expenditure on the project.

---

**Test your understanding 5 – Scone**

During the year ended 31 December 20X1, Scone spent $2 million on researching and developing a new product. The entity has recognised all $2 million as an intangible asset. A breakdown of the expenditure is provided below:

|  | $m |
| --- | --- |
| Research into materials | 0.5 |
| Market research | 0.4 |
| Employee training | 0.2 |
| Development activities | 0.9 |

The expenditure on development activities was incurred evenly over the year. It was not until 1 May 20X1 that market research indicated that the product was likely to be profitable. At the reporting date, the product development was not yet complete.

**Required:**

**Discuss the correct accounting treatment of the research and development expenditure in the year ended 31 December 20X1.**

---

## Disclosures

IAS 38 states that an entity must disclose:

The amount of research and development expenditure expensed in the period

- The amortisation methods used

- For intangible assets assessed as having an indefinite useful life, the reasons supporting that assessment

- The date of any revaluations, if applicable, as well as the methods and assumptions used

- A reconciliation of the carrying amount of intangibles at the beginning and end of the reporting period.

# 6    IAS 36 Impairment of Assets

 **Definition**

**Impairment** is a reduction in the recoverable amount of an asset or cash-generating unit below its carrying amount.

 IAS 36 *Impairment of Assets* says that an entity should carry out an impairment review at least annually if:

* an intangible asset is not being amortised because it has an indefinite useful life

* goodwill has arisen on a business combination.

Otherwise, an impairment review is required only where there is an indication that impairment may have occurred.

### Indications of impairment

IAS 36 lists the following indications that an asset is impaired:

* **External sources of information:**
    - unexpected decreases in an asset's market value
    - significant adverse changes have taken place, or are about to take place, in the technological, market, economic or legal environment
    - increased interest rates have decreased an asset's recoverable amount
    - the entity's net assets are measured at more than its market capitalisation.

* **Internal sources of information:**
    - evidence of obsolescence or damage
    - there is, or is about to be, a material reduction in usage of an asset
    - evidence that the economic performance of an asset has been, or will be, worse than expected.

### Calculating an impairment loss

An impairment occurs if the carrying amount of an asset is greater than its recoverable amount.

 The **recoverable amount** is the higher of fair value less costs to sell and value in use.

**Fair value** is defined in IFRS 13 *Fair Value Measurement* as the price received when selling an asset in an orderly transaction between market participants at the measurement date.

**Costs to sell** are incremental costs directly attributable to the disposal of an asset.

**Value in use** is calculated by estimating future cash inflows and outflows from the use of the asset and its ultimate disposal, and applying a suitable discount rate to these cash flows.

With regards to estimates of cash flows, IAS 36 stipulates that:

*   The cash flow projections should be based on reasonable assumptions and the most recent budgets and forecasts

*   The cash flow projections should relate to the asset's current condition and should exclude expenditure to improve or enhance it

*   For periods in excess of five years, management should extrapolate from earlier budgets using a steady, declining or zero growth rate

*   Management should assess the accuracy of their budgets by investigating the reasons for any differences between forecast and actual cash flows.

The discount rate used to calculate value in use should reflect:

*   **'the time value of money, and**

*   **the risks specific to the asset for which the future cash flow estimates have not been adjusted'** (IAS 36, para 55).

### Carrying out an impairment test

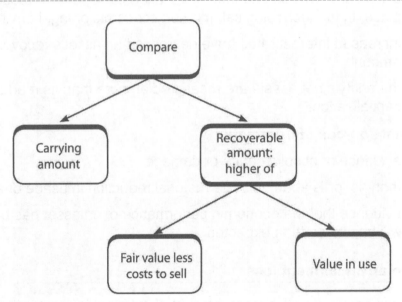

If fair value less costs to sell is higher than the carrying amount, there is no impairment and no need to calculate value in use.

## Recognising impairment losses in the financial statements

An impairment loss is normally charged immediately in the statement of profit or loss and other comprehensive income.

- If the asset has previously been revalued upwards, the impairment is recognised as a component of other comprehensive income and is debited to the revaluation reserve until the surplus relating to that asset has been reduced to nil. The remainder of the impairment loss is recognised in profit or loss.

- The recoverable (impaired) amount of the asset is then depreciated/ amortised over its remaining useful life.

### Test your understanding 6 – Impaired asset

On 31 December 20X1, an entity noticed that one of its items of plant and machinery is often left idle. On this date, the asset had a carrying amount of $500,000 and a fair value of $325,000. The estimated costs required to dispose of the asset are $25,000.

If the asset is not sold, the entity estimates that it would generate cash inflows of $200,000 in each of the next two years. Assume that the cash flows occur at the end of each year. The discount rate that reflects the risks specific to this asset is 10%.

**Required:**

(a) **Discuss the accounting treatment of the above in the financial statements for the year ended 31 December 20X1.**

(b) **How would the answer to part (a) be different if there was a balance of $10,000 in other components of equity relating to the prior revaluation of this specific asset?**

## Cash-generating units

It is not usually possible to identify cash flows relating to particular assets. For example, a factory production line is made up of many individual machines, but the revenues are earned by the production line as a whole. In these cases, value in use must be calculated for groups of assets (rather than individual assets).

These groups of assets are called cash-generating units (CGUs).

 A **cash-generating unit** is the smallest group of assets that generates independent cash flows.

**Test your understanding 7 – Cash generating units**

An entity has three stages of production:

- A – growing and felling trees

- B – creating parts of wooden furniture

- C – assembling the parts from B into finished goods.

The output of A is timber that is partly transferred to B and partly sold in an external market. If A did not exist, B could buy its timber from the market. The output of B has no external market and is transferred to C at an internal transfer price. C sells the finished product in an external market and the sales revenue achieved by C is not affected by the fact that the three stages of production are all performed by the entity.

**Required:**

**Identify the cash-generating unit(s).**

### Allocating assets to cash-generating units

The carrying amount of a cash-generating unit includes the carrying amount of assets that can be attributed to the cash-generating unit and will generate the future cash inflows used in determining the cash-generating unit's value in use.

There are two problem areas:

- **Corporate assets**: assets that are used by several cash-generating units (e.g. a head office building or a research centre). They do not generate their own cash inflows, so do not themselves qualify as cash-generating units.

- **Goodwill**, which does not generate cash flows independently of other assets and often relates to a whole business.

Corporate assets and goodwill should be allocated to cash-generating units on a reasonable and consistent basis. A cash-generating unit to which goodwill has been allocated must be tested for impairment annually.

### Allocation of an impairment to the unit's assets

If an impairment loss arises in respect of a cash-generating unit, IAS 36 requires that it is allocated among the assets in the following order:

- goodwill

- other assets in proportion to their carrying amount.

However, the carrying amount of an asset cannot be reduced below the highest of:

- fair value less costs to sell

- value in use

- nil.

## Illustration 3 – Impairment allocation within CGU

Tinud has identified an impairment loss of $41m for one of its cash-generating units. The carrying amount of the unit's net assets was $150m, whereas the unit's recoverable amount was only $109m. The draft values of the net assets of the unit are as follows:

|  | $m |
|---|---|
| Goodwill | 13 |
| Property | 20 |
| Machinery | 49 |
| Vehicles | 35 |
| Patents | 14 |
| Net monetary assets | 19 |
|  | ___ |
|  | 150 |
|  | ___ |

The net selling price of the unit's assets were insignificant except for the property, which had a market value of $35m. The net monetary assets will be realised in full.

**Required:**

**How is the impairment loss allocated to the assets within the cash-generating unit?**

## Solution

Firstly, the impairment loss is allocated to the goodwill, reducing its carrying amount to nil.

The impairment loss cannot be set against the property because its net selling price is greater than its carrying amount.

Likewise, the impairment loss cannot be set against the net monetary assets (receivables, cash, etc.) because they will be realised in full.

The balance of the impairment loss of $28 million ($41m – $13m) is apportioned between the remaining assets in proportion to their carrying amounts. So, for example, the impairment allocated to the machinery is $14 million ((49/(49 + 35 + 14)) × 28m).

The table below shows how the impairment will be allocated.

| | Draft values | Impairment loss | Revised value |
|---|---|---|---|
| | $m | $m | $m |
| Goodwill | 13 | (13) | – |
| Property | 20 | – | 20 |
| Machinery | 49 | (14) | 35 |
| Vehicles | 35 | (10) | 25 |
| Patents | 14 | (4) | 10 |
| Net monetary assets | 19 | – | 19 |
| | 150 | (41) | 109 |

### Test your understanding 8 – Factory explosion

There was an explosion in a factory. The carrying amounts of its assets were as follows:

| | $000 |
|---|---|
| Goodwill | 100 |
| Patents | 200 |
| Machines | 300 |
| Computers | 500 |
| Buildings | 1,500 |
| | 2,600 |

The factory operates as a cash-generating unit. An impairment review reveals a net selling price of $1.2 million for the factory and value in use of $1.95 million. Half of the machines have been blown to pieces but the other half can be sold for at least their carrying amount. The patents have been superseded and are now considered worthless.

**Required:**

**Discuss, with calculations, how any impairment loss will be accounted for.**

**Impairment if reasonable allocation is impossible**

If no reasonable allocation of corporate assets or goodwill is possible, then a group of cash-generating units must be tested for impairment together in a two-stage process.

**Example**

An entity acquires a business comprising three cash-generating units, D, E and F, but there is no reasonable way of allocating goodwill to them. After three years, the carrying amount and the recoverable amount of the net assets in the cash-generating units and the purchased goodwill are as follows:

|  | D | E | F | Goodwill | Total |
|---|---|---|---|---|---|
|  | $000 | $000 | $000 | $000 | $000 |
| Carrying amount | 240 | 360 | 420 | 150 | 1,170 |
| Recoverable amount | 300 | 420 | 360 |  | 1,080 |

**Step 1:** Review the individual units for impairment.

F is impaired. A loss of $60,000 is recognised and its carrying amount is reduced to $360,000.

**Step 2:** Compare the carrying amount of the business as a whole, including the goodwill, with its recoverable amount.

The total carrying amount of the business is now $1,110,000 ($1,170,000 – $60,000). A further impairment loss of $30,000 must then be recognised in respect of the goodwill ($1,110,000 – $1,080,000).

### Reversal of an impairment loss

The calculation of impairment losses is based on predictions of what may happen in the future. Sometimes, actual events turn out to be better than predicted. If this happens, the recoverable amount is re-calculated and the previous write-down is reversed.

- Impaired assets should be reviewed at each reporting date to see whether there are indications that the impairment has reversed.

- A reversal of an impairment loss is recognised immediately as income in profit or loss. If the original impairment was charged against the revaluation surplus, it is recognised as other comprehensive income and credited to the revaluation reserve.

- The reversal must not take the value of the asset above the amount it would have been if the original impairment had never been recorded. The depreciation that would have been charged in the meantime must be taken into account.

- The depreciation charge for future periods should be revised to reflect the changed carrying amount.

An impairment loss recognised for goodwill cannot be reversed in a subsequent period.

### Test your understanding 9 – Boxer

Boxer purchased a non-current asset on 1 January 20X1 at a cost of $30,000. At that date, the asset had an estimated useful life of ten years. Boxer does not revalue this type of asset, but accounts for it on the basis of depreciated historical cost. At 31 December 20X2, the asset was subject to an impairment review and had a recoverable amount of $16,000.

At 31 December 20X5, the circumstances which caused the original impairment to be recognised have reversed and are no longer applicable, with the result that recoverable amount is now $40,000.

**Required:**

**Explain, with supporting computations, the impact on the financial statements of the two impairment reviews.**

### Test your understanding 10 – CGUs and impairment reversals

On 31 December 20X2, an impairment review was conducted on a cash generating unit and the results were as follows:

| Asset | Carrying amount pre-impairment | Impairment | Carrying amount post-impairment |
|---|---|---|---|
| | $000 | $000 | $000 |
| Goodwill | 100 | (100) | Nil |
| Property, plant and equipment | 300 | (120) | 180 |
| | 400 | (220) | 180 |

The property, plant and equipment was originally purchased for $400,000 on 1 January 20X1 and was attributed a useful life of 8 years.

At 31 December 20X3, the circumstances which caused the original impairment have reversed and are no longer applicable. The recoverable amount of the cash generating unit is now $420,000.

**Required:**

**Explain, with supporting computations, the impact of the impairment reversal on the financial statements for the year ended 31 December 20X3.**

## Disclosures

IAS 36 requires disclosure of the following:

- impairment losses recognised during the period

- impairment reversals recognised during the period.

For each material loss or reversal:

- the amount of loss or reversal and the events causing it

- the recoverable amount of the asset (or cash generating unit)

- the level of fair value hierarchy (per IFRS 13) used in determining fair value less costs to sell

- the discount rate(s) used.

## 7    Non-current assets held for sale (IFRS 5)

 **Definitions**

IFRS 5 *Non-current Assets Held for Sale and Discontinued Operations* says that a non-current asset or disposal group should be classified as 'held for sale' if its carrying amount will be recovered primarily through a sale transaction rather than through continuing use.

 A **disposal group** is a group of assets (and possibly liabilities) that the entity intends to dispose of in a single transaction.

### Classification as 'held for sale'

IFRS 5 requires the following conditions to be met before an asset or disposal group can be classified as 'held for sale':

- The item is available for immediate sale in its present condition.

- The sale is highly probable.

- Management is committed to a plan to sell the item.

- An active programme to locate a buyer has been initiated.

- The item is being actively marketed at a reasonable price in relation to its current fair value.

- The sale is expected to be completed within one year from the date of classification.

- It is unlikely that the plan will change significantly or be withdrawn.

Assets that are to be abandoned or wound down gradually cannot be classified as held for sale because their carrying amounts will not be recovered principally through a sale transaction.

**Test your understanding 11 – Hyssop**

Hyssop is preparing its financial statements for the year ended 31 December 20X7.

(a) On 1 December 20X7, the entity became committed to a plan to sell a surplus office property and has already found a potential buyer. On 15 December 20X7 a survey was carried out and it was discovered that the building had dry rot and substantial remedial work would be necessary. The buyer is prepared to wait for the work to be carried out, but the property will not be sold until the problem has been rectified. This is not expected to occur until summer 20X8.

**Required:**

**Can the property be classified as 'held for sale'?**

(b) A subsidiary entity, B, is for sale at a price of $3 million. There has been some interest from prospective buyers but no sale as of yet. One buyer has made an offer of $2 million but the Directors of Hyssop rejected the offer. The Directors have just received advice from their accountants that the fair value of the business is $2.5 million. They have decided not to reduce the sale price of B at the moment.

**Required:**

**Can the subsidiary be classified as 'held for sale'?**

**Measurement of assets and disposal groups held for sale**

Items classified as held for sale should, according to IFRS 5, be measured at the lower of their carrying amount and fair value less costs to sell.

- Where fair value less costs to sell is lower than carrying amount, the item is written down and the write down is treated as an impairment loss.

- If a non-current asset is measured using a revaluation model and it meets the criteria to be classified as being held for sale, it should be revalued to fair value immediately before it is classified as held for sale. It is then revalued again at the lower of the carrying amount and the fair value less costs to sell. The difference is the selling costs and these should be charged against profits in the period.

- When a disposal group is being written down to fair value less costs to sell, the impairment loss reduces the carrying amount of assets in the order prescribed by IAS 36.

- A gain can be recognised for any subsequent increase in fair value less costs to sell, but not in excess of the cumulative impairment loss that has already been recognised, either when the assets were written down to fair value less costs to sell or previously under IAS 36.

An asset held for sale is not depreciated, even if it is still being used by the entity.

## Test your understanding 12 – AB

On 1 January 20X1, AB acquires a building for $200,000 with an expected life of 50 years. On 31 December 20X4 AB puts the building up for immediate sale. Costs to sell the building are estimated at $10,000.

**Required**

**Outline the accounting treatment of the above if the building had a fair value at 31 December 20X4 of:**

(a)  **$220,000**

(b)  **$110,000.**

## Test your understanding 13 – Nash

Nash purchased a building for its own use on 1 January 20X1 for $1m and attributed it a 50 year useful life. Nash uses the revaluation model to account for buildings.

On 31 December 20X2, this building was revalued to $1.2m.

On 31 December 20X3, the building met the criteria to be classified as held for sale. Its fair value was deemed to be $1.1m and the costs necessary to sell the building were estimated to be $50,000.

Nash does not make a reserves transfer in respect of excess depreciation.

**Required:**

**Discuss the accounting treatment of the above.**

### Presentation in the statement of financial position

IFRS 5 states that assets classified as held for sale should be presented separately from other assets in the statement of financial position.

The liabilities of a disposal group classified as held for sale should be presented separately from other liabilities in the statement of financial position.

The major classes of assets and liabilities classified as held for sale must be separately disclosed either on the face of the statement of financial position or in the notes.

Where an asset or disposal group is classified as held for sale after the reporting date, but before the issue of the financial statements, details should be disclosed in the notes (this is a non-adjusting event after the reporting period).

**Presentation**

**Statement of financial position (showing non-current assets held for sale)**

|  | 20X2 $m | 20X1 $m |
|---|---|---|
| **ASSETS** | | |
| Non-current assets | | |
| Property, plant and equipment | X | X |
| Goodwill | X | X |
| Financial assets | X | X |
| | X | X |
| Current assets | | |
| Inventories | X | X |
| Trade receivables | X | X |
| Cash and cash equivalents | X | X |
| **Non-current assets classified as held for sale** | X | X |
| | X | X |
| Total assets | X | X |

### Changes to a plan of sale

If a sale does not take place within one year, IFRS 5 says that an asset (or disposal group) can still be classified as held for sale if:

- the delay has been caused by events or circumstances beyond the entity's control

- there is sufficient evidence that the entity is still committed to the sale.

If the criteria for 'held for sale' are no longer met, then the entity must cease to classify the assets or disposal group as held for sale. The assets or disposal group must be measured at the lower of:

- **'its carrying amount before it was classified as held for sale adjusted for any depreciation, amortisation or revaluations that would have been recognised had it not been classified as held for sale**

- **its recoverable amount at the date of the subsequent decision not to sell'** (IFRS 5, para 27).

Any adjustment required is recognised in profit or loss as a gain or loss from continuing operations.

## Disclosures

In the period in which a non-current asset or disposal group has been classified as held for sale, or sold, IFRS 5 says that the entity must disclose:

- a description of the non-current asset (or disposal group)
- a description of the facts and circumstances of the sale or expected sale
- any impairment losses or reversals recognised.

## 8    Chapter summary

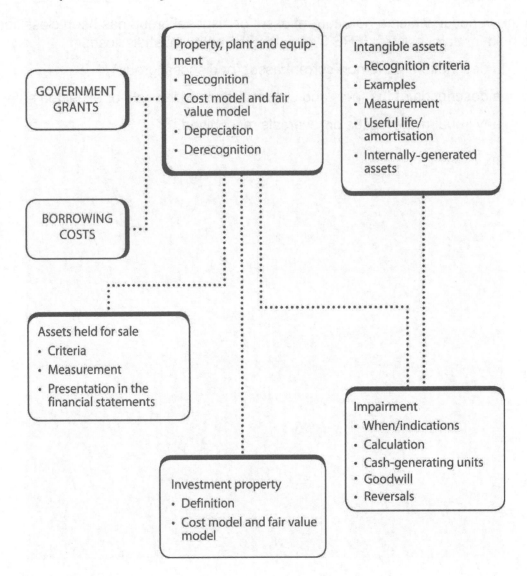

# Test your understanding answers

### Test your understanding 1 – Cap

**The building**

The building would have been recognised on 1 January 20X1 at a cost of $3m ($2.9m purchase price + $0.1m legal fees). Recoverable sales tax is excluded from the cost of property, plant and equipment. General administrative costs of $0.2m will have been expensed to profit or loss as incurred.

Depreciation of $0.06m ($3m/50 years) would have been charged to profit or loss in each of the years ended 31 December 20X1, 20X2, 20X3 and 20X4.

Prior to the revaluation on 31 December 20X4, the carrying amount of the building was $2.76m (46/50 × $3m). In the year ended 31 December 20X4, a gain on revaluation of $1.84m ($4.6m – $2.76m) would have been recognised in other comprehensive income and held within equity.

In the year ended 31 December 20X5, the building would have been depreciated over its remaining useful life of 46 (50 – 4) years. The depreciation charge in the year ended 31 December 20X5 would therefore have been $0.1m ($4.6m/46) leaving a carrying amount at the disposal date of $4.5m ($4.6m – $0.1m).

On 31 December 20X5, a profit on disposal of $0.5m ($5m – $4.5m) would be recorded in the statement of profit or loss.

The revaluation gains previously recognised within OCI and held within equity are not reclassified to profit or loss on the disposal of the asset. However, Cap could do a transfer within equity as follows:

Dr Other components of equity                  $1.84m

Cr Retained earnings                           $1.84m

**The machine**

The machine would be recognised on 1 January 20X3 at $100,000 and depreciated over 10 years. Depreciation of $10,000 ($100,000/10) will be charged in the years ended 31 December 20X3 and December 20X4.

On 1 January 20X5, Cap changes its estimate of the machine's useful life. This is a change in accounting estimate and therefore dealt with prospectively. The carrying amount of the asset at the date of the estimate change is $80,000 (8/10 × $100,000). This remaining carrying amount will be written off over the revised life of 4 years. This means that the depreciation charge is $20,000 ($80,000/4) in the year ended 31 December 20X5.

### Test your understanding 2 – Clock

Government grants should be recognised when there is reasonable assurance that:

- the entity will comply with any conditions attached, and

- the grant will be received.

The only condition attached to the grant is the purchase of the new building. Therefore, the grant should be accounted for on 1 October 20X1.

A receivable will be recognised for the $1m due from the local government. Clock could then choose to either:

(a) Reduce the cost of the building by $1m

In this case, the building will have a cost of $9m ($10m – $1m). This will be depreciated over its useful life of 50 years. The depreciation charge in profit or loss for the year ended 31 December 20X1 will be $15,000 (($9m/50 years) × 1/12) and the building will have a carrying amount of $8,985,000 ($9m – $15,000) as at 31 December 20X1.

(b) Recognise deferred income of $1m.

In this case, the building is recognised at its cost of $10m. This will be depreciated over its useful life of 50 years. The depreciation charge in profit or loss for the year ended 31 December 20X1 will be $16,667 (($10m/50 years) × 1/12) and the building will have a carrying value of $9,983,333 ($10m – $16,667) as at 31 December 20X1.

The deferred income will be amortised to profit or loss over the building's useful life. Therefore, income of $1,667 (($1m/50) × 1/12) will be recorded in profit or loss for the year ended 31 December 20X1. The carrying amount of the deferred income balance within liabilities on the statement of financial position will be $998,333 ($1m – $1,667) as at 31 December 20X1.

## Test your understanding 3 – Hi-Rise

An entity must capitalise borrowing costs that are directly attributable to the production of a qualifying asset. The new office building is a qualifying asset because it takes a substantial period of time to get ready for its intended use.

Hi-Rise should start capitalising borrowing costs when all of the following conditions have been met:

- It incurs expenditure on the asset – 1 March 20X1.

- It incurs borrowing costs – 1 April 20X1.

- It undertakes activities necessary to prepare the asset for intended use – 1 January 20X1.

Capitalisation of borrowing costs should therefore commence on 1 April 20X1. Capitalisation of borrowing costs ceases for the month of July because active development was suspended. In total, 8 months' worth of borrowing costs should be capitalised in the year ended 31 December 20X1.

The total borrowing costs to be capitalised are $333,333 ($5m × 10% × 8/12). These will be added to the cost of the building, giving a carrying amount of $12,333,333 as at 31 December 20X1. The building is not ready for use, so no depreciation is charged.

## Test your understanding 4 – Innovate

According to IAS 38, an intangible asset can be recognised if:

- it is probable that expected future economic benefits attributable to the asset will flow to the entity

- the cost of the asset can be measured reliably.

Cash flow projections suggest that the Our Sports brand will lead to future economic benefits. However, the asset has been internally generated and therefore the cost of the asset cannot be measured reliably. This means that the Our Sports brand cannot be recognised in the financial statements.

The Pets & Me brand has been purchased for $1 million. Therefore, its cost can be measured reliably. An intangible asset should be recognised in respect of the Pets & Me brand at its cost of $1 million.

In subsequent periods, the Pets & Me brand will be amortised over its expected useful life.

## Test your understanding 5 – Scone

Expenditure on research, market research and employee training cannot be capitalised and so must be written off to profit or loss.

In relation to development activities, $0.3 million (4/12 × $0.9m) was incurred before the product was known to be commercially viable. This amount must also be written off to profit or loss.

In total, $1.4 million ($0.5m + $0.4m + $0.2m + $0.3m) must be written off from intangible assets to profit or loss:

| | |
|---|---|
| Dr Profit or loss | $1.4m |
| Cr Intangible assets | $1.4m |

The intangible asset recognised on the statement of financial position will be $0.6 million ($2m – $1.4m). No amortisation will be charged because the product is not yet complete.

## Test your understanding 6 – Impaired asset

(a) The value in use is calculated as the present value of the asset's future cash inflows and outflows

| | Cash flow $000 | Discount rate | PV $000 |
|---|---|---|---|
| Year 1 | 200 | 1/1.10 | 182 |
| Year 2 | 200 | $1/1.10^2$ | 165 |
| | | | 347 |

The recoverable amount is the higher of the fair value less costs to sell of $300,000 ($325,000 – $25,000) and the value in use of $347,000.

The carrying amount of the asset of $500,000 exceeds the recoverable amount of $347,000. Therefore, the asset is impaired and must be written down by $153,000 ($500,000 – $347,000). This impairment loss would be charged to the statement of profit or loss.

| | |
|---|---|
| Dr Profit or loss | $153,000 |
| Cr PPE | $153,000 |

(b) The asset must still be written down by $153,000. However, $10,000 of this would be recognised in other comprehensive income and the remaining $143,000 ($153,000 – $10,000) would be charged to profit or loss.

| | |
|---|---|
| Dr Profit or loss | $143,000 |
| Dr Other comprehensive income | $10,000 |
| Cr PPE | $153,000 |

## Test your understanding 7 – Cash generating units

A forms a cash-generating unit and its cash inflows should be based on the market price for its output. B and C together form one cash-generating unit because there is no market available for the output of B. In calculating the cash outflows of the cash-generating unit B + C, the timber received by B from A should be priced by reference to the market, not any internal transfer price.

## Test your understanding 8 – Factory explosion

The patents have been superseded and have a recoverable amount of $nil. They therefore should be written down to $nil and an impairment loss of $200,000 must be charged to profit or loss.

Half of the machines have been blown to pieces. Therefore, half of the carrying amount of the machines should be written off. An impairment loss of $150,000 will be charged to profit or loss.

The recoverable amount of the other assets cannot be determined so therefore they must be tested for impairment as part of their cash generating unit.

The total carrying amount of the CGU after the impairment of the patents and machines is $2,250,000 (see working below), whereas the recoverable amount is $1,950,000. A further impairment of $300,000 is therefore required.

This is firstly allocated to goodwill and then to other assets on a pro-rata basis. No further impairment should be allocated to the machines as these have already been written down to their recoverable amount.

**Allocation of impairment loss to CGU**

|  | Draft | Impairment | Revised |
|---|---|---|---|
|  | $000 | $000 | $000 |
| Goodwill | 100 | (100) | Nil |
| Patents | nil | – | Nil |
| Machines | 150 | – | 150 |
| Computers | 500 | (50) | 450 |
| Buildings | 1,500 | (150) | 1,350 |
|  | 2,250 | (300) | 1,950 |

The total impairment charged to profit or loss is $650,000 ($200,000 + $150,000 + $300,000).

**Test your understanding 9 – Boxer**

**Year ended 31 December 20X2**

|  | $ |
|---|---|
| Asset carrying amount ($30,000 × 8/10) | 24,000 |
| Recoverable amount | 16,000 |
| | |
| Impairment loss | 8,000 |

The asset is written down to $16,000 and the loss of $8,000 is charged to profit or loss. The depreciation charge per annum in future periods will be $2,000 ($16,000 × 1/8).

**Year ended 31 December 20X5**

|  | $ |
|---|---|
| Asset carrying amount ($16,000 × 5/8) | 10,000 |
| Recoverable amount | 40,000 |
| | |
| Impairment loss | nil |

There has been no impairment loss. In fact, there has been a complete reversal of the first impairment loss. The asset can be reinstated to its depreciated historical cost i.e. to the carrying amount at 31 December 20X5 if there never had been an earlier impairment loss.

Year 5 depreciated historical cost (30,000 × 5/10) = $15,000

Carrying amount: $10,000

Reversal of the loss: $5,000

The reversal of the loss is now recognised. The asset will be increased by $5,000 ($15,000 – $10,000) and a gain of $5,000 will be recognised in profit or loss.

It should be noted that the whole $8,000 original impairment cannot be reversed. The impairment can only be reversed to a maximum amount of depreciated historical cost, based upon the original cost and estimated useful life of the asset.

### Test your understanding 10 – CGUs and impairment reversals

The goodwill impairment cannot be reversed.

The impairment of the PPE can be reversed. However, this is limited to the carrying amount of the asset had no impairment loss been previously recognised.

The carrying amount of the PPE as at 31 December 20X3 is $150,000 ($180,000 × 5/6).

If the PPE had not been impaired, then its value at 31 December 20X3 would have been $250,000 ($400,000 × 5/8).

Therefore, the carrying amount of the PPE can be increased from $150,000 to $250,000. This will give rise to a gain of $100,000 in profit or loss.

### Test your understanding 11 – Hyssop

(a)   IFRS 5 states that in order to be classified as 'held for sale' the property should be available for immediate sale in its present condition. The property will not be sold until the work has been carried out, demonstrating that the facility is not available for immediate sale. Therefore the property cannot be classified as 'held for sale'.

(b)   The subsidiary B does not meet the criteria for classification as 'held for sale'. Although actions to locate a buyer are in place, the subsidiary is not for sale at a price that is reasonable compared with its fair value – the fair value of the subsidiary is $2.5 million, but it is advertised for sale at $3 million. It cannot be classified as 'held for sale' until the sales price is reduced.

**Test your understanding 12 – AB**

Until 31 December 20X4 the building is a non-current asset and its accounting treatment is prescribed by IAS 16. The annual depreciation charge was $4,000 ($200,000/50). As such, the carrying amount at 31 December 20X4, prior to reclassification, was $184,000 ($200,000 – (4 × $4,000)).

(a)  On 31 December 20X4 the building is reclassified as a non-current asset held for sale. It is measured at the lower of carrying amount ($184,000) and fair value less costs to sell ($220,000 – $10,000 = $210,000). This means that the building will continue to be measured at $184,000.

(b)  On 31 December 20X4 the building is reclassified as a non-current asset held for sale. It is measured at the lower of carrying amount ($184,000) and fair value less costs to sell ($110,000 – $10,000 = $100,000). The building will therefore be measured at $100,000 as at 31 December 20X4. An impairment loss of $84,000 ($184,000 – $100,000) will be charged to the statement of profit or loss.

**Test your understanding 13 – Nash**

The building would have been recognised on 1 January 20X1 at its cost of $1m and depreciated over its 50 year life.

By 31 December 20X2, the carrying amount of the building would have been $960,000 ($1m – (($1m/50) × 2 years)).

The building was revalued on 31 December 20X2 to $1.2m, giving a gain on revaluation of $240,000 ($1.2m – $960,000). This gain will have been recorded in other comprehensive income and held within a revaluation surplus (normally as a part of other components of equity).

The building would then have been depreciated over its remaining useful life of 48 years. Depreciation in the year ended 20X3 was therefore $25,000 ($1.2m/48). The building had a carrying amount at 31 December 20X3 of $1,175,000 ($1.2m – $25,000).

At 31 December 20X3, the building is held for sale. Because it is held under the revaluation model, it must initially be revalued downwards to its fair value of $1,100,000. This loss of $75,000 ($1,175,000 – $1,100,000) is recorded in other comprehensive income because there are previous revaluation gains relating to this asset within equity.

The building will then be revalued to fair value less costs to sell. Therefore, the asset must be reduced in value by a further $50,000. This loss is charged to the statement of profit or loss.

# Agriculture and inventories

## Chapter learning objectives

Upon completion of this chapter you will be able to:

- Discuss and apply the principles behind the initial recognition and subsequent measurement of a biological asset or agricultural produce

- Discuss and apply the principles behind the initial recognition and subsequent measurement of inventories.

**PER**

One of the PER performance objectives (PO6) is to record and process transactions and events. You need to use the right accounting treatments for transactions and events. These should be both historical and prospective – and include non-routine transactions. Working through this chapter should help you understand how to demonstrate that objective.

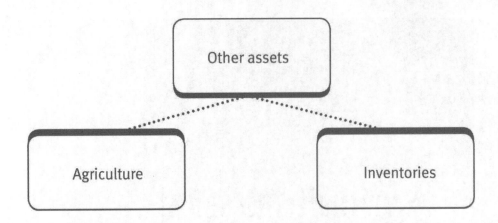

 **Progression**

The IFRS Standards in this chapter were also examined in Financial Reporting. The SBR exam will feature more open-ended questions and real-life scenarios.

## 1 Agriculture

IAS 41 *Agriculture* applies to biological assets and to agricultural produce at the point of harvest.

### Definitions

A biological asset is **'a living plant or animal'** (IAS 41, para 5).

Agricultural produce is **'the harvested product of the entity's biological assets'** (IAS 41, para 5).

Harvest is **'the detachment of produce from a biological asset or the cessation of a biological asset's life processes'** (IAS 41, para 5).

### Application of IAS 41 definitions

| | |
|---|---|
| A farmer buys a dairy calf. | The calf is a biological asset. |
| The calf grows into a mature cow. | Growth is a type of biological transformation. |
| The farmer milks the cow. | The milk has been harvested. Milk is agricultural produce. |

### Biological assets

### Recognition criteria

A biological asset should be recognised if

- it is probable that future economic benefits will flow to the entity from the asset
- the cost or fair value of the asset can be reliably measured
- the entity controls the asset.

## Initial recognition

Biological assets are initially measured at fair value less estimated costs to sell.

Gains and losses may arise in profit or loss when a biological asset is first recognised. For example:

- A loss can arise because estimated selling costs are deducted from fair value.

- A gain can arise when a new biological asset (such as a lamb or a calf) is born.

## Subsequent measurement

At each reporting date, biological assets are revalued to fair value less costs to sell.

Gains and losses arising from changes in fair value are recognised in profit or loss for the period in which they arise.

The fair value of a biological asset may change because of its age, or because prices in the market have changed. IAS 41 recommends separate disclosure of physical and price changes because this information is likely to be of interest to users of the financial statements. However, this is not mandatory.

Biological assets are presented separately on the face of the statement of financial position within non-current assets.

## Inability to measure fair value

IAS 41 presumes that the fair value of biological assets should be capable of being measured reliably.

If market prices are not readily available then the biological asset should be measured at cost less accumulated depreciation and accumulated impairment losses.

Once the asset's fair value can be measured reliably, it should be remeasured to fair value less costs to sell.

**Test your understanding 1 – Cows**

On 1 January 20X1, a farmer had a herd of 100 cows, all of which were 2 years old. At this date, the fair value less point of sale costs of the herd was $10,000. On 1 July 20X1, the farmer purchased 20 cows (each two and half years old) for $60 each.

As at 31 December 20X1, three year old cows sell at market for $90 each.

Market auctioneers have charged a sales levy of 2% for many years.

**Required:**

**Discuss the accounting treatment of the above in the financial statements for the year ended 31 December 20X1.**

## Agricultural produce

At the date of harvest, agricultural produce should be recognised and measured at fair value less estimated costs to sell.

Gains and losses on initial recognition are included in profit or loss (operating profit) for the period.

After produce has been harvested, it becomes an item of inventory. Therefore, IAS 41 ceases to apply. The initial measurement value at the point of harvest is the deemed 'cost' for the purpose of IAS 2 Inventories, which is applied from then onwards.

## Assets outside the scope of IAS 41 Agriculture

IAS 41 does not apply to intangible assets (such as production quotas), bearer plants, or to land related to agricultural activity.

- In accordance with IAS 38, intangible assets are measured at cost less amortisation or fair value less amortisation.

- Bearer plants are used to produce agricultural produce for more than one period. Examples include grape vines or tea bushes. Bearer plants are accounted for in accordance with IAS 16 Property, Plant and Equipment.

  - However, any unharvested produce growing on a bearer plant, such as grapes on a grape vine, is a biological asset and so is accounted for in accordance with IAS 41.

- Land is not a biological asset. It is treated as a tangible non-current asset and accounted for under IAS 16 *Property, Plant and Equipment*.

  - When valuing a forest, for example, the trees must be accounted for separately from the land that they grow on.

### Test your understanding 2 – GoodWine

GoodWine is a company that grows and harvests grapes. Grape vines, which produce a new harvest of grapes each year, are typically replaced every 30 years. Harvested grapes are sold to wine producers. With regards to property, plant and equipment, GoodWine accounts for land using the revaluation model and all other classes of assets using the cost model.

On 30 June 20X1, its grape vines had a carrying amount of $300,000 and a remaining useful life of 20 years. The grapes on the vines, which are generally harvested in August each year, had a fair value of $500,000. The land used for growing the grape vines had a fair value of $2m.

> On 30 June 20X2, grapes with a fair value of $100,000 were harvested early due to unusual weather conditions. The grapes left on the grape vines had a fair value of $520,000. The land had a fair value of $2.1m.
>
> All selling costs are negligible and should be ignored.
>
> **Required:**
>
> **Discuss the accounting treatment of the above in the financial statements of GoodWine for the year ended 30 June 20X2.**

### Agriculture and government grants

If a government grant relates to a biological asset measured at its cost less accumulated depreciation and accumulated impairment losses, it is accounted for under IAS 20 *Accounting for Government Grants and Disclosure of Government Assistance*.

If a government grant relates to biological assets measured at fair value less costs to sell, then it is accounted for under IAS 41 *Agriculture* as follows:

* An **unconditional** government grant related to a biological asset measured at its fair value less costs to sell shall be recognised in profit or loss when it becomes receivable.

* A **conditional** government grant related to a biological asset measured at its fair value less costs to sell, shall be recognised in profit or loss when the conditions attaching to the government grant are met.

### Disclosures

IAS 41 says that an entity must disclose:

* A description of each group of biological assets

* Methods and significant assumptions used when determining fair value

* A reconciliation of the carrying amounts of biological assets between the beginning and the end of the reporting period.

## 2 Inventories

### Initial measurement

Inventories are initially measured at cost.

The cost of an item of inventory, according to IAS 2 *Inventories*, includes purchase costs, conversion costs, and any other costs required to get it to its current condition and location.

* **Purchase costs** include the purchase price (less discounts and rebates), import duties, irrecoverable taxes, transport and handling costs and any other directly attributable costs.

- **Conversion costs** include all direct costs of conversion (materials, labour, expenses, etc.), and a proportion of the fixed and variable production overheads. The allocation of fixed production overheads must be based on the normal level of activity.

- Abnormal wastage, storage costs, administration costs and selling costs must be excluded from the valuation and charged as expenses in the period in which they are incurred.

IAS 2 allows three methods of arriving at the cost of inventories:

- actual unit cost

- first-in, first-out (FIFO)

- weighted average cost (AVCO).

Actual unit cost must be used where items of inventory are not ordinarily interchangeable.

### Subsequent measurement

Inventories may be sold below cost if they are damaged, if there is a decline in demand, or if the market is increasingly competitive. It may also be that items or work in progress are overstated if there has been a rise in the costs required to complete the asset and make the sale.

As such, IAS 2 requires inventories to be written down to the **lower of cost and net realisable value** (NRV) on a line-by-line basis.

Net realisable value is the estimated proceeds from selling the inventory less completion and selling costs.

The NRV of inventory held to satisfy a sales contract is normally evidenced by that contract. However, in other cases, NRV must be estimated. Sales of inventory after the reporting date provide strong evidence about its NRV as at the reporting date.

When measuring NRV, the standard permits similar items to be grouped together, assuming they are sold in the same market.

Raw materials are not written down below cost if the finished good they will form a part of will be sold at a profit. However, a decline in raw material prices would suggest that their NRV has fallen below purchase cost. In such cases, the replacement cost of the raw materials provides evidence of their NRV.

### Disclosure requirements

Entities should disclose:

- the total carrying amount of inventories by category

- details of inventories carried at net realisable value.

**Illustration 1 – Valuation of inventories**

An entity has the following items of inventory.

(a) Raw materials costing $12,000 bought for processing and assembly for a profitable special order. Since buying these items, the cost price of the raw materials has fallen to $10,000.

(b) Equipment constructed for a customer for an agreed price of $18,000. This has recently been completed at a cost of $16,800. It has now been discovered that, in order to meet certain regulations, conversion with an extra cost of $4,200 will be required. The customer has accepted partial responsibility and agreed to meet half the extra cost.

**Required:**

**In accordance with IAS 2 *Inventories*, at what amount should the above items be valued?**

 **Solution**

(a) Raw materials are not written down below cost if the finished good they will form a part of will be sold at a profit. Therefore the inventory should be valued at its cost of $12,000.

(b) The net realisable value is $15,900 (contract price $18,000 – constructor's share of modification cost $2,100). The net realisable value is below the cost price. Therefore the inventory should be held at $15,900.

### 3 Chapter summary

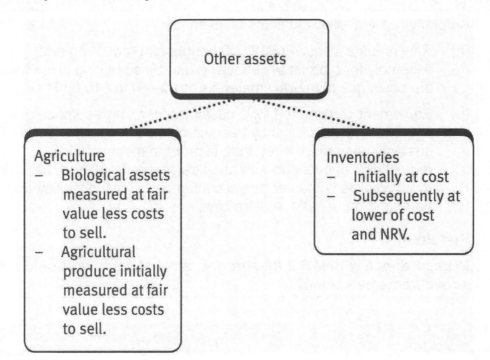

Other assets

Agriculture
- Biological assets measured at fair value less costs to sell.
- Agricultural produce initially measured at fair value less costs to sell.

Inventories
- Initially at cost
- Subsequently at lower of cost and NRV.

## Test your understanding answers

### Test your understanding 1

Cows are biological assets and should be initially recognised at fair value less costs to sell.

The cows purchased in the year should be initially recognised at $1,176 ((20 × $60) × 98%). This will give rise to an immediate loss of $24 ((20 × $60) − $1,176) in the statement of profit or loss.

At year end, the whole herd should be revalued to fair value less costs to sell. Any gain or loss will be recorded in the statement of profit or loss.

The herd of cows will be held at $10,584 ((120 × $90) × 98%) on the statement of financial position.

This will give rise to a further loss of $592 (W1) in the statement of profit or loss.

### (W1) Loss on revaluation

|  | $ |
|---|---|
| Value at 1 January 20X1 | 10,000 |
| New purchase | 1,176 |
| Loss (bal. fig) | (592) |
|  | ——— |
| Value at 31 December 20X1 | 10,584 |
|  | ——— |

**Test your understanding 2 – GoodWine**

Land is accounted for in accordance with IAS 16 *Property, Plant and Equipment*. If the revaluation model is chosen, then gains in the fair value of the land should be reported in other comprehensive income.

At 30 June 20X2, the land should be revalued to $2.1m and a gain of $100,000 ($2.1m – $2.0m) should be reported in other comprehensive income and held within a revaluation reserve in equity.

The grape vines are used to produce agricultural produce over many periods. This means that they are bearer plants and are therefore also accounted for under IAS 16. Except for land, GoodWine uses the cost model for property, plant and equipment. Therefore, depreciation of $15,000 ($300,000/20 years) will be charged to profit or loss in the year and the grape vines will have a carrying amount of $285,000 ($300,000 – $15,000) at 30 June 20X2.

The grapes growing on the vines are biological assets. They should be revalued at the year end to fair value less costs to sell with any gain or loss reported in profit or loss. GoodWine's biological assets should therefore be revalued to $520,000. A gain of $20,000 ($520,000 – $500,000) should be reported in profit or loss.

The grapes are agricultural produce and should initially be recognised at fair value less costs to sell. Any gain or loss on initial recognition is reported in profit or loss. The harvested grapes should be initially recognised at $100,000 with a gain of $100,000 reported in profit or loss. The harvested grapes are now accounted for in accordance with IAS 2 *Inventories* and will have a deemed cost of $100,000.

# Foreign currency in individual financial statements

## Chapter learning objectives

Upon completion of this chapter you will be able to:

- Outline and apply the translation of foreign currency amounts and transactions into the functional currency and the presentation currency.

**PER** One of the PER performance objectives (PO6) is to record and process transactions and events. You need to use the right accounting treatments for transactions and events. These should be both historical and prospective – and include non-routine transactions. Working through this chapter should help you understand how to demonstrate that objective.

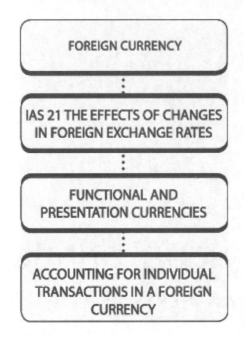

 **Progression**

The content of this chapter was also examined in Financial Reporting. SBR will test more complicated scenarios – particularly with regards to determining an entity's functional currency.

## 1 IAS 21 *The Effects of Changes in Foreign Exchange Rates*

IAS 21 deals with

- the definition of functional and presentation currencies
- accounting for individual transactions in a foreign currency
- translating the financial statements of a foreign operation.

Translating the financial statements of a foreign operation is covered in a later chapter.

### Functional and presentation currencies

An entity maintains its day-to-day financial records in its functional currency.

 **Functional currency** is the **'currency of the primary economic environment where the entity operates'** (IAS 21, para 8).

IAS 21 (para 9) says that an entity should consider the following primary factors when determining its functional currency:

- **'the currency that mainly influences sales prices for goods and services**

- **the currency of the country whose competitive forces and**

- **regulations mainly determine the sales price of goods and services**

- **the currency that mainly influences labour, materials and other costs of providing goods and services'.**

If the primary factors are inconclusive then the following secondary factors should also be considered:

- the currency in which funds from financing activities are generated

- the currency in which receipts from operating activities are retained.

There are times when a foreign subsidiary, rather than applying the above rules, should simply use the same functional currency as its parent. In determining this, IAS 21 says that the following factors should be considered:

- whether the foreign operation operates as an extension of the parent, rather than having significant autonomy

- the level of transactions with the parent

- whether cash flows are readily available for remittance to its parent

- whether the foreign operation has sufficient cash flows to service its debts without needing funds from its parent.

The **presentation currency** is defined by IAS 21 as the currency in which the entity presents its financial statements. This can be different from the functional currency.

### Test your understanding 1 – Chive

Chive is an entity located in a country whose currency is dollars ($).

Seventy per cent of Chive's sales are denominated in dollars and 30% of them are denominated in sterling (£). Chive does not convert receipts from customers into other currencies. Chive buys most of its inventories, and pays for a large proportion of operating costs, in sterling.

Chive has two bank loans outstanding. Both of these loans are denominated in dollars.

**Required:**

**What is the functional currency of Chive?**

## 2 Accounting for transactions designated in a foreign currency

Where an entity enters into a transaction denominated in a currency other than its functional currency, that transaction must be translated into the functional currency before it is recorded.

The exchange rate used to initially record transactions should be either:

- the spot exchange rate on the date the transaction occurred, or
- an average rate over a period of time, providing the exchange rate has not fluctuated significantly.

### Cash settlement

When cash settlement occurs, such as when cash is received from an overseas credit customer, the settled amount should be translated into the functional currency using the spot exchange rate on the settlement date. If this amount differs from that used when the transaction occurred, there will be an exchange difference.

### Exchange differences on settlement

IAS 21 requires that exchange gains or losses on settlement of individual transactions are recognised in profit or loss in the period in which they arise.

IAS 21 is not definitive in stating where in profit or loss any such gains or losses are classified. It would seem reasonable to regard them as items of operating expense or income. However, other profit or loss headings may also be appropriate.

---

 **Exchange differences on settlement**

On 7 May 20X6 an entity with a functional currency of dollars ($) sold goods to a German entity for €48,000. On this date, the rate of exchange was $1 = € 3.2.

The sale is translated into the functional currency using the exchange rate in place on the transaction date.

|  | $ |
|---|---|
| Dr Receivables (€48,000/3.2) | 15,000 |
| Cr Revenue | 15,000 |

On 20 July 20X6 the customer paid the outstanding balance. On this date, the rate of exchange was $1 = €3.17.

The settlement is translated into the functional currency using the exchange rate in place on the settlement date.

|  | $ |
|---|---|
| Dr Cash (€48,000/3.17) | 15,142 |
| Cr Receivables | 15,000 |
| Cr Profit or loss (exchange gain) | 142 |

The $142 exchange gain forms part of the profit for the year.

---

## Treatment of year-end balances

The treatment of any overseas items remaining in the statement of financial position at the year-end depends on whether they are monetary or non-monetary:

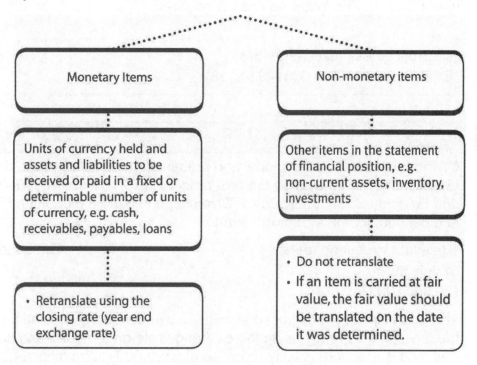

## Exchange differences on retranslation of monetary items

As with exchange differences arising on settlement, IAS 21 requires that exchange differences arising on retranslation of monetary assets and liabilities must be recognised in profit or loss.

IAS 21 does not specify the heading(s) under which such exchange gains or losses should be classified. It would seem reasonable to regard them as items of operating income or operating expense as appropriate.

 **Monetary items**

On 7 May 20X6 an entity with a functional currency of dollars ($) sold goods to a German entity for €48,000. On this date, the rate of exchange was $1 = €3.2.

The sale is translated into the functional currency using the exchange rate in place on the transaction date.

|  | $ |
| --- | --- |
| Dr Receivables (€48,000/3.2) | 15,000 |
| Cr Revenue | 15,000 |

By the reporting date of 31 July 20X6, the invoice had not been settled. On this date, the rate of exchange was $1 = €3.4.

Receivables are a monetary item so must be retranslated into the entity's functional currency at the year-end using the closing exchange rate.

The receivable at year end should therefore be held at $14,118 (€48,000/3.4). The following entry is required:

|  | $ |
|---|---|
| Dr Profit or loss (exchange loss) | 882 |
| Cr Receivables ($15,000 – $14,118) | 882 |

## Non-monetary items

Olympic, which has a functional and presentation currency of the dollar ($), accounts for land using the cost model in IAS 16 *Property, Plant and Equipment*. On 1 July 20X5, Olympic purchased a plot of land in another country for 1.2 million dinars.

| Relevant exchange rates: | Dinars to $1 |
|---|---|
| 1 July 20X5 | 4.0 |
| 30 June 20X6 | 3.0 |

The land is initially recognised at cost. This should be translated into the functional currency using the exchange rate on the purchase date. The land is therefore initially recorded at $300,000 (1.2m dinars/4.0).

Land is not a monetary item so is therefore not retranslated. In accordance with IAS 16, no depreciation is charged. This means that the land remains at $300,000.

## Non-monetary items at fair value

Pallot, which has a functional and presentation currency of the dollar ($), accounts for land using the revaluation model in IAS 16 *Property, Plant and Equipment*. On 1 July 20X5, Pallot purchased a plot of land in another country for 1.2 million dinars. At 30 June 20X6, the fair value of the plot of land was 1.5 million dinars.

| Relevant exchange rates: | Dinars to $1 |
|---|---|
| 1 July 20X5 | 4.0 |
| 30 June 20X6 | 3.0 |

The land is initially recognised at cost. This should be translated into the functional currency using the exchange rate on the purchase date. The land is therefore initially recorded at $300,000 (1.2m dinars/4.0).

Land is not a monetary item so its cost is not retranslated. However, in accordance with the revaluation model in IAS 16, a fair value has been determined. This valuation is in dinars and so must be translated into the functional currency using the exchange rate in place when the fair value was determined. This means that the land must be revalued to $500,000 (1.5m dinars/3.0).

The increase in the carrying value of the land of $200,000 ($500,000 – $300,000) will be reported as a revaluation gain in other comprehensive income for the year and a revaluation reserve will be included within other components of equity on the statement of financial position at the reporting date.

### Test your understanding 2 – Butler, Waiter and Attendant

(a) An entity, Butler, has a reporting date of 31 December and a functional currency of dollars ($). On 27 November 20X6 Butler plc buys goods from a Swedish supplier for SwK 324,000.

On 19 December 20X6 Butler plc pays the Swedish supplier in full.

Exchange rates were as follows:

27 November 20X6 – SwK 11.15: $1

19 December 20X6 – SwK 10.93: $1

**Required:**

**Describe how the above transaction should be accounted for in the financial statements of Butler for the year ended 31 December 20X6.**

(b) An entity, Waiter, has a reporting date of 31 December and the dollar ($) as its functional currency. Waiter borrows in the foreign currency of the Kram (K). The loan of K120,000 was taken out on 1 January 20X7. A repayment of K40,000 was made on 1 March 20X7.

Exchange rates were as follows

1 January 20X7 – K1: $2

1 March 20X7 – K1: $3

31 December 20X7 – K1: $3.5

**Required:**

**Describe how the above should be accounted for in the financial statements of Waiter for the year ended 31 December 20X7.**

(c) An entity, Attendant, has a reporting date of 31 December and has the dollar ($) as its functional currency. Attendant purchased a plot of land overseas on 1 March 20X0. The entity paid for the land in the currency of the Rylands (R). The purchase cost of the land at 1 March 20X0 was R60,000. The value of the land at the reporting date was R80,000.

Exchange rates were as follows:

1 March 20X0 – R8 : $1

31 December 20X0 – R10 : $1

**Required:**

**Describe how the above transaction should be accounted for in the financial statements of Attendant for the year ended 31 December 20X0 if the land is measured at:**

- **cost**

- **fair value.**

## Test your understanding 3 – Highlight

(a) Highlight is an entity whose functional currency is the dollar ($) and has an annual reporting date of 31 December.

On 1 July 20X3, Highlight purchased an item of plant and equipment on credit for Dn400,000. On 1 November 20X3, Highlight made a payment of Dn180,000 to the supplier. The balance of the invoice remains outstanding.

Highlight has a policy of applying historical cost accounting and depreciating plant and equipment at the rate of 20% per annum. The item of plant and equipment is not expected to have any residual value at the end of its useful life.

Relevant exchange rates to $1 are as follows:

|  | Dn |
| --- | --- |
| 1 July 20X3 | 10.0 |
| 1 November 20X3 | 7.2 |
| 1 December 20X3 | 9.0 |
| 31 December 20X3 | 8.0 |

**Required:**

**Prepare relevant extracts from Highlight's financial statements for the year ended 31 December 20X3 to illustrate the impact of the above transactions.**

(b) During 20X3, Highlight entered into a number of transactions with Eraser, an overseas customer.

On 1 November 20X3, Highlight made credit sales to Eraser on 3 months credit for Dn360,000. On 1 December 20X3, Highlight made further credit sales to Eraser on 3 months credit for Dn540,000.

By 31 December 20X3, Highlight had received no payment from Eraser. As the receivables were still within their credit period, they were not regarded as being impaired.

Relevant exchange rates to $1 are as follows:

|  | Dn |
| --- | --- |
| 1 July 20X3 | 10.0 |
| 1 November 20X3 | 7.2 |
| 1 December 20X3 | 9.0 |
| 31 December 20X3 | 8.0 |

**Required:**

**Prepare relevant extracts from Highlight's financial statements for the year ended 31 December 20X3 to illustrate the impact of the above transactions.**

## 3 Criticisms of IAS 21

In relation to IAS 21, the following criticisms have been made:

### Lack of theoretical underpinning

It is not clear why foreign exchange gains and losses on monetary items are recorded in profit or loss, yet foreign exchange gains and losses arising on consolidation of a foreign operation (see Chapter 20) are reported in other comprehensive income (OCI).

It is argued that recording foreign exchange gains or losses on monetary items in profit or loss increases the volatility of reported profits. As such, it has been suggested that foreign exchange gains or losses should be recorded in OCI if there is a high chance of reversal.

### Long-term items

It is argued that retranslating long-term monetary items using the closing rate does not reflect economic substance. This is because a current exchange rate is being used to translate amounts that will be repaid in the future.

Foreign exchange gains and losses on long-term items are highly likely to reverse prior to repayment/receipt, suggesting that such gains and losses are unrealised. This provides further weight to the argument that foreign exchange gains and losses on at least some monetary items should be recorded in OCI.

### The average rate

IAS 21 does not stipulate how to determine the average exchange rate in the reporting period. This increases the potential for entities to manipulate their net assets or total comprehensive income.

The use of different average rates will limit comparability between reporting entities.

### Monetary/non-monetary

The distinction between monetary and non-monetary items can be ambiguous and would benefit from further clarification.

### Foreign operations

IAS 21 uses a restrictive definition of a 'foreign operation' – a subsidiary, associate, joint venture or branch whose activities are based in a country or currency other than that of the reporting entity. It is argued that IAS 21 should instead use a definition of a foreign operation that is based on substance, rather than legal form.

## 4 Chapter summary

```
┌─────────────────────────┐
│    FOREIGN CURRENCY     │
└─────────────────────────┘
            ┊
┌─────────────────────────┐
│   IAS 21 THE EFFECTS OF  │
│   CHANGES IN FOREIGN     │
│    EXCHANGE RATES        │
└─────────────────────────┘
            ┊
┌─────────────────────────┐
│ Functional currency:    │
│ The currency of the primary │
│ economic environment where │
│ the entity operates     │
│                         │
│ Presentation currency:  │
│ The currency in which the entity │
│ presents its financial statements │
└─────────────────────────┘
            ┊
┌─────────────────────────┐
│ Accounting for individual │
│ transactions in a foreign currency │
│ • At transaction date   │
│ • On settlement         │
│ • At reporting date     │
└─────────────────────────┘
```

## Test your understanding answers

### Test your understanding 1 – Chive

Firstly, the primary indicators of functional currency should be applied. Most of Chive's sales are denominated in dollars and so this would suggest that the dollar is its functional currency. However, since a lot of the costs of the business are denominated in sterling, it could be argued that its functional currency is sterling.

Since the primary indicators of functional currency are not clear cut, it is important to look at the secondary indicators. Receipts are retained in both dollars and sterling. However, funding is generated in the form of dollar loans, which further suggests that the dollar might be Chive's functional currency.

All things considered, it would seem that the functional currency of Chive is dollars. This means that any business transactions that are denominated in sterling must be translated into dollars in order to record them.

### Test your understanding 2 – Butler, Waiter and Attendant

(a)    The transaction on 27 November 20X6 must be translated using the exchange rate on the transaction date.

The transaction is recorded at $29,058 (SwK324,000/11.15).

| | |
|---|---|
| Dr Purchases | $29,058 |
| Cr Payables | $29,058 |

The cash settlement on 19 December 20X6 must be translated using the exchange rate on the settlement date.

The cash settlement is recorded at $29,643 (SwK324,000/10.93).

| | |
|---|---|
| Dr Payables | $29,058 |
| Dr Profit or loss | $585 |
| Cr Cash | $29,643 |

An exchange loss of $585 has arisen and this is recorded in the statement of profit or loss.

(b) On 1 January 20X7, money was borrowed in Krams. This must be translated into the functional currency using the exchange rate on the transaction date. The transaction is recorded at $240,000 (K120,000 × 2).

| | |
|---|---|
| Dr Cash | $240,000 |
| Cr Loans | $240,000 |

The cash settlement on 1 March 20X7 must be translated into the functional currency using the exchange rate on the settlement date. The cash settlement is recorded at $120,000 (K40,000 × 3).

| | |
|---|---|
| Dr Loans | $120,000 |
| Cr Cash | $120,000 |

Loans are a monetary liability. At the reporting date, the remaining loan of K80,000 (K120,000 – K40,000) must be translated at the year-end exchange rate. This gives a closing liability of $280,000 (K80,000 × 3.5).

The exchange loss on retranslation is calculated as follows:

| | K | Rate | $ |
|---|---|---|---|
| 1 January 20X7 | 120,000 | 2.0 | 240,000 |
| 1 March 20X7 | (40,000) | 3.0 | (120,000) |
| Exchange loss (bal. fig) | | | 160,000 |
| 31 December 20X7 | 80,000 | 3.5 | 280,000 |

The double entry to record this loss:

| | |
|---|---|
| Dr Profit or loss | $160,000 |
| Cr Loans | $160,000 |

(c) The asset is initially recognised at cost. This should be translated into the functional currency using the exchange rate on the purchase date. The land is therefore initially recorded at $7,500 ($60,000/8).

Land is not a monetary item so is not retranslated. If held under the cost model, it will remain at $7,500.

If the land is held at fair value, then the valuation must be translated into dollars using the exchange rate in place when determined. Therefore, the land will be revalued to $8,000 (R80,000/10). The carrying amount of the land must be increased by $500 ($8,000 – $7,500).

If the land is held under IAS 40 *Investment Property*, then the gain will be recorded in profit or loss. If the land is held under IAS 16 *Property, Plant and Equipment*, then the gain will be recorded in other comprehensive income.

**Test your understanding 3 – Highlight**

(a) Both the purchase of plant and equipment and the associated payable are recorded using the rate ruling at the date of the transaction (Dn10 = $1), giving a value of $40,000. The part-payment made on 1 November is recorded using the rate applicable on that date, with the remaining dinar liability being restated in dollars at the closing rate at the reporting date. The exchange difference, in this case a loss of $12,500 (see calculation below), is taken to profit or loss as an operating expense.

|  |  | Dn | Rate | $ |
|---|---|---|---|---|
| 1/7/X3 | Payable recorded | 400,000 | 10.0 | 40,000 |
| 1/11/X3 | Part-payment made | (180,000) | 7.2 | (25,000) |
|  | Exchange loss (bal. fig) |  |  | 12,500 |
| 31/12/X3 | Payable outstanding | 220,000 | 8.0 | 27,500 |

Plant and equipment, as a non-monetary item, is accounted for at historic cost and is therefore not retranslated. The depreciation charge is $4,000 ($40,000 × 1/5 × 6/12).

Extracts of the financial statements for the year ended 31 December 20X3 are as follows:

| **Statement of profit or loss:** | $ |
|---|---|
| Cost of sales (depreciation) | (4,000) |
| Operating expenses (exchange loss) | (12,500) |
| **Statement of financial position:** | |
| Property, plant and equipment ($40,000 – $4,000) | 36,000 |
| Current liabilities | 27,500 |

(b) Each of the sales invoices denominated in Dn must be translated into $ using the spot rate on the date of each transaction. Each transaction will result in recognition of revenue and a trade receivable at the following amounts.

1 November 20X3: Dn360,000/7.2 = $50,000

1 December 20X3: Dn540,000/9.0 = $60,000

Both amounts remain outstanding at the reporting date and must be restated into dollars using the closing rate of Dn8 = $1. The exchange difference, in this case a gain of $2,500 (see calculation below), is taken to profit or loss as an item of other operating income.

| | | Dn | Rate | $ |
|---|---|---|---|---|
| 1/11/X3 | Receivable recorded | 360,000 | 7.2 | 50,000 |
| 1/12/X3 | Receivable recorded | 540,000 | 9.0 | 60,000 |
| | Exchange gain (bal. fig) | | | 2,500 |
| 31/12/X3 | Receivable outstanding | 900,000 | 8.0 | 112,500 |

Extracts of the financial statements for the year ended 31 December 20X3 are as follows:

**Statement of profit or loss:** $

Revenue ($50,000 + $60,000) 110,000

Other operating income (exchange gain) 2,500

**Statement of financial position:**

Receivables 112,500

# Leases

## Chapter learning objectives

Upon completion of this chapter you will be able to:

- Discuss and apply the lessee accounting requirements for leases including the identification of a lease and the measurement of the right of use asset and liability

- Discuss and apply the accounting for leases by lessors

- Discuss and apply the circumstances where there may be re-measurement of the lease liability

- Discuss and apply the reasons behind the separation of the components of a lease contract into lease and non-lease elements

- Discuss the recognition exemptions under the current leasing standard

- Discuss and apply the principles behind accounting for sale and leaseback transactions.

**PER**

One of the PER performance objectives (PO6) is to record and process transactions and events. You need to use the right accounting treatments for transactions and events. These should be both historical and prospective – and include non-routine transactions. Working through this chapter should help you understand how to demonstrate that objective.

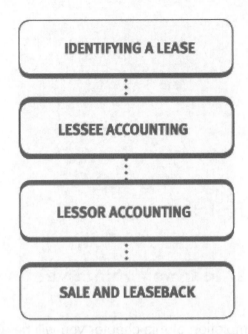

 **Progression**

Most of the content of this chapter was also examined in Financial Reporting, with the exception of lessor accounting. Entities might attempt to under-report lease liabilities, so this can be an area of audit risk in Advanced Audit and Assurance.

##  1 Leases: definitions

IFRS 16 *Leases* provides the following definitions:

A **lease** is a contract, or part of a contract, that conveys the right to use an underlying asset for a period of time in exchange for consideration.

The **lessor** is the entity that provides the right-of-use asset and, in exchange, receives consideration.

The **lessee** is the entity that obtains use of the right-of-use asset and, in exchange, transfers consideration.

A **right-of-use asset** is the lessee's right to use an underlying asset over the lease term.

## 2 Identifying a lease

IFRS 16 *Leases* requires lessees to recognise an asset and a liability for all leases, unless they are short-term or of a minimal value. As such, it is vital to assess whether a contract contains a lease, or whether it is simply a contract for a service.

A contract contains a lease if it conveys **'the right to control the use of an identified asset for a period of time in exchange for consideration'** (IFRS 16, para 9).

The customer controls the asset's use if it has:

- the right to substantially all of the identified asset's economic benefits, and

- the right to direct the identified asset's use.

The right to direct the use of the asset can still exist if the lessor puts restrictions on its use within a contract (such as by capping the maximum mileage of a vehicle, or limiting which countries an asset can be used in). These restrictions define the scope of a lessee's right of use, rather than preventing them from directing use.

IFRS 16 says that a customer does not have the right to use an identified asset if the supplier has the practical ability to substitute the asset for an alternative and if it would be economically beneficial for them to do so.

### Test your understanding 1 – Coffee Bean

Coffee Bean enters into a contract with an airport operator to use some space in the airport to sell its goods from portable kiosks for a three-year period. Coffee Bean owns the portable kiosks. The contract stipulates the amount of space and states that the space may be located at any one of several departure areas within the airport. The airport operator can change the location of the space allocated to Coffee Bean at any time during the period of use, and the costs that the airport operator would incur to do this would be minimal. There are many areas in the airport that are suitable for the portable kiosks.

**Required:**

**Does the contract contain a lease?**

### Test your understanding 2 – AFG

AFG enters into a contract with Splash, the supplier, to use a specified ship for a five-year period. Splash has no substitution rights. During the contract period, AFG decides what cargo will be transported, when the ship will sail, and to which ports it will sail. However, there are some restrictions specified in the contract. Those restrictions prevent AFG from carrying hazardous materials as cargo or from sailing the ship into waters where piracy is a risk.

Splash operates and maintains the ship and is responsible for the safe passage of the cargo on board the ship. AFG is prohibited from hiring another operator for the ship, and from operating the ship itself during the term of the contract.

**Required:**

**Does the contract contain a lease?**

## 3 Lessee accounting

### Basic principle

At the commencement of the lease, IFRS 16 requires that the lessee recognises a lease liability and a right-of-use asset.

**The *Conceptual Framework***

The *Conceptual Framework* defines an asset as an economic resource that, as a result of a past event, is controlled by an entity.

A 'right-of-use' asset meets this definition, because the lessee determines how the asset is used during the lease term. This use will generate economic benefits for the lessee. The lessor is unable to use the asset during this period.

The *Conceptual Framework* defines a liability as a present obligation, arising from a past event, to transfer an economic resource.

A lease liability meets this definition because the lessee has an obligation to transfer consideration to the lessor once the asset has been made available. Consideration, normally in the form of cash, is an economic resource.

### Initial measurement

### The liability

The lease liability is initially measured at the present value of the lease payments that have not yet been paid.

IFRS 16 states that lease payments include the following:

- Fixed payments

- Variable payments that depend on an index or rate, initially valued using the index or rate at the lease commencement date

- Amounts expected to be payable under residual value guarantees

- Options to purchase the asset that are reasonably certain to be exercised

- Termination penalties, if the lease term reflects the expectation that these will be incurred.

A residual value guarantee is when the lessor is promised that the underlying asset at the end of the lease term will not be worth less than a specified amount.

The discount rate should be the rate implicit in the lease. If this cannot be determined, then the entity should use its incremental borrowing rate (the rate at which it could borrow funds to purchase a similar asset).

## The right-of-use asset

The right-of-use asset is initially recognised at cost.

IFRS 16 says that the initial cost of the right-of-use asset comprises:

- The amount of the initial measurement of the lease liability (see above)

- Lease payments made at or before the commencement date

- Initial direct costs

- The estimated costs of removing or dismantling the underlying asset as per the conditions of the lease.

## The lease term

To calculate the initial value of the liability and right-of-use asset, the lessee must consider the length of the lease term. IFRS 16 says that the lease term comprises:

- Non-cancellable periods

- Periods covered by an option to extend the lease if reasonably certain to be exercised

- Periods covered by an option to terminate the lease if reasonably certain not to be exercised.

### Test your understanding 3 – Dynamic

On 1 January 20X1, Dynamic entered into a two year lease for a lorry. The contract contains an option to extend the lease term for a further year. Dynamic believes that it is reasonably certain to exercise this option. Lorries have a useful life of ten years.

Lease payments are $10,000 per year for the initial term and $15,000 per year for the option period. All payments are due at the end of the year. To obtain the lease, Dynamic incurs initial direct costs of $3,000. The lessor immediately reimburses $1,000 of these costs.

The interest rate within the lease is not readily determinable. Dynamic's incremental rate of borrowing is 5%.

**Required:**

**Calculate the initial carrying amount of the lease liability and the right-of-use asset and provide the double entries needed to record these amounts in Dynamic's financial records.**

## Subsequent measurement

### The liability

The carrying amount of the lease liability is increased by the interest charge. This interest is also recorded in the statement of profit or loss:

| | |
|---|---|
| Dr Finance costs (P/L) | X |
| Cr Lease liability | X |

The carrying amount of the lease liability is reduced by cash repayments:

| | |
|---|---|
| Dr Lease liability | X |
| Cr Cash | X |

### The right-of-use asset

The right-of-use asset is measured using the cost model (unless another measurement model is chosen). This means that it is measured at its initial cost less accumulated depreciation and impairment losses.

Depreciation is calculated as follows:

- If ownership of the asset transfers to the lessee at the end of the lease term then depreciation should be charged over the asset's remaining useful life

- Otherwise, depreciation is charged over the shorter of the useful life and the lease term (as defined previously).

### Other measurement models

If the lessee measures investment properties at fair value then IFRS 16 requires that right-of-use assets that meet the definition of investment property should also be measured using the fair value model (e.g. right-of-use assets that are sub-leased under operating leases in order to earn rental income).

If the right-of-use asset belongs to a class of property, plant and equipment that is measured using the revaluation model, an entity **may** apply the IAS 16 *Property, Plant and Equipment* revaluation model to all right-of-use assets within that class.

**Test your understanding 4 – Dynamic (cont.)**

This question follows on from the previous 'test your understanding'.

**Required:**

**Explain the subsequent treatment of Dynamic's lease in the year ended 31 December 20X1.**

## Separating components

A contract may contain a lease component and a non-lease component.

Unless an entity chooses otherwise, the consideration in the contract should be allocated to each component based on the stand-alone selling price of each component.

Entities can, if they prefer, choose to account for the lease and non-lease component as a single lease. This decision must be made for each class of right-of-use asset. However this choice would increase the lease liability recorded at the inception of the lease, which may negatively impact perception of the entity's financial position.

### Illustration 1 – Swish

On 1 January 20X1 Swish entered into a contract to lease a crane for three years. The lessor agrees to maintain the crane during the three year period. The total contract cost is $180,000. Swish must pay $60,000 each year with the payments commencing on 31 December 20X1. Swish accounts for non-lease components separately from leases.

If contracted separately it has been determined that the standalone price for the lease of the crane is $160,000 and the standalone price for the maintenance services is $40,000.

Swish can borrow at a rate of 5% a year.

**Required:**

**Explain how the above will be accounted for by Swish in the year ended 31 December 20X1.**

### Solution

**Allocation of payments**

The annual payments of $60,000 should be allocated between the lease and non-lease components of the contract based on their standalone selling prices:

Lease of Crane: ($160/$160 + $40) × $60,000 = $48,000

Maintenance ($40/$160 + $40) × $60,000 = $12,000

## Lease of Crane

The lease liability is calculated as the present value of the lease payments, as follows:

| Date | Cash flow ($) | Discount rate | Present value ($) |
|---|---|---|---|
| 31/12/X1 | 48,000 | 1/1.05 | 45,714 |
| 31/12/X2 | 48,000 | $1/1.05^2$ | 43,537 |
| 31/12/X3 | 48,000 | $1/1.05^3$ | 41,464 |
| | | | ———— |
| | | | 130,715 |
| | | | ———— |

There are no direct costs so the right-of-use asset is recognised at the same amount:

| | |
|---|---|
| Dr Right-of-use asset | $130,715 |
| Cr Lease liability | $130,715 |

Interest of $6,536 (W1) is charged on the lease liability.

| | |
|---|---|
| Dr Finance costs (P/L) | $6,536 |
| Cr Lease liability | $6,536 |

The cash payment reduces the liability.

| | |
|---|---|
| Dr Lease liability | $48,000 |
| Cr Cash | $48,000 |

The liability has a carrying amount of $89,251 at the reporting date.

The right-of-use asset is depreciated over the three year lease term. This gives a charge of $43,572 ($130,715/3 years).

| | |
|---|---|
| Dr Depreciation (P/L) | $43,572 |
| Cr Right-of-use asset | $43,572 |

The carrying amount of the right-of-use asset will be reduced to $87,143 ($130,715 – $43,572).

### (W1) Lease liability table

| Year-ended | Opening | Interest (5%) | Payments | Closing |
|---|---|---|---|---|
| | $ | $ | $ | $ |
| 31/12/X1 | 130,715 | 6,536 | (48,000) | 89,251 |

### Maintenance

The cost of one year's maintenance will be expensed to profit or loss:

| | |
|---|---|
| Dr P/L | $12,000 |
| Cr Cash | $12,000 |

## Reassessing the lease liability

If changes to lease payments occur then the lease liability must be re-calculated and its carrying amount adjusted. A corresponding adjustment is posted against the carrying amount of the right-of-use asset.

IFRS 16 says that the lease liability should be re-calculated using a revised discount rate if:

- the lease term changes

- the entity's assessment of an option to purchase the underlying asset changes.

The revised discount rate should be the interest rate implicit in the lease for the remainder of the lease term. If this cannot be readily determined, the lessee's incremental borrowing rate at the date of reassessment should be used.

### Test your understanding 5 – Kingfisher

On 1 January 20X1, Kingfisher enters into a four year lease of property with annual lease payments of $1 million, payable at the beginning of each year. According to the contract, lease payments will increase every year on the basis of the increase in the Consumer Price Index for the preceding 12 months. The Consumer Price Index at the commencement date is 125. The interest rate implicit in the lease is not readily determinable. Kingfisher's incremental borrowing rate is 5 per cent per year.

At the beginning of the second year of the lease the Consumer Price Index is 140.

**Required:**

**Discuss how the lease will be accounted for:**

- **during the first year of the contract**

- **on the first day of the second year of the contract.**

## Short-term leases and low value assets

If the lease is short-term (twelve months or less at the inception date) or of a low value then a simplified treatment is allowed.

IFRS 16 does not specify a particular monetary amount below which an asset would be considered 'low value' but instead gives the following examples of low value assets:

- tablets

- small personal computers

- telephones

- small items of furniture.

The assessment of whether an asset qualifies as having a 'low value' must be made based on its value when new. Therefore, a car would not qualify as a low value asset, even if it was very old at the commencement of the lease.

In these cases, the lessee can choose to recognise the lease payments in profit or loss on a straight line basis. No lease liability or right-of-use asset would therefore be recognised.

### Lessee disclosures

If right-of-use assets are not presented separately on the face of the statement of financial position then they should be included within the line item that would have been used if the assets were owned. The entity must disclose which line item includes right-of-use assets.

IFRS 16 requires lessees to disclose the following amounts:

- The depreciation charged on right-of-use assets

- Interest expenses on lease liabilities

- The expense relating to short-term leases and leases of low value assets

- Cash outflows for leased assets

- Right-of-use asset additions

- The carrying amount of right-of-use assets

- A maturity analysis of lease liabilities.

## 4 Lessor accounting

A lessor must classify its leases as finance leases or operating leases.

 IFRS 16 provides the following definitions:

A **finance lease** is a lease where substantially all of the risks and rewards of the underlying asset transfer to the lessee.

An **operating lease** is a lease that does not meet the definition of a finance lease.

### How to classify a lease

IFRS 16 *Leases* states that a lease is probably a finance lease if one or more of the following apply:

Ownership is transferred to the lessee at the end of the lease

- The lessee has the option to purchase the asset for less than its expected fair value at the date the option becomes exercisable and it is reasonably certain that the option will be exercised

- The lease term (including any secondary periods) is for the major part of the asset's economic life

- At the inception of the lease, the present value of the lease payments amounts to at least substantially all of the fair value of the leased asset

- The leased assets are of a specialised nature so that only the lessee can use them without major modifications being made

- The lessee will compensate the lessor for their losses if the lease is cancelled

- Gains or losses from fluctuations in the fair value of the residual fall to the lessee (for example, by means of a rebate of lease payments)

- The lessee can continue the lease for a secondary period in exchange for substantially lower than market rent payments.

---

**Test your understanding 6 – DanBob**

DanBob is a lessor and is drawing up a lease agreement for a building.

The building has a remaining useful life of 50 years. The lease term, which would commence on 1 January 20X0, is for 30 years.

DanBob would receive 40% of the asset's value upfront from the lessee. At the end of each of the 30 years, DanBob will receive 6% of the asset's fair value as at 1 January 20X0.

Legal title at the end of the lease remains with DanBob, but the lessee can continue to lease the asset indefinitely at a rental that is substantially below its market value. If the lessee cancels the lease, it must make a payment to DanBob to recover its remaining investment.

**Required:**

**Per IFRS 16 *Leases*, should the lease be classified as an operating lease or a finance lease?**

---

### Finance leases

#### Initial treatment

At the inception of a lease, lessors present assets held under a finance lease as a receivable. The value of the receivable is calculated as the present value of:

- Fixed payments

- Variable payments that depend on an index or rate, valued using the index or rate at the lease commencement date

- Residual value guarantees

- Unguaranteed residual values

- Purchase options that are reasonably certain to be exercised

- Termination penalties, if the lease term reflects the expectation that these will be incurred.

## Subsequent treatment

The subsequent treatment of the finance lease is as follows:

- The carrying amount of the lease receivable is increased by finance income earned, which is also credited to the statement of profit or loss.

- The carrying amount of the lease receivable is reduced by cash receipts.

### Test your understanding 7 – Vache

Vache leases machinery to Toro. The lease is for four years at an annual cost of $2,000 payable annually in arrears. The present value of the lease payments is $5,710. The implicit rate of interest is 15%.

**Required:**

**How should Vache account for their net investment in the lease?**

## Operating leases

A lessor recognises income from an operating lease on a straight line basis over the lease term.

Any direct costs of negotiating the lease are added to the cost of the underlying asset. The underlying asset should be depreciated in accordance with IAS 16 *Property, Plant and Equipment* or IAS 38 *Intangible Assets*.

### Test your understanding 8 – Oroc

Oroc hires out industrial plant on long-term operating leases. On 1 January 20X1, it entered into a seven-year lease on a mobile crane. The terms of the lease are $175,000 payable on 1 January 20X1, followed by six rentals of $70,000 payable on 1 January 20X2 – 20X7. The crane will be returned to Oroc on 31 December 20X7. The crane originally cost $880,000 and has a 25-year useful life with no residual value.

**Required:**

**Discuss the accounting treatment of the above in the year ended 31 December 20X1.**

## Lessor disclosures

The underlying asset should be presented in the statement of financial position according to its nature.

For finance leases, IFRS 16 requires lessors to disclose:

*   Profit or loss arising on the sale

*   Finance income

*   Data about changes in the carrying amount of the net investment in finance leases

*   A maturity analysis of lease payments receivable.

For operating leases, lessors should disclose a maturity analysis of undiscounted lease payments receivable.

### The *Conceptual Framework*

When developing IFRS Standards, the Board assesses whether the benefits of reporting particular information outweighs the costs involved in providing it.

IFRS 16 *Leases,* which replaced IAS 17 *Leases*, radically changed lessee accounting by requiring all lessees to recognise an asset and liability at the inception of a lease (unless short-term or of minimal value). However, IFRS 16 did not change the accounting treatment of leases by lessors. This was because most stakeholders did not believe that the requirements relating to lessors in IAS 17 were 'broken'. The perceived time and costs involved in implementing substantial changes to lessor accounting were believed to outweigh the benefits.

## 5 Sale and leaseback

If an entity (the seller-lessee) transfers an asset to another entity (the buyer-lessor) and then leases it back, IFRS 16 requires that both entities assess whether the transfer should be accounted for as a sale.

For this purpose, entities must apply IFRS 15 *Revenue from Contracts with Customers* to decide whether a performance obligation has been satisfied. This normally occurs when the customer obtains control of a promised asset. Control of an asset refers to the ability to obtain substantially all of the remaining benefits.

### The Conceptual Framework

IFRS 16 *Leases* provides a faithful representation of sale and leaseback transactions by requiring preparers of financial statements to consider the economic substance of the arrangement. If a 'sale' has not taken place then the underlying asset should not be derecognised.

## Transfer is not a sale

If the transfer is not a sale then IFRS 16 states that:

- The seller-lessee continues to recognise the transferred asset and will recognise a financial liability equal to the transfer proceeds.

- The buyer-lessor will not recognise the transferred asset and will recognise a financial asset equal to the transfer proceeds.

In simple terms, the transfer proceeds are treated as a loan. The detailed accounting treatment of financial assets and financial liabilities is covered in Chapter 12.

## Transfer is a sale

If the transfer does qualify as a sale then IFRS 16 states that:

- The seller-lessee must measure the right-of-use asset as the proportion of the previous carrying amount that relates to the rights retained.

  - This means that the seller-lessee will recognise a profit or loss based only on the rights transferred to the buyer-lessor.

- The buyer-lessor accounts for the asset purchase using the most applicable accounting standard (such as IAS 16 *Property, Plant and Equipment*). The lease is accounted for by applying lessor accounting requirements.

### Test your understanding 9 – Painting

On 1 January 20X1, Painting sells an item of machinery to Collage for its fair value of $3 million. The asset had a carrying amount of $1.2 million prior to the sale. This sale represents the satisfaction of a performance obligation, in accordance with IFRS 15 *Revenue from Contracts with Customers*. Painting enters into a contract with Collage for the right to use the asset for the next five years. Annual payments of $500,000 are due at the end of each year. The interest rate implicit in the lease is 10%.

The present value of the annual lease payments is $1.9 million. The remaining useful life of the machine is much greater than the lease term.

### Required:

**Explain how the transaction will be accounted for on 1 January 20X1 by both Painting and Collage.**

## Transactions not at fair value

If the sales proceeds or lease payments are not at fair value, IFRS 16 requires that:

- below market terms (e.g. when the sales proceeds are less than the asset's fair value) are treated as a prepayment of lease payments

- above market terms (e.g. when the sales proceeds exceed the asset's fair value) are treated as additional financing.

### Illustration 2 – Mosaic

On 1 January 20X1, Mosaic sells an item of machinery to Ceramic for $3 million. Its fair value was $2.8 million. The asset had a carrying amount of $1.2 million prior to the sale. This sale represents the satisfaction of performance obligation, in accordance with IFRS 15 *Revenue from Contracts with Customers*.

Mosaic enters into a contract with Ceramic for the right to use the asset for the next five years. Annual payments of $500,000 are due at the end of each year. The interest rate implicit in the lease is 10%. The present value of the annual lease payments is $1.9 million.

**Required:**

**Explain how the transaction will be accounted for on 1 January 20X1 by both Mosaic and Ceramic.**

### Solution

The excess sales proceeds are $0.2 million ($3m – $2.8m). This is treated as additional financing.

The present value of the lease payments was $1.9 million. It is assumed that $0.2 million relates to the additional financing that Mosaic has been given. The remaining $1.7 million relates to the lease.

**Mosaic**

Mosaic must remove the carrying amount of the machine from its statement of financial position. It should instead recognise a right-of-use asset. This right-of-use asset will be measured as the proportion of the previous carrying amount that relates to the rights retained by Mosaic:

(1.7m/2.8m) × $1.2 million = $0.73 million.

The entry required is as follows:

| | |
|---|---|
| Dr Cash | $3.00m |
| Dr Right-of-use asset | $0.73m |
| Cr Machine | $1.20m |
| Cr Lease liability | $1.70m |
| Cr Financial liability | $0.20m |
| Cr Profit or loss (bal. fig.) | $0.63m |

Note: The gain in profit or loss is the proportion of the overall $1.6 million gain on disposal ($2.8m – $1.2m) that relates to the rights transferred to Ceramic. This can be calculated as follows:

((2.8m – 1.7m)/2.8m) × $1.6 million = $0.63 million.

The right of use asset and the lease liability will then be accounted for using normal lessee accounting rules. The financial liability is accounted for in accordance with IFRS 9 *Financial Instruments*.

### Ceramic

Ceramic will post the following:

| | |
|---|---|
| Dr Machine | $2.80m |
| Dr Financial asset | $0.20m |
| Cr Cash | $3.00m |

It will then account for the lease using normal lessor accounting rules.

### Note

The payments/receipts will be allocated between the lease and the additional finance. This is based on the proportion of the total present value of the payments that they represent:

- The payment/receipt allocated to the lease will be $447,368 ((1.7/1.9) × $500,000).

- The payment/receipt allocated to the additional finance will be $52,632 ((0.2/1.9) × $500,000).

## 6 Chapter summary

```
┌─────────────────────────────────────┐
│         IDENTIFYING A LEASE          │
│          A contract that conveys     │
│      the right to control the use of an │
│        identified asset for a period of │
│   time in exchange for consideration. │
└─────────────────────────────────────┘
                  ⋮
┌─────────────────────────────────────┐
│          LESSEE ACCOUNTING           │
│        Recognise a lease liability   │
│   and a right-of-use asset (unless the │
│    lease is short-term or of low value) │
└─────────────────────────────────────┘
                  ⋮
┌─────────────────────────────────────┐
│          LESSOR ACCOUNTING           │
│           Classify the lease as a    │
│    finance lease or an operating lease │
└─────────────────────────────────────┘
                  ⋮
┌─────────────────────────────────────┐
│         SALE AND LEASEBACK           │
│         Determine whether the        │
│     transfer qualifies as a 'sale'   │
└─────────────────────────────────────┘
```

## Test your understanding answers

### Test your understanding 1 – Coffee Bean

The contract does not contain a lease because there is no identified asset.

The contract is for space in the airport, and the airport operator has the practical right to substitute this during the period of use because:

- There are many areas available in the airport that would meet the contract terms, providing the operator with a practical ability to substitute

- The airport operator would benefit economically from substituting the space because there would be minimal cost associated with it. This would allow the operator to make the most effective use of its available space, thus maximising profits.

### Test your understanding 2 – AFG

AFG has the right to use an identified asset (a specific ship) for a period of time (five years). Splash cannot substitute the specified ship for an alternative.

AFG has the right to control the use of the ship throughout the five-year period of use because:

- it has the right to obtain substantially all of the economic benefits from use of the ship over the five-year period due to its exclusive use of the ship throughout the period of use.

- it has the right to direct the use of the ship. Although contractual terms limit where the ship can sail and what cargo can be transported, this acts to define the scope of AFG's right to use the ship rather than restricting AFG's ability to direct the use of the ship. Within the scope of its right of use, AFG makes the relevant decisions about how and for what purpose the ship is used throughout the five-year period of use because it decides whether, where and when the ship sails, as well as the cargo it will transport.

Splash's operation and maintenance of the ship does not prevent AFG from directing how, and for what purpose, the ship is used.

Therefore, based on the above, the contract contains a lease.

## Test your understanding 3 – Dynamic

The lease term is three years. This is because the option to extend the lease is reasonably certain to be exercised.

The lease liability calculated as follows:

| Date | Cash flow ($) | Discount rate | Present value ($) |
|---|---|---|---|
| 31/12/X1 | 10,000 | $1/1.05$ | 9,524 |
| 31/12/X2 | 10,000 | $1/1.05^2$ | 9,070 |
| 31/12/X3 | 15,000 | $1/1.05^3$ | 12,958 |
| | | | ——— |
| | | | 31,552 |
| | | | ——— |

The initial cost of the right-of-use asset is calculated as follows:

| | $ |
|---|---|
| Initial liability value | 31,552 |
| Direct costs | 3,000 |
| Reimbursement | (1,000) |
| | ——— |
| | 33,552 |
| | ——— |

The double entries to record this are as follows:

| | |
|---|---|
| Dr Right-of-use asset | $31,552 |
| Cr Lease liability | $31,552 |
| Dr Right-of-use asset | $3,000 |
| Cr Cash | $3,000 |
| Dr Cash | $1,000 |
| Cr Right-of-use asset | $1,000 |

**Test your understanding 4 – Dynamic (cont.)**

Interest of $1,578 (W1) is charged on the lease liability.

| | |
|---|---|
| Dr Finance costs (P/L) | $1,578 |
| Cr Lease liability | $1,578 |

The cash payment reduces the liability.

| | |
|---|---|
| Dr Liability | $10,000 |
| Cr Cash | $10,000 |

The liability has a carrying amount of $23,130 at the reporting date. Of this, $14,287 (W1) is non-current and $8,843 ($23,130 – $14,287) is current.

The right-of-use asset is depreciated over the three year lease term, because it is shorter than the useful life. This gives a charge of $11,184 ($33,552/3 years).

| | |
|---|---|
| Dr Depreciation (P/L) | $11,184 |
| Cr Right-of-use asset | $11,184 |

The carrying amount of the right-of-use asset will be reduced to $22,368 ($33,552 – $11,184).

**(W1)  Lease liability table**

| Year-ended | Opening | Interest (5%) | Payments | Closing |
|---|---|---|---|---|
| | $ | $ | $ | $ |
| 31/12/X1 | 31,552 | 1,578 | (10,000) | 23,130 |
| 31/12/X2 | 23,130 | 1,157 | (10,000) | 14,287 |

## Test your understanding 5 – Kingfisher

### The first year

The first payment occurs on the commencement date so is included in the initial cost of the right-of-use asset:

| | |
|---|---|
| Dr Right-of-use asset | $1m |
| Cr Cash | $1m |

The liability should be measured at the present value of the lease payments not yet made. The payments are variable as they depend on an index. They should be valued using the index at the commencement date (i.e. it is assumed that the index will remain at 125 and so the payments will remain at $1 million a year).

| Date | Cash flow ($m) | Discount rate | Present value ($m) |
|---|---|---|---|
| 1/1/X2 | 1.0 | $1/1.05$ | 0.95 |
| 1/1/X3 | 1.0 | $1/1.05^2$ | 0.91 |
| 1/1/X4 | 1.0 | $1/1.05^3$ | 0.86 |
| | | | _____ |
| | | | 2.72 |
| | | | _____ |

| | |
|---|---|
| Dr Right-of-use asset | $2.72m |
| Cr Lease liability | $2.72m |

The asset is depreciated over the lease term of four years, giving a charge of $0.93 million (($1m + $2.72m)/4).

| | |
|---|---|
| Dr Depreciation (P/L) | $0.93m |
| Cr Right-of-use asset | $0.93m |

The asset has a carrying amount at the reporting date of $2.79 million ($1m + $2.72m – $0.93m).

The interest charge on the liability is $0.14 million (W1).

| | |
|---|---|
| Dr Finance costs (P/L) | $0.14m |
| Cr Lease liability | $0.14m |

The liability has a carrying amount at the reporting date of $2.86m (W1).

### (W1) Lease liability table

| Year-ended | Opening $m | Interest (5%) $m | Closing $m |
|---|---|---|---|
| 31/12/X1 | 2.72 | 0.14 | 2.86 |

**The first day of the second year**

There are three remaining payments to make. The payment for the second year that is now due is $1.12 million ($1m × 140/125). The lease liability is remeasured to reflect the revised lease payments (three payments of $1.12 million).

| Date | Cash flow ($m) | Discount rate | Present value ($m) |
|---|---|---|---|
| 1/1/X2 | 1.12 | 1 | 1.12 |
| 1/1/X3 | 1.12 | 1/1.05 | 1.07 |
| 1/1/X4 | 1.12 | $1/1.05^2$ | 1.02 |
| | | | ――― |
| | | | 3.21 |
| | | | ――― |

The lease liability must be increased by $0.35 million ($3.21 – $2.86m). A corresponding adjustment is made to the right-of-use asset:

| | |
|---|---|
| Dr Right-of-use asset | $0.35m |
| Cr Lease liability | $0.35m |

The payment of $1.12 million will then reduce the lease liability:

| | |
|---|---|
| Dr Lease liability | $1.12m |
| Cr Cash | $1.12m |

The right-of-use asset's carrying amount of $3.14 million ($2.79 + $0.35m) will be depreciated over the remaining lease term of three years.

**Test your understanding 6 – DanBob**

A finance lease is defined by IFRS 16 as a lease where substantially all of the risks and rewards of ownership transfer from the lessor to the lessee.

Key indications, according to IFRS 16, that a lease is a finance lease are as follows:

- The lease transfers ownership of the asset to the lessee by the end of the lease term.

- The lease term is for the major part of the asset's economic life.

- At the inception of the lease, the present value of the lease payments amounts to at least substantially all of the fair value of the leased asset.

- If the lessee can cancel the lease, the lessor's losses are borne by the lessee.

- The lessee can continue the lease for a secondary period in exchange for substantially lower than market rent payments.

The lease term is only for 60% (30 years/50 years) of the asset's useful life. Legal title also does not pass at the end of the lease. These factors suggest that the lease is an operating lease.

However, the lessee can continue to lease the asset at the end of the lease term for a value that is substantially below market value. This suggests that the lessee will benefit from the building over its useful life and is therefore an indication of a finance lease.

The lessee is also unable to cancel the lease without paying DanBob. This is an indication that DanBob is guaranteed to recoup its investment and therefore that they have relinquished the risks of ownership.

It also seems likely that the present value of the minimum lease payments will be substantially all of the asset's fair value. The minimum lease payments (ignoring discounting) equate to 40% of the fair value, payable upfront, and then another 180% (30 years × 6%) of the fair value over the lease term. Therefore this again suggests that the lease is a finance lease.

All things considered, it would appear that the lease is a finance lease.

## Test your understanding 7 – Vache

Vache recognises the net investment in the lease as a receivable. This is the present value of the lease payments of $5,710.

The receivable is increased by finance income. The receivable is reduced by the cash receipts.

| Year | Opening balance | Finance income (15%) | Cash received | Closing balance |
|---|---|---|---|---|
| | $ | $ | $ | $ |
| 1 | 5,710 | 856 | (2,000) | 4,566 |
| 2 | 4,566 | 685 | (2,000) | 3,251 |
| 3 | 3,251 | 488 | (2,000) | 1,739 |
| 4 | 1,739 | 261 | (2,000) | – |

**Extract from the statement of financial position at the end of Year 1**

|  | $ |
|---|---|
| Non-current assets: | |
| Net investment in finance leases (see note) | 3,251 |
| Current assets: | |
| Net investment in finance leases | 1,315 |

**Note:** the current asset is the next instalment less next year's interest ($2,000 – $685). The non-current asset is the remainder ($4,566 – $1,315).

## Test your understanding 8 – Oroc

Oroc holds the crane in its statement of financial position and depreciates it over its useful life. The annual depreciation charge is $35,200 ($880,000/25 years).

Rental income must be recognised in profit or loss on a straight line basis. Total lease receipts are $595,000 ($175,000 + ($70,000 × 6 years)). Annual rental income is therefore $85,000 ($595,000/7 years). The statement of financial position includes a liability for deferred income of $90,000 ($175,000 – $85,000).

## Test your understanding 9 – Painting

### Painting

Painting must remove the carrying amount of the machine from its statement of financial position. It should instead recognise a right-of-use asset. This right-of-use asset will be measured as the proportion of the previous carrying amount that relates to the rights retained by Painting:

(1.9m/3m) × $1.2 million = $0.76 million.

The entry required is as follows:

| | |
|---|---|
| Dr Cash | $3.00m |
| Dr Right-of-use asset | $0.76m |
| Cr Machine | $1.20m |
| Cr Lease liability | $1.90m |
| Cr Profit or loss (bal. fig.) | $0.66m |

Note: The gain in profit or loss is the proportion of the overall $1.8 million gain on disposal ($3m – $1.2m) that relates to the rights transferred to Collage. This can be calculated as follows:

((3m – 1.9m)/3m) × $1.8m = $0.66 million.

The right-of-use asset and the lease liability will then be accounted for using normal lessee accounting rules.

### Collage

Collage will post the following:

| | |
|---|---|
| Dr Machine | $3.00m |
| Cr Cash | $3.00m |

Normal lessor accounting rules apply. The lease is an operating lease because the present value of the lease payments is not substantially the same as the asset's fair value, and the lease term is not for the majority of the asset's useful life. Collage will record rental income in profit or loss on a straight line basis.

# Employee benefits

## Chapter learning objectives

Upon completion of this chapter you will be able to:

- Discuss and apply the accounting treatment of short term and long term employee benefits and defined contribution and defined benefit plans
- Account for gains and losses on settlements and curtailments
- Account for the "Asset Ceiling" test and the reporting of actuarial gains and losses.

**PER**

One of the PER performance objectives (PO6) is to record and process transactions and events. You need to use the right accounting treatments for transactions and events. These should be both historical and prospective – and include non-routine transactions. Working through this chapter should help you understand how to demonstrate that objective.

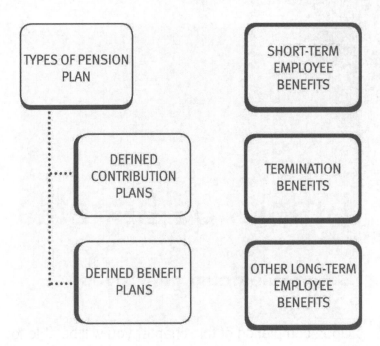

## 1 Introduction

**Types of employee benefit**

IAS 19 *Employee Benefits* identifies four types of employee benefit as follows:

- **Post-employment benefits.** This normally relates to retirement benefits.

- **Short-term employee benefits.** This includes wages and salaries, bonuses and other benefits.

- **Termination benefits.** Termination benefits arise when benefits become payable upon employment being terminated, either by the employer or by the employee accepting terms to have employment terminated.

- **Other long-term employee benefits.** This comprises other items not within the above classifications and will include long-service leave or awards, long-term disability benefits and other long-service benefits.

Each will be considered within this chapter, with particular emphasis upon post-employment defined benefit plans.

 **Progression**

This topic is not examined in Financial Reporting and so is likely to be new to you.

## 2 Post-employment benefit plans

A pension plan (sometimes called a post-employment benefit plan or scheme) consists of a pool of assets, together with a liability for pensions owed. Pension plan assets normally consist of investments, cash and (sometimes) properties. The return earned on the assets is used to pay pensions.

There are two main types of pension plan:

- defined contribution plans
- defined benefit plans.

 **Defined contribution plans** are benefit plans where the entity **'pays fixed contributions into a separate entity and will have no legal or constructive obligation to pay further contributions if the fund does not hold sufficient assets to pay all employee benefits relating to their service'** (IAS 19, para 8).

**Defined benefit plans** are post-employment plans that are not defined contribution plans.

 **A defined contribution plan**

An entity pays fixed contributions of 5% of employee salaries into a pension plan each month. The entity has no obligation outside of its fixed contributions.

The lack of any obligation to contribute further assets into the fund means that this is a defined contribution plan.

 **A defined benefit plan**

An entity guarantees a particular level of pension benefit to its employees upon retirement. The annual pension income that employees will receive is based on the following formula:

Salary at retirement × (no. of years worked/60 years)

The entity has an obligation to pay extra funds into the pension plan to meet this promised level of pension benefits. This is therefore a defined benefit plan.

**Test your understanding 1 – Deller**

Deller has a defined contribution pension scheme. However, during the year, it introduced a new post-employment plan (the Fund) for its employees as a way of enhancing the benefits they will receive when they retire. Deller makes monthly contributions into the Fund that are equal to a set percentage of the salary cost.

Upon retirement, employees will receive annual payments from the Fund based on their number of years of service and their final salary.

The Fund is voluntary and Deller can cancel it at any point.

Deller has a history of paying employees benefits that are substantially above the national average, with annual increases in excess of inflation. Deller has won many accolades as a 'top employer' and received positive coverage from the national press when the Fund was announced. The leadership team are well trusted by the employees.

**Required:**

**Advise Deller on whether the Fund is a defined benefit plan or a defined contribution plan.**

## 3 Accounting for defined contribution plans

The entity should charge the agreed pension contribution to profit or loss as an employment expense in each period.

The expense of providing pensions in the period is often the same as the amount of contributions paid. However, an accrual or prepayment arises if the cash paid does not equal the value of contributions due for the period.

**Test your understanding 2 – Defined contribution scheme**

An entity makes contributions to the pension fund of employees at a rate of 5% of gross salaries. For convenience, the entity pays $10,000 per month into the pension scheme with any balance being paid in the first month of the following accounting year. The wages and salaries for 20X6 are $2.7 million.

**Required:**

**Calculate the pension expense for 20X6, and the accrual/ prepayment at the end of the year.**

## 4  Accounting for defined benefit plans

### The statement of financial position

Under a defined benefit plan, an entity has an obligation to its employees. The entity therefore has a long-term liability that must be measured at present value.

The entity will also be making regular contributions into the pension plan. These contributions will be invested and the investments will generate returns. This means that the entity has assets held within the pension plan, which IAS 19 states must be measured at fair value.

On the statement of financial position, an entity offsets its pension obligation and its plan assets and reports the net position:

- If the obligation exceeds the assets, there is a plan deficit (the usual situation) and a liability is reported in the statement of financial position.

- If the assets exceed the obligation, there is a surplus and an asset is reported in the statement of financial position.

It is difficult to calculate the size of the defined benefit pension obligation and plan assets. It is therefore recommended that entities use an expert known as an actuary.

### The year-on-year movement

An entity must account for the year-on-year movement in its defined benefit pension scheme deficit (or surplus).

The following proforma shows the movement on the defined benefit deficit (surplus) over a reporting period:

|  | $000 |
|---|---|
| Net deficit/(asset) brought forward | X/(X) |
| (Obligation bfd – assets bfd) | |
| Net interest component | X/(X) |
| Service cost component | X |
| Contributions into plan | (X) |
| Benefits paid | – |
| | X/(X) |
| Remeasurement component (bal. fig) | X/(X) |
| Net deficit/(asset) carried forward (Obligation cfd – assets cfd) | X/(X) |

### Net interest component

This is charged (or credited) to profit or loss and represents the change in the net pension liability (or asset) due to the passage in time. It is computed by applying the discount rate at the start of the year to the net defined benefit liability (or asset).

### Service cost component

This is charged to profit or loss and is comprised of three elements

- **'Current service cost, which is the increase in the present value of the obligation arising from employee service in the current period. period.**

- **Past service cost, which is the change in the present value of the obligation for employee service in prior periods, resulting from a plan amendment or curtailment.**

- **Any gain or loss on settlement'** (IAS 19, para 8).

**Past service costs** arise when there has been an improvement in the benefits to be provided under the plan or when there has been a curtailment.

**A curtailment** is a significant reduction in the number of employees covered by a pension plan. This may be a consequence of employees being made redundant.

Past service costs are recognised at the earlier of:

- **'when the plan amendment or curtailment occurs**

- **when the entity recognises related restructuring costs or termination benefit'** (IAS 19, para 103).

**A settlement** occurs when an entity enters into a transaction to eliminate the obligation for part or all of the benefits under a plan. For example, an employee may leave the entity for a new job elsewhere, and a payment is made from that pension plan to the pension plan operated by the new employer.

The gain or loss on settlement is the difference between the fair value of the plan assets paid out and the reduction in the present value of the defined benefit obligation. The gain or loss forms part of the service cost component.

### Contributions into the plan

These are the cash payments paid into the plan during the reporting period by the employer. This has no impact on the statement of profit or loss and other comprehensive income.

## Benefits paid

These are the amounts paid out of the plan assets to retired employees during the period. These payments reduce both the plan obligation and the plan assets. Therefore, this has no overall impact on the net pension deficit (or asset).

## Remeasurement component

After accounting for the above, the net pension deficit will differ from the amount calculated by the actuary as at the current year end. This is for a number of reasons:

- The actuary's calculation of the value of the plan obligation and assets is based on assumptions, such as life expectancy and final salaries, and these will have changed year-on-year.

- The actual return on plan assets is different from the amount taken to profit or loss as part of the net interest component.

An adjustment, known as the **remeasurement component,** must therefore be posted. This is charged or credited to other comprehensive income for the year and identified as an item that will not be reclassified to profit or loss in future periods.

**The** *Conceptual Framework*

When developing or amending IFRS Standards, the Board notes that it might decide that certain income or expenses should be presented in other comprehensive if they result from remeasuring an item to current value and if this means that:

- profit or loss provides more relevant information, or

- it provides a more faithful representation of an entity's performance.

IAS 19 requires that the remeasurement component is recorded in other comprehensive income. A defined benefit plan is long-term in nature and so the Board believes it is inappropriate to recognise short-term fluctuations in profit or loss. This protects the statement of profit or loss as the primary source of information about an entity's financial performance in the period.

According to the *Conceptual Framework*, income and expenditure included in other comprehensive income should be reclassified to profit or loss when doing so results in profit or loss providing more relevant information. However, the Board may decide that reclassification is not appropriate.

The remeasurement component is not reclassified to profit or loss. The Board argues that there is no clear basis to determine the amount or the timing of reclassification.

## Summary of the amounts recognised in the financial statements

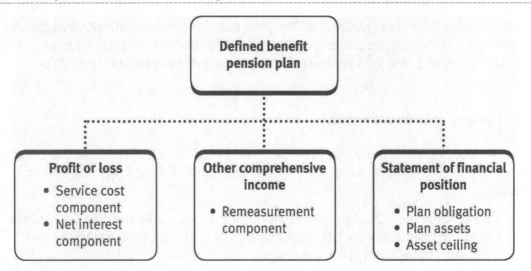

 **Illustration 1 – Defined benefit plan – Celine**

The following information is provided in relation to a defined benefit plan operated by Celine. At 1 January 20X4, the present value of the obligation was $140 million and the fair value of the plan assets amounted to $80 million.

| | 20X4 | 20X5 |
|---|---|---|
| Discount rate at start of year | 4% | 3% |
| Current and past service cost ($m) | 30 | 32 |
| Benefits paid ($m) | 20 | 22 |
| Contributions into plan ($m) | 25 | 30 |
| Present value of obligation at 31 December ($m) | 200 | 230 |
| Fair value of plan assets at 31 December ($m) | 120 | 140 |

**Required:**

**Determine the net plan obligation or asset at 31 December 20X4 and 20X5 and the amounts to be taken to profit or loss and other comprehensive income for both financial years.**

 **Solution**

**The statement of financial position**

| | 20X4 | 20X5 |
|---|---|---|
| | $m | $m |
| PV of plan obligation | 200.0 | 230.0 |
| FV of plan assets | (120.0) | (140.0) |
| | | |
| Closing net liability | 80.0 | 90.0 |

## The statement of profit or loss and other comprehensive income

Both the service cost component and the net interest component are charged to profit or loss for the year. The remeasurement component, which comprises actuarial gains and losses, together with returns on plan assets to the extent that they are not included within the net interest component, is taken to other comprehensive income.

|  | 20X4 $m | 20X5 $m |
|---|---|---|
| **Profit or loss** |  |  |
| Service cost component | 30.0 | 32.0 |
| Net interest component | 2.4 | 2.4 |
|  | 32.4 | 34.4 |
| **Other comprehensive income** |  |  |
| Remeasurement component | 12.6 | 5.6 |
| Total comprehensive income charge for year | 45.0 | 40.0 |

## Reconciliation of the net obligation for 20X4 and 20X5

|  | 20X4 $m | 20X5 $m |
|---|---|---|
| Obligation bal b/fwd 1 January | 140.0 | 200.0 |
| Asset bal b/fwd at 1 January | (80.0) | (120.0) |
| Net obligation b/fwd at 1 January | 60.0 | 80.0 |
| Service cost component | 30.0 | 32.0 |
| Net interest component |  |  |
| 4% × $60m | 2.4 |  |
| 3% × $80m |  | 2.4 |
| Contributions into plan | (25.0) | (30.0) |
| Benefits paid | – | – |
| Remeasurement component (bal. fig.) | 12.6 | 5.6 |
| Net obligation c/fwd at 31 December | 80.0 | 90.0 |

## Illustration 2 – Past service costs

An entity operates a pension plan that provides a pension of 2% of final salary for each year of service. On 1 January 20X5, the entity improves the pension to 2.5% of final salary for each year of service, including service before this date. Employees must have worked for the entity for at least five years in order to obtain this increased benefit. At the date of the improvement, the present value of the additional benefits for service from 1 January 20X1 to 1 January 20X5, is as follows:

|  | $000 |
|---|---|
| Employees with more than five years' service at 1.1.X5 | 150 |
| Employees with less than five years' service at 1.1.X5 (average length of service: two years) | 120 |
|  | ─── |
|  | 270 |
|  | ─── |

**Required:**

**Explain how the additional benefits are accounted for in the financial statements of the entity.**

## Solution

The entity recognises all $270,000 immediately as an increase in the defined benefit obligation following the amendment to the plan on 1 January 20X5. This will form part of the service cost component. Whether or not the benefits have vested by the reporting date is not relevant to their recognition as an expense in the financial statements.

## Illustration 3 – Curtailments

AB decides to close a business segment. The segment's employees will be made redundant and will earn no further pension benefits after being made redundant. Their plan assets will remain in the scheme so that the employees will be paid a pension when they reach retirement age (i.e. this is a curtailment without settlement).

Before the curtailment, the scheme assets had a fair value of $500,000, and the defined benefit obligation had a present value of $600,000. It is estimated that the curtailment will reduce the present value of the future obligation by 10%, which reflects the fact that employees will not benefit from future salary increases and therefore will be entitled to a smaller pension than previously estimated.

**Required:**

**What is net gain or loss on curtailment and how will this be treated in the financial statements?**

## Solution

The obligation is to be reduced by 10% × $600,000 = $60,000, with no change in the fair value of the assets as they remain in the plan. The reduction in the obligation represents a gain on curtailment which should be included as part of the service cost component and taken to profit or loss for the year. The net position of the plan following curtailment will be:

|  | Before | On curtailment | After |
|---|---|---|---|
|  | $000 | $000 | $000 |
| Present value of obligation | 600 | (60) | 540 |
| Fair value of plan assets | (500) | – | (500) |
| Net obligation in SFP | 100 | (60) | 40 |

The gain on curtailment is $60,000 and this will be included as part of the service cost component in profit or loss for the year.

## Test your understanding 3 – Fraser

The following information relates to a defined benefit plan operated by Fraser. At 1 January 20X1, the present value of the obligation was $1,000,000 and the fair value of the plan assets amounted to $900,000.

|  | 20X1 | 20X2 | 20X3 |
|---|---|---|---|
| Discount rate at start of year | 10% | 9% | 8% |
| Current and past service cost ($000) | 125 | 130 | 138 |
| Benefits paid ($000) | 150 | 155 | 165 |
| Contributions paid into plan ($000) | 90 | 95 | 105 |
| PV of obligation at 31 December ($000) | 1,350 | 1,340 | 1,450 |
| FV of plan assets at 31 December ($000) | 1,200 | 1,150 | 1,300 |

**Required:**

**Show how the defined benefit plan would be shown in the financial statements for each of the years ended 31 December 20X1, 20X2 and 20X3 respectively.**

## Test your understanding 4 – TC

TC has a defined benefit pension plan and prepares financial statements to 31 March each year. The following information is relevant for the year ended 31 March 20X3:

- The net pension obligation at 31 March 20X3 was $55 million. At 31 March 20X2, the net obligation was $48 million, comprising the present value of the plan obligation stated at $100 million, together with plan assets stated at fair value of $52 million.

- The discount rate relevant to the net obligation was 6.25% and the actual return on plan assets for the year was $4 million.

- The current service cost was $12 million.

- At 31 March 20X3, TC granted additional benefits to those currently receiving benefits that are due to vest over the next four years and which have a present value of $4 million at that date. They were not allowed for in the original actuarial assumptions.

- During the year, TC made pension contributions of $8 million into the scheme and the scheme paid pension benefits in the year amounting to $3 million.

**Required:**

**Explain the accounting treatment of the TC pension scheme for the year to 31 March 20X3, together with supporting calculations.**

## Test your understanding 5 – Mickleover

On 1 July 20X3 Mickleover started a defined benefit pension scheme for its employees and immediately contributed $4m cash into the scheme. The actuary has stated that the net obligation was $0.4m as at 30 June 20X4. The interest rate for good quality corporate bonds was 10% at 1 July 20X3 but 12% by 30 June 20X4. The actual return on the plan assets was 11%. The increased cost from the employee's service in the year was $4.2m which can be assumed to accrue at the year end.

On 30 June 20X4 Mickleover paid $0.3m in settlement of a defined benefit obligation with a present value of $0.2m. This related to staff that were to be made redundant although, as at 30 June 20X4, they still had an average remaining employment term of one month. The redundancies were not foreseen at the start of the year.

**Required:**

**Discuss the correct accounting treatment of the above transaction in the financial statements of Mickleover for the year ended 30 June 20X4.**

## 5 The asset ceiling

Most defined benefit pension plans are in deficit (i.e. the obligation exceeds the plan assets) although some defined benefit pension plans show a surplus.

If a defined benefit plan is in surplus, IAS 19 states that the surplus must be measured at the lower of:

- the amount calculated as normal (per earlier examples and illustrations)

- the total of the present value of any economic benefits available in the form of refunds from the plan or reductions in future contributions to the plan.

This is known as applying the 'asset ceiling'. It means that a surplus can only be recognised to the extent that it will be recoverable in the form of refunds or reduced contributions in the future. This ensures that an asset is only recognised if it has the potential to bring economic benefits to the reporting entity.

### Illustration 4 – The asset ceiling

The following information relates to a defined benefit plan:

|  | $000 |
| --- | --- |
| Fair value of plan assets | 950 |
| Present value of pension liability | 800 |
| Present value of future refunds and reductions in future contributions | 70 |

**Required:**

**What is the value of the asset that should be recognised in the financial statements?**

### Solution

The amount that can be recognised is the lower of:

|  | $000 |
| --- | --- |
| Present value of plan obligation | 800 |
| Fair value of plan assets | (950) |
|  | ——— |
|  | (150) |
|  | ——— |

|  | $000 |
| --- | --- |
| PV of future refunds and/or reductions in future contributions | (70) |
|  | ——— |

Therefore the asset that can be recognised is restricted to $70,000.

### Test your understanding 6 – Arc

The following information relates to the defined benefit plan operated by Arc for the year ended 30 June 20X4:

|  | $m |
|---|---|
| FV of plan assets b/fwd at 30 June 20X3 | 2,600 |
| PV of obligation b/fwd at 30 June 20X3 | 2,000 |
| Current service cost for the year | 100 |
| Benefits paid in the year | 80 |
| Contributions into plan | 90 |
| FV of plan assets at 30 June 20X4 | 3,100 |
| PV of plan obligation at 30 June 20X4 | 2,400 |

Discount rate for the defined benefit obligation – 10%

Arc has identified that the asset ceiling at 30 June 20X3 and 30 June 20X4, based upon the present value of future refunds from the plan and/or reductions in future contributions amounts to $200m at 30 June 20X3 and 30 June 20X4.

**Required:**

**Explain, with supporting calculations, the accounting treatment of the pension scheme for the year ended 30 June 20X4.**

## 6 Other issues

### Other employee benefits

IAS 19 covers a number of other issues in addition to post-employment benefits as follows:

### Short-term employee benefits

This includes a number of issues including:

- **Wages and salaries and bonuses and other benefits.** The general principle is that wages and salaries costs are expenses as they are incurred on a normal accruals basis, unless capitalisation is permitted in accordance with another reporting standard. Bonuses and other short-term payments are recognised using normal criteria of establishing an obligation based upon past events which can be reliably measured.

- **Compensated absences.** This covers issues such as holiday pay, sick leave, maternity leave, jury service, study leave and military service. The key issue is whether the absences are regarded as being accumulating or non-accumulating:

    - accumulating benefits are earned over time and are capable of being carried forward. In this situation, the expense for future compensated absences is recognised over the period services are provided by the employee. This will typically result in the recognition of a liability at the reporting date for the expected cost of the accumulated benefit earned but not yet claimed by an employee. An example of this would be a holiday pay accrual at the reporting date where unused holiday entitlement can be carried forward and claimed in a future period.

    - for non-accumulating benefits, an expense should only be recognised when the absence occurs. This may arise, for example, where an employee continues to receive their normal remuneration whilst being absent due to illness or other permitted reason. A charge to profit or loss would be made only when the authorised absence occurs; if there is no such absence, there will be no charge to profit or loss.

- **Benefits in kind.** Recognition of cost should be based on the same principles as benefits payable in cash; it should be measured based upon the cost to the employer of providing the benefit and recognised as it is earned.

### Termination benefits

Termination benefits may be defined as benefits payable as a result of employment being terminated, either by the employer, or by the employee accepting voluntary redundancy. Such payments are normally in the form of a lump sum; entitlement to such payments is not accrued over time, and only become available in a relatively short period prior to any such payment being agreed and paid to the employee.

The obligation to pay such benefits is recognised either when the employer can no longer withdraw the offer of such benefits (i.e. they are committed to paying them), or when it recognises related restructuring costs (normally in accordance with IAS 37). Payments which are due to be paid more than twelve months after the reporting date should be discounted to their present value.

### Other long-term employee benefits

This comprises other items not within the above classifications and will include long-service leave, long-term disability benefits and other long-service benefits. These employee benefits are accounted for in a similar manner to accounting for post-employment benefits, as benefits are payable more than twelve months after the period in which services are provided by an employee.

## Disclosure requirements

IAS 19 has extensive disclosure requirements. An entity should disclose the following information about defined benefit plans:

- Significant actuarial assumptions used to determine the net defined benefit obligation or assets.

- a general description of the type of plan operated

- a reconciliation of the assets and liabilities recognised in the statement of financial position

- the charge to total comprehensive income for the year, separated into the appropriate components

- analysis of the remeasurement component to identify returns on plan assets, together with actuarial gains and losses arising on the net plan obligation

- sensitivity analysis and narrative description of how the defined benefit plan may affect the nature, timing and uncertainty of the entity's future cash flows.

### Investor perspective

IAS 19 recommends the use of an actuary to calculate the defined benefit obligation. The use of an independent expert should reduce the potential for management bias. However, even when using an actuary, the net defined benefit obligation is still susceptible to volatility because the long-term assumptions used are likely to change over time.

As such, IAS 19 requires entities to disclose the results of a sensitivity analysis. This shows the potential impact on the net deficit of changes in the main actuarial assumptions.

An example is provided below:

|  | $m |
|---|---|
| Defined benefit deficit as at 31 December 20X1 | 500 |
| Sensitivity of 0.1% increase in: |  |
|     Discount rate | (69) |
|     Inflation | 50 |
|     Salary increases | 18 |
| Sensitivity of one year increase in life expectancy | 104 |

This information will help investors to understand the risks underlying amounts recognised in the financial statements. Some investors may be deterred by the impact of these reasonably possible changes and therefore decide to invest in other entities which are less susceptible to volatility.

## Criticisms

Retirement benefit accounting continues to be a controversial area. Commentators have perceived the following problems with IAS 19:

- **Classification** – some types of pension plans cannot be easily classified as 'defined benefit' or 'defined contribution'.

- **Volatility** – the fair values of defined benefit plan assets may be volatile or difficult to measure reliably.

- **Short-term** – IAS 19 requires defined benefit plan assets to be valued at fair value. However, most pension scheme assets and liabilities are held for the long term.

- **Complexity** – the treatment of defined benefit pension costs in the statement of profit or loss and other comprehensive income is complex and may not be easily understood by users of the financial statements. It has been argued that all the components of the pension cost are so interrelated that it does not make sense to present them separately.

- **Conceptual Framework** – the requirement to reflect future salary increases and unvested benefits when measuring the defined benefit obligation seems to be at odds with the *Conceptual Framework's* definition of a liability because there is no current obligation to pay these.

# 7 Chapter summary

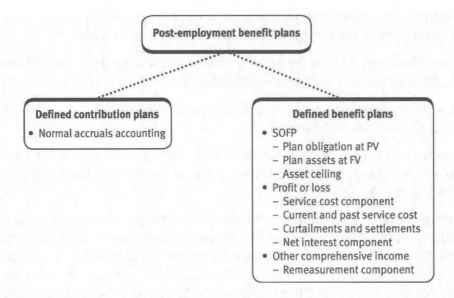

**Other long-term employee benefits**
- Account for in similar way to defined benefit pension plans – spread cost over service period

**Short-term employee benefits**
- Normal accruals accounting
- Cumulating or non-cumulating

**Termination benefits**
- Recognise when an obligation or when related restructuring costs recognised

## Test your understanding answers

### Test your understanding 1 – Deller

It is possible that there will be insufficient assets in the Fund to pay the benefits due to retired employees, particularly if final salaries or life expectancy rise substantially. Deller therefore bears actuarial and investment risk because, if it continues with the Fund, it would need to make up for any shortfall.

Although the Fund is voluntary and can be cancelled, Deller has a history of remunerating its employees above the national average as well as a strong reputation as a good and honest employer. Deller therefore has a constructive obligation to continue with the Fund and to ensure that its level of assets is sufficient.

As a result of the above, the Fund should be accounted for as a defined benefit plan.

### Test your understanding 2 – Defined contribution scheme

This appears to be a defined contribution scheme.

The charge to profit or loss should be:

$2.7m × 5% = $135,000

The statement of financial position will therefore show an accrual of $15,000, being the difference between the $135,000 expense and the $120,000 ($10,000 × 12 months) cash paid in the year.

## Test your understanding 3 – Fraser

### Statement of financial position

|  | 20X1 $000 | 20X2 $000 | 20X3 $000 |
|---|---|---|---|
| Net pension (asset)/liability | 150 | 190 | 150 |

### Profit or loss and other comprehensive income for the year

|  | 20X1 $000 | 20X2 $000 | 20X3 $000 |
|---|---|---|---|
| **Profit or loss** |  |  |  |
| Service cost component | 125 | 130 | 138 |
| Net interest component | 10 | 14 | 15 |
|  | —— | —— | —— |
| Charge to profit or loss | 135 | 144 | 153 |
| **Other comprehensive income:** |  |  |  |
| Remeasurement component | 5 | (9) | (88) |
|  | —— | —— | —— |
| Total charge to comprehensive income | 140 | 135 | 65 |
|  | —— | —— | —— |

### The remeasurement component on the net obligation

|  | 20X1 $000 | 20X2 $000 | 20X3 $000 |
|---|---|---|---|
| Net obligation at start of the year | 100 | 150 | 190 |
| Net interest component (10% X1/9% X2/8% X3) | 10 | 14 | 15 |
| Service cost component | 125 | 130 | 138 |
| Contributions into plan | (90) | (95) | (105) |
| Remeasurement (gain)/loss (bal. fig) | 5 | (9) | (88) |
|  | —— | —— | —— |
| Net obligation at end of the year | 150 | 190 | 150 |
|  | —— | —— | —— |

## Test your understanding 4 – TC

|  | $m | $m |
|---|---|---|
| Net obligation brought forward |  | 48 |
| Net interest component (6.25% × 48) |  | 3 |
| Service cost component: |  |  |
| Current service cost | 12 |  |
| Past service cost | 4 |  |
|  | ——— |  |
|  |  | 16 |
| Contributions into the plan |  | (8) |
| Benefits paid |  | – |
| Remeasurement component (bal. fig.) |  | (4) |
|  |  | ——— |
| Net obligation carried forward |  | 55 |
|  |  | ——— |

**Explanation:**

- The discount rate is applied to the net obligation brought forward. The net interest component is $3m and this is charged to profit or loss.

- The current year service cost, together with the past service cost forms the service cost component. Past service cost is charged in full, usually when the scheme is amended, rather than when the additional benefits vest. The total service cost component is $16m and this is charged to profit or loss.

- To the extent that there has been a return on assets in excess of the amount identified by application of the discount rate to the fair value of plan assets, this is part of the remeasurement component (i.e. $4m – $3.25m ($52m × 6.25%) = $0.75m).

- Contributions paid into the plan during the year of $8m reduce the net obligation.

- Benefits paid of $3 million will reduce both the scheme assets and the scheme obligation, so have no impact on the net obligation.

- The statement of financial position as at 31 March 20X3 will show a net deficit (a liability) of $55m.

### Test your understanding 5 – Mickleover

The accounting treatment of a defined benefit plan is as follows:

- the amount recognised in the statement of financial position is the present value of the defined benefit obligation less the fair value of the plan assets as at the reporting date.

- The opening net position should be unwound using a discount rate that applies to good quality corporate bonds. This should be charged/credited to profit or loss.

- The increased cost from the employees' service during the past year is known as a current service cost. This should be expensed against profits as part of the service cost component and credited to the pension scheme obligation.

- Curtailments should be recognised at the earlier of when the curtailment occurs or when the related termination benefits are recognised.

- The remeasurement component should be included in other comprehensive income and identified as an item which will not be reclassified to profit and loss in future periods.

In relation to Mickleover:

- The net liability on the statement of financial position as at 30 June 20X4 is $0.4m.

- Although this is the first year of the scheme cash of $4m was introduced at the start of the year and so this should be unwound at 10%.

- The net interest component credited to profit and loss will therefore be $0.4m (10% × $4m). The service cost arises at the year end and so is not unwound.

- Although the employees have not yet been made redundant, the costs related to the redundancy will have been recognised during the current reporting period. Therefore, a loss on curtailment of $0.1m ($0.3m – $0.2m) should also be recognised in the current year. As the curtailment was not foreseen and would not have been included within the actuarial assumptions, the $0.1m should be charged against profits within the service cost component.

- The remeasurement loss, which includes the difference between the actual returns on plan assets and the amount taken to profit or loss as part of the net interest component, is $0.5m (W1).

**(W1) Remeasurement component**

| | $m |
|---|---:|
| Net obligation brought forward | 0 |
| Contributions | (4) |
| Net interest component (10% × $4m) | (0.4) |
| Service cost component | |
| Current service cost | 4.2 |
| Loss on curtailment | 0.1 |
| | 4.3 |
| Benefits paid | – |
| **Remeasurement component (bal fig)** | 0.5 |
| Net obligation carried forward | 0.4 |

**Test your understanding 6 – Arc**

| | Net plan asset before ceiling adj | Ceiling adj* | Net plan asset after ceiling adj | Note |
|---|---:|---:|---:|---:|
| | $m | $m | $m | |
| Balance b/fwd | (600) | 400 | (200) | 1 |
| Net interest component (10%) | (60) | 40 | (20) | 2 |
| Service cost component | 100 | – | 100 | 3 |
| Benefits paid | – | – | – | 4 |
| Contributions in | (90) | – | (90) | 5 |
| Sub-total: | (650) | 440 | (210) | |
| Remeasurement component | (50) | 60 | 10 | 6 |
| Balance c/fwd | (700) | 500 | (200) | |

* note that this is effectively a balancing figure.

**Explanation:**

1   The asset ceiling adjustment at the previous reporting date of 30 June 20X3 measures the net defined benefit asset at the amount recoverable by refunds and/or reduced future contributions, stated at $200m. In effect, the value of the asset was reduced for reporting purposes at 30 June 20X3.

2   Interest charged on the obligation or earned on the plan assets is based upon the discount rate for the obligation, stated at 10%. This will then require adjustment to agree with the net return on the net plan asset at the beginning of the year. Net interest earned is taken to profit or loss for the year.

3   The current year service cost increases the plan obligation, which therefore reduces the net plan asset. The current year service cost is taken to profit or loss for the year.

4   Benefits paid in the year reduce both the plan obligation and the plan assets by the same amount.

5   Contributions into the plan increase the fair value of plan assets, and also the net plan asset during the year.

6   The remeasurement component, including actuarial gains and losses for the year, is identified to arrive at the present value of the plan obligation and the fair value of the plan assets at 30 June 20X4. As there is a net asset of $700m ($3,100m – $2,400m) for the defined benefit pension plan, the asset ceiling test is applied to restrict the reported asset to the expected future benefits in the form of refunds and/or reduced future contributions. This is stated in the question to be $200m. To the extent that an adjustment is required to the net asset at the reporting date, this is part of the net remeasurement component.

**Statement of financial position**

|  | $000 |
|---|---|
| Net pension asset | 200 |

**Profit or loss and other comprehensive income for the year**

|  | $000 |
|---|---|
| **Profit or loss** | |
| Service cost component | 100 |
| Net interest component | (20) |
| Charge to profit or loss | 80 |
| **Other comprehensive income:** | |
| Remeasurement component | 10 |
| Total charge to comprehensive income | 90 |

# Share-based payment

## Chapter learning objectives

Upon completion of this chapter you will be able to:

- Discuss and apply the recognition and measurement of share-based payment transactions
- Account for modifications, cancellations and settlements of share-based payment transactions.

**PER**

One of the PER performance objectives (PO6) is to record and process transactions and events. You need to use the right accounting treatments for transactions and events. These should be both historical and prospective – and include non-routine transactions. Working through this chapter should help you understand how to demonstrate that objective.

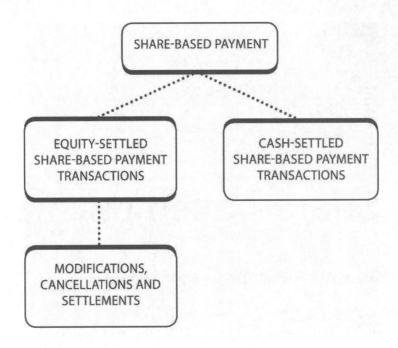

## 1    Share-based payment

### Introduction

Share-based payment schemes have become increasingly common. A share-based payment occurs when an entity buys goods or services from other parties (such as employees or suppliers) and:

- settles the amounts payable by issuing its shares or share options, or

- incurs liabilities for cash payments based on its share price.

### The problem

If a company pays for goods or services in cash, an expense is recognised in profit or loss. If a company 'pays' for goods or services in share options, there is no cash outflow and therefore, under traditional accounting, no expense would be recognised.

If a company issues shares to employees, a transaction has occurred. The employees have provided a valuable service to the entity, in exchange for the shares or share options. It is inconsistent not to recognise this transaction in the financial statements.

IFRS 2 *Share-based Payment* was issued to deal with this accounting anomaly. IFRS 2 requires that all share-based payment transactions must be recognised in the financial statements when the transaction takes place.

## Types of transaction

IFRS 2 applies to all share-based payment transactions. There are two main types.

- **Equity-settled share-based payments**: the entity acquires goods or services in exchange for equity instruments of the entity (e.g. shares or share options)

- **Cash-settled share-based payments**: the entity acquires goods or services in exchange for amounts of cash measured by reference to the entity's share price.

A **share option** allows the holder to buy a share in the future for a fixed price (the 'exercise price'). If the exercise price is less than the fair value of a share at the exercise date then the option holder is essentially getting a discount and so the option is said to be 'in the money'.

The most common type of share-based payment transaction is where share options are granted to employees or directors as part of their remuneration.

> **Progression**
>
> This topic is not examined in Financial Reporting and so is likely to be new to you.

## 2    Equity-settled share-based payments

### Accounting treatment

When an entity receives goods or services as a result of an equity-settled share-based payment transaction, it posts the following double entry:

Dr Expense/asset

Cr Equity

The entry to equity is normally reported in 'other components of equity'. Share capital is not affected until the share-based payment has 'vested' (covered later in the chapter).

### Measurement

The basic principle is that share-based payment transactions are measured at fair value. However, there are complications as to how this is determined:

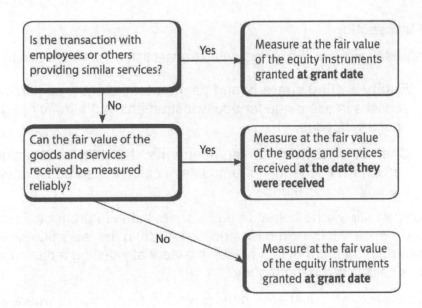

 The **grant date** is the date at which the entity and another party agree to the arrangement.

## Timing

Some equity instruments vest immediately. In other words, the holder is unconditionally entitled to the instruments. In this case, the transaction should be accounted for in full on the grant date.

However, when share options are granted to employees, there are normally conditions attached. For example, a service condition may exist that requires employees to complete a specified period of service.

 IFRS 2 states that an entity should account for services as they are rendered during the vesting period (the period between the grant date and the vesting date).

 The **vesting date** is the date on which the counterparty (e.g. the employee) becomes entitled to receive the cash or equity instruments under the arrangement.

The expense recognised at each reporting date should be based on the best estimate of the number of equity instruments expected to vest.

On the vesting date, the entity shall revise the estimate to equal the number of equity instruments that ultimately vest.

## Illustration 1 – When to recognise the transaction

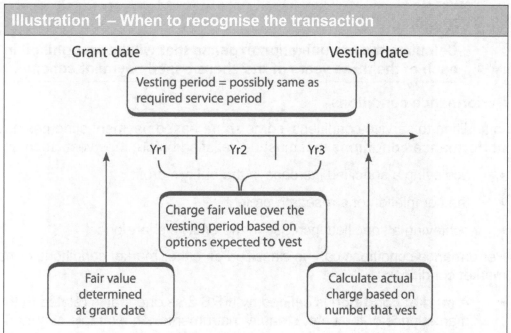

## Test your understanding 1 – Liminal

On 1 January 20X8 Liminal purchased a patent. The fair value of the patent was reliably estimated to be $3 million. The consideration transferred was 1 million of Liminal's own $1 ordinary shares. On the purchase date, the patent had a remaining useful life of three years. The fair value of one of Liminal's ordinary shares was $3.50 on 1 January 20X8 and $3.20 on 30 June 20X8.

**Required:**

**Discuss the correct accounting treatment of the above in the year ended 30 June 20X8.**

## Test your understanding 2 – Equity-settled share-based payment

An entity has a reporting date of 31 December.

On 1 January 20X1 it grants 100 share options to each of its 500 employees. Each grant is conditional upon the employee working for the entity until 31 December 20X3. At the grant date the fair value of each share option is $15.

During 20X1, 20 employees leave and the entity estimates that a total of 20% of the 500 employees will leave during the three-year period.

During 20X2, a further 20 employees leave and the entity now estimates that only 15% of the original 500 employees will leave during the three-year period.

During 20X3, a further 10 employees leave.

> **Required:**
>
> **Calculate the remuneration expense that will be recognised in each of the three years of the share-based payment scheme.**

## Performance conditions

In addition to service conditions, some share based payment schemes have **performance conditions** that must be satisfied before they vest, such as:

- achieving a specified increase in the entity's profit
- the completion of a research project
- achieving a specified increase in the entity's share price.

Performance conditions can be classified as either market conditions or non-market conditions.

- A **market condition** is defined by IFRS 2 as one that is related to the market price of the entity's equity instruments. An example of a market condition is that the entity must attain a minimum share price by the vesting date for scheme members to be eligible to participate in the share-based payment scheme.

- **Non-market performance conditions** are not related to the market price of the entity's equity instruments. Examples of non-market performance conditions include EPS or profit targets.

## Conditions attaching to share-based payment transactions: a summary

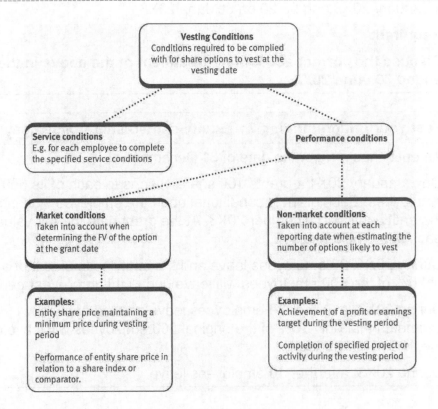

## The impact of performance conditions

- **Market-based conditions** have already been factored into the fair value of the equity instrument at the grant date. Therefore, an expense is recognised irrespective of whether market conditions are satisfied.

- **Non-market based conditions** must be taken into account in determining whether an expense should be recognised in a reporting period.

### Test your understanding 3 – Market based conditions

On 1 January 20X1, one hundred employees were given 50 share options each. These will vest if the employees still work for the entity on 31 December 20X2 and if the share price on that date is more than $5.

On 1 January 20X1, the fair value of the options was $1. The share price on 31 December 20X1 was $3 and it was considered unlikely that the share price would rise to $5 by 31 December 20X2. Ten employees left during the year ended 31 December 20X1 and a further ten are expected to leave in the following year.

**Required:**

**How should the above transaction be accounted for in the year ended 31 December 20X1?**

### Test your understanding 4 – Blueberry

On 1 January 20X4 an entity, Blueberry, granted share options to each of its 200 employees, subject to a three-year vesting period, provided that the volume of sales increases by a minimum of 5% per annum throughout the vesting period. A maximum of 300 share options per employee will vest, dependent upon the increase in the volume of sales throughout each year of the vesting period as follows:

- If the volume of sales increases by an average of between 5% and 10% per year, each eligible employee will receive 100 share options.

- If the volume of sales increases by an average of between 10% and 15% per year, each eligible employee will receive 200 share options.

- If the volume of sales increases by an average of over 15% per year, each eligible employee will receive 300 share options.

At the grant date, Blueberry estimated that the fair value of each option was $10 and that the increase in the volume of sales each year would be between 10% and 15%. It was also estimated that a total of 22% of employees would leave prior to the end of the vesting period. At each reporting date within the vesting period, the situation was as follows:

| Reporting date | Employees leaving in year | Further leavers expected prior to vesting date | Annual increase in sales volume | Expected sales volume increase over remaining vesting period | Average annual increase in sales volume to date |
|---|---|---|---|---|---|
| 31 Dec X4 | 8 | 18 | 14% | 14% | 14% |
| 31 Dec X5 | 6 | 4 | 18% | 16% | 16% |
| 31 Dec X6 | 2 | | 16% | | 16% |

**Required:**

**Calculate the impact of the above share-based payment scheme on Blueberry's financial statements in each reporting period.**

## Accounting after the vesting date

IFRS 2 states that no further adjustments to **total equity** should be made after the vesting date. This applies even if some of the equity instruments do not vest (for example, because a market based condition was not met).

Entities may, however, transfer any balance from 'other components of equity' to retained earnings.

### Test your understanding 5 – Beginner

Beginner offered directors an option scheme conditional on a three-year period of service. The number of options granted to each of the ten directors at the inception of the scheme was 1 million. The options were exercisable shortly after the end of the third year. Upon exercise of the share options, those directors eligible would be required to pay $2 for each share of $1 nominal value.

The fair value of the options and the estimates of the number of options expected to vest at various points in time were as follows:

| Year | Rights expected to vest | Fair value of the option $ |
|---|---|---|
| Start of Year One | 8m | 0.30 |
| End of Year One | 7m | 0.33 |
| End of Year Two | 8m | 0.37 |

At the end of year three, 9 million rights actually vested.

**Required:**

(a)  **Show how the option scheme will affect the financial statements for each of the three years of the vesting period.**

(b)  **Show the accounting treatment at the vesting date for each of the following situations:**

(i)  **The fair value of a share was $5 and all eligible directors exercised their share options immediately.**

(ii)  **The fair value of a share was $1.50 and all eligible directors allowed their share options to lapse.**

## Modifications to the terms on which equity instruments are granted

An entity may alter the terms and conditions of share option schemes during the vesting period. For example:

- it might increase or reduce the exercise price of the options (the price that the holder of the options has to pay for shares when the options are exercised). This makes the scheme less favourable or more favourable to employees.

- it might change the vesting conditions, to make it more likely or less likely that the options will vest.

If a modification to an equity-settled share-based payment scheme occurs, the entity must continue to recognise the grant date fair value of the equity instruments in profit or loss, unless the instruments do not vest because of a failure to meet a non-market based vesting condition.

If the modification increases the fair value of the equity instruments, then an extra expense must be recognised:

- The difference between the fair value of the new arrangement and the fair value of the original arrangement (the incremental fair value) at the date of the modification must be recognised as a charge to profit or loss.

- The extra expense is spread over the period from the date of the change to the vesting date.

### Test your understanding 6 – Modifications

An entity grants 100 share options to each of its 500 employees, provided that they remain in service over the next three years. The fair value of each option is $20.

During year one, 50 employees leave. The entity estimates that a further 60 employees will leave during years two and three.

At the end of year one the entity reprices its share options because the share price has fallen. The other vesting conditions remain unchanged. At the date of repricing, the fair value of each of the original share options granted (before taking the repricing into account) was $10. The fair value of each repriced share option is $15.

During year two, a further 30 employees leave. The entity estimates that a further 30 employees will leave during year three.

During year three, a further 30 employees leave.

**Required:**

**Calculate the amounts to be recognised in the financial statements for each of the three years of the scheme.**

## Cancellations and settlements

An entity may cancel or settle a share option scheme before the vesting date.

- If the cancellation or settlement occurs during the vesting period, the entity immediately recognises the amount that would otherwise have been recognised for services received over the vesting period (**'an acceleration of vesting'** (IFRS 2, para 28a)).

- Any payment made to employees up to the fair value of the equity instruments granted at cancellation or settlement date is accounted for as a deduction from equity.

- Any payment made to employees in excess of the fair value of the equity instruments granted at the cancellation or settlement date is accounted for as an expense in profit or loss.

**Test your understanding 7 – Cancellations and settlements**

An entity introduced an equity-settled share-based payment scheme on 1 January 20X0 for its 5 directors. Under the terms of the scheme, the entity will grant 1,000 options to each director if they remain in employment for the next three years. All five directors are expected to stay for the full three years. The fair value of each option at the grant date was $8.

On 30 June 20X1, the entity decided to base its share-based payment schemes on profit targets instead. It therefore cancelled the existing scheme. On 30 June 20X1, it paid compensation of $10 per option to each of the 5 directors. The fair value of the options at 30 June 20X1 was $9.

**Required:**

**Explain, with calculations, how the cancellation and settlement of the share-based payment scheme should be accounted for in the year ended 31 December 20X1.**

## 3 Cash-settled share-based payments

Examples of cash-settled share-based payment transactions include:

- share appreciation rights (SARs), where employees become entitled to a future cash payment based on the increase in the entity's share price from a specified level over a specified period of time

- the right to shares that are redeemable, thus entitling the holder to a future payment of cash.

 **Accounting treatment**

The double entry for a cash-settled share-based payment transaction is:

Dr Profit or loss/Asset

Cr Liabilities

 **Measurement**

The entity remeasures the fair value of the liability arising under a cash-settled scheme at each reporting date.

This is different from accounting for equity-settled share-based payments, where the fair value is fixed at the grant date.

### Allocating the expense to reporting periods

Where services are received in exchange for cash-settled share-based payments, the expense is recognised over the period that the services are rendered (the vesting period).

This is the same principle as for equity-settled transactions.

 **Illustration 2 – Cash-settled share-based payment transactions**

An entity has a reporting date of 31 December.

On 1 January 20X1 the entity grants 100 share appreciation rights (SARs) to each of its 300 employees, on the condition that they continue to work for the entity until 31 December 20X3.

During 20X1, 20 employees leave. The entity estimates that a further 40 will leave during 20X2 and 20X3.

During 20X2, 10 employees leave. The entity estimates that a further 20 will leave during 20X3.

During 20X3, 10 employees leave.

The fair value of a SAR at each reporting date is shown below:

|  | $ |
|---|---|
| 20X1 | 10.00 |
| 20X2 | 12.00 |
| 20X3 | 15.00 |

**Required:**

**Calculate the expense for each of the three years of the scheme, and the liability to be recognised in the statement of financial position as at 31 December for each of the three years.**

### Solution

|  | Liability at year-end | Expense for year |
|---|---|---|
|  | $000 | $000 |
| 20X1 ((300 – 20 – 40) × 100 × $10 × 1/3) | 80 | 80 |
| 20X2 ((300 – 20 – 10 – 20) × 100 × $12 × 2/3) | 200 | 120 |
| 20X3 ((300 – 20 – 10 – 10) × 100 × $15) | 390 | 190 |

Note that the fair value of the liability is remeasured at each reporting date. The expense is spread over the vesting period.

**The value of share appreciation rights (SARs)**

SARs may be exercisable over a period of time. The fair value of each SAR comprises the intrinsic value (the cash amount payable based upon the share price at that date) together with its time value (based upon the fact that the share price will vary over time).

When SARs are exercised, they are accounted for at their intrinsic value at the exercise date. The fair value of a SAR could exceed its intrinsic value at this date. This is because SAR holders who do not exercise their rights at that time have the ability to benefit from future share price rises.

At the end of the exercise period, the intrinsic value of a SAR will equal its fair value. The liability will be cleared and any remaining balance taken to profit or loss.

## Test your understanding 8 – Growler

On 1 January 20X4 Growler granted 200 share appreciation rights (SARs) to each of its 500 employees on the condition that they continue to work for the entity for two years. At 1 January 20X4, the entity expects that 25 of those employees will leave each year.

During 20X4, 20 employees leave Growler. The entity expects that the same number will leave in the second year.

During 20X5, 24 employees leave.

The SARs vest on 31 December 20X5 and can be exercised during 20X6 and 20X7. On 31 December 20X6, 257 of the eligible employees exercised their SARs in full. The remaining eligible employees exercised their SARs in full on 31 December 20X7.

The fair value and intrinsic value of each SAR was as follows:

| Reporting date | FV per SAR | Intrinsic value per SAR |
|---|---|---|
| 31 December 20X4 | $5 | |
| 31 December 20X5 | $7 | |
| 31 December 20X6 | $8 | $7 |
| 31 December 20X7 | $10 | $10 |

**Required:**

(a)  **Calculate the amount to be recognised as a remuneration expense in the statement of profit or loss, together with the liability to be recognised in the statement of financial position, for each of the two years to the vesting date.**

(b)  **Calculate the amount to be recognised as a remuneration expense and reported as a liability in the financial statements for each of the two years ended 31 December 20X6 and 20X7.**

### Replacing a cash-settled scheme with an equity-settled scheme

An entity may modify the terms of a cash-settled share-based payment scheme so that it becomes classified as an equity-settled scheme. If this is the case, IFRS 2 requires the entity to:

- Measure the transaction by reference to the modification fair value of the equity instruments granted

- Derecognise the liability and recognise equity to the extent of the services rendered by the modification date

- Recognise a profit or loss for the difference between the liability derecognised and the equity recognised.

# 4 Other issues

## Hybrid transactions

If a share-based payment transaction gives the entity a choice over whether to settle in cash or by issuing equity instruments, IFRS 2 states that:

- The scheme should be accounted for as a cash-settled share-based payment transaction if the entity has an obligation to settle in cash.

- If no obligation exists to settle in cash, then the entity accounts for the transaction as an equity-settled share-based payment scheme.

Some entities enter into share-based payment transactions that give the counterparty the choice of settling in cash or in equity instruments. In this case, the entity has granted a compound instrument that must be split accounted (part is recorded as debt and part is recorded as equity).

## Group share-based payments

A subsidiary might receive goods or services from employees or suppliers but the parent (or another entity in the group) might issue equity or cash settled share-based payments as consideration.

In accordance with IFRS 2, the entity that receives goods or services in a share-based payment arrangement must account for those goods or services irrespective of which entity in the group settles the transaction, or whether the transaction is settled in shares or cash.

## Disclosures

The main disclosures required by IFRS 2 are as follows:

- a description of share-based payment arrangements

- the number of share options granted or exercised during the year

- the total share-based payment expense.

IFRS 2 requires disclosures that enable users to understand how fair values have been determined.

The *Conceptual Framework* defines an expense as a decrease in economic benefits that results in decreases to equity (other than those related to distributions to equity participants). In the case of a cash-settled share-based payment, the entity has an obligation to pay cash in the future. This clearly meets the definition of an expense.

In the case of an equity-settled share-based payment, the entity is providing equity as payment for the good or service. There is therefore no reduction in an asset or increase in a liability in accordance with the definition of an expense. IFRS 2 *Share Based Payment* requires the recognition of an expense for equity-settled schemes with employees, but it can be argued that this is not in accordance with the definitions in the Framework.

The Board disagrees with the above argument. It argues that employee service is an asset that is received by the reporting entity but then simultaneously consumed. It might be easier to conceptualise this as two double entries:

Dr Employee service (asset) X

Cr Equity X

*To recognise the receipt of the employee service asset*

Dr Employee service (P/L) X

Cr Employee service (asset) X

*To recognise the consumption of employee service as an expense.*

In practice, and as noted earlier in this chapter, entities simply post the net entry, as follows:

Dr Employee service (P/L) X

Cr Equity X

The recognition of an expense from share-based payment transactions receives strong support from investors. Omitting these expenses from financial statements would reduce comparability between entities. The reduction in transparency, particularly if the share-based payment was with directors, would also raise concerns about corporate governance and stewardship.

## 5 Chapter summary

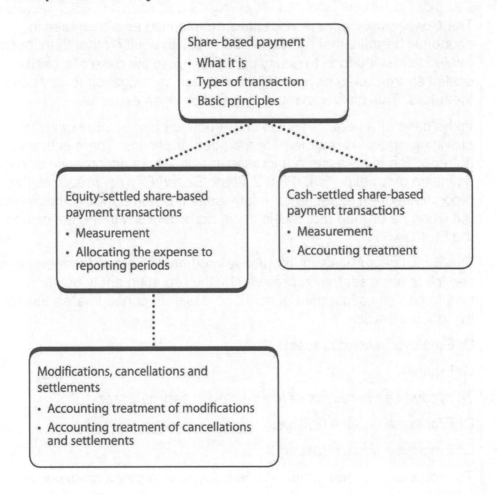

# Test your understanding answers

## Test your understanding 1 – Liminal

The consideration for the patent purchase was 1 million of Liminal's own shares and so the transaction should be accounted for in accordance with IFRS 2 *Share-based Payment*.

On the purchase date all vesting conditions have been met so the transaction is accounted for in full.

The patent is an intangible asset because, per IAS 38 *Intangible Assets*, it is a non-monetary asset that has no physical substance. The fair value of the patent can be reliably measured at $3 million and so an intangible asset should be recognised for this amount. A corresponding credit for $3 million should be made to equity. Of this $1 million will be recorded in share capital and $2 million in share premium/other components of equity.

The patent should be amortised over its useful economic life of three years. The amortisation charge amounts to $0.5 million (($3m/3 years) × 6/12). This will be charged to profit or loss and will reduce the carrying amount of the patent to $2.5 million.

## Test your understanding 2 – Equity-settled share-based payment

The total expense recognised is based on the fair value of the share options granted at the grant date (1 January 20X1). The entity recognises the remuneration expense as the employees' services are received during the three-year vesting period.

### Year ended 31 December 20X1

At 31 December 20X1, the entity must estimate the number of options expected to vest by predicting how many employees will remain in employment until the vesting date. It believes that 80% of the employees will stay for the full three years and therefore calculates an expense based on this assumption:

(500 employees × 80%) × 100 options × $15 FV × 1/3 = $200,000

Therefore, an expense is recognised for $200,000 together with a corresponding increase in equity.

**Year ended 31 December 20X2**

The estimate of the number of employees staying for the full three years is revised at each year end. At 31 December 20X2, it is estimated that 85% of the 500 employees will stay for the full three years. The calculation of the share based payment expense is therefore as follows:

|  | $ |
|---|---|
| (500 employees × 85%) × 100 options × $15 FV × 2/3 | 425,000 |
| Less previously recognised expense | (200,000) |
| | |
| Expense in year ended 31 December 20X2 | 225,000 |

Equity will be increased by $225,000 to $425,000 ($200,000 + $225,000).

**Year ended 31 December 20X3**

A total of 50 (20 + 20 + 10) employees left during the vesting period. The expense recognised in the final year of the scheme is as follows:

|  | $ |
|---|---|
| (500 – 50 employees) × 100 options × $15 FV × 3/3 | 675,000 |
| Less previously recognised expense | (425,000) |
| | |
| Expense in year ended 31 December 20X3 | 250,000 |

The financial statements will include the following amounts:

| Statement of profit or loss | 20X1 | 20X2 | 20X3 |
|---|---|---|---|
|  | $ | $ | $ |
| Staff costs | 200,000 | 225,000 | 250,000 |

| Statement of financial position | 20X1 | 20X2 | 20X3 |
|---|---|---|---|
|  | $ | $ | $ |
| Other components of equity | 200,000 | 425,000 | 675,000 |

**Test your understanding 3 – Market based conditions**

The expense recognised is based on the fair value of the options at the grant date. This should be spread over the vesting period.

There are two types of conditions attached to the share based payment scheme:

- A service condition (employees must complete a minimum service period)

- A market based performance condition (the share price must be $5 at 31 December 20X2).

Although it looks unlikely that the share price target will be hit, this condition has already been factored into the fair value of the options at the grant date. Therefore, this condition can be ignored when determining the charge to the statement of profit or loss.

The expense to be recognised should therefore be based on how many employees are expected to satisfy the service condition only. The calculation is as follows:

(100 employees – 10 – 10) × 50 options × $1 FV × 1/2 = $2,000.

The entry to recognise this is:

| | |
|---|---|
| Dr Profit or loss | $2,000 |
| Cr Equity | $2,000 |

**Test your understanding 4 – Blueberry**

| Rep. date | Calculation of equity | Equity $000 | Expense $000 | Note |
|---|---|---|---|---|
| 31/12/X4 | (174 × 200 × $10) × 1/3 | 116 | 116 | 1 |
| 31/12/X5 | (182 × 300 × $10) × 2/3 | 364 | 248 | 2 |
| 31/12/X6 | (184 × 300 × $10) × 3/3 | 552 | 188 | 3 |

**Notes:**

1   At 31/12/X4 a total of 26 employees (8 + 18) are expected to leave by the vesting date meaning that 174 are expected to remain. Blueberry estimates that average annual growth in sales volume will be 14%. Consequently, it is estimated that eligible employees would each receive 200 share options at the vesting date.

2   At 31/12/X5, a total of 18 employees (8 + 6 + 4) are expected to leave by the vesting date meaning that 182 are expected to remain. Blueberry estimates that the average growth in sales volume will be 16%. Consequently, it is estimated that eligible employees will each receive 300 share options at the vesting date.

3   A t 31/12/X6, it is known that total of 16 employees (8 + 6 + 2) have left at some point during the vesting period, leaving 184 eligible employees. As average annual growth in sales volume over the vesting period was 16%, eligible employees are entitled to 300 share options each.

## Test your understanding 5 – Beginner

| Year | | Equity $000 | Expense $000 |
|------|--|-------------|--------------|
| Year 1 | (7m × $0.3 × 1/3) | 700 | 700 |
| Year 2 | (8m × $0.3 × 2/3) | 1,600 | 900 |
| Year 3 | (9m × $0.3) | 2,700 | 1,100 |

**Note:** Equity-settled share-based payments are measured using the fair value of the instrument at the grant date (the start of year one).

(i) All eligible directors exercised their options:

The entity will post the following entry:

| | |
|---|---|
| Dr Cash (9m × $2) | $18.0m |
| Dr Equity reserve | $2.7m |
| Cr Share capital (9m × $1) | $9.0m |
| Cr Share premium (bal. fig.) | $11.7m |

(ii) No options are exercised

The amount recognised in equity ($2.7m) remains. The entity can choose to transfer this to retained earnings.

## Test your understanding 6 – Modifications

The repricing means that the total fair value of the arrangement has increased. The entity must account for an increased remuneration expense. The increased cost is based upon the difference in the fair value of the option, immediately before and after the repricing. Under the original arrangement, the fair value of the option at the date of repricing was $10, which increased to $15 following the repricing of the options, for each share estimated to vest. The additional cost is recognised over the remainder of the vesting period (years two and three).

The amounts recognised in the financial statements for each of the three years are as follows:

|  | Equity $ | Expense $ |
|---|---|---|
| Year one original | | |
| $(500 - 50 - 60) \times 100 \times \$20 \times 1/3$ | 260,000 | 260,000 |
| | | |
| Year two original | | |
| $(500 - 50 - 30 - 30) \times 100 \times \$20 \times 2/3$ | 520,000 | 260,000 |
| Incremental | | |
| $(500 - 50 - 30 - 30) \times 100 \times \$5 \times 1/2$ | 97,500 | 97,500 |
| | | |
| | 617,500 | 357,500 |
| | | |
| Year three original | | |
| $(500 - 50 - 30 - 30) \times 100 \times \$20$ | 780,000 | 260,000 |
| Incremental | | |
| $(500 - 50 - 30 - 30) \times 100 \times \$5$ | 195,000 | 97,500 |
| | | |
| | 975,000 | 357,500 |

**Test your understanding 7 – Cancellations and settlements**

The share option scheme has been cancelled. This means that all the expense not yet charged through profit or loss must now be recognised in the year ended 31 December 20X1:

|  | $ |
| --- | --- |
| Total expense | 40,000 |
| (5 directors × 1,000 options × $8) | |
| Less expense recognised in year ended 31 December 20X0 | (13,333) |
| (5 directors × 1,000 options × $8 × 1/3) | |
| | |
| Expense to be recognised | 26,667 |

To recognise the remaining expense, the following entry must be posted:

| | |
| --- | --- |
| Dr Profit or loss | $26,667 |
| Cr Equity | $26,667 |

Any payment made in compensation for the cancellation that is up to the fair value of the options is recognised as a deduction to equity. Any payment in excess of the fair value is recognised as an expense.

The compensation paid to the director for each option exceeded the fair value by $1 ($10 – $9). Therefore, an expense of $1 per option should be recognised in profit or loss.

The following accounting entry is required:

| | |
| --- | --- |
| Dr Equity (5 directors × 1,000 options × $9) | $45,000 |
| Dr Profit or loss (5 directors × 1,000 options × $1) | $5,000 |
| Cr Cash (5 directors × 1,000 options × $10) | $50,000 |

**Test your understanding 8 – Growler**

(a) The liability is remeasured at each reporting date, based upon the current information available relating to known and expected leavers, together with the fair value of the SAR at each date. The remuneration expense recognised is the movement in the liability from one reporting date to the next as summarised below:

| Rep. date | Workings | Liability (SFP) $ | Expense (P/L) $ |
|---|---|---|---|
| 31/12/X4 | (500 – 20 – 20) × 200 × $5 × 1/2 | 230,000 | 230,000 |
| 31/12/X5 | (500 – 20 – 24) × 200 × $7 × 2/2 | 638,400 | 408,400 |

(b) The number of employees eligible for a cash payment is 456 (500 – 20 – 24). Of these, 257 exercise their SARs at 31/12/X6 and the remaining 199 exercise their SARs at 31/12/X7.

The liability is measured at each reporting date, based upon the current information available at that date, together with the fair value of each SAR at that date. Any SARs exercised are reflected at their intrinsic value at the date of exercise.

**Year ended 31/12/X6**

| | $ |
|---|---|
| Liability b/fwd | 638,400 |
| Cash payment (257 × 200 × $7) | (359,800) |
| Profit or loss (bal. fig) | 39,800 |
| | |
| Liability c/fwd (199 × 200 × $8) | 318,400 |

**Year ended 31/12/X7**

| | $ |
|---|---|
| Liability b/fwd | 318,400 |
| Cash payment (199 × 200 × $10) | (398,000) |
| Profit or loss (bal. fig) | 79,600 |
| | |
| Liability c/fwd | nil |

# Events after the reporting period, provisions and contingencies

## Chapter learning objectives

Upon completion of this chapter you will be able to:

- Discuss and apply the recognition, de-recognition and measurement of provisions, contingent liabilities and contingent assets including environmental provisions and restructuring provisions

- Discuss and apply the accounting for events after the reporting period.

**PER**

One of the PER performance objectives (PO6) is to record and process transactions and events. You need to use the right accounting treatments for transactions and events. These should be both historical and prospective – and include non-routine transactions. Working through this chapter should help you understand how to demonstrate that objective.

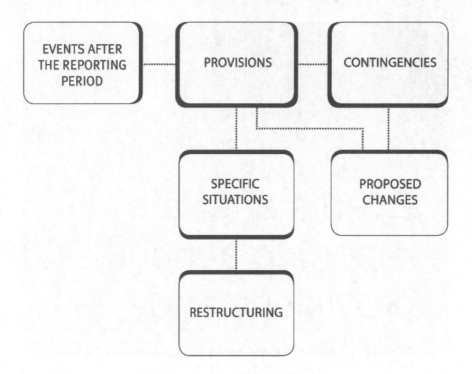

## 1 IAS 10 *Events after the Reporting Period*

**Definition**

 **Events after the reporting period** are events **'that occur between the reporting date and the date on which the financial statements are authorised for issue'** (IAS 10, para 3).

There are two types of event after the reporting period:

- adjusting events
- non-adjusting events.

Financial statements are prepared on the basis of conditions existing at the reporting date.

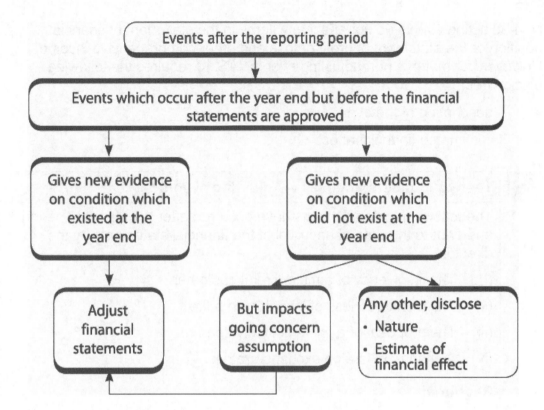

Examples of **adjusting events** provided by IAS 10 include:

- the sale of inventory after the reporting date – this gives evidence about the net realisable value of inventory at the reporting date

- the bankruptcy of a customer after the reporting date – this confirms that an allowance is required against a receivables balance at the reporting date

- the discovery of fraud or errors – this shows that the financial statements are incorrect

- the settlement after the reporting period of a court case – this confirms the existence and value of the entity's obligation at the reporting date.

Examples of **non-adjusting events** provided by IAS 10 include:

- a major business combination after the reporting date or the disposal of a major subsidiary

- announcing a plan after the reporting date to discontinue an operation

- major purchases and disposals of assets after the reporting date

- destruction of assets by a fire after the reporting date

- announcing or commencing a major restructuring after the reporting date

- large changes after the reporting date in foreign exchange rates

- equity dividends declared or proposed after the reporting date.

Non-adjusting events do not affect any items in the statement of financial position or the statement of profit or loss and other comprehensive income. However, for material non-adjusting events, IAS 10 requires the following disclosures:

- a description of the event
- its estimated financial effect.

**Test your understanding 1 – Adjusting events**

The following material events have occurred after the reporting period and prior to the date of approval of the financial statements by the directors.

(i) The insolvency of a major credit customer

(ii) The uninsured loss of inventory in a fire

(iii) The proposal of a final equity dividend

(iv) A change in foreign exchange rates.

**Required:**

**State whether the above are adjusting or non-adjusting events.**

### Going concern issues arising after the reporting date

 There is an exception to the rule that the financial statements reflect conditions at the reporting date. If, after the reporting date, management decides to liquidate the entity or cease trading (or decides that it has no realistic alternative to these actions), the financial statements cannot be prepared on a going concern basis.

If the going concern assumption is no longer appropriate then IAS 10 states that a fundamental change in the basis of accounting is required. In this case, entities will prepare their financial statements using the 'break up' basis and disclose this fact.

In accordance with IAS 1 *Presentation of Financial Statements*, management must disclose any material uncertainties relating to events or conditions that cast significant doubt upon an entity's ability to continue trading. This applies if the events have arisen since the reporting period.

## 2 Provisions

### Introduction

Most liabilities can be measured accurately. For example, if you take out a bank loan then you know exactly how much you have to repay, and when the repayments are due. Provisions, however, involve uncertainty.

 According to IAS 37 *Provisions, Contingent Liabilities and Contingent Assets* (para 10), **'a provision is a liability of uncertain timing or amount'**.

Note that the definition of a liability in IAS 37 was not revised as a result of the issue of the 2018 *Conceptual Framework*. IAS 37 defines a liability as a present obligation arising from a past event that is expected to lead to an outflow of economic resources.

### Recognition

IAS 37 (para 14) requires that a provision should be recognised when and only when:

*   **'an entity has a present obligation (legal or constructive) as a result of a past event**
*   **it is probable that an outflow of resources embodying economic benefits will be required to settle the obligation**
*   **a reliable estimate can be made of the amount of the obligation'.**

An obligation is something that cannot be avoided:

*   **A constructive obligation** arises when an entity's past practice or published policies creates a valid expectation amongst other parties that it will discharge certain responsibilities.
*   **A legal obligation** arises from a contract or from laws and legislation.

Only in extremely rare cases is it impossible to make a reliable estimate of the amount of the obligation.

### Measurement

IAS 37 requires that provisions are measured at the **best estimate** of the expenditure required to settle the obligation as at the reporting date.

The best estimate of a provision will be:

*   the most likely amount payable for a single obligation (such as a court case)
*   an expected value for a large population of items (such as a warranty provision).

An entity should use its own judgement in deriving the best estimate, supplemented by past experience and the advice of experts (such as lawyers).

If the effect of the time value of money is material, then the provision should be discounted to present value. The discount rate should be pre-tax and risk-specific.

## Test your understanding 2 – Warranty

Clean sells domestic appliances such as washing machines.

On 31 December 20X1, Clean decides to start selling washing machines with a warranty. Under the terms of the warranty, Clean will repair washing machines at no charge to the customer if they break within the warranty period. The entity estimates, based on past-correspondence with customers, that 20% of the washing machines sold will require repair within the warranty period at an average cost to Clean of $50 per machine.

Clean sold 200 washing machines on 31 December 20X1.

The time value of money should be ignored.

**Required:**

**Calculate the warranty provision required.**

## The *Conceptual Framework*

Provisions are liabilities where the amount required to settle them, or the timing of the settlement, is uncertain.

To be useful, financial information must be relevant and must offer a faithful representation of the underlying transaction. The measurement of provisions requires estimation, and this increases the risk of manipulation and error.

When measuring provisions, it is vital that accountants adhere to the ACCA *Code of Ethics and Conduct*. One of the core principles of this code is objectivity.

To ensure that provisions are faithfully represented, IAS 37 has extensive disclosure requirements. Preparers of financial statements are required to outline the estimation techniques used and uncertainties relating to the amount or timing of the eventual payments.

### Subsequent measurement

If a provision has been discounted to present value, then the discount must be unwound and presented in finance costs in the statement of profit or loss:

> Dr Finance costs (P/L)
>
> Cr Provisions (SFP)

Provisions should be remeasured to reflect the best estimate of the expenditure required to settle the liability as at each reporting date.

## Derecognition

IAS 37 states that provisions should be used only for expenditure that relates to the matter for which the provision was originally recognised.

At the reporting date, a provision should be reversed if it is no longer probable that an outflow of economic benefits will be required to settle the obligation.

## 3 Contingent liabilities

 A contingent liability is defined by IAS 37 as:

- a possible obligation that arises from past events and whose existence will be confirmed by the outcome of uncertain future events which are outside of the control of the entity, or

- a present obligation that arises from past events, but does not meet the criteria for recognition as a provision. This is either because an outflow of economic benefits is not probable or (more rarely) because it is not possible to make a reliable estimate of the obligation.

A contingent liability is disclosed, unless the possibility of a future outflow of economic benefits is remote.

> **The *Conceptual Framework***
>
> The *Conceptual Framework* states that an item should only be recognised in the financial statements if it meets the definition of an element. However, not all items meeting the definition of an element are recognised. One example of this is contingent liabilities.
>
> Recognition of contingent liabilities in the financial statements would not provide a faithful representation of the underlying transaction. Depending on the nature of the contingent liability, this might be because:
>
> - there is not enough certainty that an obligation exists, or
> - the probability of an outflow of economic resource is too low, or
> - the level of measurement uncertainty is too high.

If an outflow of economic benefits becomes probable then contingent liabilities are reclassified as provisions.

## 4    Contingent assets

 IAS 37 defines a contingent asset as a possible asset that arises from past events and whose existence will be confirmed by uncertain future events that are outside of the entity's control.

A contingent asset should not be recognised:

*   A contingent asset should be disclosed if the inflow of future economic benefits is at least probable

*   If the future inflow of benefits is virtually certain, then it ceases to be a contingent asset and should be recognised as a normal asset.

### Summary

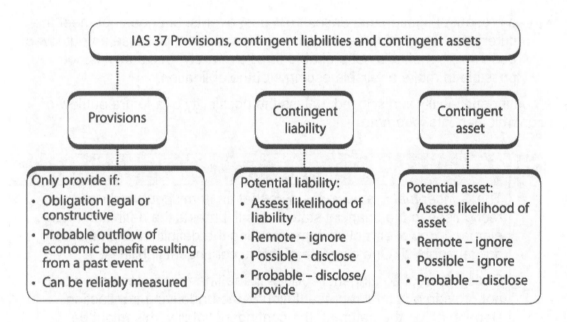

## 5    Provisions and contingencies: specific situations

### Future operating losses

IAS 37 says that provisions should not be recognised for future operating losses because:

*   They relate to future, rather than past, events

*   The loss-making business could be closed and the losses avoided, meaning that there is no obligation to make the losses.

An expectation of future operating losses is an indication that assets may be impaired. An impairment review should be conducted in accordance with IAS 36 *Impairment of Assets*.

## Onerous contracts

IAS 37 defines an onerous contract as one **'in which the unavoidable costs of meeting the contract exceed the economic benefits expected to be received under it'** (IAS 37, para 10).

If an entity has an onerous contract, a provision should be recognised for the present obligation under the contract. The provision is measured at the lower of:

- the cost of fulfilling the contract, or

- the cost of terminating it and suffering any penalties.

Some assets may have been bought specifically for use in fulfilling the onerous contract. These should be reviewed for impairment before any separate provision is made for the contract itself.

## Future repairs to assets

Some assets need to be repaired or to have parts replaced every few years. For example, an airline may be required by law to overhaul all its aircraft every three years.

Provisions cannot normally be recognised for the cost of future repairs or replacement parts. This is because there is no current obligation to incur the expense – even if the future expenditure is required by law, the entity could avoid it by selling the asset.

### Test your understanding 3 – Danboy

Danboy, a company that owns several shops, has a year end of 31 December 20X1.

One of the shops is loss-making. At 31 December 20X1, Danboy forecasts that this shop will make a loss of $50,000 in the year ended 31 December 20X2.

As at 31 December 20X1, one of the shop buildings requires repair. The cost has been estimated at the reporting date at $10,000. The repair is made in the following accounting period at a cost of $12,000.

**Required:**

**Discuss the accounting treatment of the above in the financial statements for the year ended 31 December 20X1.**

**Test your understanding 4 – Smoke filters**

Under new legislation, an entity is required to fit smoke filters to its factories by 31 December 20X7. At the reporting date of 30 June 20X7, the entity has not fitted the smoke filters.

**Required:**

**Should a provision be made at the reporting date for the estimated cost of fitting the filters?**

## Environmental provisions

Environmental provisions are often referred to as clean-up costs because they usually relate to the cost of decontaminating and restoring an industrial site after production has ceased.

A provision is recognised if a past event has created an obligation to repair environmental damage:

- A provision can only be set up to rectify environmental damage that has already happened. There is no obligation to restore future environmental damage because the entity could cease its operations.

- Merely causing damage or intending to clean-up a site does not create an obligation.

  - An entity may have a constructive obligation to repair environmental damage if it publicises policies that include environmental awareness or explicitly undertakes to clean up the damage caused by its operations.

The full cost of an environmental provision should be recognised as soon as the obligation arises.

- The effect of the time value of money is usually material. Therefore, an environmental provision is normally discounted to its present value.

- If the expenditure results in future economic benefits then an equivalent asset can be recognised. This is depreciated over its useful life, which is the same as the 'life' of the provision.

## Test your understanding 5 – Environmental provisions

(a) An entity has a policy of only carrying out work to rectify damage caused to the environment when it is required to do so by local law. For several years the entity has been operating an overseas oil rig which causes environmental damage. The country in which the oil rig is located has not had legislation in place that required this damage to be rectified.

A new government has recently been elected in the country. At the reporting date, it is virtually certain that legislation will be enacted that will require damage rectification. This legislation will have retrospective effect.

(b) Under a licence granted by a local government, an entity has constructed a rock-crushing plant to process material mined from the surrounding area. Mining activities have already started. Under the terms of the licence, the entity must remove the rock-crushing plant when mining activities have been completed and must landscape the mined area, so as to create a national park.

**Required:**

**For each of the situations, explain whether a provision should be recognised.**

## Test your understanding 6 – Scrubber

On 1 January 20X6, Scrubber spent $5m on erecting infrastructure and machinery near to an area of natural beauty. These assets will be used over the next three years. Scrubber is well-known for its environmentally friendly behaviour and is therefore expected to restore the site after its use.

The estimated cost of removing these assets and cleaning up the area on 1 January 20X9 is $3m.

The pre-tax, risk-specific discount rate is 10%. Scrubber has a reporting date of 31 December.

**Required:**

**Explain how the above should be treated in the financial statements of Scrubber.**

## 6 Restructuring

### Definition

A **restructuring** is a programme that is planned and controlled by management and has a material effect on:

- the scope of a business undertaken by the reporting entity in terms of the products or services it provides

- the manner in which a business undertaken by the reporting entity is conducted.

IAS 37 says that a restructuring could include:

- the closure or sale of a line of business

- the closure of business locations in a country

- the relocation of business activities from one country to another.

### When can a provision be recognised?

A restructuring provision can only be recognised where an entity has a **constructive obligation** to carry out the restructuring.

A board decision alone does not create a constructive obligation. IAS 37 states that a constructive obligation exists only if:

- there is a detailed formal plan for restructuring, that identifies the businesses, locations and employees affected as well as an estimate of the cost and timings involved

- the employees affected have a valid expectation that the restructuring will be carried out, either because the plan has been formally announced or because the plan has started to be implemented.

The constructive obligation must exist at the reporting date. An obligation arising after the reporting date requires disclosure as a non-adjusting event under IAS 10 *Events after the Reporting Period*.

### Measuring a restructuring provision

A restructuring provision should only include the direct costs of restructuring. These must be both:

- **'necessarily entailed by the restructuring**

- **not associated with the ongoing activities of the entity'** (IAS 37, para 80).

IAS 37 prohibits the following costs from being included in a restructuring provision:

- retraining and relocating staff

- marketing products

- expenditure on new systems

- future operating losses (unless these arise from an onerous contract)

- profits on disposal of assets.

The amount recognised should be the best estimate of the expenditure required and it should take into account expected future events. This means that expenses should be measured at their actual cost, where this is known, even if this was only discovered after the reporting date (this is an adjusting event after the reporting period per IAS 10).

### Test your understanding 7 – Restructuring provisions

On 15 January 20X5, the Board of Directors of Shane voted to proceed with two reorganisation schemes involving the closure of two factories. Shane's reporting date is 31 March, and the financial statements will be authorised for issue on 30 June.

**Scheme 1**

The closure costs will amount to $125,000. The closure will be announced in June, and will commence in August.

**Scheme 2**

The costs will amount to $45,000 (after crediting $105,000 profit on disposal of certain machines). The closure will take place in July, but redundancy negotiations began with the staff in March.

**Required:**

**For each of the two schemes discuss whether a provision should be recognised and, if so, at what amount.**

**Test your understanding 8 – Delta**

On 30 June 20X2, the directors of Delta decided to close down a division. This decision was announced to the employees affected on 15 July 20X2 and the actual closure occurred on 31 August 20X2, prior to the 20X2 financial statements being authorised for issue on 15 September.

Expenses and other items connected with the closure were as follows:

|  | $m |
|---|---|
| Redundancy costs (estimated) | 22 |
| Staff retraining (actual) | 10 |
| Operating loss for the 2 months to 31 August 20X2 (estimated at 30 June) | 12 |
| Profit on sale of property | 5 |

The actual redundancy costs were $20 million and the actual operating loss for the two months to 31 August 20X2, was $15 million.

**Required:**

**What is the amount of the restructuring provision to be recognised in the financial statements of Delta plc for the year ended 31 July 20X2?**

## 7 Criticisms of IAS 37

The following criticisms have been made of IAS 37:

- **Judgement** – provisions are estimated liabilities and IAS 37 requires the exercise of judgement. This may increase the risk of bias and reduce comparability between entities.

- **Inconsistent** – before recognising a provision, an entity must assess if the outflow of economic benefits is probable. This is inconsistent with other standards, such as IFRS 9 *Financial Instruments*.

- **Out-dated** – IAS 37 was issued many years ago and does not reflect the current thinking of the International Accounting Standards Board.

- **Best estimates** – provisions for single obligations are recognised at the 'best estimate' of the expenditure that will be incurred, but guidance in this area is lacking.

- **Types of costs** – IAS 37 does not specify what types of costs should be included when measuring a provision. For example, some entities include legal costs within provisions, but others do not.

- **Risk** – IAS 37 states that entities may need to make a risk adjustment to provisions, but it does not explain when to do this or how to calculate the adjustment.

- **Contingent assets** – these are not recognised unless the inflow of benefits is 'virtually certain'. There is a lack of guidance about the meaning of 'virtually certain'.

- **Timing** – there can be timing differences between when one entity recognises a contingent liability and when the other entity recognises a contingent asset.

- **Contradictory guidance.** IAS 37 defines an obligating event as one where the entity has no realistic alternative but to settle the obligation. However, the standard also states that no provision should be recognised if the liability can be avoided by future actions – even if those actions are unrealistic (e.g. a change in the nature of the entity's operations).

---

**Investor perspective**

IAS 37 requires entities to provide a description of the nature of each class of provision, and to include information amount uncertainties relating to the expected timing or amount of the expenditure required. An example is provided below:

|  | Service guarantee | Restructuring |
|---|---|---|
|  | $m | $m |
| 31 December 20X1 | 14 | – |
| Charged to profit or loss | 4 | 5 |
| Utilised | (3) | – |
| 31 December 20X2 | 15 | 5 |

*Provisions for service guarantee costs reflect the entity's expected liability for future repair costs for warranties and extended warranties based on estimated failure rates and unit repair costs for the classes of goods sold. The directors estimate that $5 million of this amount will be settled within the next twelve months.*

*The Restructuring provision relates to amounts provided as a result of the cost reduction programme initiated during 20X2. The provision represents the directors' best estimate of the liability arising. The directors believe these amounts will be settled within the next twelve months.*

Provisions are obligations where the measurement or timing involves a degree of uncertainty. This provisions disclosure provides relevant information to current and potential investors because it will help them to assess the risks to which the entity is exposed. In fact, disclosures related to provisions and contingencies are one of the few areas where financial statements provide information that is not solely historical.

---

## 8 Chapter summary

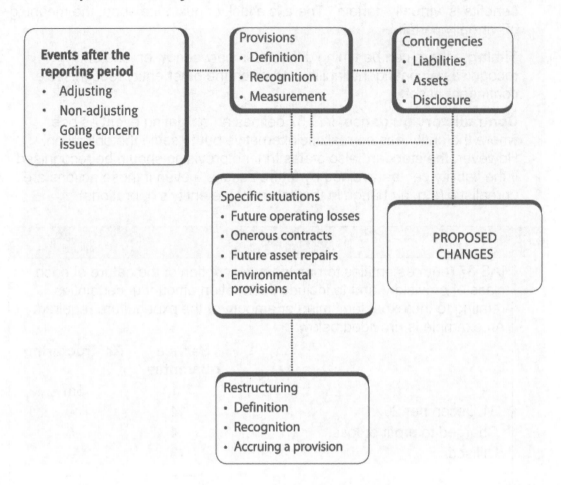

# Test your understanding answers

## Test your understanding 1 – Adjusting events

(i)   Adjusting.

(ii)  Non-adjusting.

(iii) Non-adjusting.

(iv)  Non-adjusting.

## Test your understanding 2 – Warranty

A provision is required.

A past event (the sale) has created a legal obligation to spend money on repairing machines in the future.

The best estimate can be determined using an expected value:

200 machines × 20% × $50 = $2,000.

## Test your understanding 3 – Danboy

IAS 37 states that no provision should be made for future operating losses. Therefore, no provision should be made for the $50,000 forecast losses.

No provision should be made for future repairs despite it being probable and capable of being reliably measured. This is because there is no obligation at the year end. The repairs expenditure of $12,000 is expensed to profit or loss as it is incurred.

## Test your understanding 4 – Smoke filters

No provision should be made for this future expenditure despite it being probable and capable of being reliably measured. There has been no obligating past event (the fitting of the filters).

### Test your understanding 5 – Environmental provision

For each situation, ask two questions.

(a)   Is there a present obligation as the result of a past event?

(b)   Is an outflow of economic benefits probable as a result?

A provision should be recognised if the answer to both questions is yes. In the absence of information to the contrary, it is assumed that any future costs can be estimated reliably.

(a)   Present obligation? Yes. Because the new legislation with retrospective effect is virtually certain to be enacted, the damage caused by the oil rig is the past event that gives rise to a present obligation.

   Outflow of economic benefits probable? Yes.

   Conclusion – Recognise a provision.

(b)   Present obligation? Yes. There is a legal obligation under the licence to remove the rock-crushing plant and to make good damage caused by the mining activities to date (but not any that may be caused by these activities in the future, because mining activities could be stopped and no such damage caused).

   Outflow of economic benefits probable? Yes.

   Conclusion – Recognise a provision for the best estimate of the eventual costs of rectifying the damage caused up to the reporting date.

### Test your understanding 6 – Scrubber

Scrubber has a constructive obligation to restore the area to its original condition as a result of a past event (erecting the infrastructure). Therefore, it should recognise a provision at 1 January 20X6. The best estimate of the expenditure is $3m, but this must be discounted to its present value of $2,253,000 ($3m × 0.751).

Scrubber could not carry out its operations without incurring the clean-up costs. This means that incurring the costs gives it access to future economic benefits. The estimated clean-up costs are therefore included in the cost of the property, plant and equipment (PPE):

Dr PPE                                                              $2,253,000

Cr Provisions                                                      $2,253,000

Each year, the discount unwinds and the provision increases. The unwinding of the discount is charged to the statement of profit or loss as a finance cost.

| Movement on provision | 20X6 $000 | 20X7 $000 | 20X8 $000 | 20X9 $000 |
|---|---|---|---|---|
| Opening balance | 2,253 | 2,478 | 2,727 | 3,000 |
| Finance cost at 10% | 225 | 249 | 273 | – |
| Utilisation | – | – | – | (3,000) |
| Closing balance | 2,478 | 2,727 | 3,000 | – |

| Initial cost of PPE | $000 |
|---|---|
| Cash paid 1 January 20X6 | 5,000 |
| PV of clean-up costs | 2,253 |
| Total | 7,253 |

The effect on the financial statements is shown below:

| Statements of profit or loss | 20X6 $000 | 20X7 $000 | 20X8 $000 | 20X9 $000 |
|---|---|---|---|---|
| Operating costs | | | | |
| Depreciation ($7,253/3 years) | 2,418 | 2,418 | 2,417 | – |
| Finance costs | | | | |
| Unwinding of discount | 225 | 249 | 273 | – |

| Statements of financial position | 20X6 $000 | 20X7 $000 | 20X8 $000 | 20X9 $000 |
|---|---|---|---|---|
| PPE | | | | |
| Cost | 7,253 | 7,253 | 7,253 | – |
| Depreciation | (2,418) | (4,836) | (7,253) | – |
| Carrying value | 4,835 | 2,417 | – | – |
| Liabilities | | | | |
| Clean-up provision | 2,478 | 2,727 | 3,000 | – |

### Test your understanding 7 – Restructuring provisions

**Scheme 1**

The obligating event is the announcement of the plan, which occurs in June. This is after the year-end, so there can be no provision. However, the announcement in June should be disclosed as a non-adjusting event after the reporting date.

**Scheme 2**

Although the closure will not begin until July, the employees will have had a valid expectation that it would happen when the redundancy negotiations began in March. Therefore, a provision should be recognised. The provision will be for $150,000 because the expected profit on disposal cannot be netted off against the expected costs.

### Test your understanding 8 – Delta

The only item which can be included in the provision is the redundancy costs, measured at the actual amount of $20 million.

IAS 37 prohibits the recognition of future operating losses, staff retraining and profits on the disposal of assets.

# Financial instruments

## Chapter learning objectives

Upon completion of this chapter you will be able to:

- Discuss and apply the initial recognition and measurement of financial instruments

- Discuss and apply the subsequent measurement of financial assets and financial liabilities

- Discuss and apply the derecognition of financial assets and financial liabilities

- Discuss and apply the reclassification of financial assets

- Account for derivative financial instruments, and simple embedded derivatives

- Outline and apply the qualifying criteria for hedge accounting and account for fair value hedges and cash flow hedges including hedge effectiveness

- Discuss and apply the general approach to impairment of financial instruments

- Discuss the implications of a significant increase in credit risk

- Discuss and apply the treatment of purchased or originated credit impaired financial assets.

**PER**

One of the PER performance objectives (PO6) is to record and process transactions and events. You need to use the right accounting treatments for transactions and events. These should be both historical and prospective – and include non-routine transactions. Working through this chapter should help you understand how to demonstrate that objective.

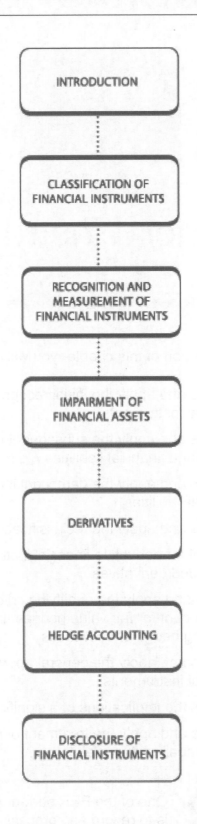

## 1 Introduction

**Progression**

Some of the content of this chapter was also examined in Financial Reporting. The situations you will encounter in the SBR exam will be more difficult. Moreover, you will need to study more complex issues, such as impairment and hedge accounting.

## Definitions

 A financial instrument is **'any contract that gives rise to a financial asset of one entity and a financial liability or equity instrument of another entity'** (IAS 32, para 11).

 A **financial asset** is any asset that is:

- **'cash**

- **an equity instrument of another entity**

- **a contractual right to receive cash or another financial asset from another entity**

- **a contractual right to exchange financial instruments with another entity under conditions that are potentially favourable to the entity**

- **a non-derivative contract for which the entity is or may be obliged to receive a variable number of the entity's own equity instruments'** (IAS 32, para 11).

 A **financial liability** is any liability that is a:

- **'contractual obligation to deliver cash or another financial asset to another entity**

- **contractual obligation to exchange financial instruments with another entity under conditions that are potentially unfavourable**

- **a non-derivative contract for which the entity is or may be obliged to deliver a variable number of the entity's own equity instruments.'** (IAS 32, para 11).

 An equity instrument is **'any contract that evidences a residual interest in the assets of an entity after deducting all of its liabilities'** (IAS 32, para 11).

## Reporting standards

There are three accounting standards in the Strategic Business Reporting syllabus that deal with financial instruments:

- IAS 32 *Financial Instruments: Presentation*

- IFRS 7 *Financial Instruments: Disclosures*

- IFRS 9 *Financial Instruments*

IAS 32 deals with the classification of financial instruments and their financial statement presentation.

IFRS 7 deals with the disclosure of financial instruments in financial statements.

IFRS 9 is concerned with the initial and subsequent measurement of financial instruments.

## 2 Financial liabilities and equity

### Classification

IAS 32 provides rules on classifying financial instruments.

The issuer of a financial instrument must classify it as a financial liability or equity instrument on initial recognition according to its substance and the definitions provided at the start of this chapter.

---

 **Test your understanding 1 – Liabilities or equity?**

Coasters wishes to purchase a new ride for its 'Animation Galaxy' theme park but requires extra funding. On 30 September 20X3, Coasters issued the following preference shares:

- 1 million preference shares for $3 each. No dividends are payable. Coasters will redeem the preference shares in three years' time by issuing ordinary shares worth $3 million. The exact number of ordinary shares issuable will be based on their fair value on 30 September 20X6.

- 2 million preference shares for $2.80 each. No dividends are payable. The preference shares will be redeemed in two years' time by issuing 3 million ordinary shares.

- 4 million preference shares for $2.50 each. They are not mandatorily redeemable. A dividend is payable if, and only if, dividends are paid on ordinary shares.

**Required:**

**Discuss whether these financial instruments should be classified as financial liabilities or equity in the financial statements of Coasters for the year ended 30 September 20X3.**

---

Note that the Board have issued a discussion paper on the topic of financial liabilities and equity. This is an examinable current issue and is covered in Chapter 23.

### Interest, dividends, losses and gains

The accounting treatment of interest, dividends, losses and gains relating to a financial instrument follows the treatment of the instrument itself.

- Dividends paid in respect of preference shares classified as a liability will be charged as a finance expense through profit or loss

- Dividends paid on shares classified as equity will be reported in the statement of changes in equity.

## Offsetting

IAS 32 states that a financial asset and a financial liability may only be offset in very limited circumstances. The net amount may only be reported when the entity:

- **'has a legally enforceable right to set off the amounts**

- **intends either to settle on a net basis, or to realise the asset and settle the liability simultaneously'** (IAS 32, para 42).

---

 **Investor perspective**

The classification of a financial instrument as either a liability or as equity will have a major impact on the financial statements, thus affecting investors' perceptions of an entity's financial performance and position:

- If an entity issues an instrument and classifies it as a liability, then gearing will rise and the entity will appear more risky to potential investors. The servicing of the finance will be charged to profit or loss reducing profits and earnings per share.

- If an entity issues an instrument and classifies it as equity then gearing will fall. The servicing of the finance will be charged directly to retained earnings and so will not impact profit or earnings per share.

In order to ensure that the instrument is faithfully represented in the financial statements, the directors will need to apply the principles in IAS 32 to the substance of the arrangement.

---

 **3   Recognition and measurement of financial liabilities**

### Initial recognition of financial liabilities

At initial recognition, financial liabilities are measured at fair value.

- If the financial liability will be held at fair value through profit or loss, transaction costs should be expensed to the statement of profit or loss.

- If the financial liability will not be held at fair value through profit or loss, transaction costs should be deducted from its carrying amount.

### Subsequent measurement of financial liabilities

The subsequent treatment of a financial liability is that they can be measured at either:

- amortised cost

- fair value through profit or loss.

## Amortised cost

Most financial liabilities, such as borrowings, are subsequently measured at amortised cost using the effective interest method. This is considered in more detail below:

### Effective rate of interest

Assume that a company takes out a $10m bank loan for 5 years. Interest of 10% is payable annually in arrears:

- The interest payable each year is $1m ($10m × 10%)

- The total cost of the loan is $5m ($1m × 5 years).

Now assume that a company issues a bond. This has a nominal value of $10m and interest of 10% is payable annually in arrears. However, the company issues the bond for only $9m and has agreed to repay $12m to the bond holders in five years' time.

- Interest of $1 m ($10m × 10%) will be paid per year.

- Total interest payments over the life of the bond are $5m ($1m × 5 years).

- On top of this interest, the entity must pay back $3m more ($12m − $9m) than it received.

The total cost of the loan is actually $8m ($5m + $3m) and, in accordance with the accruals concept, this should be spread over the 5 year period. This is achieved by charging interest on the liability using the **effective rate of interest**. The effective rate is the internal rate of return of the investment.

### Calculating amortised cost

The initial carrying amount of a financial liability measured at amortised cost is its fair value less any transaction costs (the 'net proceeds' from issue).

A finance cost is charged on the liability using the effective rate of interest. This will increase the carrying amount of the liability:

Dr Finance cost (P/L)

Cr Liability

The liability is reduced by any cash payments made during the year:

Dr Liability

Cr Cash

## Amortised cost table

In the exam, assuming interest is paid in arrears, you might find the following working useful:

| Opening liability | Finance cost (op. liability × effective %) | Cash payments (nom. value × coupon %) | Closing liability |
|---|---|---|---|
| X | X | (X) | X |

The finance cost is charged to the statement of profit or loss.

The cash payment will be part of 'interest paid' in the statement of cash flows.

The closing liability will appear on the statement of financial position.

## Illustration 1 – Loan issues at a discount

On 1 January 20X1 James issued a loan note with a $50,000 nominal value. It was issued at a discount of 16% of nominal value. The costs of issue were $2,000. Interest of 5% of the nominal value is payable annually in arrears. The bond must be redeemed on 1 January 20X6 (after 5 years) at a premium of $4,611.

The effective rate of interest is 12% per year.

**Required:**

**How will this be reported in the financial statements of James over the period to redemption?**

## Solution

The liability will be initially recognised at the net proceeds received:

|  | $ |
|---|---|
| Face value | 50,000 |
| Less: 16% discount | (8,000) |
| Less: Issue costs | (2,000) |
|  | ——— |
| Initial recognition of liability | 40,000 |
|  | ——— |

The liability is then measured at amortised cost:

| Year | Opening balance | Finance cost (Liability × 12%) | Cash payments ($50,000 × 5%) | Closing balance |
|------|-----------------|-------------------------------|------------------------------|-----------------|
| | $ | $ | $ | $ |
| 1 | 40,000 | 4,800 | (2,500) | 42,300 |
| 2 | 42,300 | 5,076 | (2,500) | 44,876 |
| 3 | 44,876 | 5,385 | (2,500) | 47,761 |
| 4 | 47,761 | 5,731 | (2,500) | 50,992 |
| 5 | 50,992 | 6,119 | (2,500) | 54,611 |
| | | 27,111 | (12,500) | |
| | | To: Profit or loss | To: Statement of cash flows | To: SOFP |

According to the above working, the total cost of the loan over the five year period is $27,111.

This is made up as follows:

| | $ | $ |
|---|---|---|
| Repayments: | | |
| Capital | 50,000 | |
| Premium | 4,611 | |
| | | 54,611 |
| Interest ($50,000 × 5% × 5 years) | | 12,500 |
| | | 67,111 |
| Cash received | | (40,000) |
| Total finance cost | | 27,111 |

The finance charge taken to profit or loss in each year is greater than the actual interest paid. This means that the value of the liability increases over the life of the instrument until it equals the redemption value at the end of its term.

In years 1 to 4 the balance shown as a liability is less than the amount that will be payable on redemption. Therefore the full amount payable must be disclosed in the notes to the financial statements.

## Test your understanding 2 – Hoy

Hoy raised finance on 1 January 20X1 by the issue of a two-year 2% bond with a nominal value of $10,000. It was issued at a discount of 5% and is redeemable at a premium of $1,075. Issue costs can be ignored. The bond has an effective rate of interest of 10%.

Wiggins raised finance by issuing $20,000 6% four-year loan notes on 1 January 20X4. The loan notes were issued at a discount of 10%, and will be redeemed after four years at a premium of $1,015. The effective rate of interest is 12%. The issue costs were $1,000.

Cavendish raised finance by issuing zero coupon bonds at par on 1 January 20X5 with a nominal value of $10,000. The bonds will be redeemed after two years at a premium of $1,449. Issue costs can be ignored. The effective rate of interest is 7%.

The reporting date for each entity is 31 December.

### Required:

**Illustrate and explain how these financial instruments should be accounted for by each company.**

## Fair value through profit or loss

Out of the money derivatives and liabilities held for trading are measured at fair value through profit or loss.

It is also possible to measure a liability at fair value when it would normally be measured at amortised cost if it would eliminate or reduce an accounting mismatch. In this case, IFRS 9 says that any movement in fair value is split into two components:

- the fair value change due to own credit risk (the risk that the entity which has issued the financial liability will be unable to repay or discharge it), which is presented in other comprehensive income

- the remaining fair value change, which is presented in profit or loss.

### Illustration 2 – Fair value through profit or loss

On 1 January 20X1, McGrath issued a financial liability for its nominal value of $10 million. Interest is payable at a rate of 5% in arrears. The liability is repayable on 31 December 20X3. McGrath trades financial liabilities in the short-term.

At 31 December 20X1, market rates of interest have risen to 10%.

### Required:

**Discuss the accounting treatment of the liability at 31 December 20X1.**

## Solution

The financial liability is traded in the short-term and so is measured at fair value through profit or loss.

The liability must be remeasured to fair value at the reporting date. Assuming that the fair value of the liability cannot be observed from an active market, it can be calculated by discounting the future cash flows at a market rate of interest.

| Date | Cash flow ($m) | Discount rate | Present value ($m) |
|------|----------------|---------------|--------------------|
| 31/12/X2 | 0.5* | $1/1.1$ | 0.45 |
| 31/12/X3 | 10.5 | $1/1.1^2$ | 8.68 |
| | | | 9.13 |

\* The interest payments are $10m × 5% = $0.5m

The fair value of the liability at the year-end is $9.13 million.

The following adjustment is required:

Dr Liability ($10m – $9.13m)                                        $0.87m

Cr Profit or loss       $0.87m

## Test your understanding 3 – Bean

Bean regularly invests in assets that are measured at fair value through profit or loss. These asset purchases are funded by issuing bonds. If the bonds were not remeasured to fair value, an accounting mismatch would arise. Therefore, Bean designates the bonds to be measured at fair value through profit or loss.

The fair value of the bonds fell by $30m during the reporting period, of which $10m related to Bean's credit worthiness.

**Required:**

**How should the bonds be accounted for?**

## 4 Compound instruments

 A **compound instrument** is a financial instrument that has characteristics of both equity and liabilities. An example would be debt that can be redeemed either in cash or in a fixed number of equity shares.

### Presentation of compound instruments

IAS 32 requires compound financial instruments be split into two components:

* a financial liability (the liability to repay the debt holder in cash)

* an equity instrument (the option to convert into shares).

These two elements must be shown separately in the financial statements.

### The initial recognition of compound instruments

On initial recognition, a compound instrument must be split into a liability component and an equity component:

* The liability component is calculated as the present value of the repayments, discounted at a market rate of interest for a similar instrument without conversion rights.

* The equity component is calculated as the difference between the cash proceeds from the issue of the instrument and the value of the liability component.

---

 **Illustration 3 – Compound instruments**

On 1 January 20X1 Daniels issued a $50m three-year convertible bond at par.

* There were no issue costs.

* The coupon rate is 10%, payable annually in arrears on 31 December.

* The bond is redeemable at par on 1 January 20X4.

* Bondholders may opt for conversion in the form of shares. The terms of conversion are two 25-cent equity shares for every $1 owed to each bondholder on 1 January 20X4.

* Bonds issued by similar entities without any conversion rights currently bear interest at 15%.

* Assume that all bondholders opt for conversion in shares.

**Required:**

**How will this be accounted for by Daniels?**

---

## Solution

On initial recognition, the proceeds received must be split between liabilities and equity.

- The liability component is calculated as the present value of the cash repayments at the market rate of interest for an instrument similar in all respects, except that it does not have conversion rights.

- The equity component is the difference between the proceeds of the issue and the liability component.

### 1 Splitting the proceeds

The cash payments on the bond should be discounted to their present value using the interest rate for a bond without the conversion rights, i.e. 15%.

| Date | | Cash flow | Discount factor (15%) | Present value |
|------|--|-----------|----------------------|---------------|
| | | $000 | | $000 |
| 31-Dec-X1 | Interest | 5,000 | $1/1.15$ | 4,347.8 |
| 31-Dec-X2 | Interest | 5,000 | $1/1.15^2$ | 3,780.7 |
| 31-Dec-X3 | Interest | 5,000 | $1/1.15^3$ | 3,287.6 |
| 1-Jan-X4 | Principal | 50,000 | $1/1.15^3$ | 32,875.8 |
| | | | | |
| Liability component | A | | | 44,291.9 |
| Net proceeds of issue | B | | | 50,000.0 |
| Equity component | B – A | | | 5,708.1 |

### 2 Measuring the liability at amortised cost

The liability component is measured at amortised cost. The working below shows the finance costs recorded in the statement of profit or loss for each year as well as the carrying value of the liability in the statement of financial position at each reporting date.

| | Opening bal. | Finance cost (15%) | Payments | Closing bal. |
|------|-------------|--------------------|----------|--------------|
| | $000 | $000 | $000 | $000 |
| 20X1 | 44,291.9 | 6,643.8 | (5,000) | 45,935.7 |
| 20X2 | 45,935.7 | 6,890.4 | (5,000) | 47,826.1 |
| 20X3 | 47,826.1 | 7,173.9 | (5,000) | 50,000.0 |

KAPLAN PUBLISHING

3 **The conversion of the bond**

The carrying amounts at 1 January 20X4 are:

|  | $000 |
|---|---|
| Equity | 5,708.1 |
| Liability – bond | 50,000.0 |
|  | 55,708.1 |

The conversion terms are two 25-cent equity shares for every $1. Therefore 100m shares ($50m × 2), will be issued which have a nominal value of $25m. The remaining $30,708,100 should be classified as the share premium, also within equity. There is no remaining liability, because conversion has extinguished it.

The double entry is as follows:

|  | $000 |
|---|---|
| Dr Other components of equity | 5,708.1 |
| Dr Liability | 50,000.0 |
| Cr Share capital | 25,000.0 |
| Cr Share premium | 30,708.1 |

**Test your understanding 4 – Craig**

Craig issues a $100,000 4% three-year convertible loan on 1 January 20X6. The market rate of interest for a similar loan without conversion rights is 8%. The conversion terms are one equity share ($1 nominal value) for every $2 of debt. Conversion or redemption at par takes place on 31 December 20X8.

**Required:**

**How should this be accounted for:**

(a) **if all holders elect for the conversion?**

(b) **no holders elect for the conversion?**

Note that the Board have issued a discussion paper on the topic of financial liabilities and equity, including compound instruments. This is an examinable current issue and is covered in Chapter 23.

## 5 Initial recognition of financial assets

IFRS 9 says that an entity should recognise a financial asset **'when, and only when, the entity becomes party to the contractual provisions of the instrument'** (IFRS 9, para 3.1.1).

Examples of this principle are as follows:

- A trading commitment to buy or sell goods is not recognised until one party has fulfilled its part of the contract. For example, a sales order will not be recognised as revenue and a receivable until the goods have been delivered.

- Forward contracts are accounted for as derivative financial assets and are recognised on the commitment date, not on the date when the item under contract is transferred from seller to buyer.

- Option contracts are accounted for as derivative financial assets and are recognised on the date the contract is entered into, not on the date when the item subject to the option is acquired.

 ## 6 Accounting for investments in equity instruments

### Classification

Investments in equity instruments (such as an investment in the ordinary shares of another entity) are measured at either:

- fair value through profit or loss, or
- fair value through other comprehensive income.

### Fair value through profit or loss

The normal expectation is that equity instruments will have the designation of fair value through profit or loss.

### Fair value through other comprehensive income

It is possible to designate an equity instrument as fair value through other comprehensive income, provided that the following conditions are complied with:

- the equity instrument must not be held for trading, and
- there must have been an irrevocable choice for this designation upon initial recognition of the asset.

## Measurement

### Fair value through profit or loss

Investments in equity instruments that are classified as fair value through profit or loss are initially recognised at fair value. Transaction costs are expensed to profit or loss.

At the reporting date, the asset is revalued to fair value with the gain or loss recorded in the statement of profit or loss.

### Fair value through other comprehensive income

Investments in equity instruments that are classified as fair value through other comprehensive income are initially recognised at fair value plus transaction costs.

At each reporting date, and immediately prior to disposal, the asset is revalued to fair value with the gain or loss recorded in other comprehensive income. This gain or loss will not be reclassified to profit or loss in future periods.

> ### Test your understanding 5 – Americano
>
> The directors of Americano designated the entity's investments in equity to be measured at fair value through other comprehensive income on the grounds that this minimises volatility in profit or loss and therefore has a positive impact on Americano's share price. They argue that this accounting treatment enables them to fulfil their duty to maximise shareholder wealth. Americano buys equity investments to trade in the short-term.
>
> **Required:**
>
> **Discuss the accounting and ethical issues raised by the above.**

## Summary

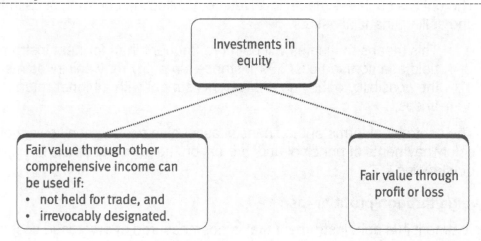

**7    Accounting for investments in debt instruments**

### Classification

Financial assets that are debt instruments can be measured in one of three ways:

- Amortised cost
- Fair value through other comprehensive income
- Fair value through profit or loss.

### Amortised cost

IFRS 9 says that an investment in a debt instrument is measured at amortised cost if:

- The entity's business model is to collect the asset's contractual cash flows.
  - This means that the entity does not plan on selling the asset prior to maturity but rather intends to hold it until redemption.
- The contractual terms of the financial asset give rise to cash flows that are solely payments of principal, and interest on the principal amount outstanding.
  - For example, the interest rate on convertible bonds is lower than market rate because the holder of the bond gets the benefit of choosing to take redemption in the form of cash or shares. The contractual cash flows are therefore not solely payments of principal and interest on the principal amount outstanding.

### Fair value through other comprehensive income

An investment in a debt instrument is measured at fair value through other comprehensive income if:

- The entity's business model involves both collecting contractual cash flows and selling financial assets.
  - This means that sales will be more frequent than for debt instruments held at amortised cost. For instance, an entity may sell investments if the possibility of buying another investment with a higher return arises.
- The contractual terms of the financial asset give rise to cash flows that are solely payments of principal and interest on the principal amount outstanding.

### Fair value through profit or loss

An investment in a debt instrument that is not measured at amortised cost or fair value through other comprehensive income will be measured, according to IFRS 9, at fair value through profit or loss.

## Test your understanding 6 – Paloma

Paloma purchased a new financial asset on 31 December 20X3. The asset is a bond that will mature in three years. Paloma buys debt investments with the intention of holding them to maturity although has, on occasion, sold some investments if cash flow deteriorated beyond acceptable levels. The bond pays a market rate of interest. The Finance Director is unsure as to whether this financial asset can be measured at amortised cost.

**Required:**

**Advise the Finance Director on how the bond will be measured.**

## Reclassification

Financial assets are classified in accordance with IFRS 9 when initially recognised.

If an entity changes its business model for managing financial assets, all affected financial assets are reclassified (e.g. from fair value through profit or loss to amortised cost). This only applies to investments in debt.

## Measurement

### Amortised cost

For investments in debt that are measured at amortised cost:

- The asset is initially recognised at fair value plus transaction costs.

- Interest income is calculated using the effective rate of interest.

### Fair value through other comprehensive income

For investments in debt that are measured at fair value through other comprehensive income:

- The asset is initially recognised at fair value plus transaction costs.

- Interest income is calculated using the effective rate of interest.

- At the reporting date, the asset will be revalued to fair value with the gain or loss recognised in other comprehensive income. This will be reclassified to profit or loss when the asset is disposed.

### Fair value through profit or loss

For investments in debt that are measured at fair value through profit or loss:

- The asset is initially recognised at fair value, with any transaction costs expensed to the statement of profit or loss.

- At the reporting date, the asset will be revalued to fair value with the gain or loss recognised in the statement of profit or loss.

## Note on loss allowances

For debt instruments measured at amortised cost or at fair value through other comprehensive income, a loss allowance must also be recognised. This detail is covered in the next section.

### Test your understanding 7 – Tokyo

On 1 January 20X1, Tokyo bought a $100,000 5% bond for $95,000, incurring issue costs of $2,000. Interest is received in arrears. The bond will be redeemed at a premium of $5,960 over nominal value on 31 December 20X3. The effective rate of interest is 8%.

The fair value of the bond was as follows:

31/12/X1      $110,000

31/12/X2      $104,000

**Required:**

**Explain, with calculations, how the bond will have been accounted for over all relevant years if:**

(a)   **Tokyo's business model is to hold bonds until the redemption date.**

(b)   **Tokyo's business model is to hold bonds until redemption but also to sell them if investments with higher returns become available.**

(c)   **Tokyo's business model is to trade bonds in the short-term. Assume that Tokyo sold this bond for its fair value on 1 January 20X2.**

**The requirement to recognise a loss allowance on debt instruments held at amortised cost or fair value through other comprehensive income should be ignored.**

### Test your understanding 8 – Magpie

On 1 January 20X1, Magpie lends $2 million to an important supplier. The loan, which is interest-free, will be repaid in two years' time. The asset is classified to be measured at amortised cost. There are no transaction fees.

Market rates of interest are 8%. The loss allowance is highly immaterial and can be ignored.

**Required:**

**Explain the accounting entries that Magpie needs to post in the year ended 31 December 20X1 to account for the above.**

## Summary

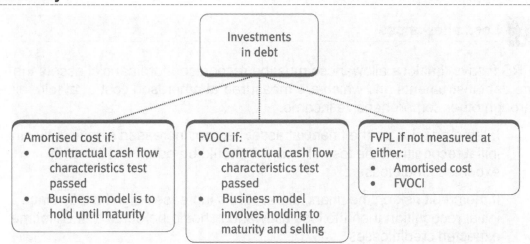

**The *Conceptual Framework***

The *Conceptual Framework* identifies two measurement bases:

- historical cost, such as amortised cost

- current value, such as fair value.

When selecting a measurement basis, the *Conceptual Framework* states that relevance is maximised if it takes into account the characteristics of the asset or liability and the way in which it contributes to future cash flows. IFRS 9 provides a good example of this because the measurement of financial assets is highly dependent on the reporting entity's business model.

If an entity's business model is to sell financial assets in the short-term then the asset is revalued to fair value at each reporting date and the gain or loss is presented in profit or loss. Measuring the asset at its fair value will help users of the financial statements to more accurately predict the entity's future cash inflows when it sells the asset.

Amortised cost reflects the present value of the future cash flows associated with the financial asset over its life. This measurement base helps users to assess the contractual cash flows that the reporting entity will receive from holding the financial asset until maturity.

## 8 Impairment of financial assets

 **Loss allowances**

IFRS 9 says that loss allowances must be recognised for financial assets that are debt instruments and which are measured at amortised cost or at fair value through other comprehensive income.

- If the credit risk on the financial asset has not increased significantly since initial recognition, the loss allowance should be equal to 12-month expected credit losses.

- If the credit risk on the financial asset has increased significantly since initial recognition then the loss allowance should be equal to the lifetime expected credit losses.

Adjustments to the loss allowance are charged (or credited) to the statement of profit or loss.

Unless credit impaired, interest income is recognised on the asset's gross carrying amount (i.e. excluding the loss allowance).

 **Definitions**

**Credit loss**: The present value of the difference between the contractual cash flows and the cash flows that the entity expects to receive.

**Expected credit losses**: The weighted average credit losses.

**Lifetime expected credit losses**: The expected credit losses that result from all possible default events.

**12-month expected credit losses**: The portion of lifetime expected credit losses that result from default events that might occur 12 months after the reporting date.

### Significant increases in credit risk

To assess whether there has been a significant increase in credit risk, IFRS 9 requires entities to compare the asset's risk of default at the reporting date with its risk of default at the date of initial recognition.

Entities should not rely solely on past information when determining if credit risk has increased significantly.

An entity can assume that credit risk has not increased significantly if the instrument has a low credit risk at the reporting date.

Credit risk can be assumed to have increased significantly if contractual payments are more than 30 days overdue at the reporting date.

**Test you understanding 9 – Tahoe**

San Fran is a company that has issued a public bond. It reports to its shareholders on a bi-annual basis.

Tahoe, a company which holds financial assets until maturity, is one of many investors in San Fran's bond. On purchase, Tahoe deemed the bond to have a low credit risk due to San Fran's strong capacity to fulfil its short-term obligations. It was perceived, however, that adverse changes in the economic environment could have a detrimental impact on San Fran's liquidity.

At Tahoe's reporting date, it has access to the following information about San Fran:

- Sales have declined 15% over the past 6 months

- External agencies are reviewing its credit rating, but no changes have yet been made

- Although market bond prices have remained static, San Fran's bond price has fallen dramatically.

**Required:**

**Discuss the accounting treatment of the bond in Tahoe's financial statements at the reporting date.**

**Measuring expected losses**

An entity's estimate of expected credit losses should be:

- unbiased and probability-weighted

- reflective of the time value of money

- based on information about past events, current conditions and forecasts of future economic conditions.

If an asset is credit impaired at the reporting date, IFRS 9 says that the expected credit losses should be measured as the difference between the asset's gross carrying amount and the present value of the estimated future cash flows when discounted at the original effective rate of interest.

IFRS 9 says that the following events may suggest the asset is credit-impaired:

- significant financial difficulty of the issuer or the borrower

- a breach of contract, such as a default

- the borrower being granted concessions

- it becoming probable that the borrower will enter bankruptcy.

If an asset is credit-impaired, interest income is calculated on the asset's net carrying amount (i.e. the gross carrying amount less the loss allowance).

## Test your understanding 10 – Napa

On 1 January 20X1, Napa purchased a bond for $1 m which is measured at amortised cost. Interest of 10% is payable in arrears. Repayment is due on 31 December 20X3. The effective rate of interest is 10%.

On 31 December 20X1, Napa received interest of $100,000. It estimated that the probability of default on the bond within the next 12 months would be 0.5%. If default occurs within the next 12 months then Napa estimated that no further interest will be received and that only 50% of the capital will be repaid on 31 December 20X3.

The asset's credit risk at 31 December 20X1 is low.

**Required:**

**Discuss the accounting treatment of the financial asset at 31 December 20X1.**

## Test your understanding 11 – Eve

On 1 February 20X6, Eve made a four-year loan of $10,000 to Fern. The coupon rate on the loan is 6%, the same as the effective rate of interest. Interest is received at the end of each year.

On 1 February 20X9, Fern tells Eve that it is in significant financial difficulties. At this time the current market interest rate is 8%.

Eve estimates that it will receive no more interest from Fern. It also estimates that only $6,000 of the capital will be repaid on the redemption date.

Eve has already recognised a loss allowance of $1,000 in respect of its loan to Fern.

**Required:**

**How should this be accounted for?**

### Purchased or originated credit-impaired financial asset

A purchased or originated credit-impaired financial asset is one that is credit-impaired on initial recognition. Interest income is calculated on such assets using the **credit-adjusted effective interest rate**.

The credit adjusted effective interest rate incorporates all the contractual terms of the financial asset as well as expected credit losses. In other words, the higher the expected credit losses, the lower the credit adjusted effective interest rate.

Since credit losses anticipated at inception will be recognised through the credit-adjusted effective interest rate, the loss allowance on purchased or originated credit-impaired financial assets should be measured only as the **change in the lifetime expected credit losses** since initial recognition.

### Debt instruments at fair value through other comprehensive income

These assets are held at fair value at the reporting date and therefore the loss allowance should not reduce the carrying amount of the asset in the statement of financial position. Instead, the allowance is recorded against other comprehensive income.

---

**Test your understanding 12 – FVOCI and expected losses**

An entity purchases a debt instrument for $1,000 on 1 January 20X1. The interest rate on the bond is the same as the effective rate. After accounting for interest for the year to 31 December 20X1, the carrying amount of the bond is still $1,000.

At the reporting date of 31 December 20X1, the fair value of the instrument has fallen to $950. There has not been a significant increase in credit risk since inception so expected credit losses should be measured at 12-month expected credit losses. This is deemed to amount to $30.

**Required:**

**Explain how the revaluation and impairment of the financial asset should be accounted for.**

---

### Simplifications

IFRS 9 permits some simplifications:

- The loss allowance should always be measured at an amount equal to lifetime credit losses for trade receivables and contract assets (recognised in accordance with IFRS 15 *Revenue from Contracts with Customers*) if they do not have a significant financing component.

- For lease receivables, as well as trade receivables and contract assets with a significant financing component, the entity can choose as its accounting policy to measure the loss allowance at an amount equal to lifetime credit losses.

### Impairment reversals

At each reporting date, the loss allowance is recalculated.

It may be that the allowance was previously equal to lifetime credit losses but now, due to reductions in credit risk, only needs to be equal to 12-month expected credit losses. As such, there may be a substantial reduction in the allowance required.

Gains or losses on remeasurement of the loss allowance are recorded in profit or loss.

## 9 Derecognition of financial instruments

**The *Conceptual Framework***

According to the *Conceptual Framework*, derecognition normally occurs when the entity:

- loses control of the asset, or

- has no present obligation for the liability.

Accounting for derecognition should faithfully represent the changes in an entity's net assets, as well as any assets or liabilities retained.

This is achieved by:

- derecognising any transferred, expired or consumed component, and

- recognising a gain or loss on the above, and

- recognising any retained component.

Sometimes an entity might appear to have transferred an asset or liability. However, derecognition would not be appropriate if exposure to variations in the element's economic benefits is retained.

As you will see below, IFRS 9 *Financial Instruments* is consistent with the *Conceptual Framework* with regards to the issue of derecognition.

A **financial asset** should be derecognised if one of the following has occurred:

- The contractual rights have expired (for example, an option held by the entity has lapsed and become worthless)

- The financial asset has been sold and substantially all the risks and rewards of ownership have been transferred from the seller to the buyer.

The analysis of where the risks and rewards of ownership lie after a transaction is critical. If an entity has retained substantially all of the risks and rewards of a financial asset then it should not be derecognised, even if it has been legally 'sold' to another entity.

A **financial liability** should be derecognised when the obligation is discharged, cancelled or expires.

The accounting treatment of derecognition is as follows:

- The difference between the carrying amount of the asset or liability and the amount received or paid for it should be recognised in profit or loss for the period.

- For investments in equity instruments held at fair value through other comprehensive income, the cumulative gains and losses recognised in other comprehensive income **are not** reclassified to profit or loss on disposal.

- For investments in debt instruments held at fair value through other comprehensive income, the cumulative gains and losses recognised in other comprehensive income **are** reclassified to profit or loss on disposal.

## Test your understanding 13 – Ming

Ming has two receivables that it has factored to a bank in return for immediate cash proceeds. Both receivables are due from long standing customers who are expected to pay in full and on time. Ming had agreed a three-month credit period with both customers.

The first receivable is for $200,000. In return for assigning the receivable, Ming has received $180,000 from the factor. Under the terms of the factoring arrangement, Ming will not have to repay this money, even if the customer does not settle the debt (the factoring arrangement is said to be 'without recourse').

The second receivable is for $100,000. In return for assigning the receivable, Ming has received $70,000 from the factor. The terms of this factoring arrangement state that Ming will receive a further $5,000 if the customer settles the account on time.

If the customer does not settle the account in accordance with the agreed terms then the receivable will be reassigned back to Ming who will then be obliged to refund the factor with the original $70,000 (this factoring arrangement is said to be 'with recourse').

### Required:

**Discuss the accounting treatment of the two factoring arrangements.**

## Test your understanding 14 – Case

Case holds equity investments at fair value through profit or loss. Due to short-term cash flow shortages, Case sold some equity investments for $5 million when the carrying amount was $4 million. The terms of the disposal state that Case has the right to repurchase the shares at any point over the next two years at their fair value on the repurchase date. Case has not derecognised the investment because its directors believe that a repurchase is highly likely.

### Required:

**Advise the directors of Case as to the acceptability of the above accounting treatment.**

## Test your understanding 15 – Jones

Jones bought an investment in equity shares for $40 million plus associated transaction costs of $1 million. The asset was designated upon initial recognition as fair value through other comprehensive income. At the reporting date the fair value of the financial asset had risen to $60 million. Shortly after the reporting date the financial asset was sold for $70 million.

**Required:**

(a) **How should the investment be accounted for?**

(b) **How would the answer have been different if the investment had been classified to be measured at fair value through profit and loss?**

## 10 Derivatives

### Definitions

IFRS 9 says that a derivative is a financial instrument with the following characteristics:

(a) Its value changes in response to the change in a specified interest rate, security price, commodity price, foreign exchange rate, index of prices or rates, a credit rating or credit index or similar variable (called the 'underlying').

(b) It requires little or no initial net investment relative to other types of contract that have a similar response to changes in market conditions.

(c) It is settled at a future date.

A contract to buy or sell a non-financial item (such as inventory or property, plant and equipment) is only a derivative if:

- it can be settled net in cash (or using another financial asset), and

- the contract was not entered into for the purpose of receipt or delivery of the item to meet the entity's operating requirements.

IFRS 9 says that a contract to buy or sell a non-financial item is considered to be settled net in cash when:

- the terms of the contract permit either party to settle the contract net

- the entity has a practice of settling similar contracts net

- the entity, for similar contracts, has a practice of taking delivery of the item and then quickly selling it in order to benefit from fair value changes

- the non-financial item is readily convertible to cash.

If the contract is not a derivative then it is a simple executory contract. Such contracts are not normally accounted for until the sale or purchase date.

### The *Conceptual Framework*

The *Conceptual Framework* defines an executory contract as a contract that is equally unperformed. This might mean that neither party to the contract has fulfilled any of its obligations.

An example would be a contract to pay employees $10 for every hour that they work. If the employee has not yet worked any hours then the entity has no obligation to pay the employee.

Executory contracts are not normally recognised in financial statements unless they are onerous, in which case a provision would be recognised in accordance with IAS 37 *Provisions, Contingent Assets and Contingent Liabilities*.

## Common derivatives

### Forward contracts

The holder of a forward contract is obliged to buy or sell a defined amount of a specific underlying asset, at a specified price at a specified future date.

### Futures contracts

Futures contracts oblige the holder to buy or sell a standard quantity of a specific underlying item at a specified future date.

Futures contracts are very similar to forward contracts. The difference is that futures contracts have standard terms and are traded on a financial exchange, whereas forward contracts are tailor-made and are not traded on a financial exchange.

### Swaps

Two parties agree to exchange periodic payments at specified intervals over a specified time period. For example, in an interest rate swap, the parties may agree to exchange fixed and floating rate interest payments calculated by reference to a notional principal amount.

### Options

These give the holder the right, but not the obligation, to buy or sell a specific underlying asset on or before a specified future date.

## Measurement of derivatives

On initial recognition, derivatives should be measured at fair value. Transaction costs are expensed to the statement of profit or loss.

At the reporting date, derivatives are remeasured to fair value. Movements in fair value are recognised in profit or loss.

## Accounting for derivatives

Entity A has a reporting date of 30 September. It enters into an option on 1 June 20X5, to purchase 10,000 shares in another entity on 1 November 20X5 for $10 per share. The purchase price of each option is $1. This is recorded as follows:

| | | |
|---|---|---|
| Debit | Option (10,000 × $1) | $10,000 |
| Credit | Cash | $10,000 |

By 30 September the fair value of each option has increased to $1.30. This increase is recorded as follows:

| | | |
|---|---|---|
| Debit | Option (10,000 × ($1.30 – $1)) | $3,000 |
| Credit | Profit or loss | $3,000 |

On 1 November, the fair value per option increases to $1.50. The share price on the same date is $11.50. A exercises the option on 1 November and the shares are classified at fair value through profit or loss. Financial assets are recognised at fair value so the shares are initially measured at $115,000 (10,000 × $11.50):

| | | |
|---|---|---|
| Debit | Investment in shares (at fair value) | $115,000 |
| Credit | Cash (10,000 × $10) | $100,000 |
| Credit | Option ($10,000 + $3,000) | $13,000 |
| Credit | Profit or loss (gain on option) | $2,000 |

## Test your understanding 16 – Hoggard

Hoggard buys 100 options on 1 January 20X6 for $5 per option. Each option gives Hoggard the right to buy a share in Rowling on 31 December 20X6 for $10 per share.

**Required:**

**How should this be accounted for, given the following outcomes?**

(a) **The options are sold on 1 July 20X6 for $15 each.**

(b) **On 31 December 20X6, Rowling's share price is $8 and Hoggard lets the option lapse unexercised.**

(c) **The option is exercised on 31 December when Rowling's share price is $25. The shares are classified as held for trading.**

## 11 Embedded derivatives

### Definition

An embedded derivative is a **'component of a hybrid contract that also includes a non-derivative host, with the effect that some of the cash flows of the combined instrument vary in a way similar to a standalone derivative'** (IFRS 9, para 4.3.3).

### Accounting treatment

With regards to the accounting treatment of an embedded derivative, if the host contract is within the scope of IFRS 9 then the entire contract must be classified and measured in accordance with that standard.

If the host contract is not within the scope of IFRS 9 (i.e. it is not a financial asset or liability), then the embedded derivative can be separated out and measured at fair value through profit or loss if:

(i) **'the economic risks and characteristics of the embedded derivative are not closely related to those of the host contract**

(ii) **a separate instrument with the same terms as the embedded derivative would meet the definition of a derivative, and**

(iii) **the entire instrument is not measured at fair value with changes in fair value recognised in profit or loss'** (IFRS 9, para 4.3.3).

Because of the complexity involved in splitting out and measuring an embedded derivative, IFRS 9 permits a hybrid contract where the host element is outside the scope of IFRS 9 to be measured at fair value through profit or loss in its entirety.

For the vast majority of embedded derivatives, the whole contract will simply be measured at fair value through profit or loss.

 **An investment in a convertible bond**

An entity has an investment in a convertible bond, which can be converted into a fixed number of equity shares at a specified future date. The bond is a non-derivative host contract and the option to convert to shares is therefore a derivative element.

The host contract, the bond, is a financial asset and so is within the scope of IFRS 9. This means that the rules of IFRS 9 must be applied to the entire contract.

The bond would fail the contractual cash flow characteristics test and therefore the entire contract should be measured at fair value through profit or loss.

## 12 Hedge accounting

**Investor perspective – derivatives**

An entity has inventories of gold that cost $8m and whose value has increased to $10m. The entity is worried that the fair value of this inventory will fall, so it enters into a futures contract on 1 October 20X1 to sell the inventory for $10m in 6 months' time.

By the reporting date, the fair value of the inventory had fallen by $1m to $9m. There was a $1m increase in the fair value of the derivative.

In accordance with IFRS 9, the $1m gain on the derivative will be recognised through profit or loss:

| | |
|---|---:|
| Dr Derivative | $1m |
| Cr Profit or loss | $1m |

In accordance with IAS 2, the $1m decline in the inventory's fair value will not be recognised because inventories are measured at the lower of cost ($8m) and NRV ($9m, assuming no selling costs).

The derivative has created volatility in profit or loss, which will also make 'earnings per share' volatile. Potential investors may be deterred by this, because they may assume that their dividend receipts will also be volatile. Although some investors are risk-seeking, others prefer steady and predictable returns.

If the entity had chosen to apply hedge accounting, this volatility would have been eliminated. This section of the text will outline the criteria for, and accounting treatment of, hedge accounting in more detail.

 **Definitions**

**Hedge accounting** is a method of managing risk by designating one or more hedging instruments so that their change in fair value is offset, in whole or in part, by the change in fair value or cash flows of a hedged item.

A **hedged item** is an asset or liability that exposes the entity to risks of changes in fair value or future cash flows (and is designated as being hedged). There are 3 types of hedged item:

- A recognised asset or liability

- An unrecognised firm commitment – a binding agreement for the exchange of a specified quantity of resources at a specified price on a specified future date

- A highly probable forecast transaction – an uncommitted but anticipated future transaction.

A **hedging instrument** is a designated derivative, or a non-derivative financial asset or financial liability, whose fair value or cash flows are expected to offset changes in fair value or future cash flows of the hedged item.

KAPLAN PUBLISHING

## Types of hedge accounting

IFRS 9 identifies three types of hedge. Two of these are in the SBR syllabus:

1   **'Fair value hedge: a hedge of the exposure to changes in fair value of a recognised asset or liability or an unrecognised firm commitment that is attributable to a particular risk and could affect profit or loss (or other comprehensive income for equity investments measured at fair value through other comprehensive income).**

2   **Cash flow hedge: a hedge of the exposure to variability in cash flows that is attributable to a particular risk associated with a recognised asset or liability or a highly probable forecast transaction and that could affect profit or loss'** (IFRS 9, para 6.5.2).

### Criteria for hedge accounting

Under IFRS 9, hedge accounting rules can only be applied if the hedging relationship meets the following criteria:

1   The hedging relationship consists only of eligible hedging instruments and hedged items.

2   At the inception of the hedge there must be formal documentation identifying the hedged item and the hedging instrument.

3   The hedging relationship meets all effectiveness requirements (see latter section for more details).

## Accounting treatment of a fair value hedge

At the reporting date:

*   The hedging instrument will be remeasured to fair value

*   The carrying amount of the hedged item will be adjusted for the change in fair value since the inception of the hedge.

The gain (or loss) on the hedging instrument and the loss (or gain) on the hedged item will be recorded:

*   in profit or loss in most cases, but

*   in other comprehensive income if the hedged item is an investment in equity that is measured at fair value through other comprehensive income.

## Investor perspective – hedge accounting

An entity has inventories of gold that cost $8m but whose value has increased to $10m. The entity is worried that the fair value of this inventory will fall, so it enters into a futures contract on 1 October 20X1 to sell the inventory for $10m in 6 months' time. This was designated as a fair value hedge.

By the reporting date of 31 December 20X1, the fair value of the inventory had fallen from $10m to $9m. There was a $1m increase in the fair value of the derivative.

The entity believes that all effectiveness criteria have been met.

Under a fair value hedge, the movement in the fair value of the item and instrument since the inception of the hedge are accounted for. The gains and losses will be recorded in profit or loss.

The $1 m gain on the future and the $1m loss on the inventory will be accounted for as follows:

| | |
|---|---|
| Dr Derivative | $1m |
| Cr Profit or loss | $1m |
| | |
| Dr Profit or loss | $1m |
| Cr Inventory | $1m |

By applying hedge accounting, the profit impact of remeasuring the derivative to fair value has been offset by the movement in the fair value of the inventory. Volatility in profits and 'earnings per share' has, in this example, been eliminated. This may make the entity look less risky to current and potential investors.

Note that the inventory will now be held at $7m (cost of $8m – $1m fair value decline). This is neither cost nor NRV. The normal accounting treatment of inventory has been changed by applying hedge accounting rules.

### Test your understanding 17 – Fair value hedge

On 1 January 20X8 an entity purchased equity instruments for their fair value of $900,000. They were designated upon initial recognition to be classified as fair value through other comprehensive income.

At 30 September 20X8, the equity instrument was still worth $900,000 but the entity became worried about the risk of a decline in value. It therefore entered into a futures contract to sell the shares for $900,000 in six months' time. It identified the futures contract as a hedging instrument as part of a fair value hedging arrangement. The fair value hedge was correctly documented and designated upon initial recognition. All effectiveness criteria have been complied with.

By the reporting date of 31 December 20X8, the fair value of the equity instrument had fallen to $800,000, and the fair value of the futures contract had risen by $90,000.

**Required:**

**Explain the accounting treatment of the fair value hedge arrangement based upon the available information.**

### Test your understanding 18 – Firm commitments

Chive has a firm commitment to buy an item of machinery for CU2m on 31 March 20X2. The Directors are worried about the risk of exchange rate fluctuations.

On 1 October 20X1, when the exchange rate is CU2:$1, Chive enters into a futures contract to buy CU2m for $1m on 31 March 20X2.

At 31 December 20X1, CU2m would cost $1,100,000. The fair value of the futures contract has risen to $95,000. All effectiveness criteria have been complied with.

**Required:**

**Explain the accounting treatment of the above in the financial statements for the year ended 31 December 20X1 if:**

(a) **Hedge accounting was not used.**

(b) **On 1 October 20X1, the futures contract was designated as a fair value hedge of the movements in the fair value of the firm commitment to purchase the machine.**

**Accounting treatment of a cash flow hedge**

For cash flow hedges, the hedging instrument will be remeasured to fair value at the reporting date. The gain or loss is recognised in other comprehensive income.

However, if the gain or loss on the hedging instrument since the inception of the hedge is greater than the loss or gain on the hedged item then the **excess** gain or loss on the instrument must be recognised in profit or loss.

 **Test your understanding 19 – Cash flow hedge**

A company enters into a derivative contract in order to protect its future cash inflows relating to a recognised financial asset. At inception, when the fair value of the hedging instrument was nil, the relationship was documented as a cash flow hedge.

By the reporting date, the loss in respect of the future cash flows amounted to $9,100 in fair value terms. It has been determined that the hedging relationship meets all effectiveness criteria.

**Required:**

**Explain the accounting treatment of the cash flow hedge if the fair value of the hedging instrument at the reporting date is:**

(a)   **$8,500**

(b)   **$10,000.**

If the hedged item eventually results in the recognition of a financial asset or a financial liability, the gains or losses that were recognised in equity shall be reclassified to profit or loss as a reclassification adjustment in the same period during which the hedged forecast cash flows affect profit or loss (e.g. in the period when the hedged forecast sale occurs).

If the hedged item eventually results in the recognition of a non-financial asset or liability, the gain or loss held in equity must be adjusted against the carrying amount of the non-financial asset/liability. This is not a reclassification adjustment and therefore it does not affect other comprehensive income.

### Test your understanding 20 – Bling

On 31 October 20X1, Bling had inventories of gold which cost $6.4m to buy and which could be sold for $7.7m. The management of Bling are concerned about the risk of fluctuations in future cash inflows from the sale of this gold.

To mitigate this risk, Bling entered into a futures contract on 31 October 20X1 to sell the gold for $7.7m. The contracts mature on 31 March 20X2. The hedging relationship was designated and documented at inception as a cash flow hedge. All effectiveness criteria are complied with.

On 31 December 20X1, the fair value of the gold was $8.6m. The fair value of the futures contract had fallen by $0.9m.

There is no change in fair value of the gold and the futures contract between 31 December 20X1 and 31 March 20X2. On 31 March 20X2, the inventory is sold for its fair value and the futures contract is settled net with the bank.

**Required:**

(a) **Discuss the accounting treatment of the hedge in the year ended 31 December 20X1.**

(b) **Outline the accounting treatment of the inventory sale and the futures contract settlement on 31 March 20X2.**

### Test your understanding 21 – Grayton

In January, Grayton, whose functional currency is the dollar ($), decided that it was highly probable that it would buy an item of plant in one year's time for KR 200,000. As a result of being risk averse, it wished to hedge the risk that the cost of buying KRs would rise and so entered into a forward rate agreement to buy KR 200,000 in one year's time for the fixed sum of $100,000. The fair value of this contract at inception was zero and it was designated as a hedging instrument.

At Grayton's reporting date of 31 July, the KR had depreciated and the value of KR 200,000 was $90,000. The fair value of the derivative had declined by $10,000. These values remained unchanged until the plant was purchased.

**Required:**

**How should this be accounted for?**

## Hedge effectiveness

Hedge accounting can only be used if the hedging relationship meets all effectiveness requirements. In the examples so far, it has been assumed that this is the case.

According to IFRS 9, an entity must assess at the inception of the hedging relationship, and at each reporting date, whether a hedging relationship meets the hedge effectiveness requirements. The assessment should be **forward-looking**.

The hedge effectiveness requirements are as follows

1   **'There must be an economic relationship between the hedged item and the hedging instrument'** (IFRS 9, para 6.4.1).

   –   For example, if the price of a share falls below $10, the fair value of a futures contract to sell the share for $10 rises.

2   **'The effect of credit risk does not dominate the value changes that result from that economic relationship'** (IFRS 9, para 6.4.1).

   –   Credit risk may lead to erratic fair value movements in either the hedged item or the hedging instrument. For example, if the counterparty of a derivative experiences a decline in credit worthiness, the fair value of the derivative (the hedging instrument) may fall substantially. This movement is unrelated to changes in the fair value of the item and would lead to hedge ineffectiveness.

3   **'The hedge ratio of the hedging relationship is the same as that resulting from the quantity of the hedged item that the entity actually hedges and the quantity of the hedging instrument that the entity actually uses to hedge that quantity of hedged item'** (IFRS 9, para 6.4.1).

**Hedge ratios**

An entity owns 120,000 gallons of oil. It enters into 1 futures contract to sell 40,000 gallons of oil at a fixed price.

It wishes to designate this as a fair value hedge, with 120,000 gallons of oil as the hedged item and the futures contract as the hedging instrument. If deemed effective, this would mean that the fair value gain or loss on the hedged item (the oil) and the fair value loss or gain on the hedging instrument (the futures contract) would be recorded and recognised in profit or loss.

> However, the hedge ratio means that the gain or loss on the item would probably be much bigger than the loss or gain on the instrument. This would create volatility in profit or loss that is at odds with the purpose of hedge accounting. Therefore, the hedge ratio must be adjusted to avoid the imbalance.
>
> It may be that the hedged item should be designated as 40,000 gallons of oil, with the hedging instrument as 1 futures contract. The other 80,000 gallons of oil would be accounted for in accordance with normal accounting rules (IAS 2 *Inventories*).

### Discontinuing hedge accounting

An entity must cease hedge accounting if any of the following occur:

- The hedging instrument expires or is exercised, sold or terminated.

- The hedge no longer meets the hedging criteria.

- A forecast future transaction that qualified as a hedged item is no longer highly probable.

The discontinuance should be accounted for prospectively (entries posted to date are not reversed).

Upon discontinuing a cash flow hedge, the treatment of the accumulated gains or losses on the hedging instrument within reserves depends on the reason for the discontinuation. IFRS 9 says:

- If the forecast transaction is no longer expected to occur, gains and losses recognised in other comprehensive income must be taken to profit or loss immediately.

- If the transaction is still expected to occur, the gains and losses will be retained in equity until the former hedged transaction occurs.

## 13 Disclosure of financial instruments

IFRS 7 *Financial Instruments: Disclosures* provides the disclosure requirements for financial instruments.

The main disclosures required are:

1 Information about the significance of financial instruments for an entity's financial position and performance.

2 Information about the nature and extent of risks arising from financial instruments.

## Significance of financial instruments

- An entity must disclose the **significance** of financial instruments for their financial position and performance. The disclosures must be made for each class of financial instruments.

- An entity must disclose items of income, expense, gains, and losses, with separate disclosure of gains and losses from each class of financial instrument.

## Nature and extent of risks arising from financial instruments

### Qualitative disclosures

The qualitative disclosures describe:

- risk exposures for each type of financial instrument

- management's objectives, policies, and processes for managing those risks

- changes from the prior period.

### Quantitative disclosures

The quantitative disclosures provide information about the extent to which the entity is exposed to risk, based on information provided internally to the entity's key management personnel. These disclosures include:

- summary quantitative data about exposure to each risk at the reporting date

- disclosures about credit risk, liquidity risk, and market risk

- concentrations of risk.

### Test your understanding 22 – Lizzer

Lizzer is a debt issuer whose business is the securitisation of a portfolio of underlying investments and financing their purchase through the issuing of listed, limited recourse debt. The repayment of the debt is dependent upon the performance of the underlying investments. Debt-holders bear the ultimate risks and rewards of ownership of the underlying investments. Given the debt specific nature of the underlying investments, the risk profile of individual debt may differ.

Lizzer does not consider its debt-holders as being amongst the primary users of the financial statements and, accordingly, does not wish to provide disclosure of the debt-holders' exposure to risks in the financial statements, as distinct from the risks faced by the company's shareholders, in accordance with IFRS 7 *Financial Instruments: Disclosures*.

**Required:**

**Discuss the directors' view that no further information regarding the above should be disclosed in the financial statements because it would be 'excessive'.**

## 14 Chapter summary

**Classification of liabilities and equity:**
- Liabilities include a contractual obligation to pay cash or issue a variable number of equity instruments
- Equity – no such obligations.

**Financial liabilities:**
Measured at either:
- Fair value through profit or loss
- Amortised cost

**Derivatives (assets and liabilities):**
- Measured at fair value through profit or loss
- Volatility can be reduced by
  - fair value hedging
  - cash flow hedging

**Financial assets:**
- Measured at either
  - Fair value through profit or loss
  - Fair value through other comprehensive income
  - Amortised cost

**Impairment of financial assets:**
- Loss allowances required for investments in debt measured at amortised cost or FVOCI

**Disclosure requirements:**
- Significance of financial instruments
- Nature and extents of risks
- Qualitative and quantitative issues

## Test your understanding answers

### Test your understanding 1 – Liabilities or equity?

**1m preference shares**

The definition of a financial liability includes any contract that may be settled in a variable number of the entity's own equity instruments.

Therefore, a contract that requires the entity to deliver as many of the entity's own equity instruments as are equal in value to a certain amount should be treated as debt.

Coasters must redeem the first set of preference shares by issuing ordinary shares equal to the value of $3 million. The $3 million received from the preference share issue should be classified as a liability on the statement of financial position.

**2m preference shares**

A contract that will be settled by the entity delivering a fixed number of its own equity instruments is an equity instrument.

Coasters will redeem the second preference share issue with a fixed number of ordinary shares. Therefore, the $5.6 million from the second preference share issue should be classified as equity in the statement of financial position.

**4m preference shares**

A financial liability exists if there is a contractual obligation to deliver cash or another financial asset.

There is no obligation for Coasters to repay the instrument.

Dividends are only payable if they are also paid on ordinary shares. There is no obligation to pay dividends on ordinary shares so there is no obligation to pay dividends on these preference shares.

The instrument is not a financial liability. The proceeds from the preference share issue should therefore be classified as equity in the statement of financial position.

## Test your understanding 2 – Hoy

**Hoy** has a financial liability to be measured at amortised cost.

The financial liability is initially recorded at the fair value of the consideration received (the net proceeds of issue). This amount is then increased each year by interest at the effective rate and reduced by the actual repayments.

Hoy has no issue costs, so the net proceeds of issue were $9,500 ($10,000 less 5%). The annual cash payment is $200 (the 2% coupon rate multiplied by the $10,000 nominal value of the debt).

|  | Bal b/fwd | Finance costs (10%) | Cash paid | Bal c/fwd |
|---|---|---|---|---|
|  | $ | $ | $ | $ |
| 31 Dec X1 | 9,500 | 950 | (200) | 10,250 |
| 31 Dec X2 | 10,250 | 1,025 | (200) |  |
|  |  |  | (11,075) |  |
|  |  | ───── |  |  |
|  |  | 1,975 |  |  |
|  |  | ───── |  |  |

**Wiggins** has a liability that will be classified and accounted for at amortised cost and thus initially measured at the fair value of consideration received less the transaction costs:

|  | $ |
|---|---|
| Cash received ($20,000 × 90%) | 18,000 |
| Less the transaction costs | (1,000) |
|  | ───── |
| Initial recognition | 17,000 |
|  | ───── |

The effective rate is used to determine the finance cost for the year – this is charged to profit or loss. The coupon rate is applied to the nominal value of the loan notes to determine the cash paid to the holder of the loan notes:

|  | Bal b/fwd | Finance costs (12%) | Cash paid | Bal c/fwd |
|---|---|---|---|---|
|  | $ | $ | $ | $ |
| 31 Dec X4 | 17,000 | 2,040 | (1,200) | 17,840 |
| 31 Dec X5 | 17,840 | 2,141 | (1,200) | 18,781 |
| 31 Dec X6 | 18,781 | 2,254 | (1,200) | 19,835 |
| 31 Dec X7 | 19,835 | 2,380 | (1,200) |  |
|  |  |  | (21,015) |  |
|  |  | ───── |  |  |
|  |  | 8,815 |  |  |
|  |  | ───── |  |  |

**Cavendish** has a financial liability to be measured at amortised cost.

It is initially recorded at the fair value of the consideration received. There is no discount on issue, nor is there any issue costs to deduct from the initial measurement.

The opening balance is increased each year by interest at the effective rate. The liability is reduced by the cash repayments – there are no interest repayments in this example because it is a zero rate bond.

|  | Bal b/fwd | Finance costs (7%) | Cash paid | Bal c/fwd |
|---|---|---|---|---|
|  | $ | $ | $ | $ |
| 31 Dec X5 | 10,000 | 700 | Nil | 10,700 |
| 31 Dec X6 | 10,700 | 749 | (11,449) |  |

### Test your understanding 3 – Bean

When a financial liability is designated to be measured at fair value through profit or loss to reduce an accounting mis-match, the fair value movement must be split into:

- fair value movement due to own credit risk, which is presented in other comprehensive income (OCI)

- the remaining fair value movement, which is presented in profit or loss.

The value of Bean's liability will be reduced by $30 million. A credit of $10 million will be recorded in OCI and a credit of $20 million will be recorded in profit or loss.

### Test your understanding 4 – Craig

Up to 31 December 20X8, the accounting entries are the same under both scenarios.

1    **Splitting the proceeds**

The cash payments on the bond should be discounted to their present value using the interest rate for a bond without the conversion rights, i.e. 8%.

| Date |  | Cash flow $ | Discount factor (8%) | Present value $ |
|---|---|---|---|---|
| 31/12/X6 | Interest | 4,000 | 1/1.08 | 3,704 |
| 31/12/X7 | Interest | 4,000 | $1/1.08^2$ | 3,429 |
| 31/12/X8 | Interest and principal | 104,000 | $1/1.08^3$ | 82,559 |
| Liability component |  |  | A | 89,692 |
| Net proceeds of issue were |  |  | B | 100,000 |
| Equity component |  |  | B – A | 10,308 |

**2  The annual finance costs and year end carrying amounts**

|  | Opening balance $ | Finance cost (8%) $ | Cash paid $ | Closing balance $ |
|---|---|---|---|---|
| X6 | 89,692 | 7,175 | (4,000) | 92,867 |
| X7 | 92,867 | 7,429 | (4,000) | 96,296 |
| X8 | 96,296 | 7,704 | (4,000) | 100,000 |

**3  (a)  Conversion**

The carrying amounts at 31 December 20X8 are:

| | $ |
|---|---|
| Equity | 10,308 |
| Liability – bond | 100,000 |
| | 110,308 |

If the conversion rights are exercised, then 50,000 ($100,000 ÷ 2) equity shares of $1 are issued and $60,308 is classified as share premium.

**(b)  Redemption**

The carrying amounts at 31 December 20X8 are the same as under 3a. On redemption, the $100,000 liability is extinguished by cash payments. The equity component remains within equity, probably as a non-distributable reserve.

### Test your understanding 5 – Americano

Equity investments can be measured at fair value through other comprehensive income if the investment is not held for short-term trading and if an irrevocable designation has been made. If equity investments are acquired for short-term trading then IFRS 9 *Financial Instruments* stipulates that they must be measured at fair value through profit or loss. Therefore, Americano should measure its investments in equity instruments at fair value through profit or loss.

Directors are appointed by shareholders and have a responsibility to act in their best interests and this may be considered to be by maximising profits. However, at the same time, accountants are trusted by the public to produce financial statements that faithfully represent the financial performance, position and cash flows of an entity. These financial statements are relied on by users to make economic decisions. To ensure that this trust is not broken, accountants are bound by a *Code of Ethics and Conduct*.

Integrity is defined as being honest and straight-forward. Manipulating financial asset measurement categories shows a lack of integrity.

It would appear that fair value through other comprehensive income has been selected as a way to produce a particular performance profile in profit or loss. This demonstrates a lack of objectivity.

Therefore, despite the director's claim about the impact on shareholder wealth, the directors have an ethical responsibility to faithfully represent Americano's underlying performance and position. This is achieved through compliance with IFRS Standards.

### Test your understanding 6 – Paloma

A debt instrument can be held at amortised cost if

* the entity intends to hold the financial asset to collect contractual cash flows, rather than selling it to realise fair value changes.

* the contractual cash flows of the asset are solely payments of principal and interest based upon the principal amount outstanding.

Paloma's objective is to hold the financial assets and collect the contractual cash flows. Making some sales when cash flow deteriorates does not contradict that objective.

The bond pays a market level of interest, and therefore the interest payments received provide adequate compensation for the time value of money or the credit risk associated with the principal amount outstanding.

This means that the asset can be measured at amortised cost.

## Test your understanding 7 – Tokyo

(a) The business model is to hold the asset until redemption. Therefore, the debt instrument will be measured at amortised cost.

The asset is initially recognised at its fair value plus transaction costs of $97,000 ($95,000 + $2,000).

Interest income will be recognised in profit or loss using the effective rate of interest.

|  | Bfd | Interest (8%) | Receipt | Cfd |
|---|---|---|---|---|
|  | $ | $ | $ | $ |
| y/e 31/12/X1 | 97,000 | 7,760 | (5,000) | 99,760 |
| y/e 31/12/X2 | 99,760 | 7,981 | (5,000) | 102,741 |
| y/e 31/12/X3 | 102,741 | 8,219 | (5,000) | nil |
|  |  |  | (105,960) |  |

In the year ended 31 December 20X1, interest income of $7,760 will be recognised in profit or loss and the asset will be held at $99,760 on the statement of financial position.

In the year ended 31 December 20X2, interest income of $7,981 will be recognised in profit or loss and the asset will be held at $102,741 on the statement of financial position.

In the year ended 31 December 20X3, interest income of $8,219 will be recognised in profit or loss.

(b) The business model is to hold the asset until redemption, but sales may be made to invest in other assets will higher returns. Therefore, the debt instrument will be measured at fair value through other comprehensive income.

The asset is initially recognised at its fair value plus transaction costs of $97,000 ($95,000 + $2,000).

Interest income will be recognised in profit or loss using the effective rate of interest.

The asset must be revalued to fair value at the year end. The gain will be recorded in other comprehensive income.

|  | Bfd | Interest (per (a)) | Receipt | Total | Gain/(loss) | Cfd |
|---|---|---|---|---|---|---|
|  | $ | $ | $ | $ | $ | $ |
| y/e 31/12/X1 | 97,000 | 7,760 | (5,000) | 99,760 | 10,240 | 110,000 |
| y/e 31/12/X2 | 110,000 | 7,981 | (5,000) | 112,981 | (8,981) | 104,000 |
| y/e 31/12/X3 | 104,000 | 8,219 | (5,000) (105,960) | 1,259 | (1,259) | nil |

Note that the amounts recognised in profit or loss as interest income must be the same as if the asset was simply held at amortised cost. Therefore, the interest income figures are the same as in part (a).

In the year ended 31 December 20X1, interest income of $7,760 will be recognised in profit or loss and a revaluation gain of $10,240 will be recognised in other comprehensive income. The asset will be held at $110,000 on the statement of financial position.

In the year ended 31 December 20X2, interest income of $7,981 will be recognised in profit or loss and a revaluation loss of $8,981 will be recognised in other comprehensive income. The asset will be held at $104,000 on the statement of financial position.

In the year ended 31 December 20X3, interest income of $8,219 will be recognised in profit or loss and a revaluation loss of $1,259 will be recognised in other comprehensive income.

(c)     The bond would be classified as fair value through profit or loss.

The asset is initially recognised at its fair value of $95,000. The transaction costs of $2,000 would be expensed to profit or loss.

In the year ended 31/12/X1, interest income of $5,000 ($100,000 × 5%) would be recognised in profit or loss. The asset would be revalued to $110,000 with a gain of $15,000 ($110,000 – $95,000) recognised in profit or loss.

On 1/1/X2, the cash proceeds of $110,000 would be recognised and the financial asset would be derecognised.

### Test your understanding 8 – Magpie

The loan is a financial asset because Magpie has a contractual right to receive cash in two years' time.

Financial assets are initially recognised at fair value. Fair value is the price paid in an orderly transaction between market participants at the measurement date.

Market participants would receive 8% interest on loans of this type, whereas the loan made to the supplier is interest-free. It would seem that the transaction has not occurred on fair value terms.

The financial asset will not be recognised at the price paid of $2 million as this is not the fair value. Instead, the fair value must be determined. This can be achieved by calculating the present value of the future cash flows from the loan (discounted using a market rate of interest).

The financial asset will therefore be initially recognised at $1.71 million ($2m × 1/1.08²). The entry required to record this is as follows:

| | |
|---|---|
| Dr Financial asset | $1.71m |
| Dr Profit or loss | $0.29m |
| Cr Cash | $2.00m |

The financial asset is subsequently measured at amortised cost:

| | 1 Jan X1 | Interest (8%) | Receipt | 31 Dec X1 |
|---|---|---|---|---|
| | $m | $m | $m | $m |
| y/e 31 /12/X1 | 1.71 | 0.14 | – | 1.85 |

Interest income of $0.14 million is recorded by posting the following:

| | |
|---|---|
| Dr Financial asset | $0.14m |
| Cr Profit or loss | $0.14m |

The loan is interest-free, so no cash is received during the period.

The financial asset will have a carrying amount of $1.85 million as at 31 December 20X1.

By 31 December 20X2, the financial asset will have a carrying amount of $2 million. This amount will then be repaid by the supplier.

### Test your understanding 9 – Tahoe

Using available information, Tahoe needs to assess whether the credit risk on the bond has increased significantly since inception.

It would seem that San Fran's performance has declined and this may have an impact on its liquidity.

The review of San Fran's credit rating by external agencies is suggestive of wider concerns about the performance and position of San Fran.

The fact that market bond prices are static suggests that the decline in San Fran's bond price is entity specific. This is likely to be a response to San Fran's increased credit risk.

Based on the above, it would seem that the credit risk of the bond is no longer low. As a result, it can be concluded that credit risk has increased significantly since inception.

This means that Tahoe must recognise a loss allowance equal to lifetime expected credit losses on the bond.

### Test your understanding 10 – Napa

The credit risk on the financial asset has not significantly increased. Therefore, a loss allowance should be made equal to 12-month expected credit losses. The loss allowance should factor in a range of possible outcomes, as well as the time value of money.

The credit loss on the asset is $586,777 (W1). This represents the present value of the difference between the contractual cash flows and the expected receipts if a default occurs.

The expected credit loss is $2,934 ($586,777 credit loss × 0.5% probability of occurrence). A loss allowance of $2,934 will be created and an impairment loss of $2,934 will be charged to profit or loss in the year ended 31 December 20X1.

The net carrying amount of the financial asset on the statement of financial position is $997,066 ($1,000,000 – $2,934).

Note: Interest in future periods will continue to be charged on the asset's gross carrying amount of $1,000,000.

| Date | Expected cash shortfall | Discount rate | PV |
|---|---|---|---|
| | $ | | $ |
| 31/12/X2 | 100,000 | $1/1.1$ | 90,909 |
| 31/12/X3 | 100,000 | $1/1.1^2$ | 82,645 |
| 31/12/X3 | 500,000 | $1/1.1^2$ | 413,223 |
| | | | ——— |
| | | | 586,777 |
| | | | ——— |

## Test your understanding 11 – Eve

Evidence about the significant financial difficulties of Fern mean that the asset is now credit impaired.

Expected losses on credit impaired assets are calculated as the difference between the asset's gross carrying amount and the present value of the expected future cash flows discounted using the original effective rate of interest.

Because the coupon and the effective interest rate are the same, the carrying amount of the asset will remain constant at $10,000.

The present value of the future cash flows discounted using the original effective rate is $5,660 ($6,000 × 1/1.06).

The expected losses are therefore $4,340 ($10,000 – $5,660) and so a loss allowance should be recognised for this amount. Therefore, the existing loss allowance must be increased by $3,340 ($4,340 – $1,000) with an expense charged to profit or loss.

The asset is credit impaired and so interest income will now be calculated on the net carrying amount of $5,660 (the gross amount of $10,000 less the loss allowance of $4,340). Consequently, in the last year of the loan, interest income of $340 (5,660 × 6%) will be recognised in profit or loss.

## Test your understanding 12 – FVOCI and expected losses

A loss of $50 ($1,000 – $950) arising on the revaluation of the asset to fair value will be recognised in other comprehensive income.

| | |
|---|---|
| Dr OCI | $50 |
| Cr Financial asset | $50 |

The 12-month expected credit losses of $30 will be debited to profit or loss. The credit entry is not recorded against the carrying amount of the asset but rather against other comprehensive income:

| | |
|---|---|
| Dr Impairment loss (P/L) | $30 |
| Cr OCI | $30 |

There is therefore a cumulative loss in OCI of $20 (the fair value change of $50 offset by the impairment amount of $30).

**Test your understanding 13 – Ming**

The principle at stake with derecognition or otherwise of receivables is whether, under the factoring arrangement, the risks and rewards of ownership pass from Ming to the factor. The key risk with regard to receivables is the risk of bad debt.

In the first arrangement the $180,000 has been received as a one-off, non-refundable sum. This is factoring without recourse for bad debts. The risk of bad debt has clearly passed from Ming to the factoring bank. Accordingly Ming should derecognise the receivable and there will be an expense of $20,000 recognised.

In the second arrangement the $70,000 is simply a payment on account. More may be received by Ming implying that Ming retains an element of reward. The monies received are refundable in the event of default and as such represent an obligation. This means that the risk of slow payment and bad debt remains with Ming who is liable to repay the monies so far received. Despite the passage of legal title the receivable should remain recognised in the accounts of Ming. In substance Ming has borrowed $70,000 and this loan should be recognised immediately. This will increase the gearing of Ming.

**Test your understanding 14 – Case**

An entity has transferred a financial asset if it has transferred the contractual rights to receive the cash flows of the asset.

IFRS 9 says that if an entity has transferred a financial asset, it must evaluate the extent to which it has retained the significant risks and rewards of ownership. If the entity transfers substantially all the risks and rewards of ownership, the entity must derecognise the financial asset.

Gains and losses on the disposal of a financial asset are recognised in the statement of profit or loss.

Case is under no obligation to buy back the shares and is therefore protected from future share price declines. Moreover, If Case does repurchase the shares, this will be at fair value rather than a pre-fixed price and therefore Case does not retain the risks and rewards related to price fluctuations.

The risks and rewards of ownership have been transferred and, as such, Case should derecognise the financial asset. A profit of $1m ($5m – $4m) should be recognised in profit or loss.

**Test your understanding 15 – Jones**

(a)  On purchase the investment is recorded at fair value. The asset is classified as fair value through other comprehensive income and, as such, transaction costs are included in the initial value:

| | |
|---|---|
| Dr Asset | 41m |
| Cr Cash | 41m |

At the reporting date the asset is remeasured to fair value and the gain of $19 million ($60m – $41 m) is recognised in other comprehensive income and taken to equity:

| | |
|---|---|
| Dr Asset | 19m |
| Cr Other comprehensive income | 19m |

Prior to disposal, the asset is remeasured to fair value with the gain of $10 million ($70m – $60m) recorded in other comprehensive income:

| | |
|---|---|
| Dr Asset | 10m |
| Cr Other comprehensive income | 10m |

The asset is then derecognised:

| | |
|---|---|
| Dr Cash | 70m |
| Cr Asset | 70m |

Note that any gains or losses recorded in OCI to-date are **not** reclassified to profit or loss upon derecognition of the financial asset, although they may be reclassified within equity.

(b)  If Jones had designated the investment as fair value through profit and loss, the transaction costs would have been recognised as an expense in profit or loss. The entry posted on the purchase date would have been:

| | |
|---|---|
| Dr Asset | 40m |
| Cr Cash | 40m |

| | |
|---|---|
| Dr Profit or loss | 1m |
| Cr Cash | 1m |

At the reporting date, the asset is remeasured to fair value and the gain of $20 million ($60m – $40m) is recognised in the statement of profit or loss:

| | |
|---|---|
| Dr Asset | 20m |
| Cr Profit or loss | 20m |

On disposal the asset is derecognised and the profit on disposal is recorded in the statement of profit or loss:

| | |
|---|---|
| Dr Cash | 70m |
| Cr Asset | 60m |
| Cr Profit or loss | 10m |

## Test your understanding 16 – Hoggard

In all scenarios the cost of the derivative on 1 January 20X6 is $500 ($5 × 100) and an asset is recognised in the statement of financial position.

| | |
|---|---|
| Dr Asset – option | $500 |
| Cr Cash | $500 |

### Outcome A

If the option is sold for $1,500 (100 × $15) before the exercise date, it is derecognised at a profit of $1,000.

| | |
|---|---|
| Dr Cash | $1,500 |
| Cr Asset – option | $500 |
| Cr Profit or loss | $1,000 |

### Outcome B

If the option lapses unexercised, then it is derecognised and there is a loss to be taken to profit or loss:

| | |
|---|---|
| Dr Profit or loss | $500 |
| Cr Asset – option | $500 |

### Outcome C

If the option is exercised then the option is derecognised, the entity records the cash paid upon exercise, and the investment in shares is recognised at fair value. An immediate profit is recognised:

| | |
|---|---|
| Dr Asset – investment (100 × $25) | $2,500 |
| Cr Cash (100 × $10) | $1,000 |
| Cr Asset – option | $500 |
| Cr Profit or loss | $1,000 |

## Test your understanding 17 – Fair value hedge

The hedged item is an investment in equity that is measured at fair value through other comprehensive income (OCI). Therefore, the increase in the fair value of the derivative of $90,000 and the fall in fair value of the equity interest of $100,000 since the inception of the hedge are taken to OCI.

| | |
|---|---|
| Dr Derivative | $90,000 |
| Cr OCI | $90,000 |
| Dr OCI | $100,000 |
| Cr Equity investment | $100,000 |

The net result is a small loss of $10,000 in OCI.

## Test your understanding 18 – Firm commitments

(a) The futures contract is a derivative and is measured at fair value with all movements being accounted for through profit or loss.

The fair value of the futures contract at 1 October 20X1 was nil. By the year end, it had risen to $95,000. Therefore, at 31 December 20X1, Chive will recognise an asset at $95,000 and a gain of $95,000 will be recorded in profit or loss.

(b) If the relationship had been designated as a fair value hedge then the movement in the fair value of the hedging instrument (the future) and the fair value of the hedged item (the firm commitment) since inception of the hedge are accounted for through profit or loss.

The derivative has increased in fair value from $nil at 1 October 20X1 to $95,000 at 31 December 20X1. Purchasing CU2 million at 31 December 20X1 would cost Chive $100,000 more than it would have done at 1 October 20X1. Therefore the fair value of the firm commitment has fallen by $100,000.

At year end, the derivative will be held at its fair value of $95,000, and the gain of $95,000 will be recorded in profit or loss.

The $100,000 fall in the fair value of the commitment will also be accounted for, with an expense recognised in profit or loss.

In summary, the double entries are as follows:

| | |
|---|---|
| Dr Derivative | $95,000 |
| Cr Profit or loss | $95,000 |
| Dr Profit or loss | $100,000 |
| Cr Firm commitment | $100,000 |

The gain on the derivative and the loss on the firm commitment largely net off. There is a residual $5,000 ($100,000 – $95,000) net expense in profit or loss due to hedge ineffectiveness. Nonetheless, financial statement volatility is far less than if hedge accounting had not been used.

## Test your understanding 19 – Cash flow hedge

(a) The movement on the hedging instrument is less than the movement on the hedged item. Therefore, the instrument is remeasured to fair value and the gain is recognised in other comprehensive income.

| | |
|---|---|
| Dr Derivative | $8,500 |
| Cr OCI | $8,500 |

(b) The movement on the hedging instrument is more than the movement on the hedged item. The excess movement of $900 ($10,000 – $9,100) is recognised in the statement of profit or loss.

| | |
|---|---|
| Dr Derivative | $10,000 |
| Cr Profit or loss | $900 |
| Cr OCI | $9,100 |

## Test your understanding 20 – Bling

(a) Between 1 October 20X1 and 31 December 20X1, the fair value of the futures contract had fallen by $0.9m. Over the same time period, the hedged item (the estimated cash receipts from the sale of the inventory) had increased by $0.9m ($8.6m – $7.7m).

Under a cash flow hedge, the movement in the fair value of the hedging instrument is accounted for through other comprehensive income. Therefore, the following entry is required:

| | |
|---|---|
| Dr Other comprehensive income | $0.9m |
| Cr Derivative | $0.9m |

The loss recorded in other comprehensive income will be held within equity.

(b) The following entries are required:

| | |
|---|---|
| Dr Cash | $8.6m |
| Cr Revenue | $8.6m |
| Dr Cost of sales | $6.4m |
| Cr Inventory | $6.4m |

To record the sale of the inventory at fair value

| | |
|---|---|
| Dr Derivative | $0.9m |
| Cr Cash | $0.9m |

To record the settlement of the futures contract

| | |
|---|---|
| Dr Profit or loss | $0.9m |
| Cr OCI | $0.9m |

To reclassify the losses held in equity through profit or loss in the same period as the hedged item affects profit or loss.

### Test your understanding 21 – Grayton

The forward rate agreement has no fair value at its inception so is initially recorded at $nil.

This is a cash flow hedge. The derivative has fallen in value by $10,000 but the cash flows have increased in value by $10,000 (it is now $10,000 cheaper to buy the asset).

Because it has been designated a cash flow hedge, the movement in the value of the hedging instrument is recognised in other comprehensive income:

| | |
|---|---|
| Dr Other comprehensive income | $10,000 |
| Cr Derivative | $10,000 |

(Had this not been designated a hedging instrument, the loss would have been recognised immediately in profit or loss.)

The forward contract will be settled and closed when the asset is purchased.

Property, plant and equipment is a non-financial item. The loss on the hedging instrument held within equity is adjusted against the carrying amount of the plant.

The following entries would be posted:

| | |
|---|---|
| Dr Liability – derivative | $10,000 |
| Dr Plant | $90,000 |
| Cr Cash | $100,000 |

Being the settlement of the derivative and the purchase of the plant.

| | |
|---|---|
| Dr Plant | $10,000 |
| Cr Cash flow hedge reserve | $10,000 |

Being the adjustment of the losses held within equity against the carrying amount of the plant. Notice that the plant will be held at $100,000 ($90,000 + $10,000) and the cash spent in total was $100,000. This was the position that the derivative guaranteed.

## Test your understanding 22 – Lizzer

Lizzer's perception of who could reasonably be considered to be among the users of its financial statements is too narrow, being limited to the company's shareholders rather than including debt-holders.

IAS 1 *Presentation of Financial Statements* states that the objective of financial statements is to provide information about the financial position, financial performance and cash flows of an entity that is useful to a wide range of users in making economic decisions. The standard also states that omissions or misstatements of items are material if they could, individually or collectively, influence the economic decisions that users make on the basis of the financial statements.

The objective of IFRS 7 *Financial Instruments: Disclosures* is to require entities to provide disclosures in their financial statements that enable users to evaluate the significance of financial instruments for the entity's financial position and performance. IFRS 7 states that, amongst other matters, for each type of risk arising from financial instruments, an entity shall disclose:

- the exposures to risk and how they arise

- its objectives, policies and processes for managing the risk and the methods used to measure the risk.

Thus the risks attached to the debt should be disclosed.

# Tax

## Chapter learning objectives

Upon completion of this chapter you will be able to:

- Discuss and apply the recognition and measurement of deferred tax liabilities and deferred tax assets

- Discuss and apply the recognition of current and deferred tax as income or expense

- Discuss and apply the treatment of deferred taxation on a business combination.

**PER**

One of the PER performance objectives (PO6) is to record and process transactions and events. You need to use the right accounting treatments for transactions and events. These should be both historical and prospective – and include non-routine transactions. Working through this chapter should help you understand how to demonstrate that objective.

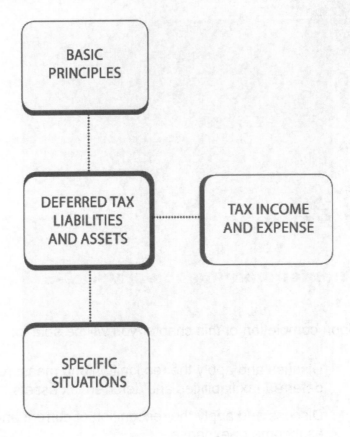

## 1 Basic principles of tax

### Taxation

Taxation is a major expense for business entities. IAS 12 *Income Taxes* notes that there are two elements to tax that an entity must deal with:

- **Current tax** – the amount payable to the tax authorities in relation to the trading activities of the current period.

- **Deferred tax** – an accounting measure used to match the tax effects of transactions with their accounting treatment. It is not a tax that is levied by the government that needs to be paid, but simply an application of the accruals concept.

In summary, the tax expense for an entity is calculated as follows:

Tax expense = current tax +/– movement in deferred tax

> **Progression**
>
> Some of the content of this chapter was tested in Financial Reporting. However, the situations you will encounter in the SBR exam will be more varied.

## 2 Current tax

### Accounting for current tax

Current tax is the amount expected to be paid to the tax authorities by applying the tax laws and tax rates in place at the reporting date.

Current tax is recognised in the financial statements by posting the following entry:

Dr Tax expense (P/L)

Cr Tax payable (SFP)

Current tax accounting is often based on estimates, and the final amount payable is often not finalised until after the financial statements have been authorised for issue:

- If the eventual amount paid is less than the estimate recognised in the current period's financial statements then this will reduce the current tax expense in the next accounting period

- If the eventual amount paid is more than the estimate recognised in the current period's financial statements then this will increase the current tax expense in the next accounting period.

## 3 Basic principles of deferred tax

### The need to provide for deferred tax

There will be differences between the principles in an accounting standard and the tax rules in a particular jurisdiction. Accounting profits therefore differ from taxable profits.

Some of these differences are temporary:

- Capital assets might be written down at different rates for tax purposes than they are in the financial statements.

Some of these differences are not temporary:

- Fines are expensed to the statement of profit or loss but are normally disallowed by the tax authorities. Therefore, these costs are eliminated ('added back') in the company's tax computation and never permitted as an expense.

Temporary differences may mean that profits are reported in the financial statements before they are taxable by the authorities. Conversely, it might mean that tax is payable to the authorities even though profits have not yet been reported in the financial statements.

According to the accruals concept, the tax effect of a transaction should be reported in the same accounting period as the transaction itself. To ensure this, entities are required to account for deferred tax on temporary differences.

A **temporary difference** is the difference between the carrying amount of an asset or liability and its tax base.

The **tax base** is the **'amount attributed to an asset or liability for tax purposes'** (IAS 12, para 5).

### Illustration 1 – Basic principles of deferred tax

Prudent prepares financial statements to 31 December each year. On 1 January 20X0, the entity purchased a non-current asset for $1.6 million that had an anticipated useful life of four years. This asset qualified for immediate tax relief of 100% of the cost of the asset.

For the year ending 31 December 20X0, the draft accounts showed a profit before tax of $2 million. The directors anticipate that this level of profit will be maintained for the foreseeable future.

Prudent pays tax at a rate of 30%. Apart from the differences caused by the purchase of the non-current asset in 20X0, there are no other differences between accounting profit and taxable profit or the tax base and carrying amount of net assets.

**Required:**

**Compute the pre, and post-tax profits for Prudent for each of the four years ending 31 December 20X0–20X3 inclusive and for the period as a whole assuming that:**

(a) **no deferred tax is recognised**

(b) **deferred tax is recognised.**

### Solution

(a) **No deferred tax**

First of all, it is necessary to compute the taxable profits of Prudent for each period and the current tax payable:

|  | Year ended 31 December | | | | Total |
|---|---|---|---|---|---|
|  | **20X0** | **20X1** | **20X2** | **20X3** |  |
|  | $000 | $000 | $000 | $000 | $000 |
| Accounting profit | 2,000 | 2,000 | 2,000 | 2,000 | 8,000 |
| Add back Depreciation | 400 | 400 | 400 | 400 | 1,600 |
| Deduct Capital allowances | (1,600) | – | – | – | (1,600) |
| Taxable profits | 800 | 2,400 | 2,400 | 2,400 | 8,000 |
| Current tax at 30% | 240 | 720 | 720 | 720 | 2,400 |

The differences between the accounting profit and the taxable profit that occur from one year to another, cancel out over the four years as a whole.

The statements of profit or loss for each period and for the four years as a whole, are given below:

| | Year ended 31 December | | | | Total |
|---|---|---|---|---|---|
| | 20X0 | 20X1 | 20X2 | 20X3 | |
| | $000 | $000 | $000 | $000 | $000 |
| Profit before tax | 2,000 | 2,000 | 2,000 | 2,000 | 8,000 |
| Current tax | (240) | (720) | (720) | (720) | (2,400) |
| Profit after tax | 1,760 | 1,280 | 1,280 | 1,280 | 5,600 |

Ignoring deferred tax produces a performance profile that suggests a declining performance between 20X0 and 20X1.

In fact the decline in profits is caused by the timing of the current tax charge on them.

In 20X0, some of the accounting profit escapes tax, but the tax is only postponed until 20X1, 20X2 and 20X3, when the taxable profit is more than the accounting profit.

(b) **Deferred tax is recognised**

The deferred tax figures that are required in the statement of financial position are given below:

| | Year ended 31 December | | | |
|---|---|---|---|---|
| | 20X0 | 20X1 | 20X2 | 20X3 |
| | $000 | $000 | $000 | $000 |
| Carrying amount | 1,200 | 800 | 400 | Nil |
| Tax base | Nil | Nil | Nil | Nil |
| Temporary difference at year end | 1,200 | 800 | 400 | Nil |
| Closing deferred tax liability (30%) | 360 | 240 | 120 | Nil |
| Opening deferred tax liability | Nil | (360) | (240) | (120) |
| So charge/(credit) to P/L | 360 | (120) | (120) | (120) |

The statements of profit or loss for the four year period including deferred tax are shown below:

|  | Year ended 31 December | | | | Total |
|  | 20X0 | 20X1 | 20X2 | 20X3 |  |
|  | $000 | $000 | $000 | $000 | $000 |
| Profit before tax | 2,000 | 2,000 | 2,000 | 2,000 | 8,000 |
| Current tax | (240) | (720) | (720) | (720) | (2,400) |
| Deferred tax | (360) | 120 | 120 | 120 | Nil |
| Profit after tax | 1,400 | 1,400 | 1,400 | 1,400 | 5,600 |

A more meaningful performance profile is presented.

## Examples of temporary differences

Temporary differences include (but are not restricted to):

- Tax deductions for the cost of non-current assets that have a different pattern to the write-off of the asset in the financial statements.

- Intra-group profits in inventory that are unrealised for consolidation purposes yet taxable in the computation of the group entity that made the unrealised profit.

- Losses reported in the financial statements but the related tax relief is only available by carry forward against future taxable profits.

- Assets are revalued upwards in the financial statements, but no adjustment is made for tax purposes.

- Development costs are capitalised and amortised to profit or loss in future periods, but were deducted for tax purposes as incurred.

- The cost of granting share options to employees is recognised in profit or loss, but no tax deduction is obtained until the options are exercised.

## Calculating temporary differences

Deferred tax is calculated by comparing the carrying amount of an asset or liability to its tax base. The tax base is the amount attributed to the asset or liability for tax purposes. To assist with determining the tax base, IAS 12 notes that:

- **'The tax base of an asset is the amount that will be deductible for tax purposes against any taxable economic benefits that will flow to an entity when it recovers the carrying amount of the asset. If those economic benefits will not be taxable, the tax base of the asset is equal to its carrying amount'** (IAS 12, para 7).

- **'The tax base of a liability is its carrying amount, less any amount that will be deductible for tax purposes in future periods. In the case of revenue which is received in advance, the tax base of the liability is its carrying amount, less any amount of the revenue that will not be taxable in future periods'** (IAS 12, para 8).

When looking at the difference between the carrying amount and the tax base of an asset or liability:

- If the carrying amount exceeds the tax base, the temporary difference is said to be a **taxable** temporary difference which will give rise to a deferred tax **liability**.

- If the tax base exceeds the carrying amount, the temporary difference is a **deductible** temporary difference which will give rise to a deferred tax **asset**.

---

**Test your understanding 1 – Dive (temporary differences)**

An entity, Dive, provides the following information regarding its assets and liabilities as at 31 December 20X1.

| | Carrying amount | Tax base | Temporary difference |
|---|---|---|---|
| **Assets** | | | |
| A machine cost $100,000. Depreciation of $18,000 has been charged to date. Tax allowances of $30,000 have been claimed. | | | |
| Interest receivable in the statement of financial position is $1,000. The interest will be taxed when received. | | | |
| Trade receivables have a carrying amount of $10,000. The revenue has already been included in taxable profit. | | | |
| Inventory has been written down by $500 to $4,500 in the financial statements. The reduction is ignored for tax purposes until the inventory is sold. | | | |

---

| Liabilities | | | |
|---|---|---|---|
| Current liabilities include accrued expenses of $1,000. This is deductible for tax on a cash paid basis. | | | |
| Accrued expenses have a carrying amount of $5,000. The related expense has been deducted for tax purposes. | | | |

**Required:**

**Complete the table with carrying amount, tax base and temporary difference for each of the assets and liabilities.**

## 4 Deferred tax liabilities and assets

### Recognition

 IAS 12 *Income Taxes* states that deferred tax should be provided for on all taxable temporary differences, unless the deferred tax liability arises from:

- goodwill, for which amortisation is not tax deductible

- the initial recognition of an item that affects neither accounting profit nor taxable profit, and which does not result from a business combination.

Deferred tax assets should be recognised on all deductible temporary differences unless:

- the exceptions above apply

- insufficient taxable profits are expected to be available in the future against which the deductible temporary difference can be utilised.

 **Recognition exemption – an example**

On the reporting date, Enchilada purchases a factory building for $1 million and recognises this as property, plant and equipment. In Enchilada's jurisdiction, the building is not deductible for tax. The tax rate is 20%.

The carrying amount of the asset is $1 million. The tax base is nil because no tax deductions are permitted. As such, a taxable temporary difference of $1 million arises.

Despite the fact that the factory building will generate taxable income of at least $1 million (otherwise the asset's carrying amount is over-stated) and thus a tax charge of at least $0.2 million over its useful life, no deferred tax liability is recognised.

> This is because the temporary difference arises from the initial recognition of an item that has not affected accounting profit (the asset was capitalised) or taxable profit (the asset is unrecognised for tax purposes).
>
> The logic behind this exemption is that recognition would not provide useful information. Think about the double entry:
>
> Dr ??? $0.2m
>
> Cr Deferred tax liability $0.2m
>
> The debit cannot be posted to profit or loss or OCI because the transaction itself has not affected those statements. To-date the transaction been recorded in PPE, but debiting PPE with a further $0.2 million would make little sense and would reduce the understandability of financial statements.

 **Measurement**

The tax rate in force (or expected to be in force) when the asset is realised or the liability is settled, should be applied to the temporary difference to calculate the deferred tax balance. IAS 12 specifies that this rate must be based on legislation enacted or substantively enacted by the reporting date.

Deferred tax assets and liabilities are **not** discounted to present value.

The entry to profit or loss and other comprehensive income in respect of deferred tax is the difference between the net liability (or asset) at the beginning of the year and the net liability (or asset) at the end of the year. It is important to note that:

- If the item giving rise to the deferred tax is dealt with in profit or loss, the related deferred tax should also be presented in profit or loss.

- If the item giving rise to the deferred tax is dealt with in other comprehensive income, the related deferred tax should also be recorded in other comprehensive income and held within equity.

### Presentation

Deferred tax liabilities and assets are presented as non-current on the statement of financial position.

IAS 12 notes that deferred tax assets and liabilities can be offset as long as:

- the entity has a legally enforceable right to set off **current** tax assets and **current** tax liabilities

- the deferred tax assets and liabilities relate to tax levied by the same tax authority.

## Test your understanding 2 – Dive (deferred tax calculation)

**Required:**

**Using the information in 'test your understanding 1', calculate Dive's deferred tax balance as at 31 December 20X1. The applicable tax rate is 30%.**

## Test your understanding 3 – Brick

Brick is a company with a reporting date of 30 April 20X4. The company obtains tax relief for research and development expenditure on a cash paid basis. The recognition of a material development asset during the year, in accordance with IAS 38, created a significant taxable temporary difference as at 30 April 20X4.

The tax rate for companies as at the reporting period was 22%. On 6 June 20X4, the government passed legislation to lower the company tax rate to 20% from 1 January 20X5.

**Required:**

**Explain which tax rate should have been used to calculate the deferred tax liability for inclusion in the financial statements for the year ended 30 April 20X4.**

## 5 Specific situations

### Revaluations

Deferred tax should be recognised on the revaluation of property, plant and equipment even if:

- there is no intention to sell the asset
- any tax due on the gain made on any sale of the asset can be deferred by being 'rolled over' against the cost of a replacement asset.

Revaluation gains are recorded in other comprehensive income and so any deferred tax arising on the revaluation must also be recorded in other comprehensive income.

## Test your understanding 4 – Dodge

An entity, Dodge, owns property, plant and equipment that cost $100,000 when purchased. Depreciation of $40,000 has been charged up to the reporting date of 31 March 20X1. The entity has claimed total tax allowances on the asset of $50,000. On 31 March 20X1, the asset is revalued to $90,000. The tax rate is 30%.

**Required:**

**Explain the deferred tax implications of this situation.**

## Share option schemes

Accounting for share option schemes involves recognising an annual remuneration expense in profit or loss throughout the vesting period. Tax relief is not normally granted until the share options are exercised. The amount of tax relief granted is based on the intrinsic value of the options (the difference between the market price of the shares and the exercise price of the option).

This delayed tax relief means that equity-settled share-based payment schemes give rise to a deferred tax asset.

The following pro-forma can be used to calculate the deferred tax asset arising on an equity-settled share-based payment scheme:

|  | $ | $ |
|---|---|---|
| Carrying amount of share-based payment | Nil | |
| Less: | | |
| Tax base of the share-based payment* | (X) | |
| | — | |
| × Tax rate % | X | |
| | — | — |
| Deferred tax asset | | X |
| | | — |

* The tax base is the expected future tax relief (based on the intrinsic value of the options) that has accrued by the reporting date.

Where the amount of the estimated future tax deduction exceeds the accumulated remuneration expense, this indicates that the tax deduction relates partly to the remuneration expense and partly to equity. Therefore, the deferred tax must be recognised partly in profit or loss and partly in equity.

### Test your understanding 5 – Splash

An entity, Splash, established a share option scheme for its four directors. This scheme commenced on 1 July 20X8. Each director will be entitled to 25,000 share options on condition that they remain with Splash for four years, from the date the scheme was introduced.

Information regarding the share options is provided below:

| | |
|---|---|
| Fair value of option at grant date | $10 |
| Exercise price of option | $5 |

The fair value of the shares at 30 June 20X9 was $17 per share.

A tax deduction is only given for the share options when they are exercised. The allowable deduction will be based on the intrinsic value of the options. Assume a tax rate of 30%.

> **Required:**
>
> **Calculate and explain the amounts to be included in the financial statements of Splash for the year ended 30 June 20X9, including explanation and calculation of any deferred tax implications.**

### Unused tax losses

Where an entity has unused tax losses, IAS 12 allows a deferred tax asset to be recognised only to the extent that it is probable that future taxable profits will be available against which the unused tax losses can be utilised.

IAS 12 advises that the deferred tax asset should only be recognised after considering:

- whether an entity has sufficient taxable temporary differences against which the unused tax losses can be offset.

- whether it is probable the entity will make taxable profits before the tax losses expire.

- whether the cause of the tax losses can be identified and whether it is likely to recur (otherwise, the existence of unused tax losses is strong evidence that future taxable profits may not be available).

- whether tax planning opportunities are available.

> **Test your understanding 6 – Red**
>
> As at 31 December 20X1, Red has tax adjusted losses of $4m which arose from a one-off restructuring exercise. Under tax law, these losses may be carried forward to relieve taxable profits in the future. Red has produced forecasts that predict total future taxable profits over the next three years of $2.5m. However, the accountant of Red is not able to reliably forecast profits beyond that date.
>
> The tax rate for profits earned during the year ended 31 December 20X1 is 30%. However, the government passed legislation during the reporting period that lowered the tax rate to 28% from 1 January 20X2.
>
> **Required:**
>
> **Explain the deferred tax implications of the above.**

## 6 Business combinations and deferred tax

Accounting for a business combination, such as the consolidation of a subsidiary, can have several deferred tax implications.

### Fair value adjustments

The identifiable assets and liabilities of the acquired subsidiary are consolidated at fair value but the tax base derives from the values in the subsidiary's individual financial statements. A temporary difference is created, giving rise to deferred tax in the consolidated financial statements.

The deferred tax recognised on this difference is treated as part of the net assets acquired and, as a result, impacts upon the amount of goodwill recognised on the acquisition of the subsidiary.

The goodwill itself does not give rise to deferred tax because IAS 12 specifically excludes it.

> **Test your understanding 7 – Tom**
>
> On 30 June 20X1 Tom acquired 100% of the shares of Jones for $300,000. At this date, the carrying amount of the net assets of Jones was $250,000. Included in this net asset figure is inventory which cost $50,000 but which had a replacement cost of $55,000. The applicable tax rate is 30%.
>
> **Required:**
>
> **Explain the deferred tax implications of the above in the consolidated financial statements of the Tom group.**

### Provisions for unrealised profit

When one company within a group sells inventory to another group company, unrealised profits remaining within the group at the reporting date must be eliminated. The following adjustment is required in the consolidated financial statements:

    Dr Cost of sales (P/L)

    Cr Inventory (SFP)

This adjustment reduces the carrying amount of inventory in the consolidated financial statements but the tax base of the inventory remains as its cost in the individual financial statements of the purchasing company.

This creates a **deductible temporary difference**, giving rise to a **deferred tax asset** in the consolidated financial statements.

Note: you may find it easier to think of this adjustment in terms of profits. The unrealised profit on the intra-group transaction is removed from the consolidated financial statements and therefore the tax charge on this profit must also be removed.

## Test your understanding 8 – Mug

Mug has owned 80% of the ordinary shares of Glass for many years. During the current year, Mug sold inventory to Glass for $250,000 making a gross profit margin of 40%. One quarter of this inventory remains unsold by Glass at the reporting date.

The tax rate is 20%.

**Required:**

**Discuss the deferred tax implications of the above transaction.**

### Unremitted earnings

A temporary difference arises when the carrying amount of investments in subsidiaries, associates or joint ventures is different from the tax base.

- The carrying amount in consolidated financial statements is the investor's share of the net assets of the investee, plus purchased goodwill. The tax base is usually the cost of the investment. The difference is the unremitted earnings (i.e. undistributed profits) of the subsidiary, associate or joint venture.

- IAS 12 says that deferred tax should be recognised on this temporary difference except when:

  - the investor controls the timing of the reversal of the temporary difference and

  - it is probable that the profits will not be distributed in the foreseeable future.

- An investor can control the dividend policy of a subsidiary, but not always that of other types of investment. This means that deferred tax does not arise on investments in subsidiaries, but may arise on investments in associates and joint ventures.

Financial assets may give rise to deferred tax if they are revalued.

## 7 Disclosure

An entity must disclose:

- the major components of its tax expense

- tax recognised directly in equity

- tax relating to items recognised directly in equity

- tax relating to each component of other comprehensive income

- an explanation of the relationship between tax expense and accounting profit.

## Test your understanding 9 – HCRM

In the year ended 31 December 20X1, HCRM recorded a profit before tax of $300 million. Its tax rate is 20%.

In accordance with IAS 12 *Income Taxes*, it has disclosed the following information in its published financial statements:

|  | $m |
|---|---|
| PBT | 300.0 |
| PBT multiplied by 20% tax rate | 60.0 |
| Adjustments to current tax in respect of prior years | 8.2 |
| Depreciation on assets not qualifying for tax relief | (1.5) |
| Sundry disallowables | (0.7) |
| Total tax charge | 66.0 |
| Effective tax rate (%) | 22 |

**Required:**

**Discuss why this disclosure provides useful information to HCRM's investors.**

## 8    Chapter summary

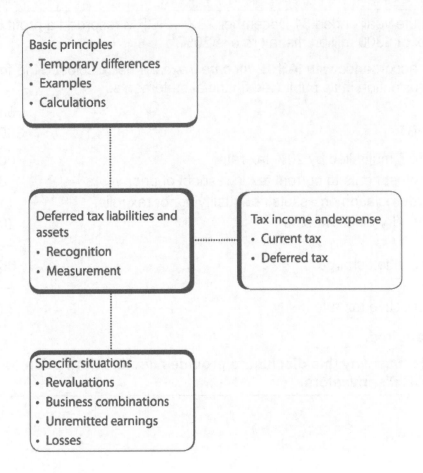

Basic principles
- Temporary differences
- Examples
- Calculations

Deferred tax liabilities and assets
- Recognition
- Measurement

Tax income andexpense
- Current tax
- Deferred tax

Specific situations
- Revaluations
- Business combinations
- Unremitted earnings
- Losses

# Test your understanding answers

## Test your understanding 1 – Dive (temporary differences)

|  | Carrying amount $ | Tax base $ | Temp. difference $ |
|---|---|---|---|
| Non-current asset | 82,000 | 70,000 | 12,000 |
| Interest receivable | 1,000 | Nil | 1,000 |
| Receivables | 10,000 | 10,000 | Nil |
| Inventory | 4,500 | 5,000 | (500) |
| Accrual (cash basis for tax) | (1,000) | Nil | (1,000) |
| Accrual (already had tax relief) | (5,000) | (5,000) | Nil |

## Test your understanding 2 – Dive (deferred tax calculation)

The net temporary difference as at the reporting date is as follows:

|  | $ |
|---|---|
| Non-current assets | 12,000 |
| Interest receivables | 1,000 |
| Receivables | – |
| Inventory | (500) |
| Accrual (cash basis for tax) | (1,000) |
| Accrual (already had tax relief) | – |
|  | 11,500 |

There will be a deferred tax liability because the carrying amount of the net assets and liabilities exceeds their net tax base. The deferred tax liability is calculated by applying the relevant tax rate to the temporary difference.

The deferred tax liability is therefore $3,450 ($11,500 × 30%).

Assuming that there is no opening deferred tax liability, the following accounting entry is required:

| Dr Tax expense (P/L) | $3,450 |
|---|---|
| Cr Deferred tax liability (SFP) | $3,450 |

## Test your understanding 3 – Brick

Deferred tax liabilities and assets should be measured using the tax rates expected to apply when the asset is realised. This tax rate must have been enacted or substantively enacted by the end of the reporting period.

The government enacted the 20% tax rate after the period end. Therefore, it should not be used when calculating the deferred tax liability for the year ended 30 April 20X4. The current 22% rate should be used instead.

Per IAS 10, changes in tax rates after the end of the reporting period are a non-adjusting event. However, if the change in the tax rate is deemed to be material then Brick should disclose this rate change and an estimate of the financial impact.

## Test your understanding 4 – Dodge

The carrying amount of the asset is $90,000 and the tax base is $50,000 ($100,000 – $50,000). The carrying amount exceeds the tax base by $40,000 ($90,000 – $50,000).

This temporary difference will give rise to a deferred tax liability of $12,000 ($40,000 × 30%).

Prior to the revaluation, the carrying amount of the asset was $60,000. The asset was then revalued to $90,000. Therefore, $30,000 ($90,000 – $60,000) of the temporary difference relates to the revaluation. Revaluation gains are recorded in other comprehensive income and so the deferred tax charge relating to this gain should also be recorded in other comprehensive income. This means that the tax charged to other comprehensive income is $9,000 ($30,000 × 30%).

The following accounting entry is required:

| | |
|---|---:|
| Dr Other comprehensive income | $9,000 |
| Dr Profit or loss (bal. fig.) | $3,000 |
| Cr Deferred tax liability | $12,000 |

The balance on the revaluation reserve within other components of equity will be $21,000 ($30,000 revaluation gain – $9,000 deferred tax).

## Test your understanding 5 – Splash

The expense recognised for an equity-settled share-based payment scheme is calculated based on the fair value of the options at the grant date. This expense is spread over the vesting period. At each reporting date, the entity should reassess the number of options expected to vest.

The expense for the scheme in the year ended 30 June 20X9 is $250,000 (4 × 25,000 × $10 × 1/4).

For tax purposes, tax relief is allowed based on the intrinsic value of the options at the date they are exercised.

At the reporting date, the shares have a market value of $17 but the options allow the holders to purchase these shares for $5. The options therefore have an intrinsic value of $12 ($17 – $5).

The deferred tax asset is calculated as follows:

|  | $ | $ |
|---|---|---|
| Carrying value of share-based payment | Nil | |
| Tax base of the share-based payment | (300,000) | |
| (4 × 25,000 × ($17 – $5) × 1/4) | | |
|  | ———— | |
| × Tax rate 30% | (300,000) | |
|  | | ———— |
| Deferred tax asset | | 90,000 |
|  | | ———— |

Where the amount of the estimated future tax deduction exceeds the accumulated remuneration expense, this indicates that the tax deduction relates partly to the remuneration expense and partly to equity.

In this case, the estimated future tax deduction is $300,000 whereas the accumulated remuneration expense is $250,000. Therefore, $50,000 of the temporary difference is deemed to relate to an equity item, and the deferred tax relating to this should be credited to equity.

The following entry is required:

| | |
|---|---|
| Dr Deferred tax asset | $90,000 |
| Cr Equity ($50,000 × 30%) | $15,000 |
| Cr Profit or loss ($250,000 × 30%) | $75,000 |

If the deferred tax asset is to be recognised, it must be regarded as recoverable.

### Test your understanding 6 – Red

A deferred tax asset can be recognised if it is deemed probable that future taxable profits will be available against which the unused losses can be utilised.

The tax losses have arisen from an exceptional event, suggesting that the entity will return to profitability. Forecasts produced by the accountant confirm this.

Red is only able to reliably forecast future profits of $2.5m. This limits the deferred tax asset that can be recognised.

Deferred tax should be calculated using the tax rate that is expected to be in force when the temporary difference reverses based on the rates enacted by the reporting date. This means that the 28% rate should be used.

The deferred tax asset that can be recognised is therefore $700,000 ($2.5m × 28%). There will be a corresponding credit to the tax expense in the statement of profit or loss.

### Test your understanding 7 – Tom

According to IFRS 3 *Business Combinations*, the net assets of the subsidiary at the acquisition date must be consolidated at fair value. The carrying amount of the inventory in the group financial statements will be $55,000. The tax base of the inventory is based on its carrying amount of $50,000 in the individual financial statements. Therefore, there is a temporary difference of $5,000 that arises on consolidation.

A deferred tax liability must be recognised in the consolidated financial statements for $1,500 ($5,000 × 30%). This is treated as a reduction in the subsidiary's net assets at the acquisition date, which will increase the goodwill arising on acquisition.

|  | $ | $ |
|---|---|---|
| Consideration |  | 300,000 |
| Net assets: |  |  |
| Carrying amount | 250,000 |  |
| Fair value uplift | 5,000 |  |
| Deferred tax liability | (1,500) |  |
|  |  | (253,500) |
| Goodwill at acquisition |  | 46,500 |

### Test your understanding 8 – Mug

There has been an intra-group sale and some of the inventory remains within the group at the reporting date. The profits held within this unsold inventory must therefore be removed from the consolidated statements.

The profit on the sale was $100,000 ($250,000 × 40%). Of this, $25,000 ($100,000 × 25%) remains within the inventory of the group. The adjustment required to eliminate the unrealised profits is:

| | |
|---|---|
| Dr Cost of sales | $25,000 |
| Cr Inventory | $25,000 |

The carrying amount of inventory in the consolidated financial statements is now $25,000 lower than its tax base, creating a deductible temporary difference of $25,000. This gives rise to a deferred tax asset of $5,000 ($25,000 × 20%) in the consolidated statement of financial position as well as a corresponding reduction to the tax expense in the consolidated statement of profit or loss. The adjustment required to account for the deferred tax is:

| | |
|---|---|
| Dr Deferred tax asset | $5,000 |
| Cr Tax expense | $5,000 |

### Test your understanding 9 – HCRM

Users of the financial statements need information to help them assess an entity's future profits and future cash flows. The tax rate reconciliation is important for understanding the tax charge reported in the financial statements and why the effective tax rate differs from the statutory rate.

The main reason for the difference between the statutory tax rate and the effective tax rate is due to current tax adjustments. HCRM under-accrued in prior periods for current tax, resulting in additional expense in the current period. Investors need to assess whether the effective tax rate is likely to be static or volatile and so must analyse comparative information to understand whether HCRM has a history of under-accruing (or over-accruing) for current tax. This will inform profit and cash flow forecasts.

One-off and unusual items can have a significant effect on the effective tax rate. Depreciation on assets that do not qualify for tax relief is likely to be a recurring item year-on-year. Other reconciling items should be explained so that investors can assess if they are likely to recur. To provide transparency, there should be minimal use of the 'sundry disallowables' category. In HCRM's reconciliation, this sundry category is relatively insignificant, although more information might be useful depending on the nature of these items.

Investors should also refer to the statement of cash flows, which will specify the tax paid in the current period.

# Segment reporting

## Chapter learning objectives

Upon completion of this chapter you will be able to:

- Determine the nature and extent of reportable segments
- Discuss the nature of segment information to be disclosed and how segmental information enhances the quality and sustainability of performance.

**PER**

One of the PER performance objectives (PO7) is to prepare external financial reports. You take part in preparing and reviewing financial statements – and all accompanying information – and you do it in accordance with legal and regulatory requirements. Working through this chapter should help you understand how to demonstrate that objective.

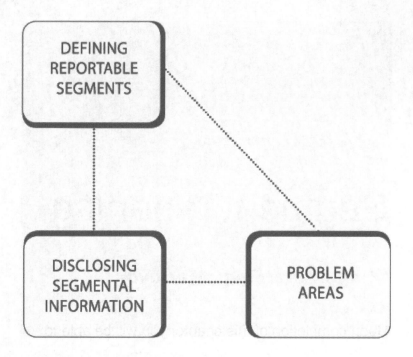

## 1 Defining reportable segments

### Introduction

| Progression |
| --- |
| You will not have studied this topic in earlier ACCA exams. |

Segmental reports are designed to reveal significant information that might otherwise be hidden by the process of presenting a single statement of profit or loss and other comprehensive income and statement of financial position for an entity.

IFRS 8 *Operating Segments* requires certain entities to disclose information about each of its operating segments that will enable users of the financial statements to evaluate the nature and financial effects of the business activities in which it engages and the economic environments in which it operates.

IFRS 8 applies to entities which trade debt or equity instruments in a public market.

 An **operating segment** is defined as a component of an entity:

- **'that engages in business activities from which it may earn revenues and incur expenses**

- **whose operating results are regularly reviewed by the entity's chief operating decision maker to make decisions about resources to be allocated to the segment and assess its performance**

- **for which discrete financial information is available'** (IFRS 8, para 5).

**How to define reportable segments**

Under IFRS 8, an operating segment is a component whose results are regularly reviewed by the entity's chief operating decision maker. This means that the segments reported in the financial statements should be the same as those reviewed in internal management reports.

Management may use more than one set of segment information. For example, they might analyse information by classes of business (different products or services) and by geographical areas. If this is the case then management must identify a **single** set of components on which to base the segmental disclosures. The basis of reporting information should be the one that best enables users to understand the business and the environment in which it operates.

Not every part of an entity is necessarily an operating segment or part of an operating segment:

- Corporate headquarters and other similar departments do not earn revenue and are therefore not operating segments.

- An entity's pension plan is not an operating segment.

## Aggregation

IFRS 8 says that two or more operating segments can be aggregated and reported as a single operating segment provided that they have similar economic characteristics, and are similar in the following respects:

- products and services

- production processes

- classes of customer

- distribution methods.

 **Test your understanding 1 – E-Games**

E-Games is a UK based company that sells computer games and hardware. Sales are made through the E-Games website as well as through high street stores. The products sold online and in the stores are the same. E-Games sells new releases for $40 in its stores, but for $30 online.

Internal reports used by the chief operating decision maker show the results of the online business separately from the stores. However, they will be aggregated together for disclosure in the financial statements.

**Required:**

**Should the online business and the high street stores be aggregated into a single segment in the operating segments disclosure?**

## Quantitative thresholds

An entity must separately report information about an operating segment that meets any of the following quantitative thresholds:

- **'its reported revenue, including both sales to external customers and inter-segment sales, is ten per cent or more of the combined revenue of all operating segments**

- **its reported profit or loss is ten per cent or more of the greater, in absolute amount, of:**
    - **the combined reported profit of all operating segments that did not report a loss and**
    - **the combined reported loss of all operating segments that reported a loss.**

- **its assets are ten per cent or more of the combined assets of all operating segments'** (IFRS 8, para 13).

At least 75% of the entity's external revenue must be included in reportable segments. Other segments should be identified as reportable segments until 75% of external revenue is reported.

Information about other business activities and operating segments that are not reportable are combined into an 'all other segments' category.

### Test your understanding 2 – Identifying reportable segments

The management of a company have identified operating segments based on geographical location. Information for these segments is provided below:

| Segment | Total revenue $000 | External revenue $000 | Internal revenue $000 | Profit/ (loss) $000 | Assets $000 |
|---|---|---|---|---|---|
| Europe | 260 | 140 | 120 | 98 | 3,400 |
| Middle East | 78 | 33 | 45 | (26) | 345 |
| Asia | 150 | 150 | – | 47 | 995 |
| North America | 330 | 195 | 135 | 121 | 3,800 |
| Central America | 85 | 40 | 45 | (15) | 580 |
| South America | 97 | 54 | 43 | 12 | 880 |
| | 1,000 | 612 | 388 | 237 | 10,000 |

**Required:**

**According to IFRS 8, which segments must be reported?**

**2 Disclosing reportable segments**

## General information

IFRS 8 requires disclosure of the following:

- Factors used to identify reportable segments
- The types of products and services sold by each reportable segment.

## Information about profit or loss and other segment items

For each reportable segment an entity should report:

- a measure of profit or loss
- a measure of total assets.

Other information should be disclosed if regularly provided to the chief operating decision maker.

IFRS 8 requires segmental reports to be based on the information reported to and used by management, even where this is prepared on a different basis from the rest of the financial statements. Therefore, an entity must provide explanations of the measurement of segment profit or loss, segment assets and segment liabilities.

 **Example of a segmental report**

| | Segment A | Segment B | Segment C | All other | Totals |
|---|---|---|---|---|---|
| | $000 | $000 | $000 | $000 | $000 |
| Revenues from external customers | 5,000 | 9,500 | 12,000 | 800 | 27,300 |
| Revenues from inter-segment transactions | – | 3,000 | 1,500 | – | 4,500 |
| Interest income | 800 | 1,000 | 1,500 | – | 3,300 |
| Interest expense | 600 | 700 | 1,100 | – | 2,400 |
| Depreciation and amortisation | 100 | 50 | 1,500 | – | 1,650 |
| Exceptional costs | 200 | – | – | – | 200 |
| Segment profit | 70 | 900 | 2,300 | 100 | 3,370 |
| Impairment of assets | 200 | – | | – | 200 |
| Segment assets | 5,000 | 3,000 | 12,000 | 400 | 20,400 |
| Additions to non-current assets | 700 | 500 | 800 | – | 2,000 |
| Segment liabilities | 3,000 | 1,800 | 8,000 | – | 12,800 |

**Notes**

1 The 'all other' column shows amounts relating to segments that fall below the quantitative thresholds.

2 Impairment of assets is disclosed as a material non-cash item.

The standards referred to in the diagram above cover a range of group accounting issues:

- IFRS 10 *Consolidated Financial Statements*

- IFRS 11 *Joint Arrangements*

- IFRS 12 *Disclosure of Interests in Other Entities*

- IAS 28 *Investments in Associates and Joint Ventures*

These standards, as well as IFRS 3 *Business Combinations*, are covered in this chapter. IFRS 9 *Financial Instruments* was dealt with earlier in the publication.

> **Progression**
>
> You have covered group accounting extensively in your prior studies. A more detailed knowledge is required for SBR. More emphasis will be placed on discussion of group accounting issues than on number-crunching.

 **2    Definitions**

IFRS 10 *Consolidated Financial Statements* says that an entity that is a parent is required to prepare consolidated financial statements. The standard provides the following definitions:

A **parent** is an entity that controls another entity.

A subsidiary is an entity that is controlled.

An investor controls an investee when:

- the investor has power over the investee, and

- the investor is exposed, or has rights, to variable returns from its involvement with the investee, and

- the investor has the ability to affect those returns through its power over the investee.

**Consolidated financial statements** present the assets, liabilities, equity, income, expenses and cash flows of the parent and its subsidiaries as if they were a single economic entity.

**The *Conceptual Framework***

In the *Conceptual Framework* the Board notes that consolidated financial statements are important for investors in the parent company. This is because their economic returns are dependent on profits made by the subsidiaries that are then distributed to the parent.

The separate (non-consolidated) financial statements of the parent company provide useful information to its investors (such as the level of distributable reserves) but are not a substitute for information provided in consolidated financial statements.

## Exam focus

Question 1 in the SBR exam will always test consolidated financial statements. However, the exam will not ask for the production of full consolidated financial statements. Instead, candidates will be required to produce extracts from these statements and to explain the accounting numbers that they have produced.

Some questions in this text require the production of full consolidated financial statements. This is to enable SBR candidates to revise, practice and develop a deeper understanding of consolidation techniques. Without this, you will find it difficult to tackle discursive exam-style questions.

 **3    Revision from prior studies**

## Consolidated statement of financial position

When required to produce a consolidated statement of financial position from the individual financial statements of group companies then the easiest method is to use five standard workings. These will assist you in understanding the structure of the group and in calculating goodwill, the non-controlling interest and group reserves.

Note that the SBR exam will not require you to prepare full consolidated financial statements. However, the following workings are still important when preparing calculations and extracts.

**(W1) Group structure**

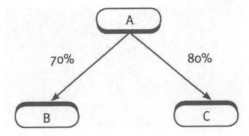

This working is useful to decide the status of any investments. If one entity is controlled by another entity then it is a subsidiary and must be consolidated.

Control is normally presumed to exist if one company owns more than half of the voting capital of another entity.

Once the group structure has been determined, set up a proforma statement of financial position.

**Group statement of financial position as at the reporting date**

|  | $000 |
|---|---|
| Goodwill (W3) | X |
| Assets (P + S) | X |
| | ___ |
| Total assets | X |
| | ___ |
| Equity capital (Parent's only) | X |
| Retained earnings (W5) | X |
| Other components of equity (W5) | X |
| Non-controlling interest (W4) | X |
| | ___ |
| Total equity | X |
| Liabilities (P + S) | X |
| | ___ |
| Total equity and liabilities | X |
| | ___ |

You will need to do the following:

–   Eliminate the carrying amount of the parent's investments in its subsidiaries (these will be replaced by goodwill)

–   Add together the assets and liabilities of the parent and its subsidiaries in full

–   Include only the parent's balances within share capital and share premium

–   Set up and complete standard workings 2 – 5 to calculate goodwill, the non-controlling interest and group reserves.

## (W2) Net assets of each subsidiary

This working sets out the fair value of the subsidiary's identifiable net assets at acquisition date and at the reporting date.

|  | At acquisition $000 | At reporting date $000 |
|---|---|---|
| Equity capital | X | X |
| Share premium | X | X |
| Other components of equity | X | X |
| Retained earnings | X | X |
| Goodwill in the accounts of the sub. | (X) | (X) |
| Fair value adjustments (FVA) | X | X |
| Post acq'n dep'n/amort. on FVA |  | (X) |
| PURP if the sub is the seller |  | (X) |
|  | X (to W3) | X |

Remember to update the face of the statement of financial position for adjustments made to the net assets at the reporting date (such as fair value uplifts and provisions for unrealised profits (PURPS)).

The fair value of the subsidiary's net assets at the acquisition date are used in the calculation of goodwill.

The movement in the subsidiary's net assets since acquisition is used to calculate the non-controlling interest and group reserves.

## (W3) Goodwill

|  | $000 |
|---|---|
| Fair value of purchase consideration | X |
| NCI at acquisition** | X |
|  | X |
| Less: fair value of identifiable net assets at acquisition (W2) | (X) |
| Goodwill at acquisition | X |
| Less: impairment to date | (X) |
| Goodwill to consolidated SFP | X |

**if full goodwill method adopted, NCI value = FV of NCI at date of acquisition. This will normally be given in a question.

**if proportionate goodwill method adopted, NCI value = NCI % of the fair value of the subsidiary's net assets at acquisition (per W2).

(W4) **Non-controlling interest**

|  | $000 |
|---|---|
| NCI value at acquisition (W3) | X |
| NCI % of post-acquisition movement in net assets (W2) | X |
| Less: NCI % of goodwill impairment (fair value method only) | (X) |
| NCI to consolidated SFP | X |

(W5) **Group reserves**

**Retained earnings**

|  | $000 |
|---|---|
| Parent's retained earnings (100%) | X |
| For each subsidiary: group share of post-acquisition retained earnings (W2) | X |
| Add: gain on bargain purchase (W3) | X |
| Less: goodwill impairment** (W3) | (X) |
| Less: PURP if the parent was the seller | (X) |
| Retained earnings to consolidated SFP | X |

** If the NCI was valued at fair value at the acquisition date, then only the parent's share of the goodwill impairment is deducted from retained earnings.

**Other components of equity**

|  | $000 |
|---|---|
| Parent's other components of equity (100%) | X |
| For each subsidiary: group share of post-acquisition other components of equity (W2) | X |
| Other components of equity to consolidated SFP | X |

### Consolidated statement of profit or loss and other comprehensive income

If required to produce a consolidated statement of profit or loss and other comprehensive income from the individual financial statements of group companies, the following four step approach will help.

**Step 1: Group structure**

This working is useful to decide the status of any investments. If one entity is controlled by another entity then it is a subsidiary and must be consolidated.

In numerical exam questions, control is normally presumed to exist if one company owns more than half of the voting capital of another entity.

## Step 2: Pro-forma

Once the group structure has been determined, set up a proforma statement of profit or loss and other comprehensive income.

Remember to leave space at the bottom to show the profit and total comprehensive income (TCI) attributable to the owners of the parent company and the profit and TCI attributable to the non-controlling interest.

**Group statement of profit or loss and other comprehensive income for the year ended 30 June 20X8**

|  | $000 |
|---|---|
| Revenue (P + S) | X |
| Cost of sales (P + S) | (X) |
|  |  |
| Gross profit | X |
| Operating costs (P + S) | (X) |
|  |  |
| Profit from operations | X |
| Investment income (P + S) | X |
| Finance costs (P + S) | (X) |
|  |  |
| Profit before tax | X |
| Income tax (P + S) | (X) |
|  |  |
| Profit for the period | X |
| Other comprehensive income (P + S) | X |
|  |  |
| Total comprehensive income | X |
|  |  |
| Profit attributable to: |  |
| Equity holders of the parent (bal. fig) | X |
| Non-controlling interest (Step 4) | X |
|  |  |
| Profit for the period | X |
|  |  |
| Total comprehensive income attributable to: |  |
| Equity holders of the parent (bal. fig) | X |
| Non-controlling interest (Step 4) | X |
|  |  |
| Total comprehensive income for the period | X |

## Step 3: Complete the pro-forma

Add together the parent and subsidiary's incomes and expenses and items of other comprehensive income on a line-by-line basis.

- If the subsidiary has been acquired mid-year, make sure that you prorate the results of the subsidiary so that only post-acquisition incomes, expenses and other comprehensive income are consolidated.

- Ensure that you eliminate intra-group incomes and expenses, unrealised profits on intra-group transactions, as well as any dividends received from the subsidiary.

## Step 4: Calculate the profit/TCI attributable to the non-controlling interest

Remember, profit for the year and TCI for the year must be split between the group and the non-controlling interest. The following proforma will help you to calculate the profit and TCI attributable to the non-controlling interest.

|  | Profit $000 | TCI $000 |
|---|---|---|
| Profit/TCI of the subsidiary for the year (pro-rated for mid-year acquisition) | X | X |
| PURP (if S is the seller) | (X) | (X) |
| Excess depreciation/amortisation | (X) | (X) |
| Goodwill impairment (under FV model only) | (X) | (X) |
|  | —— | —— |
| × NCI % | X | X |
|  | —— | —— |
| Profit/TCI attributable to the NCI | X | X |
|  | —— | —— |

## 4 Associates

### Definitions

An **associate** is defined as **'an entity over which the investor has significant influence and which is neither a subsidiary nor a joint venture of the investor'** (IAS 28, para 3).

**Significant influence** is the power to participate in, but not control, the financial and operating policy decisions of an entity. IAS 28 *Investments in Associates and Joint Ventures* states that:

- Significant influence is usually evidenced by representation on the board of directors, which allows the investing entity to participate in policy decisions.

- Holding between 20% and 50% of the voting power is presumed to give significant influence.

The existence of significant influence normally entails at least one of the following:

- representation on the board of directors

- ability to influence policy making

- significant levels of transactions between the entity and the investee

- management personnel being shared between the entity and the investee

- provision of important technical information.

### Test your understanding 1 – Sparrow

Sparrow owns 18% of the ordinary shares of Blackbird. The remaining 82% of the ordinary shares are held by hundreds of investors, and no single investor has a holding of more than 5%.

Blackbird has six directors and Sparrow is able to appoint two of these.

Blackbird is one of Sparrow's key suppliers. Sparrow's operations and human resource managers spend several days a year at Blackbird in order to ensure that trading between the two entities is as smooth as possible.

In the consolidated financial statements, the directors of Sparrow wish to account for the investment in Blackbird as a financial asset.

**Required:**

**Discuss whether the proposed accounting treatment is correct.**

## Accounting for associates

Associates are not consolidated because the investor does not have control. Instead they are accounted for using the **equity method**.

### Statement of financial position

IAS 28 requires that the carrying amount of the associate is determined as follows:

|  | $000 |
|---|---|
| Cost | X |
| P% of post-acquisition reserves | X/(X) |
| Impairment losses | (X) |
| P% of unrealised profits if P is the seller | (X) |
| P% of excess depreciation on fair value adjustments | (X) |
| Investment in associate | X |

The investment in the associate is shown in the non-current assets section of the consolidated statement of financial position.

## Statement of profit or loss and other comprehensive income

For an associate, a single line item is presented in the statement of profit or loss below operating profit. This is made up as follows:

|  | $000 |
|---|---|
| P% of associate's profit after tax | X |
| Less: Current year impairment loss | (X) |
| Less: P% of unrealised profits if associate is the seller | (X) |
| Less: P% of excess depreciation on fair value adjustments | (X) |
| Share of profit of associate | X |

Within consolidated other comprehensive income, the group should present its share of the associate's other comprehensive income (if applicable).

## Adjustments

Dividends received from the associate must be removed from the consolidated statement of profit or loss.

Transactions and balances between the associate and the parent company are not eliminated from the consolidated financial statements because the associate is not a part of the group.

The group share of any unrealised profit arising on transactions between the group and the associate must be eliminated.

- If the associate is the seller:

    Dr Share of the associate's profit (P/L)/Retained earnings (SFP)

    Cr Inventories (SFP)

- If the associate is the purchaser:

    Dr Cost of sales (P/L)/Retained earnings (SFP)

    Cr Investment in the associate (SFP)

When an investor contributes assets in exchange for an equity interest in the associate, the investor recognises the portion of the gain or loss on disposal attributable to the **other investors** in the associate (i.e. if the investor owns 40% of the associate, it recognises 60% of the gain or loss).

## General points and disclosures

IAS 28 notes the following:

- The financial statements used to equity account for the associate should be drawn up to the investor's reporting date. If this is not possible, then the difference in reporting dates should be less than three months.

- The associate's accounting policies should be harmonised with those of its investor.

- The investor should disclose its share of the associate's contingencies.

Illustration 1 – Consolidated statement of financial position

Financial statements for three entities for the year ended 30 June 20X8 are as follows:

**Statements of financial position**

| | Borough | High | Street |
|---|---|---|---|
| Assets | $ | $ | $ |
| Property, plant and equipment | 100,000 | 80,000 | 60,000 |
| Investments | 121,000 | – | – |
| Inventories | 22,000 | 30,000 | 15,000 |
| Receivables | 70,000 | 10,000 | 2,000 |
| Cash and cash equivalents | 47,000 | 25,000 | 3,000 |
| | 360,000 | 145,000 | 80,000 |
| | | | |
| **Equity and liabilities** | | | |
| Equity capital ($1 shares) | 100,000 | 75,000 | 35,000 |
| Retained earnings | 200,000 | 50,000 | 40,000 |
| Other components of equity | 10,000 | 5,000 | – |
| Liabilities | 50,000 | 15,000 | 5,000 |
| | 360,000 | 145,000 | 80,000 |

On 1 July 20X7, Borough purchased 45,000 shares in High for $100,000. At that date, High had retained earnings of $30,000 and no other components of equity. High's net assets had a fair value of $120,000 and the fair value of the non-controlling interest was $55,000. It is group policy to value the non-controlling interest at acquisition at fair value.

The excess of the fair value of High's net assets over their carrying amounts at the acquisition date relates to property, plant and equipment. This had a remaining estimated useful life of five years at the acquisition date. Goodwill has been subject to an impairment review and it was determined to be impaired by $7,000.

On 1 July 20X7, Borough purchased 10,500 equity shares in Street for $21,000. At that date, Street had retained earnings of $25,000 and no other components of equity.

During the year Borough sold goods too High for $10,000 at a margin of 50%. By the reporting date, High had only sold 80% of these goods. Included in the receivables of Borough and the liabilities of High are intragroup balances of $5,000.

On 5 July 20X8, Borough received notification that an employee was claiming damages against them as a result of a work-place accident that took place on 30 April 20X8. Lawyers have advised that there is a 60% chance that Borough will lose the case and will be required to pay damages of $30,000.

**Required:**

**Prepare the consolidated statement of financial position as at 30 June 20X8.**

### Solution

**Borough Group statement of financial position as at 30 June 20X8**

| | $ |
|---|---:|
| Non-Current Assets | |
| Goodwill (W3) | 28,000 |
| Property, plant and equipment | 192,000 |
| ($100,000 + $80,000 + $15,000 (W2) – $3,000 (W2)) | |
| Investment in Associate (W7) | 25,500 |
| Current Assets | |
| Inventories ($22,000 + $30,000 – $1,000 (W6)) | 51,000 |
| Receivables ($70,000 + $10,000 – $5,000 inter.co) | 75,000 |
| Cash and cash equivalents ($47,000 + $25,000) | 72,000 |
| | ——— |
| | 443,500 |
| | ——— |
| | |
| Equity capital | 100,000 |
| Retained earnings (W5) | 179,500 |
| Other components of equity (W5) | 13,000 |
| Non-controlling interest (W4) | 61,000 |
| | ——— |
| Total equity | 353,500 |
| Liabilities | 90,000 |
| ($50,000 + $15,000 – $5,000 inter.co + $30,000 (W8)) | |
| | ——— |
| | 443,500 |
| | ——— |

**(W1) Group structure**

Borough is the parent

High is a 60% subsidiary (45/75)

Street is a 30% associate (10.5/35)

Both acquisitions took place a year ago

**(W2) Net assets of High**

|  | Acq $ | Rep date $ |
|---|---|---|
| Equity capital | 75,000 | 75,000 |
| Other components of equity | – | 5,000 |
| Retained earnings | 30,000 | 50,000 |
| Fair value adjustment (FVA) | 15,000* | 15,000 |
| Depreciation on FVA ($15,000/5) | – | (3,000) |
| *bal fig | 120,000 | 142,000 |

**(W3) Goodwill**

|  | $ |
|---|---|
| Consideration | 100,000 |
| FV of NCI at acquisition | 55,000 |
|  | 155,000 |
| FV of net assets at acquisition (W2) | (120,000) |
| Goodwill at acquisition | 35,000 |
| Impairment | (7,000) |
| Goodwill at the reporting date | 28,000 |

**(W4) Non-controlling interest**

|  | $ |
|---|---|
| Fair value of NCI at acquisition | 55,000 |
| NCI % of post-acquisition net assets (40% × ($142,000 – $120,000) (W2)) | 8,800 |
| NCI share of goodwill impairment (40% × $7,000) | (2,800) |
|  | 61,000 |

KAPLAN PUBLISHING

**(W5) Group reserves**

**Group retained earnings**

|  | $ |
|---|---|
| Parent | 200,000 |
| Provision (W8) | (30,000) |
| Share of post-acquisition retained earnings: | |
| High: 60% × (($50,000 – $3,000) – $30,000) (W2) | 10,200 |
| Street: 30% × ($40,000 – $25,000) | 4,500 |
| Group share of goodwill impairment | (4,200) |
| (60% × $7,000) | |
| PURP (W6) | (1,000) |
| | ——— |
| | 179,500 |
| | ——— |

**Other components of equity**

|  | $ |
|---|---|
| Parent | 10,000 |
| Share of post-acquisition other components of equity: | |
| High: 60% × ($5,000 – $nil) (W2) | 3,000 |
| | ——— |
| | 13,000 |
| | ——— |

**(W6) Provision for unrealised profit**

The profit on the intra-group sale was $5,000 (50% × $10,000).

The unrealised profit still in inventory is $1,000 (20% × $5,000).

The parent was the seller, so retained earnings is adjusted in (W5)

| Dr Retained earnings | $1,000 |
|---|---|
| Cr Inventories | $1,000 |

**(W7) Investment in the associate**

|  | $ |
|---|---|
| Cost | 21,000 |
| Share of increase in retained earnings | 4,500 |
| (30% × ($40,000 – $25,000)) | |
| | ——— |
| | 25,500 |
| | ——— |

**(W8) Provision**

The obligating event, the accident, happened during the reporting period. This means that there is an obligation from a past event, and a probable outflow of resources that can be measured reliably. A provision is therefore required for the best estimate of the amount payable, which is $30,000. This is charged to the statement of profit or loss so will reduce retained earnings in (W5).

| | |
|---|---|
| Dr Retained earnings | $30,000 |
| Cr Provisions | $30,000 |

## Illustration 2 – Consolidated statement of profit or loss

H has owned 80% of the ordinary shares of S and 30% of the ordinary shares of A for many years. The information below is required to prepare the consolidated statement of profit or loss for the year ended 30 June 20X8.

**Statements of profit or loss for the year ended 30 June 20X8**

| | H | S | A |
|---|---|---|---|
| | $ | $ | $ |
| Revenue | 500,000 | 200,000 | 100,000 |
| Cost of sales | (100,000) | (80,000) | (40,000) |
| Gross profit | 400,000 | 120,000 | 60,000 |
| Distribution costs | (160,000) | (20,000) | (10,000) |
| Administrative expenses | (140,000) | (40,000) | (10,000) |
| Profit from operations | 100,000 | 60,000 | 40,000 |
| Tax | (23,000) | (21,000) | (14,000) |
| Profit after tax | 77,000 | 39,000 | 26,000 |

**Note:** There were no items of other comprehensive income in the year.

At the date of acquisition, the fair value of S's plant and machinery, which at that time had a remaining useful life of ten years, exceeded the book value by $10,000.

During the year S sold goods to H for $10,000 at a margin of 25%. By the year-end H had sold 60% of these goods.

The group accounting policy is to measure non-controlling interests using the proportion of net assets method. The current year goodwill impairment loss was $1,200, and this should be charged to administrative expenses.

By 30 June 20X8 the investment in A had been impaired by $450, of which the current year loss was $150.

On 1 January 20X8, H signed a contract to provide a customer with support services for the following twelve months. H received the full fee of $30,000 in advance and recognised this as revenue.

**Required:**

**Prepare the consolidated statement of profit or loss for the year ended 30 June 20X8.**

### Solution

**Group statement of profit or loss for the year ended 30 June 20X8**

|  | $ |
|---|---:|
| Revenue | 675,000 |
| ($500,000 + $200,000 − $10,000 (W3) − $15,000 (W4)) | |
| Cost of sales | (172,000) |
| ($100,000 + $80,000 + $1,000 (W2) − $10,000 (W3) + $1,000 (W3)) | |
| Gross profit | 503,000 |
| Distribution costs ($160,000 + $20,000) | (180,000) |
| Administrative expenses | (181,200) |
| ($140,000 + $40,000 + $1,200 GW imp) | |
| Profit from operations | 141,800 |
| Share of profit of associate | 7,650 |
| ((30% × $26,000) − $150 impairment) | |
| Profit before tax | 149,450 |
| Tax ($23,000 + $21,000) | (44,000) |
| Profit for the period | 105,450 |
| Attributable to: | |
| Equity holders of the parent (bal. fig) | 98,050 |
| Non-controlling interest (W5) | 7,400 |
| Profit for the period | 105,450 |

**Workings**

**(W1) Group structure**

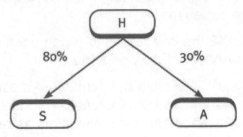

**(W2) Excess depreciation**

$10,000/10 years = $1,000.

The adjusting entry is:

| | |
|---|---|
| Dr Cost of sales | $1,000 |
| Cr PPE | $1,000 |

**(W3) Intra-group trading**

The $10,000 trading between S and H must be eliminated:

| | |
|---|---|
| Dr Revenue | $10,000 |
| Cr Cost of sales | $10,000 |

The profit on the sale was $2,500 (25% × $10,000). Of this, $1,000 ($2,500 × 40%) remains within the inventories of the group. The PURP adjustment is therefore:

| | |
|---|---|
| Dr Cost of sales | $1,000 |
| Cr Inventories | $1,000 |

**(W4) Revenue**

The performance obligation is satisfied over time. Based on the passage of time, the contract is 50% (6/12) complete so only 50% of the revenue should be recognised by the reporting date. Therefore $15,000 ($30,000 × 50%) should be removed from revenue and held as a liability on the SFP.

| | |
|---|---|
| Dr Revenue | $15,000 |
| Cr Contract liability | $15,000 |

**(W5) Profit attributable to NCI**

|  | $ | $ |
|---|---|---|
| S's profit for the year | 39,000 | |
| PURP (W3) | (1,000) | |
| Excess depreciation (W2) | (1,000) | |
| | 37,000 | |
| × 20% | | |
| Profit attributable to NCI | | 7,400 |

**Note:** If the parent had sold goods to the subsidiary then the PURP adjustment would not be included when calculating the profit attributable to the NCI.

Goodwill has been calculated using the share of net assets method. Therefore, none of the impairment loss is attributable to the NCI.

## Illustration 3 – Associates

Paint has several investments in subsidiary companies. On 1 July 20X1, it acquires 30% of the ordinary shares of Animate for $2m. This holding gives Paint significant influence over Animate.

At the acquisition date, the fair value of Animate's net assets approximate to their carrying values with the exception of a building. This building, with a remaining useful life of 10 years, had a carrying value of $1 m but a fair value of $1.8m.

Between 1 July 20X1 and 31 December 20X1, Animate sold goods to Paint for $1 million making a profit of $100,000. All of these goods remain in the inventory of Paint. This sale was made on credit and the invoice has not yet been settled.

Animate made a profit after tax of $800,000 for the year ended 31 December 20X1. At 31 December 20X1, the directors of Paint believe that the investment in the associate needs impairing by $50,000.

**Required:**

**Prepare extracts from the consolidated statement of financial position and the consolidated statement of profit or loss showing the treatment of the associate for the year ended 31 December 20X1.**

## Solution

### Consolidated statement of financial position

| | $ |
|---|---|
| Non-current assets | |
| Investment in associate (W1) | 2,058,000 |

### Consolidated statement of profit or loss

| | |
|---|---|
| Share of profit of associate (W2) | 28,000 |

Note: No adjustment is required for receivables and payables held between Paint and Animate.

### (W1) Investment in associate

| | $ |
|---|---|
| Cost | 2,000,000 |
| Share of post-acquisition profit (30% × $800,000 × 6/12) | 120,000 |
| Share of excess depreciation (30% × (($1.8m – $1m)/10 years) × 6/12) | (12,000) |
| Impairment | (50,000) |
| | ———— |
| Investment in associate | 2,058,000 |
| | ———— |

The inventory is held within the group so the parent's share of the PURP is credited against inventory rather than the investment in the associate.

### (W2) Share of profit of associate

| | $ |
|---|---|
| P's share of A's profit after tax (30% × $800,000 × 6/12) | 120,000 |
| Impairment | (50,000) |
| P's share of excess depreciation (30% × (($1.8m – $1m)/10 years) × 6/12) | (12,000) |
| P's share of PURP (30% × $100,000) | (30,000) |
| | ———— |
| Share of profit of associate | 28,000 |
| | ———— |

## 5 Control

Consolidated statements are produced if one entity controls another entity that constitutes a business. It is often presumed that control exists if a company owns more than 50% of the ordinary shares of another company. However, the Strategic Business Reporting exam might test the definition of control in more detail.

> **The *Conceptual Framework***
>
> The *Conceptual Framework* says that an entity controls a resource if it can direct its use and obtain economic benefits that may flow from it. Control includes the ability to prevent others from directing the use of the resource and from obtaining economic benefits that may flow from it.
>
> IFRS 10 *Consolidated Financial Statements* sets out how to apply the principle of control to identify whether an investor controls an investee.

According to IFRS 10, an investor **controls an investee** when:

- the investor has power over the investee, and

- the investor is exposed, or has rights, to variable returns from its involvement with the investee, and

- the investor has the ability to affect those returns through its power over the investee.

IFRS 10 identifies a range of circumstances that may need to be considered when determining whether or not an investor has power over an investee, such as:

- exercise of the majority of voting rights in an investee

- contractual arrangements between the investor and other parties

- holding less than 50% of the voting shares, with all other equity interests held by a numerically large, dispersed and unconnected group

- holding potential voting rights (such as convertible loans) that are currently capable of being exercised

- the nature of the investor's relationship with other parties that may enable that investor to exercise control over an investee.

It is therefore possible to own less than 50% of the ordinary shares of another entity and to still exercise control over it.

## Test your understanding 2 – Control

Parsley has a 40% holding in the ordinary shares of Oregano. Another investor has a 10% shareholding in Oregano whilst the remaining voting rights are held by thousands of shareholders, none of whom individually hold more than 1 per cent of the voting rights. Parsley also holds debt instruments that, as at 30 April 20X4, are convertible into ordinary shares of Oregano at a price of $4 per share. At 30 April 20X4, the shares of Oregano trade at $3.80 per share. If the debt was converted into ordinary shares, Parsley would hold 60% of the voting rights in Oregano. Parsley and Oregano undertake similar activities and would benefit from synergies.

**Required:**

**Discuss how Parsley's investment in the ordinary shares of Oregano should be treated in the consolidated financial statements for the year ended 30 April 20X4.**

## Test your understanding 3 – Vertical group

Look at the group structure below:

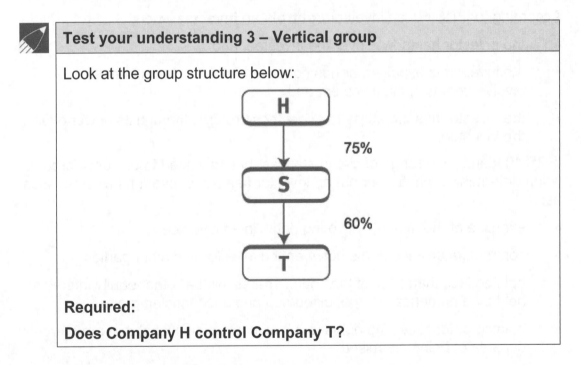

**Required:**

**Does Company H control Company T?**

## 6 Business combinations

### The definition of a business

The acquisition method (i.e. consolidation) is applied when one entity obtains control over another entity that constitutes a business. If the assets acquired are not a business, the transaction should be accounted for as the purchase of an asset

A business is not simply a collection of resources. For example, a restaurant is more than just a building with ovens, tables and chairs. It also has trained chefs who use this equipment in combination with ingredients and their knowledge of the restaurant's recipes to produce sellable finished goods.

Per IFRS 3 *Business Combinations*, a business must have processes that are able to convert acquired inputs into outputs.

**Inputs** are economic resources that can create outputs once processes are applied to them. Examples include property, plant and equipment, intangible assets, raw materials, and employees.

**Processes** are '**any system, standard, protocol, convention or rule that when applied to an input or inputs, creates outputs or has the ability to contribute to the creation of outputs**' (IFRS 3, B7b). Processes are normally documented. However, employee knowledge and experience in following rules and conventions can also constitute a process

**Outputs** result from inputs and the processes applied to inputs. Outputs include goods, services and income.

### Concentration test

The Board are aware that the definition of a business can be difficult and judgemental to apply. As such, there is an optional concentration test that preparers of financial statements can use to assess whether an acquired set of assets is **not** a business.

The concentration test is met (i.e. the acquired assets are not a business) if substantially all of the fair value of the total assets acquired is concentrated in a single identifiable asset or group of similar identifiable assets.

---

**Test your understanding 4 – Taco**

Taco purchases 100% of the shares in Fajita, a non-listed company. Fajita owns 20 houses, which are leased to tenants. The houses are located in the same area. The fair value of the consideration paid for the shares in Fajita is equal to the total fair value of the 20 houses.

**Required:**

**Apply the optional concentration test in IFRS 3 *Business Combinations* to determine whether Fajita is not a business.**

### Elements of a business

If the concentration test is not met, or if the test is not applied, a more detailed assessment of the facts and circumstances is required to ascertain if a business has been acquired.

To meet the definition of a business, there must be inputs and processes that, when applied to acquired inputs, are capable of producing outputs. The processes acquired must be important and considerable (or, as IFRS 3 says, 'substantive').

Outputs are not required for an acquisition of assets to constitute a business. This is because some early stage entities may have engaged in significant research and development activities but not, as yet, finished any projects or generated any revenue.

If there are no outputs at the acquisition date then an acquired process is only substantive if:

- it is critical to convert an input to an output, **and**

- inputs acquired include a knowledgeable, skilled, organised workforce able to perform that process on other acquired inputs to produce outputs.

If there are outputs at the acquisition date then an acquired process is substantive if it:

- is critical to continuing to produce outputs, and the inputs acquired include an organised workforce with the skills and knowledge to perform that process, **or**

- significantly contributes to the ability to continue producing outputs and is either rare or not capable of easy replacement.

**Test your understanding 5 – Shepherd and Pie**

Shepherd purchases 100% of the shares in Pie, a non-listed company. Pie owns 10 houses, which are leased to residential tenants, and two multi-story office blocks, which are leased to commercial tenants. Pie has no employees, with all property management tasks to be performed by other employees from within the Shepherd group. There are contracts in place for third parties to provide cleaning and security services to the commercial tenants. The total fair value of the houses is similar to the total fair value of the office blocks.

The directors of Shepherd wish to apply the optional concentration test to determine whether Pie is not a business.

**Required:**

**Discuss whether Pie constitutes a business.**

**Test your understanding 6 – Tahini and Kofta**

Tahini purchases 100% of the ordinary share capital of Kofta, an entity that does not yet generate revenue. Kofta operates in the biotech industry. It has engaged in research and development activities into a number of drug compounds, and also owns a headquarters, research laboratories and technical equipment. Kofta employs senior management and highly-skilled research scientists. Each of Kofta's assets has a similar fair value.

**Required:**

**Discuss whether Kofta constitutes a business.**

## 7 Acquisition accounting

### The acquisition method

The acquisition method has the following requirements:

- Identifying the acquirer

- Determining the acquisition date

- Recognising and measuring the subsidiary's identifiable assets and liabilities

- Recognising goodwill (or a gain from a bargain purchase) and any non-controlling interest.

Although you will be aware of many of these requirements from your previous studies, as well as from the illustrations earlier in this chapter, you are expected to have a more detailed knowledge of each of these elements for the SBR exam.

### Identifying the acquirer

The acquirer is the entity that has assumed control over another entity.

In a business combination, it is normally clear which entity has assumed control.

**The acquirer**

Lyra pays $1 million to obtain 60% of the ordinary shares of Pan.

Lyra is the acquiring company.

However, sometimes it is not clear as to which entity is the acquirer. For these cases, IFRS 3 provides guidance:

- The acquirer is normally the entity that has transferred cash or other assets within the business combination

- If the business combination has not involved the transfer of cash or other assets, the acquirer is usually the entity that issues its equity interests.

Other factors to consider are as follows:

- The acquirer is usually the entity whose (former) management dominates the combined entity

- The acquirer is usually the entity whose owners have the largest portion of voting rights in the combined entity

- The acquirer is normally the bigger entity.

**Test your understanding 7 – Identifying the acquirer**

Abacus and Calculator are two public limited companies. The fair values of the net assets of these two companies are $100 million and $60 million respectively.

On 31 October 20X1, Abacus incorporates a new company, Phone, in order to effect the combination of Abacus and Calculator. Phone issues its shares to the shareholders of Abacus and Calculator in return for their equity interests.

After this, Phone is 60% owned by the former shareholders of Abacus and 40% owned by the former shareholders of Calculator. On the board of Phone are 4 of the former directors of Abacus and 2 of the former directors of Calculator.

**Required:**

**With regards to the above business combination, discuss which company is the acquirer.**

## The acquisition date

The acquisition date is the date on which the acquirer obtains control over the acquiree. This will be the date at which goodwill must be calculated and from which the incomes and expenses of the acquiree will be consolidated.

## Identifiable assets and liabilities

The acquirer must measure the identifiable assets acquired and the liabilities assumed at their fair values at the acquisition date.

IFRS 3 says that an asset is identifiable if:

- It is capable of disposal separately from the business owning it, or

- It arises from contractual or other legal rights, regardless of whether those rights can be sold separately.

The identifiable assets and liabilities of the subsidiary should be recognised at fair value where:

- they meet the definitions of assets and liabilities in the 2010 *Conceptual Framework for Financial Reporting*, and

- they are exchanged as part of the business combination rather than a separate transaction.

Note that IFRS 3 was not updated to refer to the revised element definitions in the 2018 *Conceptual Framework.* The *2010 Conceptual Framework* defined assets and liabilities as follows:

- **assets** are resources controlled by an entity from a past event that are expected to lead to an inflow of economic benefits

- **liabilities** are present obligations from a past event that are expected to lead to an outflow of economic resources.

Items that are not identifiable or do not meet the definitions of assets or liabilities are subsumed into the calculation of purchased goodwill.

Watch out for the following items:

- **Contingent liabilities** are recognised at fair value at the acquisition date. This is true even where an economic outflow is not probable. The fair value will incorporate the probability of an economic outflow.

- **Provisions** for future operating losses cannot be created as this is a post-acquisition item. Similarly, restructuring costs are only recognised to the extent that a liability actually exists at the date of acquisition.

- **Intangible assets** are recognised at fair value if they are separable or arise from legal or contractual rights. This might mean that the parent recognises an intangible asset in the consolidated financial statements that the subsidiary did not recognise in its individual financial statements, e.g. an internally generated brand name.

- **Goodwill** in the subsidiary's individual financial statements is not consolidated. This is because it is not separable and it does not arise from legal or contractual rights.

There are some exceptions to the requirement to measure the subsidiary's net assets at fair value when accounting for business combinations. Assets and liabilities falling within the scope of the following standards should be valued according to those standards:

- IAS 12 *Income Taxes*

- IAS 19 *Employee Benefits*

- IFRS 2 *Share-based Payment*

- IFRS 5 *Non-current Assets Held for Sale and Discontinued Operations.*

## Test your understanding 8 – Fair value of identifiable net assets

P purchased 60% of the shares of S on 1 January 20X1. At the acquisition date, S had share capital of $10,000 and retained earnings of $190,000.

The property, plant and equipment of S includes land with a carrying value of $10,000 but a fair value of $50,000.

Included within the intangible assets of S is goodwill of $20,000 which arose on the purchase of the trade and assets of a sole-trader business. S has an internally generated brand that is not recognised (in accordance with IAS 38 *Intangible Assets*). The directors of P believe that this brand has a fair value of $150,000.

In accordance with IAS 37 *Provisions, Contingent Liabilities and Contingent Assets*, the financial statements of S disclose the fact that a customer has initiated legal proceedings against them. If the customer wins, which lawyers have advised is unlikely, estimated damages would be $1 million. The fair value of this contingent liability has been assessed as $100,000 at the acquisition date.

The directors of P wish to close one of the divisions of S. They estimate that this will cost $200,000 in redundancy payments.

**Required:**

**Discuss, with calculations, the fair value of S's identifiable net assets at the acquisition date.**

## Goodwill

Goodwill should be recognised on a business combination. This is calculated as the difference between:

1    The aggregate of the fair value of the consideration transferred and the non-controlling interest in the acquiree at the acquisition date, and

2    The fair value of the acquiree's identifiable net assets and liabilities.

## Purchase consideration

When calculating goodwill, purchase consideration transferred to acquire control of the subsidiary must be measured at fair value.

When determining the fair value of the consideration transferred:

- Contingent consideration is included even if payment is not deemed probable. Its fair value will incorporate the probability of payment occurring.

- Acquisition costs are excluded from the calculation of purchase consideration.

  - Legal and professional fees are expensed to profit or loss as incurred

  - Debt or equity issue costs are accounted for in accordance with IFRS 9 *Financial Instruments*.

## Replacement share-based payment schemes

Consideration transferred in exchange for control of a subsidiary could include replacement share-based payment schemes exchanged for share-based payments schemes held by the subsidiary's employees.

If the acquirer is obliged to issue replacement share-based payments to employees of the subsidiary in exchange for their existing schemes, then the fair value of the replacement scheme must be allocated between:

- purchase consideration, and

- post-acquisition remuneration expense.

The amount allocated as purchase consideration cannot exceed the value of the original share scheme at the date of acquisition. The amount attributable to post-acquisition service is recognised in accordance with IFRS 2 *Share-based Payments*.

### Test your understanding 9 – Purchase consideration

Following on from Test your understanding 8, the purchase consideration transferred by P in exchange for the shares in S was as follows:

- Cash paid of $300,000

- Cash to be paid in one year's time of $200,000

- 10,000 shares in P. These had a nominal value of $1 and a fair value at 1 January 20X1 of $3 each

- $250,000 to be paid in one year's time if S makes a profit before tax of more than $2m. There is a 50% chance of this happening. The fair value of this contingent consideration can be measured as the present value of the expected value.

- P is required to replace a share-based payment scheme previously granted by S to its employees. By the acquisition date, S's employees had rendered the required service for the award but had not exercised their options. The fair value of S's award at the acquisition date was $400,000. The fair value of P's replacement award, which has no post-acquisition vesting conditions attached, was $500,000.

Legal fees associated with the acquisition were $10,000.

Where required, a discount rate of 10% should be used.

**Required:**

**Discuss, with calculations, the fair value of the consideration transferred to acquire control of S.**

## Goodwill and the non-controlling interest

The calculation of goodwill will depend on the method chosen to value the non-controlling interest at the acquisition date.

IFRS 3 provides a choice in valuing the non-controlling interest at acquisition:

EITHER: OR:

| Method 1 – The proportionate share of net assets method | Method 2 – The fair value method |
|---|---|
| NCI % × fair value of the net assets of the subsidiary at the acquisition date. | Fair value of NCI at date of acquisition. This is usually given in the question. |

If the NCI is valued at acquisition as their proportionate share of the acquisition net assets, then only the acquirer's goodwill will be calculated.

If the NCI is valued at acquisition at fair value, then goodwill attributable to both the acquirer and the NCI will be calculated. This is known as the 'full goodwill method'.

The method used to measure the NCI should be decided on a transaction by transaction basis. This means that, within the same group, the NCI in some subsidiaries may have been measured at fair value at acquisition, whilst the NCI in other subsidiaries may have been measured at acquisition using the proportionate basis.

### Test your understanding 10 – Goodwill

Following on from Test your understanding 8 and 9, the fair value of the non-controlling interest at the acquisition date is $160,000.

**Required:**

Calculate the goodwill arising on the acquisition of S if the non-controlling interest at the acquisition date is valued at:

(a) fair value

(b) its proportion of the fair value of the subsidiary's identifiable net assets.

### Bargain purchase

If the share of net assets acquired exceeds the consideration transferred, then a gain on bargain purchase ('negative goodwill') arises on acquisition. The accounting treatment for this is as follows:

- IFRS 3 says that negative goodwill is rare and may suggest that errors were made when determining the fair value of the consideration transferred and the net assets acquired. The figures should be reviewed for accuracy.
- If no errors have been made, the negative goodwill is credited immediately to profit or loss.

## Measurement period

During the measurement period, IFRS 3 requires the acquirer in a business combination to retrospectively adjust the provisional amounts recognised at the acquisition date to reflect new information obtained about facts and circumstances that existed as of the acquisition date.

This would result in goodwill arising on acquisition being recalculated.

The measurement period ends no later than twelve months after the acquisition date.

### Measurement period illustration

P bought 100% of the shares of S on 31 December 20X1 for $60,000. On the acquisition date, it was estimated that the fair value of S's net assets were $40,000.

For the year ended 31 December 20X1, P would consolidate S's net assets of $40,000 and would also show goodwill of $20,000 ($60,000 – $40,000).

However, P receives further information on 30 June 20X2 which indicates that the fair value of S's net assets at the acquisition date was actually $50,000. This information was determined within the measurement period and so is retrospectively adjusted for.

Therefore, the financial statements for the year ended 31 December 20X1 will be adjusted. P will now consolidate S's net assets of $50,000 and will show goodwill of $10,000 ($60,000 – $50,000).

## 8    Impairment of goodwill

IAS 36 *Impairment of Assets* requires that goodwill is tested for impairment annually.

Goodwill does not generate independent cash inflows. Therefore, it is tested for impairment as part of a cash generating unit.

 A cash-generating unit is the **'smallest identifiable group of assets that generates cash inflows that are largely independent of the cash inflows from other assets or groups of assets'** (IAS 36, para 6).

For exam purposes, a subsidiary is normally designated as a cash-generating unit.

### Accounting for an impairment

An **impairment loss** is the amount by which the carrying amount of an asset or a cash generating unit exceeds its recoverable amount.

**Recoverable amount** is the higher of fair value less costs to sell and value in use.

Impairment losses on a subsidiary will firstly be allocated against goodwill and then against other assets on a pro-rata basis.

## Accounting for an impairment with a non-controlling interest

### NCI – fair value method

Goodwill calculated under the fair value method represents full goodwill. It can therefore be added together with the other net assets of the subsidiary and compared to the recoverable amount of the subsidiary's net assets on a like for like basis.

Any impairment of goodwill is allocated between the group and the NCI based upon their respective shareholdings.

### NCI – proportionate method

If the NCI is valued at acquisition at its share of the subsidiary's net assets then only the goodwill attributable to the group is calculated. This means that the NCI share of goodwill is not reflected in the group accounts. As such, any comparison between the carrying amount of the subsidiary (including goodwill) and the recoverable amount of its net assets will not be on a like-for-like basis.

- In order to address this problem, goodwill must be grossed up to include goodwill attributable to the NCI prior to conducting the impairment review. This grossed up goodwill is known as **total notional goodwill**.

- As only the parent's share of the goodwill is recognised in the group accounts, only the parent's share of the goodwill impairment loss should be recognised.

---

### Illustration 4 – Impairment of goodwill

A owns 80% of B. At 31 October 20X6 the carrying amount of B's net assets is $60 million, excluding goodwill of $8 million that arose on the original acquisition.

The recoverable amount of the net assets of B is $64 million.

**Required:**

**Discuss the implications of the recoverable amount of the net assets of B if:**

(a) **the NCI at acquisition was measured at fair value**

(b) **the NCI at acquisition was measured at its proportion of the fair value of the subsidiary's identifiable net assets.**

---

## Solution

### Impairment

According to IAS 36 *Impairment of Assets*, goodwill must be reviewed annually for impairment. Impairment arises when an asset's carrying amount exceeds its recoverable amount.

Goodwill does not generate independent cash flows and so must be tested for impairment as part of a cash generating unit. The calculation of the impairment loss is dependent on the method used to value the non-controlling interest at acquisition.

(a) **NCI at fair value**

If the NCI at acquisition was measured at fair value then full goodwill has been calculated. This means that the carrying amount of the subsidiary's net assets and goodwill can be compared to the subsidiary's recoverable amount on a like-for-like basis.

|  | $m |
|---|---|
| Goodwill | 8 |
| Net assets | 60 |
|  | —— |
| Carrying amount | 68 |
| Recoverable amount | 64 |
|  | —— |
| Impairment | 4 |
|  | —— |

The impairment loss will be allocated against goodwill, reducing it from $8m to $4m.

The $4m impairment expense will be charged to profit or loss. Of this, $3.2m ($4m × 80%) is attributable to the group and $0.8m ($4m × 20%) is attributable to the NCI.

**(b)** **NCI using proportionate method**

If the NCI at acquisition was measured using the proportionate method then only the group's share of the goodwill has been calculated – i.e. 80% of the goodwill This means that the carrying amount of the subsidiary's net assets and goodwill cannot be compared to the subsidiary's recoverable amount on a like-for-like basis. As such, goodwill must be grossed up to include the NCI's unrecognised 20% share.

|  | $m | $m |
|---|---|---|
| Goodwill | 8 |  |
| Unrecognised NCI (20/80 × $8m) | 2 |  |
| Total notional goodwill |  | 10 |
| Net assets |  | 60 |
| Carrying amount |  | 70 |
| Recoverable amount |  | 64 |
| Impairment |  | 6 |

The impairment loss is allocated against the total notional goodwill of $10 million.

However, only the group's share of goodwill has been recognised in the financial statements and so only the group's share (80%) of the impairment is recognised. The impairment charged to profit or loss is therefore $4.8m and goodwill will be reduced to $3.2m ($8m – $4.8m).

**Test your understanding 11 – Happy**

On 1 January 20X5, Lucky group purchased 80% of Happy for $500,000. The fair value of the identifiable net assets of Happy at the date of acquisition amounted to $590,000.

The carrying amount of Happy's net assets at 31 December is $520,000 (excluding goodwill). Happy is a cash-generating unit.

At 31 December 20X5 the recoverable amount of Happy's net assets is $530,000.

**Required:**

**Calculate the impact of the impairment review if:**

**(a)** **the NCI at acquisition was measured at its fair value of $130,000.**

**(b)** **the NCI at acquisition was measured at its share of the fair value of Happy's identifiable net assets.**

## Test your understanding 12 – Pauline

Extracts from the statements of financial position at 31 March 20X8 for three companies are below:

| | Pauline $000 | Sonia $000 | Arthur $000 |
|---|---|---|---|
| **Non-current assets** | | | |
| Property, plant and equipment | 36,800 | 20,800 | 36,000 |
| Investments in Sonia and Arthur | 26,500 | – | – |
| **Equity and liabilities** | | | |
| Equity shares of $1 each | 20,000 | 8,000 | 8,000 |
| Retained earnings | | | |
| – at 31 March 20X7 | 32,000 | 12,000 | 22,000 |
| – for year ended 31 March 20X8 | 18,500 | 5,800 | 10,000 |

The following information is relevant to the preparation of the consolidated statement of financial position.

### Sonia

On 1 April 20X7 Pauline acquired 6 million of Sonia's equity shares by an exchange of one share in Pauline for every two shares in Sonia plus $1.25 per acquired Sonia share in cash. The market price of each Pauline share at the date of acquisition was $6 and the market price of each Sonia share at the date of acquisition was $3.25.

The cash consideration transferred for the acquisition of Sonia has been recorded by Pauline in its separate financial statements but the share consideration has not been recorded. In addition $1 million of professional costs relating to the acquisition of Sonia are included in the cost of the investment.

At the date of acquisition Sonia had an internally generated brand name that was unrecognised in its separate financial statements. The directors of Pauline estimate that this brand name has a fair value of $2 million and an indefinite life.

Pauline has a policy of valuing non-controlling interests at fair value at the date of acquisition. For this purpose the share price of Sonia should be used.

Impairment tests on 31 March 20X8 concluded that the recoverable amount of the net assets of Sonia was $34 million.

### Arthur

On 1 April 20X7 Pauline acquired 30% of Arthur's equity shares at a cost of $7.50 per share in cash and recorded this in its separate financial statements.

> **Required:**
>
> (a) **Discuss how to determine the carrying amount of the goodwill arising on the acquisition of Sonia that will be reported in the consolidated statement of financial position as at 31 March 20X8.**
>
> (b) **Discuss how to account for the investment in Arthur in the consolidated statement of financial position as at 31 March 20X8.**
>
> (c) **Prepare the non-current assets section of the consolidated statement of financial position as at 31 March 20X8.**

 **Investor perspective**

The method used to measure the non-controlling interest (NCI) at acquisition will have an impact on the consolidated financial statements.

Normally, the NCI figure will be higher if measured using the fair value method rather than the proportion of net assets method. This is because goodwill and equity are increased by the goodwill attributable to the NCI. As a result, the group may look more asset-rich to potential investors.

Using the fair value method will increase goodwill on the statement of financial position, and so goodwill impairments charged to profit or loss will be greater. In the long-term, this may lead to lower reported profits.

## 9 Exemptions from consolidation

### Valid consolidation exemptions

### Intermediate parent companies

An intermediate parent entity is an entity which has a subsidiary but is also itself a subsidiary of another entity. For example:

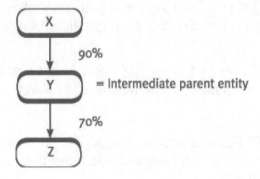

IFRS 10 permits a parent entity not to present group financial statements provided all of the following conditions apply:

- it is a wholly-owned, or partially-owned subsidiary where owners of the non-controlling interest do not object to the non-preparation

- its debt or equity instruments are not currently traded in a domestic or foreign market

- it is not in the process of having any of its debt or equity instruments traded on a domestic or foreign market

- the ultimate parent entity produces consolidated financial statements that comply with IFRS Standards and which are available to the public.

If this is the case, IAS 27 *Separate Financial Statements* requires that the following disclosures are made:

- the fact that consolidated financial statements have not been presented

- a list of significant investments (subsidiaries, joint ventures and associates) including percentage shareholdings, principal place of business and country of incorporation

- the bases on which those investments listed above have been accounted for in its separate financial statements.

### Investment entities

An investment entity is defined by IFRS 10 as an entity that:

(a) obtains funds from investors and provides them with investment management services, and

(b) invests those funds to earn returns from capital appreciation, investment income, or both, and

(c) measures the performance of its investments on a fair value basis.

Investment entities do not consolidate an investment over which they have control. Instead, the investment is measured at fair value at each reporting date with gains and losses recorded in profit or loss.

### Invalid reasons for excluding a subsidiary

In addition to the valid reasons to exclude a subsidiary from consolidation, directors of the parent entity may seek to exclude a subsidiary from group accounts for several invalid reasons, including:

- **Long-term restrictions on the ability to transfer funds to the parent**. This exclusion from consolidation is not permitted as it may still be possible to control a subsidiary in such circumstances.

- The **subsidiary undertakes different activities** and/or operates in different locations, thus being distinctive from other members of the group. This is not a valid reason for exclusion from consolidation. Indeed it could be argued that inclusion within the group accounts of such a subsidiary will enhance the relevance and reliability of the information contained within the group accounts.

- The **subsidiary has made losses or has significant liabilities** which the directors would prefer to exclude from the group accounts to improve the overall reported financial performance and position of the group. This could be motivated, for example, by determination of directors' remuneration based upon group financial performance. This is not a valid reason for exclusion from consolidation.

- The directors may seek to **disguise the true ownership of the subsidiary**, perhaps to avoid disclosure of particular activities or events, or to avoid disclosure of ownership of assets. This could be motivated, for example, by seeking to avoid disclosure of potential conflicts of interest which may be perceived adversely by users of financial statements.

- The directors may seek to exclude a subsidiary from consolidation in order for the group to **disguise its true size and extent**. This could be motivated, for example, by trying to avoid legal and regulatory compliance requirements applicable to the group or individual subsidiaries. This is not a valid reason for exclusion from consolidation.

## 10 IFRS 11 *Joint Arrangements*

**Joint arrangements** are defined **'as arrangements where two or more parties have joint control'** (IFRS 11, Appendix A). This will only apply if the relevant activities require unanimous consent of those who collectively control the arrangement.

Joint arrangements may take the form of either:

- joint operations
- joint ventures.

The key distinction between the two forms is based upon the parties' rights and obligations under the joint arrangement.

### Joint operations

Joint operations are defined as joint arrangements whereby **'the parties that have joint control have rights to the assets and obligations for the liabilities'** (IFRS 11, Appendix A). Normally, there will not be a separate entity established to conduct joint operations.

### Example of a joint operation

A and B decide to enter into a joint operation to produce a new product. A undertakes one manufacturing process and B undertakes the other. A and B have agreed that decisions regarding the joint operation will be made unanimously and that each will bear their own expenses and take an agreed share of the sales revenue from the product.

## Accounting treatment

If the joint operation meets the definition of a 'business' then the principles in IFRS 3 *Business Combinations* apply when an interest in a joint operation is acquired:

- Acquisition costs are expensed to profit or loss as incurred

- The identifiable assets and liabilities of the joint operation are measured at fair value

- The excess of the consideration transferred over the fair value of the net assets acquired is recognised as goodwill.

At the reporting date, the individual financial statements of each joint operator will recognise:

- its share of assets held jointly

- its share of liabilities incurred jointly

- its share of revenue from the joint operation

- its share of expenses from the joint operation.

The joint operator's share of the income, expenses, assets and liabilities of the joint operation are included in its individual financial statements and so they will automatically flow through to the consolidated financial statements.

## Joint ventures

Joint ventures are defined as joint arrangements whereby **'the parties have joint control of the arrangement and have rights to the net assets of the arrangement'** (IFRS 11, Appendix A). This will normally be established in the form of a separate entity to conduct the joint venture activities.

### Example of a joint venture

A and B decide to set up a separate entity, C, to enter into a joint venture. A will own 55% of the equity capital of C, with B owning the remaining 45%. A and B have agreed that decision-making regarding the joint venture will be unanimous. Neither party will have direct right to the assets, or direct obligation for the liabilities of the joint venture; instead, they will have an interest in the net assets of entity C set up for the joint venture.

### Accounting treatment

In the individual financial statements, an investment in a joint venture can be accounted for:

- at cost

- in accordance with IFRS 9 *Financial Instruments*, or

- by using the equity method.

In the consolidated financial statements, the interest in the joint venture entity will be accounted for using the equity method in accordance with IAS 28 *Investments in Associates and Joint Ventures*. The treatment of a joint venture in the consolidated financial statements is therefore identical to the treatment of an associate.

### Test your understanding 13 – A, B, C and D

A, B and C establish a new entity, which is called D. A has 50 per cent of the voting rights in the new entity, B has 30 per cent and C has 20 per cent. The contractual arrangement between A, B and C specifies that at least 75 per cent of the voting rights are required to make decisions about the activities of entity D.

**Required:**

**Discuss how A should account for its investment in D in its consolidated financial statements?**

### Illustration 5 – Joint operation - Blast

Blast has a 30% share in a joint operation. The assets, liabilities, revenues and costs of the joint operation are apportioned on the basis of shareholdings. The following information relates to the joint arrangement activity for the year ended 30 November 20X2:

- The manufacturing facility cost $30m to construct and was completed on 1 December 20X1 and is to be dismantled at the end of its estimated useful life of 10 years. The present value of this dismantling cost to the joint arrangement at 1 December 20X1, using a discount rate of 8%, was $3m.

- During the year ended 30 November 20X2, the joint operation entered into the following transactions:

  - goods with a production cost of $36m were sold for $50m

  - other operating costs incurred amounted to $1m

  - administration expenses incurred amounted to $2m.

Blast has only accounted for its share of the cost of the manufacturing facility, amounting to $9m. The revenue and costs are receivable and payable by the two other joint operation partners who will settle amounts outstanding with Blast after each reporting date.

**Required:**

**Show how Blast will account for the joint operation within its financial statements for the year ended 30 November 20X2.**

## Solution – Blast

| Profit or loss impact: | $m |
|---|---|
| Revenue ($50m × 30%) | 15.000 |
| Cost of sales ($36m × 30%) | (10.800) |
| Operating costs ($1m × 30%) | (0.300) |
| Depreciation (($30m + 3m) × 1/10 × 30%) | (0.990) |
| Administration expenses ($2m × 30%) | (0.600) |
| Finance cost ($3m × 8% × 30%) | (0.072) |
| | |
| Share of net profit re joint operation (include in retained earnings within SOFP) | 2.238 |

| Statement of financial position impact: | $m |
|---|---|
| Property, plant and equipment (amount paid = share of cost) | 9.000 |
| Dismantling cost ($3m × 30%) | 0.900 |
| Depreciation ($33m × 1/10 × 30%) | (0.990) |
| | |
| | 8.910 |
| | |
| Trade receivables (i.e. share of revenue due) | 15.000 |
| | |
| Non-current liabilities: | |
| Dismantling provision (($3m × 30%) + $0.072) | 0.972 |
| | |
| Current liabilities: | |
| Trade payables ($10.8m + $0.3m + $0.6m) (i.e. share of expenses to pay) | 11.700 |

The amounts calculated above should be classified under the appropriate headings within the statement of profit or loss for the year or statement of financial position as appropriate.

Note also that where there are amounts owed to and from a joint operating partner, it may be acceptable to show just a net amount due to or from each partner.

## 11 Other issues in group accounting

### IFRS 12 *Disclosure of Interests in Other Entities*

IFRS 12 is the single source of disclosure requirements for business combinations. Disclosure requirements include:

- disclosure of significant assumptions and judgements made in determining whether an investor has control, joint control or significant influence over an investee

- disclosure of the nature, extent and financial effects of its interests in joint arrangements and associates

- additional disclosures relating to subsidiaries with non-controlling interests, joint arrangements and associates that are individually material

- significant restrictions on the ability of the parent to access and use the assets or to settle the liabilities of its subsidiaries.

### IAS 27 *Separate Financial Statements*

IAS 27 applies when an entity has interests in subsidiaries, joint ventures or associates and either elects to, or is required to, prepare separate non-consolidated financial statements.

In separate financial statements, investments in subsidiaries, joint ventures or associates can be accounted for:

- at cost

- in accordance with IFRS 9 *Financial Instruments*, or

- by using the equity method.

In separate financial statements, dividends received from an investment are recognised in profit or loss unless the equity method is used. If the equity method has been used, then dividends received reduce the carrying amount of the investment.

### Criticisms of IFRS 3 *Business Combinations*

The Board has conducted a post-implementation review of IFRS 3. Users of the standard raised the following issues.

### Fair values

- The requirement to fair value the assets and liabilities of the acquired subsidiary at the acquisition date makes it difficult to compare entities that grow via acquisitions with those that grow organically.

- Recognising the inventory of a subsidiary at its acquisition date fair value will reduce profit margins in the next period, thus reducing comparability year-on-year.

## Intangible assets

- IFRS 3 requires entities to recognise separable intangibles at fair value at the acquisition date, but this is difficult and judgemental if no active market exists.

## Contingent consideration

- The calculation of the fair value of contingent consideration is subjective, increasing the risk of bias and reducing comparability.

- Contingent consideration may be linked to the success of a long-term development project. It has been argued that changes in the fair value of the consideration in such scenarios should be recorded against the development asset, rather than in profit or loss.

## Goodwill

- Some have argued that a gain on a bargain purchase should not be recognised in profit or loss, but rather in other comprehensive income, because it distorts the performance profile of an entity.

- Goodwill impairment reviews are complex, subjective and time-consuming.

- Performing annual impairment reviews in respect of goodwill, rather than amortising it, increases volatility in profit or loss.

- Over time, purchased goodwill will be replaced by internally generated goodwill. Per IAS 38 *Intangible Assets*, internally generated goodwill should not be recognised as an asset. As such, some argue that purchased goodwill should be amortised, rather than be subject to annual impairment review.

## NCI

- Allowing a measurement choice for the NCI at acquisition reduces comparability between entities.

- Measuring the fair value of the NCI can be problematic, and highly judgemental, if the entity is not listed.

## 12 Exam focus

Question 1 in the SBR exam will always test group accounting. However, it will not ask for the production of full consolidated financial statements. Instead, candidates will be required to produce extracts from these statements and to explain the accounting numbers that they have produced. You should attempt the SBR specimen papers and past exam papers (included in the Exam Kit) to ensure you are comfortable with this style of requirement. The following question also provides relevant practice.

## Test your understanding 14 – Fish

On 1 January 20X1, Fish acquired 80% of the ordinary shares of Lobster. The group accountant has calculated that the goodwill arising on acquisition was $40 million. However, the financial controller has uncovered a number of errors and requires advice about how to resolve them:

- No entries have been posted in respect of contingent cash consideration that will be paid in 20X5 if Lobster meets profit targets. The contingent consideration had a fair value of $4 million at acquisition and was calculated using a discount rate of 10%.

- No fair value adjustment has been recorded in respect of Lobster's non-depreciable land. This land had a carrying amount of $2 million at acquisition and a fair value of $3 million.

- Lobster's brand is internally generated and has not been recognised in the consolidated financial statements. At acquisition it had a fair value of $5 million and a remaining estimated useful life of 5 years.

Fish's policy is to value the non-controlling interest (NCI) at acquisition at fair value. The fair value of the NCI at acquisition was correctly calculated and included in the goodwill calculation.

### Required:

**Discuss how the above three issues should have been accounted for in the consolidated financial statements for the year ended 31 December 20X1. Provide the adjustments required to correct any errors. Ignore deferred tax.**

## 13 Chapter summary

Revision of group SFP:
- Group structure (W1)
- Proforma and adding
- Workings 2 – 5

Revision of group P/L and OCI:
- Group structure
- Proforma and adding
- Profit and TCI split

Revision of associates:
- Use the equity method

Control:
- Power
- Rights to variable returns
- The ability to use power to affect returns

The acquisition method:
- Identify the acquirer
- Identify the acquisition date
- Recognise net assets at fair value
- Recognise goodwill and the NCI

Impairment of goodwill:
- Goodwill calculated under the proportionate method must be grossed up.

Joint arrangements:
- Joint operations
- Joint ventures

# Test your understanding answers

### Test your understanding 1 – Sparrow

Sparrow owns less than 20% of the ordinary shares of Blackbird. As such, per IAS 28 *Investments in Associates and Joint Ventures*, it would normally be presumed that significant influence does not exist.

Despite the above, there are several indications that significant influence does exist.

Firstly, Sparrow is able to appoint two directors to Blackbird's board of directors. Moreover, Blackbird is one of Sparrow's key suppliers, which means that there are high levels of transactions between the two entities. Finally, there is interchange of management personnel between the two entities.

As such, it can be concluded that Sparrow has significant influence over Blackbird. The directors are incorrect to account for Blackbird as a financial asset in the consolidated financial statements and should instead account for the investment as an associate.

### Test your understanding 2 – Control

An investor controls an investee if the investor has:

- **'power over the investee**

- **exposure, or rights, to variable returns from its involvement with the investee**

- **the ability to use its power over the investee to affect the amount of the investor's returns'** (IFRS 10, para 7).

When assessing control, an investor considers its potential voting rights. Potential voting rights are rights to obtain voting rights of an investee, such as those arising from convertible instruments or options.

Potential voting rights are considered if the rights are substantive. This would mean that the rights need to be currently exercisable. Other factors that should be considered in determining whether potential voting rights are substantive, according to IFRS 10, include:

- whether the exercise price creates a financial barrier that would prevent (or deter) the holder from exercising its rights

- whether the party or parties that hold the rights would benefit from the exercise of those rights.

Parsley has voting rights that are currently exercisable and these should be factored into an assessment of whether control exists. The fact that the exercise price on the convertible instrument is out of the money (i.e. the exercise price is higher than the current market price) could potentially deter Parsley from taking up these voting rights.

However, these options are not deeply out of the money. This may also be compensated by the fact that synergies would arise on the acquisition. This would suggest that it is likely that Parsley will exercise the options. The potential voting rights should therefore be considered substantive.

Based on the above, Parsley has control over Oregano. Oregano should be treated as a subsidiary and consolidated.

### Test your understanding 3 – Vertical group

H controls S because the size of its shareholding gives it the ability to affect variable returns through the power it exercises.

S controls T for the same reasons as above.

H is therefore also able to exert control over T by virtue of its ability to control S.

All three companies form a group. H is a parent company and S and T are its subsidiaries.

### Test your understanding 4 – Taco

The houses are a group of similar assets and so the fair value of the total assets acquired is concentrated in a group of similar assets. This means that the purchase of Fajita's ordinary shares does not constitute a business combination. In substance, Taco is simply purchasing twenty houses.

### Test your understanding 5 – Shepherd and Pie

Pie's assets are all buildings (and, potentially, associated land). However, the risks associated with operating residential properties are very different from those associated with operating office blocks and so these assets are dissimilar. This means that the fair value of the assets acquired is not concentrated in a single group of assets.

As such, Shepherd must engage in a more detailed assessment of whether Pie constitutes a business.

Pie's assets produce outputs because there are leases in place that generate rental income. However, the purchase of Pie does not constitute a business because a substantive process has not been acquired. This is because:

- there is no organised workforce in place that can produce outputs

- the security and cleaning services are relatively minor and could be easily replaced.

As such, the acquisition of Pie is, in substance, an asset acquisition and not a business combination.

### Test your understanding 6 – Tahini and Kofta

The optional concentration test is not met because the fair value of the total assets acquired is not concentrated in a single asset or group of similar assets.

Tahini has purchased inputs (research and development, tangible assets, employees). It also appears to have purchased a substantive process because experienced employees will have knowledge of the rules and conventions that are capable of turning the other acquired inputs (in-progress research and development activities, and tangible equipment) into finished, marketable products.

As such, the acquisition of Kofta is a business combination.

### Test your understanding 7 – Identifying the acquirer

If the business combination has not involved the transfer of cash or other assets, the acquirer is usually the entity that issues its equity interests. This might point towards Phone being the acquirer, since Phone has issued shares in exchange for the shares of Abacus and Calculator.

However, other circumstances must be considered:

- The acquirer is usually the entity whose (former) management dominates the management of the combined entity.

- The acquirer is usually the entity whose owners retain or receive the largest portion of the voting rights in the combined entity.

- The acquirer is normally the entity whose size is greater than the other entities.

All three of these circumstances would point towards Abacus being the acquirer. This would appear to reflect the substance of the transaction since Phone has been incorporated by Abacus as a way of enabling a business combination with Calculator.

## Test your understanding 8 – Fair value of identifiable net assets

In the separate financial statements, the net assets are carried at $200,000 ($10,000 share capital + $190,000 retained earnings). In the consolidated financial statements, the identifiable net assets of a subsidiary must be recognised at fair value as at the acquisition date. An asset is identifiable if it is capable of separate disposal, or arises from legal or contractual rights.

Land is carried in the individual financial statements at $10,000. It should be recognised in the consolidated financial statements at $50,000. Therefore, its carrying amount must be increased by $40,000 ($50,000 – $10,000).

Goodwill in the subsidiary's own financial statements is not an identifiable asset because it cannot be disposed of separately from the rest of the business. As such, it is not recognised in the consolidated financial statements.

The brand is unrecognised in the individual financial statements but must be recognised in the consolidated financial statements at its fair value of $150,000.

The contingent liability is disclosed in the individual financial statements. However, it must be recognised in the consolidated financial statements at its fair value of $100,000. This is a liability and so reduces the total fair value of the identifiable net assets.

No adjustment is made to the fair value of the net assets for the estimated redundancy provision. This is because no obligation exists as at the acquisition date.

|  | $ |
|---|---|
| Share capital | 10,000 |
| Retained earnings | 190,000 |
| Land fair value uplift | 40,000 |
| Goodwill | (20,000) |
| Brand | 150,000 |
| Contingent liability | (100,000) |
|  | ——— |
| Fair value of identifiable net assets at acquisition | 270,000 |
|  | ——— |

### Test your understanding 9 – Purchase consideration

Purchase consideration should be measured at its fair value as at the acquisition date.

With regards to deferred cash, this should be discounted to its present value and included in the goodwill calculation at a value of $181,818 (($200,000 × (1/1.1)). A liability should be recorded for the same amount.

Share consideration should be measured at its fair value of $30,000 (10,000 × $3) at the acquisition date. Credit entries should be posted to share capital ($10,000) and share premium ($20,000).

Contingent consideration should also be measured at its fair value of $113,636 (($250,000 × 50% × (1/1.1)). This fair value will incorporate the probability of payment and the time value of money. A corresponding entry should be made to provisions.

The fair value of the replacement share-based payment scheme should be allocated between purchase consideration and a post-acquisition expense. Only $400,000 should be allocated as purchase consideration because this is the fair value of the original scheme at the acquisition date. The remaining $100,000 is recognised immediately in the consolidated statement of profit or loss as a post-acquisition expense because there are no vesting conditions to satisfy.

Legal fees are expensed to the statement of profit or loss.

The total fair value of the consideration transferred is calculated below:

|  | $ |
| --- | --- |
| Cash paid | 300,000 |
| Deferred cash | 181,818 |
| Shares | 30,000 |
| Contingent consideration | 113,636 |
| Replacement share-based payment | 400,000 |
|  |  |
| Fair value of consideration | 1,025,454 |

**Test your understanding 10 – Goodwill**

|  | Fair value method $ | Net assets method $ |
|---|---|---|
| Consideration (TYU 9) | 1,025,454 | 1,025,454 |
| Add: NCI at acquisition (part b = 40% × $270,000) | 160,000 | 108,000 |
| FV of identifiable net assets at acquisition (TYU 8) | (270,000) | (270,000) |
|  | 915,454 | 863,454 |

The fair value method calculates both the group's goodwill and the goodwill attributable to the non-controlling interest. Therefore, goodwill is higher under this method.

The proportion of net assets method only calculates the goodwill attributable to the group. Goodwill is lower under this method.

**Test your understanding 11 – Happy**

(a) **Full goodwill method**

Goodwill arising on acquisition:

|  | $000 |
|---|---|
| Fair value of consideration paid | 500 |
| NCI at acquisition | 130 |
|  | 630 |
| Less fair value of net assets at acquisition | (590) |
| Goodwill | 40 |

Impairment review:

|  | $000 |
|---|---|
| Goodwill | 40 |
| Net assets | 520 |
| Carrying amount | 560 |
| Recoverable amount | (530) |
| Impairment | 30 |

The impairment loss is allocated against goodwill, reducing it from $40,000 to $10,000.

The $30,000 impairment expense will be charged to the statement of profit or loss. Of this, $24,000 (80% × $30,000) is attributable to the group and $6,000 (20% × $30,000) is attributable to the NCI.

(b) **Proportionate method**

Goodwill arising on acquisition:

|  | $000 |
|---|---|
| Fair value of consideration paid | 500 |
| NCI at acquisition | |
| (20% × $590,000) | 118 |
| | ––––– |
| | 618 |
| Less: fair value of net assets at acquisition | (590) |
| | ––––– |
| Goodwill | 28 |
| | ––––– |

Impairment review:

|  | $000 | $000 |
|---|---|---|
| Goodwill | 28 | |
| Unrecognised NCI (20/80 × $28,000) | 7 | |
| | –––– | |
| Total notional goodwill | | 35 |
| Net assets | | 520 |
| | | ––––– |
| Carrying amount | | 555 |
| Recoverable amount | | (530) |
| | | ––––– |
| Impairment | | 25 |
| | | ––––– |

The impairment loss is firstly allocated to the notional goodwill. However, only the group's share of the goodwill was recognised in the financial statements and so only the group's share of the impairment is recognised.

The total impairment recognised is therefore $20,000 (80% × $25,000). This will be charged to the statement of profit or loss and is all attributable to the group.

**Test your understanding 12 – Pauline**

(a) **Consideration**

When calculating goodwill, IFRS 3 *Business Combinations* states that purchase consideration must be measured at fair value.

Pauline has issued 3 million shares (1/2 × 6m) and these must be valued at their fair value of $6 each. Share consideration will be included in the goodwill calculation at $18 million and a corresponding credit made to equity ($3 million share capital and $15 million share premium).

Cash consideration should be included in the goodwill calculation at its fair value of $7.5 million (6m × $1.25).

The current treatment of the $1 million professional fees is incorrect. These must be written off to the statement of profit or loss.

**Fair value of net assets**

At the acquisition date, Sonia's identifiable net assets must be measured at fair value.

The carrying amount of Sonia's net assets in its individual financial statements at acquisition is $20 million ($8m share capital + $12m retained earnings).

However, Sonia's brand name is an identifiable asset because it can be sold separately. Therefore, it must be included in the consolidated financial statements at its fair value of $2 million. This means that the fair value of Sonia's identifiable net assets at acquisition is $22 million ($20m + $2m).

The brand has an indefinite useful life so will not be amortised. It should be reviewed annually for impairment.

**Non-controlling interest**

IFRS 3 allows non-controlling interests (NCI) at acquisition to be valued at fair value or at the NCI's share of the subsidiary's identifiable net assets.

Pauline wishes to use the fair value method and so should value the NCI at $6.5 million (2m × $3.25). This will be included in the goodwill calculation and in the NCI balance within equity.

### Goodwill at acquisition

Goodwill arising at acquisition is calculated as follows:

|  | $000 |
|---|---:|
| Fair value of consideration: | |
| Share exchange | 18,000 |
| Cash paid | 7,500 |
| FV of NCI at acquisition | 6,500 |
| Less FV of net assets at acquisition | (22,000) |
| | |
| Goodwill at acquisition | 10,000 |

### Impairment

Goodwill must be reviewed annually for impairment. An impairment review involves comparing an asset's carrying amount to its recoverable amount. Goodwill does not generate independent cash flows and so must be tested for impairment as part of a cash generating unit.

Pauline valued the NCI at acquisition at fair value. Therefore, full goodwill was calculated. This can be added to the carrying amount of Sonia's other net assets in the consolidated statements and compared with the recoverable amount on a like-for-like basis (i.e. no grossing up of goodwill is required).

|  | $000 | $000 |
|---|---:|---:|
| Goodwill (see calc. above) | | 10,000 |
| Net assets: | | |
| Share capital | 8,000 | |
| Retained earnings bfd | 12,000 | |
| Profit for the period | 5,800 | |
| Brand | 2,000 | |
| | | |
| | | 27,800 |
| | | |
| Total carrying amount | | 37,800 |
| Recoverable amount | | (34,000) |
| | | |
| Impairment | | 3,800 |

The impairment loss will reduce goodwill from $10 million to $6.2 million. The loss of $3.8 million will be charged to the statement of profit or loss.

Full goodwill has been calculated so the impairment expense must be allocated between the owners of the parent company ($3.8m × 75% = $2.85 million) and the NCI ($3.8m × 25% = $0.95m) in proportion to their shareholdings.

(b) **Arthur**

Pauline has acquired 30% of the ordinary shares of Arthur. According to IAS 28 *Investments in Associates and Joint Ventures* this should be presumed to give Pauline significant influence over Arthur. This means that Arthur is an associate and should be accounted for using the equity method in the consolidated financial statements.

The investment in Arthur should be initially recognised at its cost of $18 million (8m × 30% × $7.50).

Pauline will account for its share of Arthur's post-acquisition profits. This amounts to $3 million ($10m × 30%). This will be credited to the statement of profit or loss and debited to the investment in the associate.

The investment in the associate will therefore be carried in the consolidated financial statements at $21 million ($18m + $3m).

(c) **Extract from consolidated statement of financial position as at 31 March 20X8**

| **Non-current assets** | $000 |
|---|---|
| Property, plant and equipment ($36,800 + $20,800) | 57,600 |
| Goodwill ($10m – $3.8m impairment) | 6,200 |
| Intangible assets | 2,000 |
| Investment in associate | 21,000 |
| | 86,800 |

## Test your understanding 13 – A, B, C and D

A does not control the arrangement because it needs the agreement of B when making decisions. This would imply that A and B have joint control of the arrangement because decisions about the activities of the entity cannot be made without both A and B agreeing.

In the consolidated financial statements of the A Group, D should be treated as a joint venture. This is because it is a separate entity over which A has joint control. The joint venture will be accounted for using the equity method.

## Test your understanding 14 – Fish

### Contingent consideration

Contingent consideration should be included in the goodwill calculation at its fair value at the acquisition date. This will increase the value of goodwill by $4 million. A non-current liability should also be recognised. The entry to correct this is:

| | |
|---|---|
| Dr Goodwill | $4m |
| Cr Liabilities | $4m |

The discount on the contingent consideration should be unwound over the year. This gives rise to a finance cost of $0.4 million ($4m × 10%) in the statement of profit or loss and increases the carrying amount of the liability to $4.4 million. The entry to correct this is:

| | |
|---|---|
| Dr Finance costs | $0.4m |
| Cr Liabilities | $0.4m |

### Land

IFRS 3 says that the identifiable net assets of the subsidiary should be consolidated at fair value. The property, plant and equipment balance therefore needs uplifting by $1 million. This will reduce the goodwill arising on acquisition by $1 million. The entry to correct this is:

| | |
|---|---|
| Dr Property, plant and equipment | $1m |
| Cr Goodwill | $1m |

### Brand

The brand is an identifiable asset and so should have been consolidated at its fair value of $5 million as at the acquisition date. This reduces the goodwill balance by $5 million:

| | |
|---|---|
| Dr Intangible assets | $5m |
| Cr Goodwill | $5m |

The fair value adjustment should be amortised over its remaining useful life. This will give rise to an amortisation charge of $1 million ($5m/5 years) in the statement of profit or loss, reducing the carrying amount of the brand to $4 million.

| | |
|---|---|
| Dr Profit or loss | $1m |
| Cr Intangible assets | $1m |

Of the total $1 million expense, $0.8 million is attributable to the owners of the parent company and $0.2 million is attributable to the non-controlling interest.

**Goodwill**

The total goodwill arising on the acquisition of Fish is $38 million ($40m + $4m – $1m – $5m). This should be subject to annual impairment review.

# Change in a group structure

## Chapter learning objectives

Upon completion of this chapter you will be able to:

- Apply the accounting principles relating to a business combination achieved in stages

- Discuss and apply the implications of changes in ownership interest and loss of control

- Prepare group financial statements where activities have been discontinued, or have been acquired or disposed of in the period

- Discuss and apply the treatment of a subsidiary which has been acquired exclusively with a view to subsequent disposal.

**PER**

One of the PER performance objectives (PO7) is to prepare external financial reports. You take part in preparing and reviewing financial statements – and all accompanying information – and you do it in accordance with legal and regulatory requirements. Working through this chapter should help you understand how to demonstrate that objective.

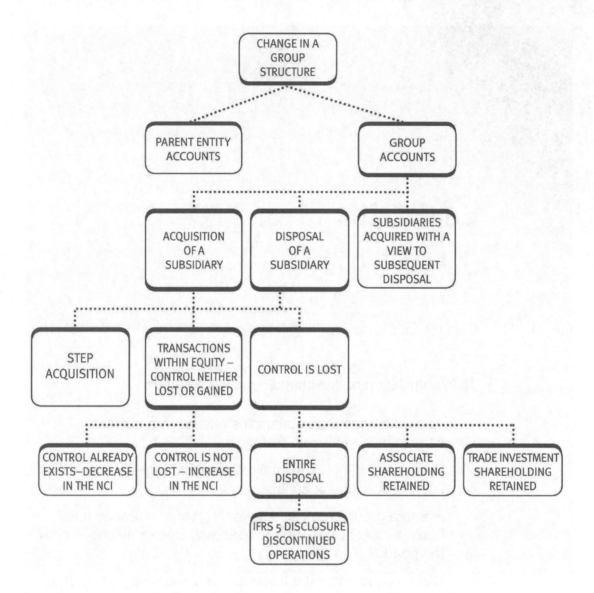

 **1 Acquisition of a subsidiary**

There are two acquisition scenarios that need to be considered in more detail:

- mid-year acquisitions
- step acquisitions.

### Mid-year acquisitions

A parent entity consolidates a subsidiary from the date that it achieves control. If this happens partway through the reporting period then it will be necessary to pro-rate the results of the subsidiary so that only the post-acquisition incomes and expenses are consolidated into the group statement of profit or loss.

## Illustration 1 – Tudor – mid-year acquisition of a subsidiary

On 1 July 20X4 Tudor purchased 1,600,000 of the 2,000,000 $1 equity shares of Windsor for $10,280,000. At the date of acquisition the retained earnings of Windsor were $6,150,000.

The statements of profit or loss for each entity for the year ended 31 March 20X5 were as follows.

|  | Tudor | Windsor |
| --- | --- | --- |
|  | $000 | $000 |
| Revenue | 60,000 | 24,000 |
| Cost of sales | (42,000) | (20,000) |
| Gross profit | 18,000 | 4,000 |
| Distribution costs | (2,500) | (50) |
| Administrative expenses | (3,500) | (150) |
| Profit from operations | 12,000 | 3,800 |
| Investment income | 75 | – |
| Finance costs | – | (200) |
| Profit before tax | 12,075 | 3,600 |
| Tax | (3,000) | (600) |
| Profit for the year | 9,075 | 3,000 |
| Retained earnings bfd | 16,525 | 5,400 |

There were no items of other comprehensive income in the year.

The following information is relevant:

1 The fair values of Windsor's net assets at the date of acquisition were equal to their carrying values with the exception of plant and equipment, which had a carrying value of $2,000,000 but a fair value of $5,200,000. The remaining useful life of this plant and equipment was four years at the date of acquisition. Depreciation is charged to cost of sales and is time apportioned on a monthly basis.

2 During the post-acquisition period Tudor sold goods to Windsor for $12 million. The goods had originally cost $9 million. During the remaining months of the year Windsor sold $10 million (at cost to Windsor) of these goods to third parties for $13 million.

3 Incomes and expenses accrued evenly throughout the year.

4    Tudor has a policy of valuing non-controlling interests using the full goodwill method. The fair value of non-controlling interest at the date of acquisition was $2,520,000.

5    The recoverable amount of the net assets of Windsor at the reporting date was $14,150,000. Any goodwill impairment should be charged to administrative expenses.

**Required:**

**Prepare a consolidated statement of profit or loss for Tudor group for the year ended 31 March 20X5.**

### Solution

**Tudor group statement of profit or loss for the year ended 31 March 20X5**

|  | $000 |
|---|---:|
| Revenue ($60,000 + (9/12 × $24,000) – $12,000) | 66,000 |
| Cost of sales | |
| ($42,000 + (9/12 × $20,000) – $12,000 + $600 (W6) + $500 (W5)) | (46,100) |
| | |
| Gross profit | 19,900 |
| Distribution costs ($2,500 + (9/12 × $50)) | (2,538) |
| Administrative expenses | |
| ($3,500 + (9/12 × $150) + $300 (W2)) | (3,912) |
| | |
| Profit from operations | 13,450 |
| Investment income ($75 + nil) | 75 |
| Finance costs (nil + (9/12 × $200)) | (150) |
| | |
| Profit before tax | 13,375 |
| Tax ($3,000 + (9/12 × $600)) | (3,450) |
| | |
| Profit after tax for the year | 9,925 |
| | |
| Profit attributable to: | |
| Owners of the parent (bal. fig) | 9,655 |
| Non-controlling interest (W7) | 270 |
| | |
| | 9,925 |

There were no items of other comprehensive income in the year.

**(W1) Group structure – Tudor owns 80% of Windsor**

- the acquisition took place three months into the year
- nine months is post-acquisition.

**(W2) Goodwill impairment**

|  | $000 |
|---|---|
| Net assets of the subsidiary (W3) | 13,000 |
| Goodwill (W4) | 1,450 |
|  | 14,450 |
| Recoverable amount | (14,150) |
| Impairment | 300 |

The impairment will be allocated against goodwill and charged to the statement of profit or loss.

Goodwill has been calculated using the fair value method so the impairment needs to be factored in when calculating the profit attributable to the NCI (W7).

**(W3) Net assets**

|  | Acq'n date | Rep. date |
|---|---|---|
|  | $000 | $000 |
| Equity capital | 2,000 | 2,000 |
| Retained earnings | 6,150 | 8,400 |
| (Rep date = $5,400 bfd + $3,000) | | |
| Fair value adjustment – PPE | | |
| ($5.2m – $2.0m) | 3,200 | 3,200 |
| Depreciation on FVA (W6) | – | (600) |
|  | 11,350 | 13,000 |

**(W4) Goodwill**

|  | $000 |
|---|---|
| Consideration | 10,280 |
| FV of NCI at acquisition | 2,520 |
|  | 12,800 |
| FV of net assets at acquisition (W3) | (11,350) |
| Goodwill pre-impairment review (W2) | 1,450 |

> **(W5) PURP**
>
> $2 million ($12m – $10m) of the $12 million intra-group sale remains in inventory.
>
> The profit that remains in inventory is $500,000 (($12m – $9m) × 2/12).
>
> **(W6) Excess depreciation**
>
> Per W3, there has been a fair value uplift in respect of PPE of $3,200,000.
>
> This uplift will be depreciated over the four year remaining life.
>
> The depreciation charge in respect of this uplift in the current year statement of profit or loss is $600,000 (($3,200,000/4 years) × 9/12).
>
> **(W7) Profit attributable to the NCI**
>
> | | $000 | $000 |
> |---|---|---|
> | Profit of Windsor (9/12 × $3,000) | 2,250 | |
> | Excess depreciation (W6) | (600) | |
> | Goodwill impairment (W2) | (300) | |
> | | 1,350 | |
> | × 20% | | |
> | Profit attributable to the NCI | | 270 |

 **Step acquisitions**

A step acquisition occurs when the parent company acquires control over the subsidiary in stages. This is achieved by buying blocks of shares at different times. Acquisition accounting is only applied at the date when control is achieved.

- Any pre-existing equity interest in an entity is accounted for according to:
  - IFRS 9 in the case of financial instruments
  - IAS 28 in the case of associates and joint ventures
  - IFRS 11 in the case of joint arrangements other than joint ventures.

- At the date when the equity interest is increased and control is achieved:

  1 re-measure the previously held equity interest to fair value

  2 recognise the resulting gain or loss in profit or loss for the year (or in other comprehensive income if the shares had been designated to be measured at fair value through other comprehensive income)

  3 calculate goodwill and the non-controlling interest on either a partial or full basis.

For the purposes of the goodwill calculation, the consideration will be the fair value of the previously held equity interest plus the fair value of the consideration transferred for the most recent purchase of shares at the acquisition date. You may wish to use the following proforma:

|  | $ |
|---|---|
| Fair value of previously held interest | X |
| Fair value of consideration for additional interest | X |
| NCI at acquisition | X |
| Less: FV of net assets at acquisition | (X) |
| | ---- |
| Goodwill at acquisition | X |
| | ---- |

- Any gains and losses recognised in other comprehensive income from the re-measurement of any previously held equity interests cannot be reclassified to profit or loss.

- Purchasing further shares in a subsidiary after control has been acquired (for example taking the group interest from 60% to 75%) is regarded as a transaction between equity holders. Goodwill is not recalculated. This situation is dealt with separately in this chapter.

## Illustration 2 – Ayre, Fleur and Byrne

Ayre has owned 90% of the ordinary shares of Fleur for many years. Ayre also has a 10% investment in the shares of Byrne, which was measured at fair value through profit or loss and held in the consolidated statement of financial position as at 31 December 20X6 at $24,000 in accordance with IFRS 9 *Financial Instruments*. On 30 June 20X7, Ayre acquired a further 50% of Byrne's equity shares at a cost of $160,000.

The draft statements of profit or loss for the three companies for the year ended 31 December 20X7 are presented below:

**Statements of profit or loss for the year ended 31 December 20X7**

|  | Ayre | Fleur | Byrne |
|---|---|---|---|
|  | $000 | $000 | $000 |
| Revenue | 500 | 300 | 200 |
| Cost of sales | (300) | (70) | (120) |
|  |  |  |  |
| Gross profit | 200 | 230 | 80 |
| Operating costs | (60) | (80) | (60) |
|  |  |  |  |
| Profit from operations | 140 | 150 | 20 |
| Income tax | (28) | (30) | (4) |
|  |  |  |  |
| Profit for the period | 112 | 120 | 16 |
|  |  |  |  |

The non-controlling interest is calculated using the fair value method. On 30 June 20X7, fair values were as follows:

- Byrne's identifiable net assets – $200,000

- The non-controlling interest in Byrne – $100,000

- The original 10% investment in Byrne – $26,000

**Required:**

**Prepare the consolidated statement of profit or loss for the Ayre Group for the year ended 31 December 20X7 and calculate the goodwill arising on the acquisition of Byrne.**

## Solution

**Group statement of profit or loss for the year ended 31 December 20X7**

|  | $000 |
|---|---|
| Revenue ($500 + $300 + (6/12 × $200)) | 900 |
| Cost of sales ($300 + $70 + (6/12 × $120)) | (430) |
| Gross profit | 470 |
| Operating costs ($60 + $80 + (6/12 × $60)) | (170) |
| Profit from operations | 300 |
| Profit on derecognition of equity investment (W1) | 2 |
|  | 302 |
| Income tax ($28 + $30 + (6/12 × $4)) | (60) |
| Profit for the period | 242 |
| Profit attributable to: |  |
| Equity holders of the parent (bal. fig) | 226.8 |
| Non-controlling interest (W2) | 15.2 |
| Profit for the period | 242 |

## Goodwill calculation

|  | $000 |
|---|---|
| FV of previously held interest | 26 |
| FV of consideration for additional interest | 160 |
| NCI at acquisition date | 100 |
| FV of net assets at acquisition | (200) |
| Goodwill | 86 |

**(W1) Group structure**

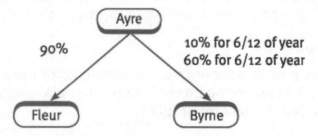

This is a step acquisition. The previous investment in shares must be revalued to fair value with the gain on revaluation recorded in the statement of profit or loss.

| Dr Investment ($26,000 – $24,000) | $2,000 |
|---|---|
| Cr Profit or loss | $2,000 |

The investment, now held at $26,000, is included in the calculation of goodwill.

Ayre had control over Byrne for 6/12 of the current year. Therefore 6/12 of the incomes and expenses of Byrne are consolidated in full.

**(W2) Profit attributable to the NCI**

|  | $000 | $000 |
|---|---|---|
| Profit of Fleur in consolidated profit or loss | 120 | |
| × 10% | | 12 |
| Profit of Byrne in consolidated profit or loss (6/12 × $16) | 8 | |
| × 40% | | 3.2 |
| Profit attributable to NCI | | 15.2 |

**Test your understanding 1 – Major and Tom**

Major, a public limited entity, has numerous subsidiaries and has prepared consolidated financial statements for many years.

Major acquired 40% of Tom's 100,000 $1 ordinary shares on 31 December 20X4 for $90,000 in cash. This holding gave Major significant influence over Tom. The retained earnings of Tom at this date were $76,000.

Major acquired a further 20% of Tom's ordinary shares on 31 December 20X6 for $70,000 in cash. On this date, the fair value of the previous 40% holding in Tom was $105,000 and Tom's retained earnings balance was $100,000. The non-controlling interest at acquisition should be valued using the proportion of net assets method.

**Required:**

**Discuss how to account for the purchase of the additional 20% holding in Tom in the consolidated financial statements for the year ended 31 December 20X6.**

## 2 Disposal of a subsidiary

During the year, one entity may sell some or all of its shares in another entity causing a loss of control.

Possible situations include:

1     the disposal of all the shares held in the subsidiary

2     the disposal of part of the shareholding, leaving a residual holding after the sale, which is regarded as an associate

3     the disposal of part of the shareholding, leaving a residual holding after the sale, which is regarded as a trade investment.

The accounting treatment of all of these situations is very similar.

### Disposals in the individual financial statements

In all of the above scenarios, the profit on disposal in the investing entity's individual financial statements is calculated as follows:

|  | $ |
|---|---|
| Sales proceeds | X |
| Carrying amount of shares sold | (X) |
|  | —— |
| Profit/(loss) on disposal | X/(X) |
|  | —— |

The profit or loss may need to be reported as an exceptional item. If so, it must be disclosed separately on the face of the parent's statement of profit or loss for the year.

There may be tax to pay on this gain, depending on the tax laws in place in the parent's jurisdiction. This would result in an increase to the parent company's tax expense in the statement of profit or loss.

 **Disposals in the consolidated financial statements**

If the sale of shares causes control over a subsidiary to be lost, then the treatment in the consolidated financial statements is as follows:

- Consolidate the incomes and expenses of the subsidiary up until the disposal date

- On disposal of the subsidiary, derecognise its assets, liabilities, goodwill and non-controlling interest and calculate a profit or loss on disposal

- Recognise any remaining investment in the shares of the former subsidiary at fair value and subsequently account for this under the relevant accounting standard

  - A holding of 20–50% of the shares would probably mean that the remaining investment is an associate, which should be accounted for using the equity method

  - A holding of less than 20% of the shares would probably mean that the remaining investment should be accounted for under IFRS 9 *Financial Instruments*.

Where control of a subsidiary has been lost, the following template should be used for the calculation of the profit or loss on disposal:

|  | $ | $ |
|---|---|---|
| Disposal proceeds |  | X |
| Fair value of retained interest |  | X |
|  |  | ––– |
|  |  | X |
|  |  |  |
| Less interest in subsidiary disposed of: |  |  |
| Net assets of subsidiary at disposal date | X |  |
| Goodwill at disposal date | X |  |
| Less: Carrying amount of NCI at disposal date | (X) |  |
|  | ––– |  |
|  |  | (X) |
|  |  | ––– |
| Profit/(loss) to the group |  | X/(X) |
|  |  | ––– |

**Illustration 3 – Rock**

Rock has held a 70% investment in Dog for two years. Goodwill has been calculated using the full goodwill method. There have been no goodwill impairments to date.

Rock disposes of all of its shares in Dog. The following information has been provided:

|  | $ |
| --- | --- |
| Cost of investment | 2,000 |
| Dog – Fair value of net assets at acquisition | 1,900 |
| Dog – Fair value of the non-controlling interest at acquisition | 800 |
| Sales proceeds | 3,000 |
| Dog – Net assets at disposal | 2,400 |

**Required:**

**Calculate the profit or loss on disposal in:**

(a) **Rock's individual financial statements**

(b) **the consolidated financial statements.**

 **Solution**

(a) **Rock's individual financial statements**

|  | $ |
| --- | --- |
| Sales proceeds | 3,000 |
| Cost of shares sold | (2,000) |
| | ——— |
| Profit on disposal | 1,000 |

(b) **Consolidated financial statements**

|  | $ | $ |
| --- | --- | --- |
| Sales proceeds | | 3,000 |
| Interest in subsidiary disposed of: | | |
| Net assets at disposal | 2,400 | |
| Goodwill at disposal (W1) | 900 | |
| Carrying amount of NCI at disposal (W2) | (950) | |
| | ——— | |
| | | (2,350) |
| | | ——— |
| Profit on disposal | | 650 |

(W1) **Goodwill**

|  | $ |
|---|---|
| Consideration | 2,000 |
| FV of NCI at acquisition | 800 |
|  | 2,800 |
| FV of net assets at acquisition | (1,900) |
| Goodwill | 900 |

(W2) **NCI at disposal date**

|  | $ |
|---|---|
| NCI at acquisition | 800 |
| NCI % of post-acquisition net assets (30% × ($2,400 – $1,900)) | 150 |
|  | 950 |

### Illustration 4 – Thomas and Percy

Thomas disposed of a 25% holding in Percy on 30 June 20X6 for $125,000. A 70% holding in Percy had been acquired five years prior to this. Thomas uses the full goodwill method. Goodwill was impaired and written off in full prior to the year of disposal.

Details of Percy are as follows:

|  | $ |
|---|---|
| Net assets at disposal date | 340,000 |
| Fair value of a 45% holding at 30 June 20X6 | 245,000 |

The carrying amount of the NCI was $80,000 at the disposal date.

**Required:**

**Discuss the accounting treatment of the above in the consolidated financial statements.**

## Solution

The group's holding in Percy has reduced from 70% to 45%. Control over Percy has been lost and a profit or loss on disposal must be calculated.

The profit on disposal to be included in the consolidated statement of profit or loss is calculated as follows:

|  | $ | $ |
|---|---|---|
| Proceeds |  | 125,000 |
| FV of retained interest |  | 245,000 |
|  |  | ――――― |
|  |  | 370,000 |
| Net assets recognised at disposal | 340,000 |  |
| Goodwill at disposal | – |  |
| Less: NCI at disposal date | (80,000) |  |
|  | ――――― |  |
|  |  | (260,000) |
|  |  | ――――― |
| Profit on disposal |  | 110,000 |
|  |  | ――――― |

On 30 June 20X6, the remaining investment in Percy will be recognised at its fair value of $245,000. A 45% shareholding would normally give the investor significant influence over the investee and so this would meet the definition of an associate. From 30 June 20X6, the investment will be accounted for using the equity method in the consolidated financial statements.

## Test your understanding 2 – Padstow

Padstow purchased 80% of the shares in St Merryn four years ago for $100,000. On 30 June it sold all of these shares for $250,000. The net assets of St Merryn at the acquisition date were $69,000 and at the disposal date were $88,000. Fifty per cent of the goodwill arising on acquisition had been written off in an earlier year. The fair value of the non-controlling interest in St Merryn at the date of acquisition was $15,000. It is group policy to account for goodwill using the full goodwill method.

**Required:**

(a) **Calculate the profit or loss arising to the parent entity on the disposal of the shares.**

(b) **Calculate the profit or loss arising to the group on the disposal of the shares.**

## Test your understanding 3 – Hague

Hague has held a 60% investment in Maude for several years, using the full goodwill method to value the non-controlling interest. Half of the goodwill has been impaired prior to the date of disposal of shares by Hague. Details are as follows:

|  | $000 |
|---|---|
| Cost of investment | 6,000 |
| Maude – Fair value of net assets at acquisition | 2,000 |
| Maude – Fair value of a 40% investment at acquisition date | 1,000 |
| Maude – Net assets at disposal | 3,000 |
| Maude – Fair value of a 25% investment at disposal date | 3,500 |

**Required:**

(a) **Assuming a full disposal of the holding and proceeds of $10 million, calculate the profit or loss arising:**

    (i)    **in Hague's individual financial statements**

    (ii)    **in the consolidated financial statements.**

(b) **Assuming a disposal of a 35% holding and proceeds of $5 million:**

    (i)    **calculate the profit or loss arising in the consolidated financial statements**

    (ii)    **explain how the residual shareholding will be accounted for.**

## Presentation of disposed subsidiary in the consolidated financial statements

There are two ways of presenting the results of the disposed subsidiary:

(i) Time-apportionment line-by-line

In the consolidated statement of profit or loss, the income and expenses of the subsidiary are consolidated up to the date of disposal. The traditional way is to time apportion each line of the disposed subsidiary's results.

The profit or loss on disposal of the subsidiary would be presented as an exceptional item.

(ii) Discontinued operation

If the subsidiary qualifies as a discontinued operation in accordance with IFRS 5 *Non-current Assets Held for Sale and Discontinued Operations* then its results are aggregated into a single line on the face of the consolidated statement of profit or loss. This is presented immediately after profit for the period from continuing operations.

This single figure comprises:

– the profit or loss of the subsidiary up to the disposal date

– the profit or loss on the disposal of the subsidiary.

## Test your understanding 4 – Kathmandu

The statements of profit or loss and extracts from the statements of changes in equity for the year ended 31 December 20X9 are as follows:

**Statements of profit or loss for the year ended 31 December 20X9**

|  | Kathmandu group $ | Nepal $ |
|---|---|---|
| Revenue | 553,000 | 450,000 |
| Operating costs | (450,000) | (400,000) |
| | | |
| Operating profits | 103,000 | 50,000 |
| Investment income | 8,000 | – |
| | | |
| Profit before tax | 111,000 | 50,000 |
| Tax | (40,000) | (14,000) |
| | | |
| Profit for the period | 71,000 | 36,000 |

**Extracts from SOCIE for year ended 31 December 20X9**

|  | Kathmandu group $ | Nepal $ |
|---|---|---|
| Retained earnings b/f | 100,000 | 80,000 |
| Profit for the period | 71,000 | 36,000 |
| Dividend paid | (25,000) | (10,000) |
| | | |
| Retained earnings c/f | 146,000 | 106,000 |

There were no items of other comprehensive income during the year.

**Additional information**

- The accounts of the Kathmandu group do not include the results of Nepal.

- On 1 January 20X5 Kathmandu acquired 70% of the shares of Nepal for $100,000 when the fair value of Nepal's net assets was $110,000. Nepal has equity capital of $50,000. At that date, the fair value of the non-controlling interest was $40,000. It is group policy to measure the NCI at fair value at the date of acquisition.

- Nepal paid its 20X9 dividend in cash on 31 March 20X9.

- Goodwill has not been impaired.

**Required:**

(a) **Prepare the group statement of profit or loss for the year ended 31 December 20X9 for the Kathmandu group on the basis that Kathmandu plc sold its holding in Nepal on 1 July 20X9 for $200,000. This disposal is not yet recognised in any way in Kathmandu group's statement of profit or loss. Assume that Nepal does not represent a discontinued operation per IFRS 5.**

(b) **Explain and illustrate how the presentation of the group statement of profit or loss would differ from part (a) if Nepal represented a discontinued activity per IFRS 5.**

(c) **Prepare the group statement of profit or loss for the year ended 31 December 20X9 for the Kathmandu group on the basis that Kathmandu sold half of its holding in Nepal on 1 July 20X9 for $100,000 This disposal is not yet recognised in any way in Kathmandu group's statement of profit or loss. The residual holding of 35% has a fair value of $100,000 and leaves the Kathmandu group with significant influence over Nepal.**

## 3 Control to control scenarios

In this chapter, we have looked at:

- share purchases that have led to control over another company being obtained

- share sales that have led to control over another company being lost.

However, some share purchases will simply increase an entity's holding in an already existing subsidiary (e.g. increasing a holding from 80% to 85%). Similarly, some share sales will not cause an entity to lose control over a subsidiary (e.g. decreasing a holding from 80% to 75%).

These 'control to control' scenarios will now be considered in more detail.

**Increasing a shareholding in a subsidiary (e.g. 80% to 85%)**

When a parent company increases its shareholding in a subsidiary, this is not treated as an acquisition in the group financial statements. For example, if the parent holds 80% of the shares in a subsidiary and buys 5% more, then the relationship remains one of a parent and subsidiary. However, the NCI holding has decreased from 20% to 15%.

The accounting treatment of the above situation is as follows:

- The NCI within equity decreases

- The difference between the consideration paid for the extra shares and the decrease in the NCI is accounted for within equity (normally, in 'other components of equity').

Note that **no profit or loss** arises on the purchase of the additional shares. Goodwill is **not recalculated**.

The following proforma will help to calculate the adjustments required to NCI and other components of equity:

|  | $ |  |
|---|---|---|
| Cash paid | X | Cr |
| Decrease in NCI | (X) | Dr |
| Decrease/(increase) to other components of equity | X/(X) | Dr/Cr (bal. entry) |

The decrease in NCI will represent the proportionate reduction in the carrying amount of the NCI at the date of the group's additional purchase of shares. For example, if the NCI shareholding reduces from 30% to 20%, then the carrying amount of the NCI must be reduced by one-third.

 **Test your understanding 5 – Gordon and Mandy**

Gordon has owned 80% of Mandy for many years.

Gordon is considering acquiring more shares in Mandy. The NCI of Mandy currently has a carrying amount of $20,000, with the net assets and goodwill having a carrying amount of $125,000 and $25,000 respectively.

Gordon is considering the following two scenarios:

(i) Gordon could buy 20% of the Mandy shares leaving no NCI for $25,000, or

(ii) Gordon could buy 5% of the Mandy shares for $4,000 leaving a 15% NCI.

**Required:**

**Calculate the adjustments required to NCI and other components of equity.**

**Sale of shares without losing control (e.g. 80% to 75%)**

From the perspective of the group accounts, a sale of shares which results in the parent retaining control over the subsidiary is simply a transaction between shareholders. If the parent company holds 80% of the shares of a subsidiary but then sells a 5% holding, a relationship of control still exists. As such, the subsidiary will still be consolidated in the group financial statements. However, the NCI has risen from 20% to 25%.

The accounting treatment of the above situation is as follows:

- The NCI within equity is increased

- The difference between the proceeds received and the increase in the non-controlling interest is accounted within equity (normally, in 'other components of equity').

Note that **no profit or loss** arises on the sale of the shares. Goodwill is **not recalculated**.

The following proforma will help to calculate the adjustments required to NCI and other components of equity:

|  | $ |  |
|---|---|---|
| Cash proceeds received | X | Dr |
| Increase in NCI | (X) | Cr |
| Increase/(Decrease) to other components of equity | X/(X) | Cr/Dr (bal. entry) |

The increase in the NCI will be the share of the net assets (always) and goodwill (fair value method only) of the subsidiary at the date of disposal which the parent has effectively sold to the NCI.

- For example, if the NCI shareholding increases from 20% to 30%, then the carrying amount of the NCI must be increased by 10% of the subsidiary's net assets and, if using the fair value method, goodwill.

 **Illustration 5 – No loss of control – Juno**

Until 30 September 20X7, Juno held 90% of Hera. On that date it sold a 10% interest in the equity capital for $15,000. At the date of the share disposal, the carrying amount of net assets and goodwill of Hera were $100,000 and $20,000 respectively. At acquisition, the NCI was valued at fair value.

**Required:**

**Discuss the treatment of the above in the Juno Group's financial statements?**

## Solution

Juno's shareholding has decreased from 90% to 80%. Juno still exercises control over Hera and therefore Hera continues to be a subsidiary.

No gain or loss on the sale of the shares is recognised in the consolidated financial statements. Goodwill is not recalculated. Instead, the transaction is accounted for in equity, as an increase to the non-controlling interest.

|  | $ |
|---|---|
| Cash proceeds | 15,000 Dr |
| Increase in NCI: 10% × ($100,000 + $20,000) | (12,000) Cr |
| | ———— |
| Increase in other components of equity (bal. fig) | 3,000 Cr |
| | ———— |

The non-controlling interest should be increased by $12,000. The difference between the proceeds received and the increase in the non-controlling interest is $3,000 and this will be recognised as an increase to the equity attributable to the owners of Juno.

## Test your understanding 6 – David and Goliath

David has owned 90% of Goliath's ordinary shares for many years. On the last day of the reporting period, David sold 5% of Goliath's ordinary shares for $5,000 (leaving it with a holding of 85%).

At the date of the sale, net assets and goodwill of Goliath were carried in the consolidated financial statements at $70,000 and $20,000 respectively. The NCI of Goliath at acquisition was valued at fair value.

**Required:**

**Discuss how the share sale should be accounted for in the consolidated financial statements of the David group?**

## Test your understanding 7 – Pepsi

Statements of financial position for three entities at the reporting date are as follows:

| | Pepsi $000 | Sprite $000 | Tango $000 |
|---|---|---|---|
| Assets | 1,000 | 800 | 500 |
| Investment in Sprite | 326 | – | – |
| Investment in Tango | 165 | – | – |
| | ———— | ———— | ———— |
| Total assets | 1,491 | 800 | 500 |
| | ———— | ———— | ———— |

| Equity | | | |
|---|---|---|---|
| Ordinary share capital ($1) | 500 | 200 | 100 |
| Retained earnings | 391 | 100 | 200 |
| | 891 | 300 | 300 |
| Liabilities | 600 | 500 | 200 |
| Total equity and liabilities | 1,491 | 800 | 500 |

### Investment in Sprite

Pepsi acquired 80% of Sprite when Sprite's retained earnings were $25,000, paying cash consideration of $300,000. It is group policy to measure NCI at fair value at the date of acquisition. The fair value of the NCI holding in Sprite at acquisition was $65,000.

At the reporting date, Pepsi purchased an additional 8% of Sprite's equity shares for cash consideration of $26,000. This amount has been debited to Pepsi's investment in Sprite.

### Investment in Tango

Pepsi acquired 75% of Tango when Tango's retained earnings were $60,000, paying cash consideration of $200,000. The fair value of the NCI holding in Tango at the date of acquisition was $50,000.

At the reporting date, Pepsi sold 10% of the equity shares of Tango for $35,000. The cash proceeds have been credited to Pepsi's investment in Tango.

### Required:

**Discuss how to account for the purchase of the additional 8% holding in Sprite's equity shares and the sale of the 10% holding in Tango's equity shares.**

## 4 Subsidiaries acquired exclusively with a view to resale

A subsidiary acquired exclusively with a view to resale is not exempt from consolidation. However, if it meets the 'held for sale' criteria in IFRS 5 *Non-current Assets Held for Sale and Discontinued Operations*:

- it is presented in the financial statements as a disposal group classified as held for sale. This is achieved by amalgamating all its assets into one line item and all its liabilities into another

- it is measured, both on acquisition and at subsequent reporting dates, at fair value less costs to sell.

The 'held for sale' criteria in IFRS 5 include the requirements that:

- the subsidiary is available for immediate sale
- the sale is highly probable
- it is likely to be disposed of within one year of the date of its acquisition.

A newly acquired subsidiary which meets these held for sale criteria automatically meets the criteria for being presented as a discontinued operation.

### Illustration 6 – IFRS 5

David acquires Rose on 1 March 20X7. Rose is a holding entity with two wholly-owned subsidiaries, Mickey and Jackie. Jackie is acquired exclusively with a view to resale and meets the criteria for classification as held for sale. David's year-end is 30 September.

On 1 March 20X7 the following information is relevant:

- the identifiable liabilities of Jackie have a fair value of $40m
- the acquired assets of Jackie have a fair value of $180m
- the expected costs of selling Jackie are $5m.

On 30 September 20X7, the assets of Jackie have a fair value of $170m.

The liabilities have a fair value of $35m and the selling costs remain at $5m.

**Discuss how Jackie will be treated in the David Group financial statements on acquisition and at 30 September 20X7.**

### Solution

On acquisition the assets and liabilities of Jackie are measured at fair value less costs to sell in accordance with IFRS 5:

|  | $m |
|---|---|
| Assets | 180 |
| Less selling costs | (5) |
|  | 175 |
| Liabilities | (40) |
| Fair value less costs to sell | 135 |

At the reporting date, the assets and liabilities of Jackie are remeasured to update the fair value less costs to sell.

|  | $m |
|---|---|
| Assets | 170 |
| Less selling costs | (5) |
|  | ——— |
|  | 165 |
| Liabilities | (35) |
|  | ——— |
| Fair value less costs to sell | 130 |
|  | ——— |

The fair value less costs to sell has decreased from $135m on 1 March to $130m on 30 September. This $5m reduction in fair value must be presented in the consolidated statement of profit or loss as part of the single line item entitled 'discontinued operations'. Also included in this line is the post-tax profit or loss earned/incurred by Jackie in the March – September 20X7 period.

The assets and liabilities of Jackie must be disclosed separately on the face of the statement of financial position. Jackie's assets will appear below the subtotal for the David group's current assets:

|  | $m |
|---|---|
| Non-current assets classified as held for sale | 165 |

Jackie's liabilities will appear below the subtotal for the David group's current liabilities:

|  | $m |
|---|---|
| Liabilities directly associated with non-current assets classified as held for sale | 35 |

No other disclosure is required.

## 5 Disposal of an associate

When significant influence over an associate is lost - most likely as a result of a share sale – then the investment in the associate is derecognised. Any shares retained are likely to fall within the scope of IFRS 9 *Financial Instruments* and should be recognised at fair value.

A profit or loss on disposal will arise in the consolidated statement of profit or loss. This is calculated as follows:

|  | $ |
|---|---|
| Disposal proceeds | X |
| Fair value of retained interest | X |
| Carrying amount of associate at disposal | (X) |
|  | ——— |
| Profit/(loss) to the group | X/(X) |
|  | ——— |

## 6 Group reorganisation

### What is a reorganisation?

A group reorganisation (or restructuring) is any of the following:

(a) the transfer of shares in a subsidiary from one group entity to another

(b) the addition of a new parent entity to a group

(c) the transfer of shares in one or more subsidiaries of a group to a new entity that is not a group entity but whose shareholders are the same as those of the group's parent

(d) the combination into a group of two or more companies that before the combination had the same shareholders

(e) the acquisition of the shares of another entity that itself then issues sufficient shares so that the acquired entity has control of the combined entity.

### Reorganisations and individual financial statements

A parent may reorganise the structure of its group by establishing a new entity as its parent. In this case, as long as certain criteria are met, the new parent records the cost of the original parent in its separate financial statements as the carrying amount of **'its share of the equity items shown in the separate financial statements of the original parent at the date of the reorganisation'** (IAS 27, para 13). The criteria that must be met are as follows:

- **'The new parent obtains control of the original parent by issuing equity instruments in exchange for existing equity instruments of the original parent**

- **The assets and liabilities of the new group and the original group are the same immediately before and after the reorganisation**

- **The owners of the original parent before the reorganisation have the same absolute and relative interests in the net assets of the original group and the new group immediately before and after the reorganisation'** (IAS 27, para 13).

The above rule also applies when an entity that is not a parent establishes a new entity as its parent.

### Reorganisations and consolidated financial statements

Assuming that all subsidiaries are 100% owned, a group reorganisation generally has no impact on the consolidated financial statements. This is because assets and investments are being moved around within the group.

## 7 Exam focus

Question 1 in the SBR exam will always test group accounting but will not ask for the production of full consolidated financial statements. Candidates will be required to produce extracts from these statements and to explain the numbers that they have produced. You should attempt the SBR specimen papers and past exam papers (included in the Exam Kit) to ensure you are comfortable with this style of requirement. The following question also provides relevant practice.

### Test your understanding 9 – Liesel

Liesel Group has a reporting date of 31 December 20X1 and prepares its financial statements in accordance with IFRS Standards. The directors of Liesel require advice about the impact of a number of share transactions on the consolidated financial statements.

**Rosa**

Six years ago, Liesel purchased 85% of the ordinary shares of Rosa. The non-controlling interest at acquisition was measured at fair value. On 31 December 20X1, Liesel sold a 5% holding in Rosa for $9 million, and therefore reduced its stake to 80%. At this date, the goodwill and net assets of Rosa were carried at $8 million and $120 million respectively. The directors of Liesel have posted the following accounting entry in the consolidated financial statements:

| | |
|---|---|
| Dr Cash | $9m |
| Cr Profit or loss | $9m |

## Hans

Several years ago Liesel purchased 70% of the ordinary shares of Hans for $105 million. At the acquisition date the carrying amount of the net assets of Hans was $100 million. The identifiable net assets of Hans were carried at fair value with the exception of freehold non-depreciable land which had a carrying amount of $5 million and a fair value of $15 million. The non-controlling interest was measured at its fair value of $36 million.

On 1 October 20X1, Liesel sold a 40% holding in the ordinary shares of Hans for $72 million. The cash received has been recognised in the consolidated financial statements and the other side of the entry has been posted to a suspense account. The directors believe that the remaining 30% holding gives Liesel significant influence over Hans. The fair value of the 30% holding on 1 October 20X1 was $51 million. Extracts from the individual (non-consolidated) financial statements of Hans for the year ended 31 December 20X1 are provided below:

|                                           | $m  |
|-------------------------------------------|-----|
| Share capital                             | 8   |
| Retained earnings as at 1 January 20X1    | 130 |
| Profit for year ended 31 December 20X1    | 20  |

The directors of Liesel Group are unsure how they should have treated the investment in Hans in the consolidated financial statements for the year ended 31 December 20X1.

**Required:**

**Explain, with calculations, how the above share transactions should be dealt with in the consolidated financial statements for the year ended 31 December 20X1.**

## 8 Chapter summary

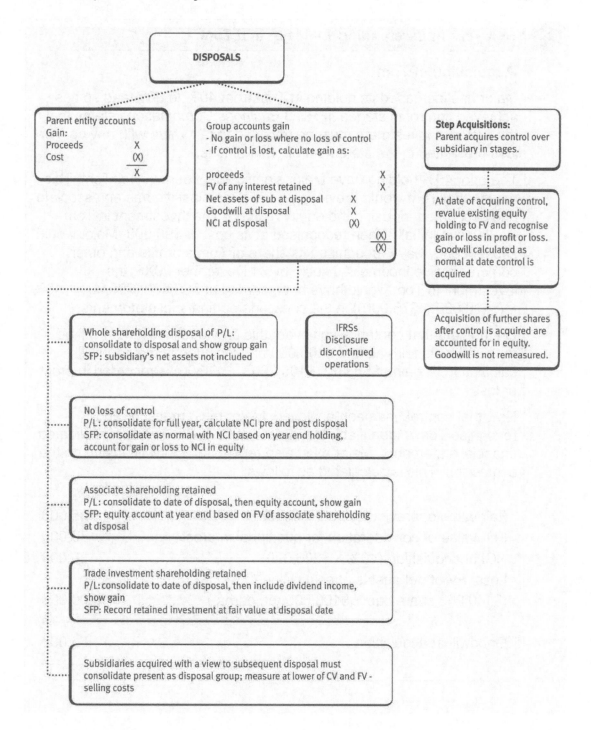

**DISPOSALS**

**Parent entity accounts**
Gain:
| | |
|---|---|
| Proceeds | X |
| Cost | (X) |
| | X |

**Group accounts gain**
- No gain or loss where no loss of control
- If control is lost, calculate gain as:

| | | |
|---|---|---|
| proceeds | | X |
| FV of any interest retained | | X |
| Net assets of sub at disposal | X | |
| Goodwill at disposal | X | |
| NCI at disposal | (X) | |
| | | (X) |
| | | (X) |

**Step Acquisitions:**
Parent acquires control over subsidiary in stages.

At date of acquiring control, revalue existing equity holding to FV and recognise gain or loss in profit or loss. Goodwill calculated as normal at date control is acquired

Whole shareholding disposal of P/L:
consolidate to disposal and show group gain
SFP: subsidiary's net assets not included

IFRSs
Disclosure
discontinued
operations

Acquisition of further shares after control is acquired are accounted for in equity. Goodwill is not remeasured.

**No loss of control**
P/L: consolidate for full year, calculate NCI pre and post disposal
SFP: consolidate as normal with NCI based on year end holding, account for gain or loss to NCI in equity

**Associate shareholding retained**
P/L: consolidate to date of disposal, then equity account, show gain
SFP: equity account at year end based on FV of associate shareholding at disposal

**Trade investment shareholding retained**
P/L: consolidate to date of disposal, then include dividend income, show gain
SFP: Record retained investment at fair value at disposal date

Subsidiaries acquired with a view to subsequent disposal must consolidate present as disposal group; measure at lower of CV and FV - selling costs

## Test your understanding answers

 **Test your understanding 1 – Major and Tom**

### Acquisition of Tom

Major has increased its holding in Tom from 40% to 60% and so has achieved control in stages. IFRS 3 *Business Combinations* states that the previous investment must be revalued to fair value with any gain or loss presented in the statement of profit or loss.

The prior 40% holding gave Major significant influence over Tom. This means that Tom would previously have been classified as an associate and accounted for using the equity method. The investment in Tom would have initially been recognised at its cost of $90,000. Major would subsequently have recognised its share of Tom's profits and other comprehensive income. As such, by 31 December 20X6, the investment in Tom would have been carried at $99,600 ($90,000 + 40% × ($100,000 − $76,000)) in the consolidated financial statements.

On the date that control is achieved, this previous investment will be revalued to its fair value of $105,000 and included in the goodwill calculation. A gain of $5,400 ($105,000 − $99,600) is recorded in profit or loss.

Now that control has been achieved, Major must measure and recognise Tom's identifiable net assets at fair value in the consolidated financial statements. Major must also recognise goodwill arising on the acquisition. This is calculated as follows:

|  | $ |
|---|---|
| Fair value of previously held interest | 105,000 |
| Fair value of consideration for additional interest | 70,000 |
| NCI at acquisition (40% × $200,000) | 80,000 |
| Less: FV of net assets at acquisition | |
| ($100,000 share cap + $100,000 ret. earns.) | (200,000) |
| | ——— |
| Goodwill at acquisition | 55,000 |
| | ——— |

## Test your understanding 2 – Padstow

**(a)  Profit to Padstow**

|  | $000 |
|---|---|
| Sales proceeds | 250 |
| Cost of shares sold | (100) |
| | |
| Profit on disposal | 150 |

**(b)  Consolidated accounts**

|  | $000 | $000 |
|---|---|---|
| Sales proceeds | | 250 |
| Net assets at disposal date | 88.0 | |
| Goodwill at disposal date (W1) | 23.0 | |
| Less: NCI at disposal date (W2) | (14.2) | |
| | | (96.8) |
| Profit on disposal | | 153.2 |

**(W1) Goodwill**

|  | $000 |
|---|---|
| Consideration | 100.0 |
| NCI at acquisition | 15.0 |
| FV of net assets at acquisition | (69.0) |
| | |
| Goodwill at acquisition | 46.0 |
| Impairment ($46 × 50%) | (23.0) |
| | |
| Goodwill at disposal date | 23.0 |

**(W2) NCI at disposal date**

|  | $000 |
|---|---|
| NCI at acquisition | 15.0 |
| NCI % of post-acq'n net assets movement (20% × ($88.0 – $69.0)) | 3.8 |
| NCI % of impairment (20% × $23.0 (W1)) | (4.6) |
| | |
| | 14.2 |

**Test your understanding 3 – Hague**

(a) **Full disposal**

   (i) **Profit in Hague's individual financial statements**

| | $000 |
|---|---:|
| Sale proceeds | 10,000 |
| Cost of shares | (6,000) |
| | |
| Profit on disposal | 4,000 |

   (ii) **Profit in consolidated financial statements**

| | $000 | $000 |
|---|---:|---:|
| Sale proceeds | | 10,000 |
| FV of retained interest | | nil |
| CV of subsidiary at disposal: | | |
| Net assets at disposal: | 3,000 | |
| Goodwill at disposal (W1) | 2,500 | |
| Less: NCI at disposal date (W2) | (400) | |
| | | (5,100) |
| | | |
| Profit on disposal | | 4,900 |

   **(W1) Goodwill**

| | $000 |
|---|---:|
| Consideration | 6,000 |
| NCI at acquisition | 1,000 |
| FV of NA at acquisition | (2,000) |
| | |
| Goodwill at acquisition | 5,000 |
| Impaired (50%) | (2,500) |
| | |
| Goodwill at disposal | 2,500 |

(W2) **NCI at disposal date**

|  | $000 |
|---|---|
| NCI at acquisition | 1,000 |
| NCI share of post-acquisition net assets (40% × ($3,000 – $2,000)) | 400 |
| Less: NCI share of goodwill impairment (40% × $2,500) (W1) | (1,000) |
|  | 400 |

(b) **Disposal of a 35% shareholding**

   (i)   **Profit in consolidated financial statements**

|  | $000 | $000 |
|---|---|---|
| Disposal proceeds | | 5,000 |
| FV of retained interest | | 3,500 |
|  | | 8,500 |
| CV of subsidiary at disposal date: | | |
| Net assets at disposal | 3,000 | |
| Goodwill at disposal (W1) | 2,500 | |
| Less: NCI at disposal date (W2) | (400) | |
|  | | (5,100) |
| Profit on disposal | | 3,400 |

   (ii)   After the date of disposal, the residual holding will be accounted for using the equity method in the consolidated financial statements:

     –   The statement of profit or loss will show the group's share of the current year profit earned by the associate from the date significant influence was obtained.

     –   The statement of financial position will show the carrying value of the investment in the associate. This will be the fair value of the retained shareholding at the disposal date plus the group's share of the increase in reserves from this date.

**Test your understanding 4 – Kathmandu**

(a) **Consolidated statement of profit or loss – full disposal**

| | $ |
|---|---:|
| Revenue ($553,000 + (6/12 × $450,000)) | 778,000 |
| Operating costs ($450,000 + (6/12 × $400,000)) | (650,000) |
| | |
| Operating profit | 128,000 |
| Investment income ($8,000 – ($10,000 × 70%)) | 1,000 |
| Profit on disposal (W1) | 80,400 |
| | |
| Profit before tax | 209,400 |
| Tax ($40,000 + (6/12 × $14,000)) | (47,000) |
| | |
| Profit for the period | 162,400 |
| | |
| Attributable to: | |
| Equity holders of Kathmandu (bal. fig) | 157,000 |
| Non-controlling interest (W5) | 5,400 |
| | |
| | 162,400 |

There were no items of other comprehensive income during the year.

(b) **Group statement of profit or loss – discontinued operations presentation**

| | $ |
|---|---:|
| Revenue | 553,000 |
| Operating costs | (450,000) |
| | |
| Operating profit | 103,000 |
| Investment income | 1,000 |
| ($8,000 – (70% × $10,000)) | |
| Profit before tax | 104,000 |
| Tax | (40,000) |
| | |
| Profit for the period from continuing operations | 64,000 |
| Profit from discontinued operations | 98,400 |
| (($36,000 × 6/12) + $80,400 (W1)) | |
| | |
| | 162,400 |

Attributable to:

| | |
|---|---:|
| Equity holders of Kathmandu (bal. fig) | 157,000 |
| Non-controlling interest (W5) | 5,400 |
| | 162,400 |

There were no items of other comprehensive income during the year.

Notice that the post-tax results of the subsidiary up to the date of disposal are presented as a one-line entry in the group statement of profit or loss. There is no line-by-line consolidation of results when this method of presentation is adopted.

(c) **Consolidated statement of profit or loss – partial disposal**

| | $ |
|---|---:|
| Revenue ($553,000 + (6/12 × $450,000) | 778,000 |
| Operating costs ($450,000 + (6/12 × $400,000)) | (650,000) |
| Operating profit | 128,000 |
| Investment income ($8,000 – (70% × $10,000) | 1,000 |
| Income from associate (35% × $36,000 × 6/12) | 6,300 |
| Profit on disposal (W6) | 80,400 |
| Profit before tax | 215,700 |
| Tax ($40,000 + (6/12 × $14,000)) | (47,000) |
| Profit for the period | 168,700 |

There were no items of other comprehensive income during the year.

Attributable to:

| | |
|---|---:|
| Equity holders of Kathmandu (bal. fig) | 163,300 |
| Non-controlling interest (W5) | 5,400 |
| | 168,700 |

---

**(W1) Profit on full disposal (part a)**

|  | $ | $ |
|---|---|---|
| Proceeds |  | 200,000 |
| Interest in subsidiary disposed of: |  |  |
| Net assets at disposal (W2) | 138,000 |  |
| Goodwill at disposal (W3) | 30,000 |  |
| NCI at date of disposal (W4) | (48,400) |  |
|  |  | (119,600) |
| Profit on disposal |  | 80,400 |

**(W2) Net assets of Nepal at disposal**

|  | $ |
|---|---|
| Share capital | 50,000 |
| Retained earnings b/f | 80,000 |
| Profit up to disposal date (6/12 × $36,000) | 18,000 |
| Dividend paid prior to disposal | (10,000) |
| Net assets at disposal | 138,000 |

**(W3) Goodwill**

|  | $ |
|---|---|
| Consideration | 100,000 |
| FV of NCI at date of acquisition | 40,000 |
| FV of net assets at date of acquisition | (110,000) |
| Goodwill | 30,000 |

**(W4) NCI at disposal date**

|  | $ |
|---|---|
| FV of NCI at date of acquisition | 40,000 |
| NCI share of post-acquisition net assets (30% × ($138,000 (W2) – $110,000) | 8,400 |
|  | 48,400 |

---

**(W5) Profit attributable to NCI**

|  | $ | $ |
|---|---|---|
| Profit of Nepal (6/12 × $36,000) | 18,000 | |
| × 30% | 18,000 | |
| Profit attributable to NCI | | 5,400 |

**(W6) Profit on part disposal (part c)**

|  | $ | $ |
|---|---|---|
| Proceeds | | 100,000 |
| FV of retained interest (per question) | | 100,000 |
| | | 200,000 |
| Net assets at disposal (W2) | 138,000 | |
| Goodwill at disposal date (W3) | 30,000 | |
| NCI at date of disposal (W4) | (48,400) | |
| | | (119,600) |
| Profit on disposal | | 80,400 |

---

### Test your understanding 5 – Gordon and Mandy

(i) **Purchase of 20% of Mandy shares**

|  | $ | |
|---|---|---|
| Cash paid | 25,000 | Cr |
| Decrease in NCI ((20%/20%) × 20,000) | (20,000) | Dr |
| Decrease in other components of equity | 5,000 | Dr |

(ii) **Purchase of 5% of Mandy shares**

|  | $ | |
|---|---|---|
| Cash paid | 4,000 | Cr |
| Decrease in NCI ((5%/20%) × 20,000) | (5,000) | Dr |
| Increase in other components of equity | (1,000) | Cr |

## Test your understanding 6 – David and Goliath

David has reduced its holding in Goliath from 90% to 85%. Goliath is a subsidiary of David both before and after the sale. As such, no gain or loss arises in the consolidated financial statements and goodwill is not remeasured.

In the consolidated financial statements, the transaction is accounted for in equity, as an increase to the non-controlling interest. The difference between the $5,000 proceeds received and the increase to the non-controlling interest of $4,500 (W1) is recognised as an increase of $500 (W1) to group equity.

(W1) **Sale of 5% of Goliath shares**

|  | $ |  |
| --- | ---: | --- |
| Cash proceeds | 5,000 | Dr |
| Increase in NCI |  |  |
| (5% × ($70,000 + $20,000) | (4,500) | Cr |
| Increase in other components of equity | 500 | Cr |

## Test your understanding 7 – Pepsi

### Purchase of additional 8% of Sprite

The purchase has increased Pepsi's holding in Sprite from 80% to 88%. Sprite was a subsidiary before and after the purchase so there has been no change in control status. This means that no gain or loss arises on the transaction in the group financial statements and goodwill is not remeasured.

The transaction is accounted for in equity as a decrease in the non-controlling interest. The decrease in NCI will represent the proportionate reduction in the carrying amount of the NCI at the date of Pepsi's additional purchase of shares.

The difference between the consideration paid of $26,000 and the decrease in the non-controlling interest of $32,000 (W1) amounts to $6,000. This will be recorded as an increase to other components of equity.

**(W1) Control to control adjustment – Sprite**

|  | $000 |  |
|---|---|---|
| Cash paid | (26) | Cr |
| Decrease in NCI (8/20 × $80 (W2)) | 32 | Dr |
| Increase to other components of equity | 6 | Cr |

**(W2) Non-controlling interest – Sprite**

|  | $000 |
|---|---|
| NCI at acquisition | 65 |
| NCI% × post acquisition reserves (20% × ($100 – $25)) | 15 |
| NCI before control to control adjustment | 80 |

**Sale of 10% of Tango**

The sale has decreased Pepsi's holding in Tango from 75% to 65%. Tango was a subsidiary before and after the sale so there has been no change in control status. This means that no gain or loss arises on the transaction in the group financial statements and goodwill is not remeasured.

The transaction is accounted for in equity as an increase in the non-controlling interest. The increase in the NCI will be the 10% share of the net assets and goodwill of Tango at the date of the sale which Pepsi has effectively sold to the NCI.

The difference between the proceeds received of $35,000 and the increase in the non-controlling interest of $39,000 (W3) amounts to $4,000. This will be recorded as a decrease to other components of equity.

**(W3) Control to control adjustment – Tango**

|  | $000 |  |
|---|---|---|
| Cash received | 35 | Dr |
| Increase in NCI (10% × ($300 (W4) + $90 (W5))) | (39) | Cr |
| Decrease to other components of equity | (4) | Dr |

**(W4) Net assets – Tango**

|  | Acquisition date $000 | Reporting date $000 |
|---|---|---|
| Share capital | 100 | 100 |
| Retained earnings | 60 | 200 |
|  | 160 | 300 |

**(W5) Goodwill – Tango**

|  | $000 |
|---|---|
| Consideration | 200 |
| FV of NCI at acquisition | 50 |
| Fair value of net assets at acquisition (W4) | (160) |
|  | 90 |

### Test your understanding 8 – Raven

The sale of the shares reduces Raven's holding from 25% to 5%. Raven has lost significant influence over Sword and so Sword is no longer an associate. The investment in the associate must be derecognised.

The associate would have been initially recognised at $1 million. Raven would have accounted for its share of the associate's profits since this date. As such, by the date of disposal, the carrying amount of the associate in the consolidated financial statements would have been $1.2 million ($1m + (25% × ($3.8m – $3m))).

A profit on disposal must be recorded in the statement of profit or loss.

|  | $m |
|---|---|
| Disposal proceeds | 2.0 |
| Fair value of shares retained | 0.5 |
| Carrying amount of associate | (1.2) |
| Profit on disposal | 1.3 |

In respect of the remaining 5% shareholding, a financial asset will be recognised at $0.5 million in accordance with IFRS 9 *Financial Instruments*. By the reporting date the financial asset will be revalued to $0.6 million with a gain of $0.1 million recorded in profit or loss. Alternatively the gain could be recorded in other comprehensive income if the shares are not held for trading and an irrevocable designation was made on 30 June to measure the shares at fair value through other comprehensive income.

## Test your understanding 9 – Liesel

### Rosa

Liesel controlled Rosa both before and after the sale of shares. As such, it is incorrect to recognise a profit (or loss) on the sale. The transaction should be accounted for in equity as an increase in the non-controlling interest. This increase amounts to $6.4 million (5% × ($8m + $120m)).

The difference between the cash proceeds and the increase in the non-controlling interest of $2.6 million ($9m – $6.4m) should be recognised as an increase to shareholders' equity.

The correcting entry is:

| | |
|---|---|
| Dr Profit or loss | $9.0m |
| Cr Non-controlling interest | $6.4m |
| Cr Other components of equity | $2.6m |

### Hans

Liesel controlled Hans for the first 9 months of the year. Therefore the Liesel Group should have consolidated the incomes and expenses of Hans that arose during these 9 months. This will have a total impact on consolidated profit of $15 million ($20m × 9/12). Of this, $10.5 million ($15m × 70%) is attributable to the equity owners of the parent and the remaining $4.5 million is attributable to the non-controlling interest.

The sale of shares caused Liesel to lose control of Hans. At this point, Hans ceases to be a subsidiary. The Liesel group should derecognise the goodwill, net assets and non-controlling interest of Hans and recognise a loss on disposal of $19.1 million. This is calculated as follows:

| | $m | $m |
|---|---|---|
| Sales proceeds | | 72 |
| Fair value of shares retained | | 51 |
| Carrying amount of subsidiary at disposal: | | |
| Goodwill at disposal date (W1) | 31 | |
| Net assets at disposal date (W2) | 163 | |
| Less: NCI at disposal date (W3) | (51.9) | |
| | ——— | (142.1) |
| | | ——— |
| Loss on disposal | | (19.1) |
| | | ——— |

After the share sale Liesel retained significant influence over Hans. As such, Liesel should have recognised its remaining investment in Hans as an associate with an initial carrying amount of $51 million. The investment would be accounted for using the equity method. In consolidated profit or loss, Liesel should report a share of profits from associate entities of $1.5 million ($20m × 3/12 × 30%). This will increase the carrying amount of the investment in the associate to $52.5 million ($51 m + $1.5m) in the consolidated statement of financial position.

**(W1) Goodwill**

|  | $m |
|---|---|
| Consideration | 105 |
| NCI at acquisition | 36 |
| FV of net assets at acquisition ($100m + ($15m – $5m)) | (110) |
| Goodwill | 31 |

**(W2) Net assets at disposal date**

|  | $m |
|---|---|
| Share capital | 8 |
| Retained earnings bfd | 130 |
| Fair value adjustment ($15m – $5m) | 10 |
| Profit to disposal ($20m × 9/12) | 15 |
|  | 163 |

**(W3) NCI at disposal date**

|  | $m |
|---|---|
| NCI at acquisition | 36.0 |
| NCI % of post-acq'n net assets movement (30% × ($163m – $110m)) | 15.9 |
|  | 51.9 |

# Group accounting – foreign currency

## Chapter learning objectives

Upon completion of this chapter you will be able to:

- Outline and apply the translation of foreign currency amounts and transactions into the functional currency and the presentational currency

- Account for the consolidation of foreign operations and their disposal.

**PER**

One of the PER performance objectives (PO7) is to prepare external financial reports. You take part in preparing and reviewing financial statements – and all accompanying information – and you do it in accordance with legal and regulatory requirements. Working through this chapter should help you understand how to demonstrate that objective.

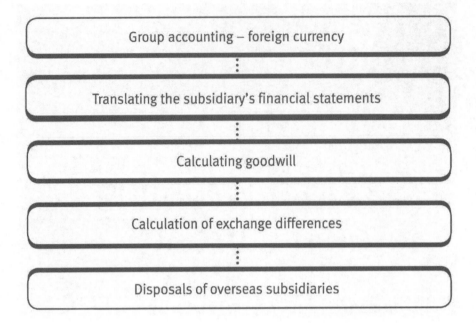

Group accounting – foreign currency

Translating the subsidiary's financial statements

Calculating goodwill

Calculation of exchange differences

Disposals of overseas subsidiaries

## 1 Key definitions

Foreign currency transactions in the individual financial statements of a company were covered earlier in this text.

Below is a reminder of some key definitions:

The **functional currency** is the currency of the **'primary economic environment where the entity operates'** (IAS 21, para 8). In most cases this will be the local currency.

The **presentation currency** is the **'currency in which the entity presents its financial statements'** (IAS 21, para 8).

## 2 Consolidation of a foreign operation

The functional currency used by a subsidiary to prepare its own individual accounting records and financial statements may differ from the presentation currency used for the group financial statements. Therefore, prior to adding together the assets, liabilities, incomes and expenses of the parent and subsidiary, the financial statements of an overseas subsidiary must be translated.

### Progression

In previous exams you did not have to consolidate a subsidiary that uses a different currency from the rest of the group.

## Translating the subsidiary's financial statements

The rules for translating an overseas subsidiary into the presentation currency of the group are as follows:

- **Income, expenses and other comprehensive income** are translated at the exchange rate in place at the date of each transaction. The average rate for the year may be used as an approximation.

- **Assets and liabilities** are translated at the closing rate of exchange.

### Illustration 1 – Dragon

This example runs through the chapter and is used to illustrate the basic steps involved in consolidating an overseas subsidiary.

Dragon bought 90% of the ordinary shares of Tattoo for DN180 million on 31 December 20X0. The retained earnings of Tattoo at this date were DN65 million. The fair value of the non-controlling interest at the acquisition date was DN14 million.

The financial statements of Dragon and Tattoo for the year ended 31 December 20X1 are presented below:

**Statements of profit or loss for year ended 31 December 20X1**

|  | Dragon $m | Tattoo DNm |
|---|---|---|
| Revenue | 1,200 | 600 |
| Costs | (1,000) | (450) |
| Profit | 200 | 150 |

**Statements of financial position as at 31 December 20X1**

|  | Dragon $m | Tattoo DNm |
|---|---|---|
| Property, plant and equipment | 290 | 270 |
| Investments | 60 | – |
| Current assets | 150 | 130 |
|  | 500 | 400 |
| Share capital | 10 | 5 |
| Retained earnings | 290 | 215 |
| Liabilities | 200 | 180 |
|  | 500 | 400 |

There has been no intra-group trading. Goodwill arising on the acquisition of Tattoo is not impaired. The presentation currency of the consolidated financial statements is the dollar ($).

Exchange rates are as follows:

|  | DN to $ |
|---|---|
| 31 December 20X0 | 3.0 |
| 31 December 20X1 | 2.0 |
| Average for year to 31 December 20X1 | 2.6 |

**Required:**

**For inclusion in the consolidated statement of profit or loss and other comprehensive income for the year ended 31 December 20X1, calculate:**

- **Revenue**
- **Costs**

**For inclusion in the consolidated statement of financial position as at 31 December 20X1, calculate:**

- **Property, plant and equipment**
- **Investments**
- **Current assets**
- **Share capital**
- **Liabilities**

### Solution

|  | $m |
|---|---|
| Revenue ($1,200 + (DN600/2.6)) | 1,430.8 |
| Costs ($1,000 + (DN450/2.6)) | (1,173.1) |
| PPE ($290 + (DN270/2)) | 425.0 |
| Investments (eliminated on consolidation) | – |
| Current assets ($150 + (DN130/2)) | 215.0 |
| Share capital (Dragon only) | 10.0 |
| Liabilities ($200 + (DN180/2)) | 290.0 |

Remember, the income and expenses of an overseas subsidiary are translated at the average rate. The assets and liabilities are translated at the closing rate.

## Translating goodwill

Goodwill should be calculated in the functional currency of the subsidiary.

According to IAS 21, goodwill should be treated like other assets of the subsidiary and translated at the reporting date using the closing rate.

### Illustration 2 – Goodwill

**Required:**

**Using the information in illustration 1, calculate goodwill for inclusion in the consolidated statement of financial position for the Dragon group as at 31 December 20X1.**

### Solution

**Goodwill calculation**

| | DNm |
|---|---|
| Consideration | 180 |
| NCI at acquisition | 14 |
| Net assets at acquisition (W) | (70) |
| | 124 |
| Goodwill impairments | – |
| | 124 |

Goodwill is translated at the closing rate to give a value of $62m (DN 124/2).

(W) **Net assets of Tattoo**

| | **Acquisition date** | **Reporting date** | **Post-acquisition** |
|---|---|---|---|
| | DNm | DNm | DNm |
| Share capital | 5 | 5 | |
| Retained earnings | 65 | 215 | 150 |
| | 70 | 220 | 150 |

**Exchange differences**

The process of translating an overseas subsidiary gives rise to exchange gains and losses. These gains and losses arise for the following reasons:

- **Goodwill:** Goodwill is retranslated each year-end at the closing rate. It will therefore increase or decrease in value simply because of exchange rate movements.

- **Opening net assets:** At the end of the prior year, the net assets of the subsidiary were translated at the prior year closing rate. This year, those same net assets are translated at this year's closing rate. Therefore, opening net assets will have increased or decreased simply because of exchange rate movements.

- **Profit:** The income and expenses (and, therefore, the profit) of the overseas subsidiary are translated at the average rate. However, making a profit increases the subsidiary's assets which are translated at the closing rate. This disparity creates an exchange gain or loss.

Current year exchange gains or losses on the translation of an overseas subsidiary and its goodwill are recorded in other comprehensive income.

**Goodwill translation**

The proforma for calculating the current year gain or loss on the retranslation of goodwill is as follows:

|  | DN | Exchange Rate | $ |
|---|---|---|---|
| Opening goodwill | X | Opening rate | X |
| Impairment loss in year | (X) | Average rate | (X) |
| **Exchange gain/(loss)** | – | **Bal fig.** | X/(X) |
|  | ____ |  | ____ |
| Closing goodwill | X | Closing rate | X |
|  | ____ |  | ____ |

If the subsidiary was purchased part-way through the current year, then substitute 'opening goodwill' for 'goodwill at acquisition'. This would then be translated at the rate of exchange on the acquisition date.

It is important to pay attention to the method of goodwill calculation:

- If the full goodwill method has been used, gain and losses will need to be apportioned between the group and the non-controlling interest.

- If the proportionate goodwill method has been used, then all of the exchange gain or loss on goodwill is attributable to the group.

**Illustration 3 – Translating goodwill**

**Required:**

**Using the information in illustration 1, calculate the exchange gain or loss arising on the translation of the goodwill that will be credited/charged through other comprehensive income in the year ended 31 December 20X1.**

**Who is this gain or loss attributable to?**

 **Solution**

|  | DNm | Exchange Rate | $m |
|---|---|---|---|
| Opening goodwill | 124.0 | 3.0 | 41.3 |
| Impairment loss in year | – | 2.6 | – |
| **Exchange gain** | – | **Bal fig.** | **20.7** |
| Closing goodwill | 124.0 | 2.0 | 62.0 |

The total translation gain of $20.7m will be credited to other comprehensive income.

This is then allocated to the group and NCI based on their respective shareholdings:

Group: $20.7m × 90% = $18.6m

NCI: $20.7m × 10% = $2.1 m

### Opening net assets and profit

The exchange gains or losses arising on the translation of opening net assets and profit for the year are generally calculated together.

The proforma for calculating the current year exchange gain or loss on the translation of the opening net assets and profit is as follows:

|  | DN | Exchange Rate | $ |
|---|---|---|---|
| Opening net assets | X | Opening rate | X |
| Profit/(loss) for the year | X/(X) | Average rate | X/(X) |
| **Exchange gain/(loss)** | – | **Bal fig.** | X/(X) |
| Closing net assets | X | Closing rate | X |

If the subsidiary was purchased part-way through the current year, then substitute 'opening net assets' and 'opening rate' for 'acquisition net assets' and 'acquisition rate'.

The gain or loss on translation of the opening net assets and profit is apportioned between the group and non-controlling interest based on their respective shareholdings.

### Illustration 4 – Opening net assets and profit

**Required:**

**Using the information in illustration 1, calculate the exchange gain or loss arising on the translation of the opening net assets and profit of Tattoo that will be credited/charged through other comprehensive income in the year ended 31 December 20X1.**

**Who are these gains or losses attributable to?**

### Solution

|  | DNm | Exchange Rate | $m |
|---|---|---|---|
| Opening net assets* | 70 | 3.0 | 23.3 |
| Profit/(loss) for the year* | 150 | 2.6 | 57.7 |
| **Exchange gain/(loss)** | – | **Bal fig.** | 29.0 |
| Closing net assets* | 220 | 2.0 | 110.0 |

*These figures are taken from the net assets working, which can be found in the solution to illustration 2.

The total translation gain of $29.0m will be credited to other comprehensive income.

This is then allocated to the group and NCI based on their respective shareholdings:

Group: 29.0m × 90% = $26.1 m

NCI: 29.0m × 10% = $2.9m

## Exchange differences on the statement of financial position

Exchange gains and losses arising from the translation of goodwill and the subsidiary's opening net assets and profit which are attributable to the group are normally held in a translation reserve, a separate component within equity.

**Illustration 5 – Reserves**

**Required:**

**Using the information in illustration 1, calculate the non-controlling interest, retained earnings and the translation reserve for inclusion in the consolidated statement of financial position as at 31 December 20X1.**

**Solution**

**Non-controlling interest**

| | $m |
|---|---|
| NCI at acquisition (DN14/3 opening rate) | 4.7 |
| NCI % of Tattoo's post-acquisition profits (10% × (DN150/2.6 average rate)) | 5.7 |
| NCI % of goodwill translation (illustration 3) | 2.1 |
| NCI % of net assets and profit translation (illustration 4) | 2.9 |
| | 15.4 |

**Retained earnings**

| | $m |
|---|---|
| 100% of Dragon | 290.0 |
| 90% of Tattoo's post-acquisition profits (90% × (DN150/2.6)) | 51.9 |
| | 341.9 |

**Translation reserve**

| | $m |
|---|---|
| Group share of goodwill forex (illustration 3) | 18.6 |
| Group share of net assets and profit forex (illustration 4) | 26.1 |
| | 44.7 |

**Illustration 6 – Completing the financial statements**

**Required:**

**Using the information in illustration 1, complete the consolidated statement of financial position and the statement of profit or loss and other comprehensive income for the Tattoo group for the year ended 31 December 20X1.**

**Solution**

**Statement of profit or loss and other comprehensive income for year ended 31 December 20X1**

|  | $m |
|---|---|
| Revenue (illustration 1) | 1,430.8 |
| Costs (illustration 1) | (1,173.1) |
| | ——— |
| Profit for the year | 257.7 |
| Other comprehensive income – items that may be classified to profit or loss in future periods | |
| Exchange differences on translation of foreign subsidiary ($20.7 (illustration 3) + $29.0 (illustration 4)) | 49.7 |
| | ——— |
| Total comprehensive income for the year | 307.4 |
| | ——— |
| Profit attributable to: | |
| Owners of Dragon (bal. fig.) | 251.9 |
| Non-controlling interest | 5.8 |
| (10% × (DN150/2.6 avg. rate)) | |
| | ——— |
| Profit for the year | 257.7 |
| | ——— |
| Total comprehensive income attributable to: | |
| Owners of Dragon (bal. fig.) | 296.6 |
| Non-controlling interest | 10.8 |
| ($5.8 (profit) + $2.1 (illustration 3) + $2.9 (illustration 4)) | |
| | ——— |
| Total comprehensive income for the year | 307.4 |
| | ——— |

**Statement of financial position as at 31 December 20X1**

|  | $m |
|---|---|
| Property, plant and equipment (illustration 1) | 425.0 |
| Goodwill (illustration 2) | 62.0 |
| Current assets (illustration 1) | 215.0 |
|  | 702.0 |
| Share capital (illustration 1) | 10.0 |
| Retained earnings (illustration 5) | 341.9 |
| Translation reserve (illustration 5) | 44.7 |
|  | 396.6 |
| Non-controlling interest (illustration 5) | 15.4 |
|  | 412.0 |
| Liabilities (illustration 1) | 290.0 |
|  | 702.0 |

### Test your understanding 1 – Parent and Overseas

Parent is an entity that owns 80% of the equity shares of Overseas, a foreign entity that has the Shilling as its functional currency. The subsidiary was acquired on 1 January 20X7 when its retained earnings were 6,000 Shillings. The reporting date is 31 December 20X7.

At the acquisition date the fair value of the net assets of Overseas was equal to the carrying amount with the exception of freehold land. The fair value of this land exceeded its carrying amount by 4,000 Shillings.

At the date of acquisition, the non-controlling interest in Overseas should be measured at its fair value of 5,000 Shillings. Goodwill at the reporting date is not impaired.

## Statements of financial position as at 31 December 20X7

|  | Parent $ | Overseas Shillings |
|---|---|---|
| Investment in Overseas at cost | 3,818 | – |
| Assets | 9,500 | 40,000 |
|  | 13,318 | 40,000 |
| **Equity and liabilities** |  |  |
| Equity capital | 5,000 | 10,000 |
| Retained earnings | 6,000 | 8,200 |
| Liabilities | 2,318 | 21,800 |
|  | 13,318 | 40,000 |

Relevant exchange rates are:

| Date | Shillings: $1 |
|---|---|
| 1 January 20X7 | 5.5 |
| 31 December 20X7 | 5.0 |
| Average for year to 31 December 20X7 | 5.2 |

### Required:

**Discuss how the goodwill arising on the acquisition of Overseas should be dealt with in the consolidated financial statements of the Parent group for the year ended 31 December 20X7.**

---

### Test your understanding 2 – Saint and Albans

On the 1 July 20X1 Saint acquired 60% of Albans, whose functional currency is Ds. The presentation currency of the Saint group is the dollar ($). The financial statements of both entities are as follows.

## Statements of financial position as at 30 June 20X2

|  | Saint $ | Albans D |
|---|---|---|
| Assets |  |  |
| Investment in Albans | 5,000 | – |
| Loan to Albans | 1,400 | – |
| Property, plant and equipment | 10,000 | 15,400 |
| Inventories | 5,000 | 4,000 |
| Receivables | 4,000 | 500 |
| Cash and cash equivalents | 1,600 | 560 |
|  | 27,000 | 20,460 |

| Equity and liabilities | $ | D |
|---|---|---|
| Equity capital ($1/D1) | 10,000 | 1,000 |
| Share premium | 3,000 | 500 |
| Retained earnings | 4,000 | 12,500 |
| Non-current liabilities | 5,000 | 5,460 |
| Current liabilities | 5,000 | 1,000 |
| | 27,000 | 20,460 |

The following information is applicable.

(i) Saint purchased the shares in Albans for D10,000 on the first day of the accounting period. At the date of acquisition the retained earnings of Albans were D500. The fair value of Albans' net assets exceeded the carrying amount by D1,000. This fair value adjustment was attributable to plant with a remaining five-year life as at the date of acquisition.

(ii) Just before the year-end Saint acquired some goods from a third party at a cost of $800, which it sold to Albans for cash at a mark-up of 50%. At the reporting date all these goods remain in the inventories of Albans.

(iii) On 1 June 20X2 Saint lent Albans $1,400. The liability is recorded at the historic rate within the non-current liabilities of Albans.

(iv) Saint measures non-controlling interests at acquisition at fair value. The fair value of the non-controlling interest in Albans at the date of acquisition was D5,000. An impairment review was performed and goodwill had reduced in value by 10% at 30 June 20X2.

(v) On 1 July 20X1, Saint received a government grant for $4,000. This grant was provided as a contribution towards the costs of training employees over the next two years. Saint has reduced its administrative expenses by the full $4,000.

(vi) Exchange rates are as follows:

| | D: $1 |
|---|---|
| 1 July 20X1 | 2.0 |
| Average rate | 3.0 |
| 1 June 20X2 | 3.9 |
| 30 June 20X2 | 4.0 |

**Required:**

**Prepare the equity section of the consolidated statement of financial position as at 30 June 20X2. With respect to Albans, your answer should explain why foreign exchange differences arise in the consolidated financial statements.**

## 3 Disposals

On the disposal of a foreign subsidiary, the cumulative exchange differences recognised as other comprehensive income and accumulated in a separate component of equity become realised.

IAS 21 requires that these exchanges differences are recycled (i.e. reclassified) on the disposal of the subsidiary as part of the profit or loss on disposal.

| **Test your understanding 3 – LUMS Group** |
|---|
| The LUMS group has sold its entire 100% holding in an overseas subsidiary for proceeds of $50,000. The net assets at the date of disposal were $20,000 and the carrying amount of goodwill at that date was $10,000. The cumulative balance on the group foreign currency reserve is a gain of $5,000.<br><br>**Required:**<br><br>**Discuss how the disposal should be accounted for in the consolidated financial statements.** |

## 4 Chapter summary

```
┌─────────────────────────────────────────────────────┐
│         Group accounting – foreign currency          │
└─────────────────────────────────────────────────────┘
                           ⋮
┌─────────────────────────────────────────────────────┐
│ Translating the subsidiary's financial statements    │
│ • Assets and liabilities at the closing rate         │
│ • Incomes, expenses and OCI at the average rate       │
└─────────────────────────────────────────────────────┘
                           ⋮
┌─────────────────────────────────────────────────────┐
│ Calculating goodwill                                 │
│ • Calculate in the subsidiary's currency             │
│ • Translate at the closing rate                      │
└─────────────────────────────────────────────────────┘
                           ⋮
┌─────────────────────────────────────────────────────┐
│ Calculation of exchange differences on:              │
│ • Goodwill                                           │
│ • Opening net assets and profit                      │
│ Current year gains and losses are recorded in OCI    │
│ and held within equity.                              │
└─────────────────────────────────────────────────────┘
                           ⋮
┌─────────────────────────────────────────────────────┐
│ Disposals of overseas subsidiaries                   │
│ • Recycle cumulative foreign exchange gains and      │
│   losses held in equity to profit or loss            │
└─────────────────────────────────────────────────────┘
```

# Test your understanding answers

### Test your understanding 1 – Parent and Overseas

Goodwill arising on the acquisition of Overseas is calculated initially in foreign currency as follows:

|  | | Shillings |
|---|---|---|
| Consideration | | 20,999 |
| ($3,818 × 5.5) | | |
| FV of NCI at acquisition | | 5,000 |
| | | ——— |
| | | 25,999 |
| FV of net assets at acquisition: | | |
| Share capital | 10,000 | |
| Retained earnings | 6,000 | |
| Fair value adjustment | 4,000 | |
| | ——— | |
| | | (20,000) |
| | | ——— |
| Goodwill at acquisition | | 5,999 |
| | | ——— |

According to IAS 21 *The Effects of Changes in Foreign Exchange Rates*, goodwill arising on the acquisition of a foreign operation is treated as the foreign operation's asset. This means that, at each reporting date, goodwill is translated using the closing rate of exchange. The goodwill of Overseas as at the reporting date is therefore $1,200 (Sh5999/5).

The foreign exchange gain arising on the translation of the goodwill of Overseas is calculated as follows:

|  | Shillings | Exchange rate | $ |
|---|---|---|---|
| Goodwill at acquisition | 5,999 | 5.5 | 1,091 |
| Impairment | – | | – |
| Exchange gain | | bal. fig | 109 |
| | ——— | | ——— |
| Closing goodwill | 5,999 | 5.0 | 1,200 |
| | ——— | | ——— |

The exchange gain of $109 is recorded in other comprehensive income and presented as an item that might be reclassified to profit or loss in the future. The exchange gain is allocated between the group and NCI because the NCI at acquisition was measured at fair value. The allocation is based on respective shareholdings:

Group: 80% × $109 = $87

NCI: 20% × $109 = $22

## Test your understanding 2 – Saint and Albans

**Extract from group statement of financial position at 30 June 20X2**

| | $ |
|---|---|
| Equity capital | 10,000 |
| Share premium | 3,000 |
| Retained earnings (W1) | 3,692 |
| Translation reserve (W2) | (2,773) |
| | ——— |
| | 13,919 |
| Non-controlling interest (W3) | 2,046 |
| | ——— |
| Total equity | 15,965 |
| | ——— |

### Discussion of exchange differences

Goodwill is translated at each reporting date at the closing rate of exchange. An exchange difference arises because goodwill at acquisition was translated at the acquisition rate but goodwill at the reporting date was translated at the closing rate.

Similarly, the net assets of Albans are retranslated each year at the closing rate of exchange and so an exchange difference arises by comparing the acquisition net assets at the rate of exchange on the acquisition date with the acquisition net assets at the closing rate of exchange.

An additional exchange difference arises because the profit of Albans is translated at the average rate of exchange for inclusion in the consolidated statement of comprehensive income. However, this profit increases the net assets of Albans which, as is indicated above, are translated at the closing rate of exchange for inclusion in the consolidated statement of financial position.

### Workings

#### (W1) Retained earnings

| | $ |
|---|---|
| Parent retained earnings | 4,000 |
| Group share of sub's post-acq'n profit | 2,332 |
| 60% × (D11,660/3 avg. rate) (W4) | |
| Group share of goodwill impairment (W5) | (240) |
| PURP (W7) | (400) |
| Government grant (W8) | (2,000) |
| | ——— |
| | 3,692 |
| | ——— |

## (W2) Translation reserve

| | $ |
|---|---|
| Group share of forex on goodwill (W5) | (1,740) |
| Group share of forex on net assets and profit (W6) | (1,033) |
| | (2,773) |

## (W3) Non-controlling interest

| | $ |
|---|---|
| FV at acquisition (D5,000/2) | 2,500 |
| NCI % of post-acquisition profit | 1,555 |
| 40% × (D11,660/3 avg rate) (W4) | |
| NCI share of goodwill impairment (W5) | (160) |
| NCI share of forex on goodwill (W5) | (1,160) |
| NCI share of forex on net assets and profit (W6) | (689) |
| | 2,046 |

## (W4) Net assets of subsidiary in functional currency

| | At acquisition D | Rep date D | Post-acq'n D |
|---|---|---|---|
| Equity capital | 1,000 | 1,000 | |
| Share premium | 500 | 500 | |
| Retained earnings | 500 | 12,500 | 12,000 |
| Fair value adjustment | 1,000 | 1,000 | |
| Depreciation (1,000/5 years) | | (200) | (200) |
| Exchange loss on loan* | | (140) | (140) |
| | 3,000 | 14,660 | 11,660 |

### *Exchange loss on loan received by Albans

The loan was initially recorded at D5,460 ($1,400 × 3.9)

The loan needs to be retranslated using the closing rate to D5,600 ($1,400 × 4.0)

There is therefore an exchange loss of D140 (D5,600 – D5,460).

| | |
|---|---|
| Dr Profit or loss/retained earnings | D140 |
| Cr Non-current liabilities | D140 |

**(W5) Goodwill**

**Goodwill calculation**

| | D |
|---|---:|
| Cost to parent ($5,000 × 2.0) | 10,000 |
| FV of NCI at acquisition | 5,000 |
| FV of NA at acquisition (W4) | (3,000) |
| | |
| Goodwill at acquisition | 12,000 |
| Impairment – 10% | (1,200) |
| | |
| Goodwill at reporting date | 10,800 |

**Exchange gain (loss) on retranslation of goodwill**

| | D | Rate | $ |
|---|---:|---:|---:|
| Goodwill at acquisition | 12,000 | 2.0 | 6,000 |
| Impairment | (1,200) | 3.0 | (400) |
| **Exchange loss** | | **bal fig** | **(2,900)** |
| | | | |
| Goodwill at reporting date | 10,800 | 4.0 | 2,700 |

The impairment loss on the goodwill is allocated between the group and NCI based on respective shareholdings:

Group: 60% × $400 = $240 (W1)
NCI: 40% × $400 = $160 (W3)

The exchange loss on retranslation of goodwill is allocated between the group and NCI based on their respective shareholdings:

Group: 60% × $2,900 = $1,740 (W2)
NCI: 40% × $2,900 = $1,160 (W3)

**(W6) Exchange differences on retranslation of net assets**

| | D | Rate | $ |
|---|---:|---:|---:|
| Acquisition net assets | 3,000 | 2.0 | 1,500 |
| Profit for year | 11,660 | 3.0 | 3,887 |
| **Exchange loss** | | **bal fig** | **(1,722)** |
| | | | |
| Closing net assets | 14,660 | 4.0 | 3,665 |

The exchange loss is allocated between the group and NCI based on respective shareholdings:

Group: 60% × $1,722 = $1,033 (W2)
NCI: 40% × $1,722 = $689 (W3)

**(W7) PURP**

The profit on the intra-group sale is $400 ((50/100) × $800).

All of these items remain in group inventory. Therefore the adjustment required is:

| | |
|---|---|
| Dr Cost of sales/retained earnings (W1) | $400 |
| Cr Inventories | $400 |

**(W8) Government grant**

This is a revenue grant. It should be recognised in profit or loss on a systematic basis. The grant is intended to cover training costs over a two year period and so it should be recognised in profit or loss over two years.

Saint should increase its expenses by $2,000 (1/2 × $4,000) and record the balance as deferred income on the SFP.

| | |
|---|---|
| Dr Admin expenses/retained earnings (W1) | $2,000 |
| Cr Current liabilities | $2,000 |

**Test your understanding 3 – LUMS Group**

The LUMS group has lost control over its overseas subsidiary. The income and expenses of the overseas subsidiary should be consolidated up to the date of disposal. On the disposal date, the goodwill and net assets of the overseas subsidiary are derecognised from the consolidated financial statements. Additionally, the foreign exchange gains previously recognised in other comprehensive income should be reclassified to profit or loss.

A gain of $25,000 should be presented in consolidated statement of profit or loss, calculated as follows:

| | $ | $ |
|---|---|---|
| Proceeds | | 50,000 |
| Net assets recorded prior to disposal: | | |
| Net assets | 20,000 | |
| Goodwill | 10,000 | |
| | | (30,000) |
| Reclassification of forex gains to P/L | | 5,000 |
| | | 25,000 |

# Group statement of cash flows

## Chapter learning objectives

Upon completion of this chapter you will be able to:

- prepare group statements of cash flows.

**PER**

One of the PER performance objectives (PO7) is to prepare external financial reports. You take part in preparing and reviewing financial statements – and all accompanying information – and you do it in accordance with legal and regulatory requirements. Working through this chapter should help you understand how to demonstrate that objective.

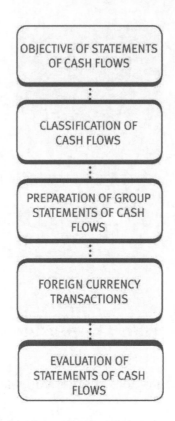

## 1 Statements of cash flows

### Exam focus

Question 1 in the SBR exam will always test consolidated financial statements. This might include consolidated statements of cash flows.

The exam will not ask for the production of a full consolidated statement. Instead, candidates will be required to produce extracts from these statements and to explain the accounting numbers that they have produced.

Some questions in this chapter do require the production of full consolidated statements of cash flows. This is to enable SBR candidates to revise, practice and develop a deeper understanding of cash flow techniques. Without this, you will find it difficult to tackle exam-style questions that focus on extracts and discussion.

 **Progression**

You learned about statements of cash flows when studying for your earlier exams. For SBR, you need to be able to discuss, and prepare extracts from, group statements of cash flows.

## Objectives of statements of cash flows

IAS 7 *Statement of Cash Flows* provides guidance on the preparation of a statement of cash flows. The objective of a statement of cash flows is to provide information on an entity's changes in cash and cash equivalents during the period.

The statement of financial position and statement of profit or loss are prepared on an accruals basis and do not show how the business has generated and used cash in the reporting period. The statement of profit or loss may show profits even though the company is suffering severe cash flow problems.

A statement of cash flows is therefore important because it enables users of the financial statements to assess the liquidity, solvency and financial adaptability of the business.

### The *Conceptual Framework*

According to the *Conceptual Framework*, investors, lenders and other creditors can only make informed decisions if provided with information that will help them to predict an entity's future cash flows. Historical cash flow information, as presented in the statement of cash flows, will help these users to assess the amount, likelihood and certainty of an entity's future cash flows.

Analysis of cash outflows may also help users to assess management's stewardship of the entity's assets.

## 2   Proforma

**Statement of cash flows for the year ended 31 December 20X1**

|  | $ | $ |
|---|---|---|
| **Cash flows from operating activities** | | |
| Profit before tax | X | |
| Add: finance costs | X | |
| Less: investment income | (X) | |
| Less: income from associate | (X) | |
| Adjust for non-cash items dealt with in arriving at operating profit: | | |
| Add: depreciation | X | |
| Less: gain on disposal of subsidiary | (X) | |
| Add: loss on disposal of subsidiary | X | |
| Add: loss on impairment charged to P/L | X | |
| Add: loss on disposal of non-current assets | X | |
| Add: increase in provisions | X | |
|  | ––– | |
|  | X/(X) | |

| | | |
|---|---|---|
| Changes in working capital: | | |
| Increase in inventory | (X) | |
| Increase in receivables | (X) | |
| Decrease in payables | (X) | |
| | ——— | |
| Cash generated/used from operations | X/(X) | |
| Interest paid | (X) | |
| Taxation paid | (X) | |
| | ——— | |
| **Net cash Inflow/(outflow) from operating activities** | | X/(X) |
| | | |
| **Cash flows from investing activities** | | |
| Payments to purchase non-current assets | (X) | |
| Receipts from non-current asset disposals | X | |
| Net cash paid to acquire subsidiary | (X) | |
| Net cash proceeds from subsidiary disposal | X | |
| Cash paid to acquire associates | (X) | |
| Dividend received from associate | X | |
| Interest received | X | |
| | ——— | |
| **Net cash inflow/(outflow) from investing activities** | | |
| | | X/(X) |
| | | |
| **Cash flows from financing activities** | | |
| Proceeds from share issue | X | |
| Proceeds from loan or debenture issue | X | |
| Cash repayment of loans or debentures | (X) | |
| Lease liability repayments | (X) | |
| Equity dividend paid by parent | (X) | |
| Dividend paid to NCI | (X) | |
| | ——— | |
| **Net cash inflow/(outflow) from financing activities** | | |
| | | X/(X) |
| | | ——— |
| **Increase/(decrease) in cash and equivalents** | | X/(X) |
| Cash and equivalents brought forward | | X/(X) |
| | | ——— |
| Cash and equivalents carried forward | | X/(X) |
| | | ——— |

# 3 Classification of cash flows

IAS 7 does not prescribe a specific format for the statement of cash flows, although it requires that cash flows are classified under one of three headings:

- **cash flows from operating activities,** defined as the entity's principal revenue earning activities and other activities that do not fall under the next two headings

- **cash flows from investing activities,** defined as the acquisition and disposal of long-term assets and other investments (excluding cash equivalents)

- **cash flows from financing activities,** defined as activities that change the size and composition of the entity's equity and borrowings.

## Cash flows from operating activities

The key figure within cash flows from operating activities is 'cash generated from operations'. There are two methods of calculating cash generated from operations:

- The **direct method** shows operating cash receipts and payments, such as cash receipts from customers, cash payments to suppliers and cash payments to and on behalf of employees.

- The **indirect method** (used in the proforma statement of cash flows presented earlier in the chapter) starts with profit before tax and adjusts it for non-cash charges and credits, deferrals or accruals of past or future operating cash receipts and payments, as well as for items that relate to investing and financing activities. The most frequently occurring adjustments required are:

    - finance costs and investment incomes

    - depreciation or amortisation charges in the year

    - impairment charged to profit or loss in the year

    - profit or loss on disposal of non-current assets

    - change in inventories

    - change in trade receivables

    - change in trade payables.

IAS 7 permits either method, although encourages the use of the direct method. A comparison between the direct and indirect method to arrive at cash generated from operations is shown below:

| Direct method: | $m | Indirect method: | $m |
|---|---|---|---|
| Cash receipts from customers | 15,424 | Profit before tax | 6,022 |
| Cash payments to suppliers | (5,824) | Depreciation charges | 899 |
| Cash payments to and on behalf of employees | (2,200) | Increase in inventories | (194) |
| Other cash payments | (511) | Increase in receivables | (72) |
| | | Increase in payables | 234 |
| Cash generated from operations | 6,889 | Cash generated from operations | 6,889 |

**Investor perspective**

Entities can choose whether to present 'cash generated from operations' using the direct or indirect method. This is a problem for users of the financial statements because it limits comparability.

The majority of companies use the indirect method for the preparation of statements of cash flow. They justify this on the grounds that the information required for the direct method is too costly and time-consuming to obtain.

The adjustments required by the indirect method are difficult to understand and can be confusing to financial statement users. In many cases these adjustments cannot be reconciled to observed changes in the statement of financial position.

Financial statement users often prefer the direct method because it reports operating cash flows in understandable categories, such as cash collected from customers, cash paid to suppliers, cash paid to employees and cash paid for other operating expenses. When presented in this way, users can assess the major trends in cash flows and can compare these to the entity's competitors. This is relevant information because it aids investment decisions.

## Cash flows from investing activities

Cash flows to appear under this heading include:

- cash paid for property, plant and equipment and other non-current assets

- cash received on the sale of property, plant and equipment and other non-current assets

- cash paid for investments in, or loans to, other entities (excluding movements on loans from financial institutions, which are shown under financing)

- cash received for the sale of investments or the repayment of loans to other entities (again excluding loans from financial institutions).

## Cash flows from financing activities

Financing cash flows mainly comprise receipts or repayments of principal from or to external providers of finance.

Financing cash inflows include:

- receipts from issuing shares or other equity instruments

- receipts from issuing debentures, loans, notes and bonds and from other long-term and short-term borrowings (other than overdrafts, which are normally included in cash and cash equivalents).

IAS 7 says that financing cash outflows include:

- repayments of amounts borrowed (other than overdrafts)

- the capital element of lease payments

- payments to reacquire or redeem the entity's shares.

## Interest and dividends

IAS 7 allows interest and dividends, whether received or paid, to be classified under any of the three headings, provided the classification is consistent from period to period.

The practice adopted in this text is to classify:

- interest received as a cash flow from investing activities

- interest paid as a cash flow from operating activities

- dividends received as a cash flow from investing activities

- dividends paid as a cash flow from financing activities.

## Test your understanding 1 – Plaster

Plaster, a public limited entity, raised considerable amounts of cash during the period by selling items of property, plant and equipment (PPE). Plaster's directors believe that presenting the proceeds received from the disposals within 'cash flows from investing activities' will jeopardise attempts to raise finance in the future. They have therefore decided to increase 'cash generated from operations' by the proceeds from the PPE disposals.

**Required:**

**Explain the likely impact of the directors' decision on users' perception of the statement of cash flows and discuss the ethical and professional issues that it raises.**

## 4 Cash and cash equivalents

The statement of cash flows reconciles cash and cash equivalents at the start of the reporting period to the end of the reporting period.

Cash equivalents are **'short-term, highly liquid investments that are readily convertible to known amounts of cash and are subject to an insignificant risk of changes in value'** (IAS 7, para 6).

IAS 7 does not define 'readily convertible' but notes that an investment would qualify as a cash equivalent if it had a short maturity of **'three months or less from the date of acquisition'** (IAS 7, para 7).

Equity investments are generally excluded from being included in cash equivalents because there is a significant risk of a change in value. IAS 7 makes an exception for preference shares with a short period to maturity and a specified redemption date.

## Test your understanding 2 – Cash and cash equivalents

The accountant for Minted, a company, is preparing a statement of cash flows. She would like advice about whether the following items can be included within 'cash and cash equivalents'.

- An overdraft of $100,000.

- A balance of $500,000 held in a high-interest account. Minted must give 28 days' notice in order to access this money, which is held with the intention of meeting working capital shortages.

- An investment in the ordinary shares of Moolah. The shares are listed and therefore could be sold immediately. The shares have a fair value of $1m.

**Required:**

**Advise the accountant of Minted whether the above items qualify as 'cash and cash equivalents'.**

## 5    Individual statements of cash flows

During your prior studies you will have learned how to prepare statements of cash flows for individual companies. It may be worthwhile taking some time to revise this knowledge using the following exercises.

---

**Test your understanding 3 – Extracts**

Calculate the required cash flows in each of the following scenarios:

1

|  | 20X1 | 20X0 |
|---|---|---|
|  | $ | $ |
| Property, plant and equipment (PPE) | 250 | 100 |

During the year depreciation charged was $20, a revaluation surplus of $60 was recorded, and PPE with a carrying amount of $15 was disposed of. The carrying amount of assets recognised through lease agreements and classified as PPE was $30.

**Required:**

**How much cash was spent on property, plant and equipment in the period?**

2

|  | 20X1 | 20X0 |
|---|---|---|
|  | $ | $ |
| Deferred tax liability | 100 | 50 |
| Income tax liability | 120 | 100 |

The income tax charge in the statement of profit or loss was $180.

**Required:**

**How much tax was paid in the period?**

3

|  | 20X1 | 20X0 |
|---|---|---|
|  | $ | $ |
| Retained earnings | 300 | 200 |

The statement of profit or loss showed a profit for the period of $150.

**Required:**

**How much was the cash dividend paid during the period?**

---

Illustration 1 – Single entities

Below are the financial statements of Single for the year ended
30 September 20X2:

**Statement of financial position as at 30 September 20X2 (including comparatives)**

|  | 20X2 $m | 20X1 $m |
|---|---|---|
| Non-current assets |  |  |
| Property, plant and equipment | 90 | 60 |
| Current assets |  |  |
| Inventories | 32 | 20 |
| Trade receivables | 20 | 27 |
| Cash and cash equivalents | 8 | 12 |
|  | 150 | 119 |
|  |  |  |
| Equity and liabilities |  |  |
| Share capital ($1 shares) | 30 | 5 |
| Retained earnings | 60 | 35 |
|  | 90 | 40 |
| Non-current liabilities: |  |  |
| Loans | 10 | 29 |
| Deferred tax | 15 | 14 |
| Current liabilities: |  |  |
| Trade payables | 23 | 25 |
| Tax payable | 12 | 11 |
|  | 150 | 119 |

## Statement of profit or loss for the year ended 30 September 20X2

|  | $m |
|---|---|
| Revenue | 450 |
| Operating expenses | (401) |
| | ——— |
| Profit from operations | 49 |
| Finance cost | (3) |
| | ——— |
| Profit before tax | 46 |
| Tax | (12) |
| | ——— |
| Profit for the period | 34 |
| | ——— |

**Notes**

1    Property, plant and equipment with a carrying amount of $9 million was disposed of for cash proceeds of $13 million. Depreciation for the year was $17 million.

2    Trade payables as at 30 September 20X2 includes accruals for interest payable of $4 million (20X1: $5 million).

**Required:**

**Prepare the statement of cash flows for Single for the year ended 30 September 20X2.**

## Solution

### Statement of cash flows

|  | $m | $m |
|---|---|---|
| **Cash flows from operating activities** | | |
| Profit before tax | 46 | |
| Finance cost | 3 | |
| Depreciation | 17 | |
| Profit on disposal of PPE | (4) | |
| ($13 – $9) | | |
| Increase in inventories | (12) | |
| ($32 – $20) | | |
| Decrease in receivables | 7 | |
| ($20 – $27) | | |
| Decrease in payables | (1) | |
| (($23 – $4) – ($25 – $5)) | | |
| | —— | |
| | 56 | |
| Interest paid (W1) | (4) | |
| Tax paid (W2) | (10) | |
| | —— | |
| | | 42 |
| **Cash flows from investing activities** | | |
| Proceeds from sale of PPE | 13 | |
| Purchases of PPE (W3) | (56) | |
| | —— | |
| | | (43) |
| **Cash flows from financing activities** | | |
| Proceeds from shares ($30 – $5) | 25 | |
| Repayment of loans ($10 – $29) | (19) | |
| Dividends paid (W4) | (9) | |
| | —— | |
| | | (3) |
| | | —— |
| Decrease in cash and cash equivalents | | (4) |
| Opening cash and cash equivalents | | 12 |
| | | —— |
| Closing cash and cash equivalents | | 8 |
| | | —— |

## Workings

### (W1) Interest

| | $m |
|---|---:|
| Balance b/fwd | 5 |
| Profit or loss | 3 |
| Cash paid (bal. fig.) | (4) |
| | |
| Balance c/fwd | 4 |

### (W2) Tax

| | $m |
|---|---:|
| Balance b/fwd ($14 + $11) | 25 |
| Profit or loss | 12 |
| Cash paid (bal. fig.) | (10) |
| | |
| Balance c/fwd ($15 + $12) | 27 |

### (W3) PPE

| | $m |
|---|---:|
| Balance b/fwd | 60 |
| Depreciation | (17) |
| Disposal | (9) |
| Cash paid (bal. fig.) | 56 |
| | |
| Balance c/fwd | 90 |

### (W4) Retained earnings

| | $m |
|---|---:|
| Balance b/fwd | 35 |
| Profit or loss | 34 |
| Cash dividends paid (bal. fig.) | (9) |
| | |
| Balance c/fwd | 60 |

## 6 Preparation of a consolidated statement of cash flows

A consolidated statement of cash flows shows the cash flows between a group and third parties. It is prepared using the consolidated statement of financial position and the consolidated statement of profit or loss. This means that intra-group transactions have already been eliminated.

When producing a consolidated statement of cash flows, there are three extra elements that need to be considered:

- acquisitions and disposals of subsidiaries
- cash paid to non-controlling interests
- associates.

### Acquisitions and disposals of subsidiaries

### Acquisitions

In the statement of cash flows we must record the actual cash flow for the purchase of the subsidiary net of any cash held by the subsidiary that is now controlled by the group.

The assets and liabilities of the acquired subsidiary must be included in any workings to calculate the cash movement for an item during the year.

---

 **Acquisition of a subsidiary**

Sparkling buys 70% of the equity shares of Still for $500,000 in cash. At the acquisition date, Still had cash and cash equivalents of $25,000.

Although Sparkling paid $500,000 for the shares, it also gained control of Still's cash of $25,000. In the consolidated statement of cash flows, this would be presented as follows:

**Cash flows from investing activities**

|  | $000 |
|---|---|
| Acquisition of subsidiary, net of cash acquired ($500,000 – $25,000) | (475) |

---

### Disposals

The statement of cash flows will show the cash received from the sale of the subsidiary, net of any cash held by the subsidiary that the group has lost control over.

The assets and liabilities of the disposed subsidiary must be included in any workings to calculate the cash movement for an item during the year.

## Disposal of a subsidiary

Sparkling owned 80% of the equity shares of Fizzy. During the period, these shares were sold for $800,000 in cash. At the disposal date, Fizzy had cash and cash equivalents of $70,000.

Although Sparkling received $800,000 for the shares, it lost control of Fizzy's cash of $70,000. In the consolidated statement of cash flows, this would be presented as follows:

**Cash flows from investing activities**

|  | $000 |
|---|---|
| Disposal of subsidiary, net of cash disposed of ($800,000 – $70,000) | 730 |

## Illustration 2 – Acquisitions and disposals

Extracts from a group statement of financial position are presented below:

|  | 20X8 | 20X7 |
|---|---|---|
|  | $000 | $000 |
| Inventories | 74,666 | 53,019 |
| Trade receivables | 58,246 | 62,043 |
| Trade payables | 93,678 | 86,247 |

During 20X8, Subsidiary A was acquired and all shares in Subsidiary B were disposed of.

Details of the working capital balances of these two subsidiaries are provided below:

|  | Working capital of Subsidiary A at acquisition | Working capital of Subsidiary B at disposal |
|---|---|---|
|  | $000 | $000 |
| Inventories | 4,500 | 6,800 |
| Trade receivables | 7,900 | 6,700 |
| Trade payables | 8,250 | 5,740 |

**Required:**

**Calculate the movement in inventories, trade receivables and trade payables for inclusion in the group statement of cash flows.**

## Solution

The net assets of Subsidiary A are being consolidated at the end of the year, but they were not consolidated at the start of the year. Conversely, the net assets of Subsidiary B are not consolidated at the end of the year, but they were consolidated at the start of the year. The working capital balances brought forward and carried forward are therefore not directly comparable.

Comparability can be achieved by calculating the movement between the closing and opening figures and then:

- Deducting the subsidiary's balances at the acquisition date for a subsidiary acquired during the year.

- Adding the subsidiary's balances at the disposal date for a subsidiary disposed of during the year.

|  | Inventories | Trade receivables | Trade payables |
|---|---|---|---|
|  | $000 | $000 | $000 |
| Bal c/fwd | 74,666 | 58,246 | 93,678 |
| Bal b/fwd | (53,019) | (62,043) | (86,247) |
|  | 21,647 | (3,797) | 7,431 |
| Less: Sub acquired in year | (4,500) | (7,900) | (8,250) |
| Add: Sub disposed in year | 6,800 | 6,700 | 5,740 |
| Movement in the year | inc 23,947 | dec (4,997) | inc 4,921 |
| Impact on cash flow | Outflow | Inflow | Inflow |

### Cash paid to non-controlling interests

When a subsidiary that is not wholly owned pays a dividend, some of that dividend is paid outside of the group to the non-controlling interest. Dividends paid to non-controlling interests should be disclosed separately in the statement of cash flows.

To calculate the dividend paid, reconcile the non-controlling interest in the statement of financial position from the opening to the closing balance. You can use a T-account or a schedule to do this.

**Illustration 3 – Cash paid to NCI**

The following information has been extracted from the consolidated financial statements of WG, which has a year end of the 31 December:

|  | 20X7 | 20X6 |
|---|---|---|
|  | $000 | $000 |
| Statement of financial position |  |  |
| Equity: |  |  |
| Non-controlling interest | 780 | 690 |
| Statement of profit or loss |  |  |
| Profit for the period attributable to the non-controlling interest | 120 | 230 |

During the year, WG bought a 70% shareholding in CC. WG uses the full goodwill method for all subsidiaries. The fair value of the non-controlling interest in CC at the acquisition date was $60,000.

During the year, WG disposed of its 60% holding in TT. At the acquisition date, the fair value of the NCI and the fair value of TT's net assets were $35,000 and $70,000 respectively. The net assets of TT at the disposal date were $100,000.

**Required:**

**What is the dividend paid to non-controlling interest in the year ended 31 December 20X7?**

 **Solution**

|  | $000 |
|---|---|
| NCI b/fwd | 690 |
| NCI re sub acquired in year | 60 |
| NCI share of profit for the year | 120 |
| NCI derecognised due to subsidiary disposal (W1) | (47) |
| Cash dividend paid in year (bal. fig.) | (43) |
|  |  |
| NCI c/fwd | 780 |

**(W1) NCI at date of TT disposal**

|  | $000 |
|---|---|
| FV of NCI at acquisition | 35 |
| NCI% of post-acquisition net assets |  |
| 40% × ($100,000 – $70,000) | 12 |
|  |  |
|  | 47 |

Alternatively, a T account can be used:

**Non-controlling interests**

| | $000 | | $000 |
|---|---|---|---|
| NCI derecognised re sub disposal (W1) | 47 | NCI Balance b/fwd | 690 |
| Dividends paid (bal fig.) | 43 | NCI recognised re acq'n of sub | 60 |
| NCI Balance c/fwd | 780 | Share of profits in year | 120 |
| | 870 | | 870 |

## Associates

An associate is a company over which an investor has significant influence. Associates are not part of the group and therefore cash flows between the group and the associate must be reported in the statement of cash flows.

Cash flows relating to associates that need to be separately reported within the statement of cash flows are as follows:

- dividends received from an associate
- loans made to associates
- cash payments to acquire associates
- cash receipts from the sale of associates.

These cash flows should be presented as cash flows from investing activities.

Remember, associates are accounted for using the equity method. This means that, in the consolidated statement of profit or loss, the group records its share of the associate's profit for the year. This is a non-cash income and so must be deducted in the reconciliation between profit before tax and cash generated from operations.

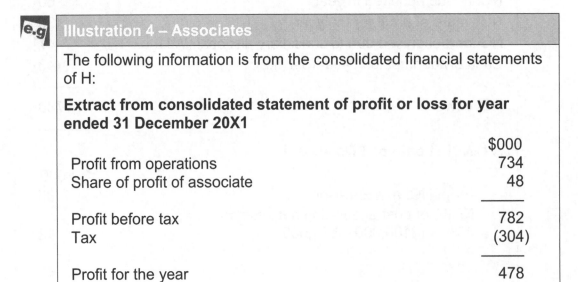

**e.g** Illustration 4 – Associates

The following information is from the consolidated financial statements of H:

**Extract from consolidated statement of profit or loss for year ended 31 December 20X1**

| | $000 |
|---|---|
| Profit from operations | 734 |
| Share of profit of associate | 48 |
| | |
| Profit before tax | 782 |
| Tax | (304) |
| | |
| Profit for the year | 478 |

**Extracts from consolidated statement of financial position as at 31 December 20X1 (with comparatives)**

| | 20X1 | 20X0 |
|---|---|---|
| | $000 | $000 |
| **Non-current assets** | | |
| Investment in associate | 466 | 456 |
| Loan to associate | 380 | 300 |

**Required:**

Calculate the relevant figures to be included in the group statement of cash flows for the year ended 31 December 20X1.

## Solution

**Extracts from statement of cash flows**

| | $000 |
|---|---|
| **Cash flows from operating activities** | |
| Profit before tax | 782 |
| Share of profit of associate | (48) |
| **Investing activities** | |
| Dividend received from associate (W1) | 38 |
| Loan to associate (380 – 300) | (80) |

**(W1) Dividend received from associate**

When dealing with the dividend from the associate, the process is the same as we have already seen with the non-controlling interest.

Set up a schedule or T account and include all the balances that relate to the associate. The balancing figure will be the cash dividend received from the associate.

| | $000 |
|---|---|
| Balance b/fwd | 456 |
| Share of profit of associate | 48 |
| Cash dividend received **(bal. fig.)** | (38) |
| | ___ |
| Balance c/fwd | 466 |
| | ___ |

Instead of a schedule, a T-account could be used:

### Associate

|  | $000 |  | $000 |
|---|---|---|---|
| Balance b/fwd | 456 | Dividend received (bal. fig.) | 38 |
| Share of profit of associate | 48 | Balance c/fwd | 466 |
|  | ———— |  | ———— |
|  | 504 |  | 504 |
|  | ———— |  | ———— |

### Test your understanding 4 – The Z group

The following information is from the consolidated financial statements of Z:

**Extract from consolidated statement of profit or loss for year ended 31 December 20X1**

|  | $000 |
|---|---|
| Profit from operations | 900 |
| Share of profit of associate | 15 |
|  | ———— |
| Profit before tax | 915 |
| Tax | (200) |
|  | ———— |
| Profit for the year | 715 |
|  | ———— |

**Extracts from consolidated statement of financial position as at 31 December 20X1 (with comparatives)**

|  | 20X1 $000 | 20X0 $000 |
|---|---|---|
| **Non-current assets** |  |  |
| Investment in associate | 600 | 580 |

During the year, Z received dividends from associates of $5,000.

**Required:**

**Based on the above information, prepare extracts showing relevant figures to be included in the group statement of cash flows for the year ended 31 December 20X1.**

## 7 Question practice

| Test your understanding 5 – Consolidated extracts |

Calculate the required cash flows in each of the following scenarios:

1

|  | 20X1 | 20X0 |
|---|---|---|
|  | $ | $ |
| Non-controlling interest | 840 | 440 |

The group statement of profit or loss and other comprehensive income reported total comprehensive income attributable to the non-controlling interest of $500.

**Required:**

**How much was the cash dividend paid to the non-controlling interest?**

2

|  | 20X1 | 20X0 |
|---|---|---|
|  | $ | $ |
| Non-controlling interest | 850 | 500 |

The group statement of profit or loss and other comprehensive income reported total comprehensive income attributable to the non-controlling interest of $600.

**Required:**

**How much was the cash dividend paid to the non-controlling interest?**

3

|  | 20X1 | 20X0 |
|---|---|---|
|  | $ | $ |
| Investment in associate | 500 | 200 |

The group statement of profit or loss reported 'share of profit of associates' of $750.

**Required:**

**How much was the cash dividend received by the group?**

4

|                          | 20X1 | 20X0 |
|--------------------------|------|------|
|                          | $    | $    |
| Investment in associate  | 3,200 | 600 |

The group statement of profit or loss reported 'share of profit of associates' of $4,000.

In addition, the associate revalued its non-current assets during the period. The group share of this gain is $500.

**Required:**

**How much was the cash dividend received by the group?**

5

|                                      | 20X1 | 20X0 |
|--------------------------------------|------|------|
|                                      | $    | $    |
| Property, plant and equipment (PPE)  | 500  | 150  |

During the year depreciation charged was $50, and the group acquired a subsidiary which held PPE of $200 at the acquisition date.

**Required:**

**How much cash was spent on property, plant and equipment in the period?**

### Test your understanding 6 – AH Group

Extracts from the consolidated financial statements of the AH Group for the year ended 30 June 20X5 are given below:

**Consolidated statement of profit or loss for the year ended 30 June 20X5**

|                        | $000    |
|------------------------|---------|
| Profit from operations | 19,850  |
| Finance cost           | (1,400) |
| Profit before tax      | 18,450  |
| Tax                    | (6,250) |
| Profit for the period  | 12,200  |

**Extract from statement of financial position, with comparatives, at 30 June 20X5**

|  | 20X5 $000 | 20X4 $000 |
|---|---|---|
| **Non-current assets** | | |
| Goodwill | 5,910 | 4,160 |
| | | |
| **Current assets** | | |
| Inventories | 33,500 | 28,750 |
| Trade receivables | 27,130 | 26,300 |
| | | |
| **Current liabilities** | | |
| Trade payables | 33,340 | 32,810 |

**Notes:**

1   On 1 January 20X5, AH acquired 75% of the issued equity shares of CJ for $6 million. The net assets of CJ at the date of acquisition had the following fair values:

| | $000 |
|---|---|
| Property, plant and equipment | 4,200 |
| Inventories | 1,650 |
| Trade receivables | 1,300 |
| Cash and cash equivalents | 50 |
| Trade payables | (1,950) |
| Tax | (250) |
| | ——— |
| | 5,000 |
| | ——— |

Goodwill relating to the acquisition of entity CJ during the year was calculated on the full goodwill basis. On 1 January 20X5 when CJ was acquired, the fair value of the non-controlling interest was $1,750,000.

Any impairments of goodwill during the year have been accounted for within operating expenses.

2   During the year, AH disposed of property, plant and equipment for proceeds of $2,250,000. The carrying amount of the asset at the date of disposal was $1,000,000. Depreciation of $7,950,000 was charged to profit or loss during the year.

**Required:**

(a) Prepare 'cash generated from operations' using the indirect method as it would appear in the consolidated statement of cash flows for the year ended 30 June 20X5.

(b) Explain the reasons behind the adjustments made to profit before tax in part (a).

## Test your understanding 7 – Pearl

Below are the consolidated financial statements of the Pearl Group for the year ended 30 September 20X2:

**Consolidated statements of financial position**

|  | 20X2 $000 | 20X1 $000 |
|---|---|---|
| Non-current assets |  |  |
| Goodwill | 1,930 | 1,850 |
| Property, plant and equipment | 2,545 | 1,625 |
| Investment in associate | 620 | 540 |
|  | 5,095 | 4,015 |
| Current assets |  |  |
| Inventories | 470 | 435 |
| Trade receivables | 390 | 330 |
| Cash and cash equivalents | 210 | 140 |
|  | 6,165 | 4,920 |
| Equity and liabilities |  |  |
| Share capital ($1 shares) | 1,500 | 1,500 |
| Retained earnings | 1,755 | 1,085 |
| Other reserves | 750 | 525 |
|  | 4,005 | 3,110 |
| Non-controlling interest | 310 | 320 |
|  | 4,315 | 3,430 |
| Non-current liabilities: |  |  |
| Loans | 500 | 300 |
| Deferred tax | 150 | 105 |
| Current liabilities: |  |  |
| Trade payables | 800 | 725 |
| Tax payable | 400 | 360 |
|  | 6,165 | 4,920 |

**Consolidated statement of profit or loss and other comprehensive income for the year ended 30 September 20X2**

|  | $000 |
|---|---|
| Revenue | 2,090 |
| Operating expenses | (1,155) |
|  |  |
| Profit from operations | 935 |
| Gain on disposal of subsidiary | 100 |
| Finance cost | (35) |
| Share of profit of associate | 115 |
|  |  |
| Profit before tax | 1,115 |
| Tax | (225) |
|  |  |
| Profit for the period | 890 |
| Other comprehensive income | 200 |
| Other comprehensive income from associate | 50 |
|  |  |
| Total comprehensive income | 1,140 |
|  |  |
| Profit for the year attributable to: |  |
| Owners of the parent | 795 |
| Non-controlling interests | 95 |
|  |  |
|  | 890 |
|  |  |
| Total comprehensive income for the year attributable to: |  |
| Owners of the parent | 1,020 |
| Non-controlling interests | 120 |
|  |  |
|  | 1,140 |

## Consolidated statement of changes in equity

| | Attributable to owners of the parent | Attributable to the NCI |
|---|---|---|
| | $000 | $000 |
| Equity brought forward | 3,110 | 320 |
| Total comprehensive income | 1,020 | 120 |
| Acquisition of subsidiary | – | 340 |
| Disposal of subsidiary | – | (420) |
| Dividends | (125) | (50) |
| | _____ | _____ |
| Equity carried forward | 4,005 | 310 |
| | _____ | _____ |

1   Depreciation of $385,000 was charged during the year. Plant with a carrying amount of $250,000 was sold for $275,000. The gain on disposal was recognised in operating costs. Certain properties were revalued during the year resulting in a revaluation gain of $200,000 being recognised.

2   During the year, Pearl acquired 80% of the equity share capital of Gem paying cash consideration of $1.5 million. The NCI holding was measured at its fair value of $340,000 at the date of acquisition. The fair value of Gem's net assets at acquisition was made up as follows:

| | $000 |
|---|---|
| Property, plant and equipment | 1,280 |
| Inventories | 150 |
| Trade receivables | 240 |
| Cash and cash equivalents | 80 |
| Trade payables | (220) |
| Tax payable | (40) |
| | _____ |
| | 1,490 |
| | _____ |

3   During the year, Pearl disposed of its 60% equity shareholding in Stone for cash proceeds of $850,000. The subsidiary had been acquired several years ago for cash consideration of $600,000. The NCI holding was measured at its fair value of $320,000 at acquisition and the fair value of Stone's net assets were $730,000. Goodwill had not suffered any impairment. At the date of disposal, the net assets of Stone were carried in the consolidated statement of financial position as follows:

|  | $000 |
|---|---|
| Property, plant and equipment | 725 |
| Inventories | 165 |
| Trade receivables | 120 |
| Cash and cash equivalents | 50 |
| Trade payables | (80) |
|  | ——— |
|  | 980 |
|  | ——— |

**Required:**

**Prepare the consolidated statement of cash flows for the Pearl group for the year ended 30 September 20X2.**

## 8   Foreign exchange and cash flow statements

### Exchange gains and losses

The values of assets and liabilities denominated in an overseas currency will increase or decrease partly due to movements in exchange rates. These movements must be factored into your workings in order to determine the actual cash payments and receipts during the year.

**Dealing with foreign exchange issues**

The loan balances of the Grey group as at 31 December 20X1 and 31 December 20X0 are presented below:

|  | 20X1 | 20X0 |
|---|---|---|
|  | $m | $m |
| Loans | 60 | 20 |

One of the subsidiaries of the Grey group prepares its financial statements in sterling (£). The exchange loss on the translation of the loans of this subsidiary was $10 million.

Remember that an exchange loss increases the carrying amount of a liability. This is not a cash flow. Therefore, the exchange loss must be factored into the cash flow workings as follows:

|  | $m |
|---|---|
| Bal b/fwd | 20 |
| Exchange loss | 10 |
| Cash received (bal. fig.) | 30 |
| | ---- |
| Bal c/fwd | 60 |
| | ---- |

The cash received from issuing new loans during the year was $30 million. This will be shown as an inflow within cash flows from financing activities.

## Overseas cash balances

If cash balances are partly denominated in a foreign currency, the effect of exchange rate movements must be reported in the statement of cash flows in order to reconcile the cash balances at the beginning and end of the period.

According to IAS 7, this reconciling item is presented separately from cash flows from operating, investing and financing activities.

### Test your understanding 8 – Boardres

Set out below is a summary of the accounts of Boardres, a public limited company, for the year ended 31 December 20X7.

**Consolidated statement of profit or loss and other comprehensive income for the year ended 31 December 20X7**

|  | $000 |
|---|---|
| Profit from operations | 5,141 |
| Income from associates | 30 |
| Finance cost | (305) |
| | ---- |
| Profit before tax | 4,866 |
| Tax | (2,038) |
| | ---- |
| Profit for the period | 2,828 |
| | ---- |

**Extracts from consolidated statements of financial position at 31 December**

|  | 20X7 | 20X6 |
| --- | --- | --- |
|  | $000 | $000 |
| **Non-current assets** |  |  |
| Property, plant and equipment | 11,157 | 8,985 |
| Investment in associate | 300 | 280 |

**Additional information**

1 **Property, plant and equipment**

Property, plant and equipment movements include the following:

|  | $000 |
| --- | --- |
| Carrying amount of disposals | 305 |
| Proceeds from disposals | 854 |
| Depreciation charge for the year | 907 |
| Exchange gain on translation of overseas subsidiary | 138 |

2 **Liberated**

During the year, the company acquired 82% of the issued equity capital of Liberated for cash consideration. Goodwill arising on the acquisition was $585,000. The non-controlling interest was valued using the proportion of net assets method. The fair values of the assets of Liberated at acquisition were as follows:

|  | $000 |
| --- | --- |
| Property, plant and equipment | 208 |
| Inventories | 612 |
| Trade receivables | 500 |
| Cash and cash equivalents | 232 |
| Trade payables | (407) |
| Debenture loans | (312) |
|  | ——— |
|  | 833 |
|  | ——— |

**Required:**

Prepare 'cash flows from investing activities' as it would appear in the consolidated statement of cash flows for the year ended 31 December 20X7. Explain your treatment of the acquisition of Liberated.

## 9 Other issues

The following criticisms have been made of IAS 7 *Statement of Cash Flows*.

### Direct and indirect method

Allowing entities to choose between using the direct or indirect method of presenting cash generated from operations limits comparability.

Many users of the financial statements will not understand the adjustments made to profit when cash generated from operations is presented using the indirect method.

### Lack of guidance and disagreements

There is insufficient guidance in IAS 7 as to how to classify cash flows. This can create the following problems:

- IAS 7 allows dividends and interest paid to be presented as cash flows from either operating or financing activities. This limits comparability between companies.

- Entities may classify cash flows related to the same transaction in different ways (a loan repayment might be split between interest paid within operating activities and the repayment of the principal in financing activities). This could hinder user understanding.

- There are disagreements about the presentation of payments related to leases. Some argue that they should be classified as a financing activity, whereas others argue that they are a form of investment activity.

- Expenditure on research is classified as an operating activity. Some argue that this should be included within investing activities, because it relates to items that are intended to generate future income and cash flows.

### Disclosures

Current cash flow disclosures are deemed to be inadequate. In particular, there is a lack of disclosure about restrictions on an entity's ability to use its cash and cash equivalents (particularly if located overseas) and whether other sources of finance would be more economical.

## 10 Chapter summary

**Objective of statements of cash flows**

- To provide information on changes in cash and cash equivalents
- To enable users to assess the liquidity, solvency and financial adaptability of a business

**Classifications of cash flows**

- IAS 7 only requires 3 headings:
  - Operating activities
  - Investing activities
  - Financing activities

**Preparation of group statements of cash flows**

- Three additional elements:
  - Cash paid to non-controlling interest
  - Associates
  - Acquisition and disposal of subsidiaries/ associates

**Foreign currency transactions**

- Exchange gains must be taken out of the statement of financial position movements as they are not cash

**Evaluation of statements of cash flows**

- Proivdes information not available in the statement of financial position and the statement of profit or loss
- Shows relationship between profitability and cash generating ability

# Test your understanding answers

## Test your understanding 1 – Plaster

The cash flow relates to the sale of property, plant and equipment (PPE) and so, per IAS 7 *Statement of Cash Flows*, should be presented as a cash flow from investing activities.

Classifying the proceeds from PPE disposals as an operating cash flow will make Plaster look more liquid, sustainable and financially secure than it really is. Plaster cannot keep selling its property, plant and equipment indefinitely. Therefore, proceeds from these disposals are unlikely to recur and cannot be relied on. It is vital that entities generate sufficient cash flows from their trading activities to meet mandatory repayments as they fall due (such as interest, tax, and borrowings).

Financial statements are used by an array of different groups, such as lenders, when making decisions about whether to advance economic resources to the reporting entity. The information presented must be reliable, truthful and neutral. Accountants are professionals, who are bestowed with status and are trusted by the public. To ensure that this trust is not broken, accountants are bound by a *Code of Ethics and Conduct*.

Integrity is defined as being honest and straight-forward. Manipulating cash flow classification shows a lack of integrity.

If the decision to misclassify cash flows has been motivated by a desire to alter user perception of the company, perhaps to facilitate the raising of finance, then this demonstrates a lack of objectivity.

The directors have a responsibility, as members of the accountancy profession, to prepare financial statements that offer a faithful representation of the Plaster's cash flows. This can be achieved through compliance with IAS 7 *Statement of Cash Flows*. False classification of cash flows will mislead key user groups and is therefore always unethical.

## Test your understanding 2 – Cash and cash equivalents

To qualify as a cash equivalent, an item must be readily convertible to cash and have an insignificant risk of a change in value. Furthermore, it should be held for the purpose of meeting short-term cash commitments.

Bank overdrafts are an integral part of most company's cash management. They are therefore generally treated as a component of cash.

The balance of $500,000 in a high interest account is readily available (only 28 days' notice is required to access it). This money is also held to meet short-term needs. Assuming that there is not a significant penalty for accessing this money, it should be included within cash equivalents.

The shares are not a cash equivalent. Shares are investments rather than a way of meeting short-term cash requirements. Moreover, there is a significant risk that the value of the shares will change. Any cash spent on shares in the period should be shown within cash flows from investing activities.

## Test your understanding 3 – Extracts

1   **Property, plant and equipment**

|  | $ |
|---|---|
| Bal b/fwd | 100 |
| Revaluation | 60 |
| Leases | 30 |
| Depreciation | (20) |
| Disposals | (15) |
| Additions (bal. fig.) | 95 |
| | ——— |
| Bal c/fwd | 250 |
| | ——— |

2   **Tax**

|  | $ |
|---|---|
| Bal b/fwd (50 + 100) | 150 |
| Profit or loss charge | 180 |
| Tax paid (bal. fig.) | (110) |
| | ——— |
| Bal c/fwd (100 + 120) | 220 |
| | ——— |

3    **Retained earnings**

|  | $ |
|---|---|
| Bal b/fwd | 200 |
| Profit or loss | 150 |
| Dividend paid (bal. fig.) | (50) |
|  | ——— |
| Bal c/fwd | 300 |
|  | ——— |

**Test your understanding 4 – The Z group**

**Extracts from statement of cash flows**

|  | $000 |
|---|---|
| **Cash flows from operating activities** |  |
| Profit before tax | 915 |
| Share of profit of associate | (15) |
| **Cash flows from investing activities** |  |
| Dividend received from associate | 5 |
| Cash paid to acquire associates (W1) | (10) |

(W1) **Associate**

|  | $000 |
|---|---|
| Balance b/fwd | 580 |
| Share of profit of associate | 15 |
| Cash dividend received | (5) |
| Cash spent on investments in associates (bal. fig.) | 10 |
|  | ——— |
| Balance c/fwd | 600 |
|  | ——— |

## Test your understanding 5 – Consolidated extracts

### 1  Non-controlling interest

|                               | $       |
|-------------------------------|--------:|
| Bal b/fwd                     | 440     |
| Total comprehensive income    | 500     |
| Dividend paid (bal. fig.)     | (100)   |
| Bal c/fwd                     | 840     |

### 2  Non-controlling interest

|                               | $       |
|-------------------------------|--------:|
| Bal b/fwd                     | 500     |
| Total comprehensive income    | 600     |
| Dividend paid (bal. fig.)     | (250)   |
| Bal c/fwd                     | 850     |

### 3  Associate

|                               | $       |
|-------------------------------|--------:|
| Bal b/fwd                     | 200     |
| Profit or loss                | 750     |
| Dividend received (bal. fig.) | (450)   |
| Bal c/fwd                     | 500     |

### 4  Associate

|                               | $       |
|-------------------------------|--------:|
| Bal b/fwd                     | 600     |
| Profit or loss                | 4,000   |
| Revaluation                   | 500     |
| Dividend received (bal. fig.) | (1,900) |
| Bal c/fwd                     | 3,200   |

### 5  Property, plant and equipment

|                               | $       |
|-------------------------------|--------:|
| Bal b/fwd                     | 150     |
| New subsidiary                | 200     |
| Depreciation                  | (50)    |
| Additions (bal. fig.)         | 200     |
| Bal c/fwd                     | 500     |

**Test your understanding 6 – AH Group**

(a) **Cash generated from operations**

|  | $000 |
|---|---|
| Profit before tax | 18,450 |
| Finance cost | 1,400 |
| Profit on disposal of property (2,250 – 1,000) | (1,250) |
| Depreciation | 7,950 |
| Goodwill impairment (W1) | 1,000 |
| Decrease in trade receivables (27,130 – 26,300 – 1,300) | 470 |
| Increase in inventories (33,500 – 28,750 – 1,650) | (3,100) |
| Decrease in trade payables (33,340 – 32,810 – 1,950) | (1,420) |
| | |
| Cash generated from operations | 23,500 |

(W1) **Goodwill**

|  | $000 |
|---|---|
| Bal b/fwd | 4,160 |
| Goodwill on sub acquired (W2) | 2,750 |
| Impairment in year (bal. fig.) | (1,000) |
| | |
| Bal c/fwd | 5,910 |

(W2) **Goodwill arising on acquisition of subsidiary**

|  | $000 |
|---|---|
| Consideration | 6,000 |
| Fair value of NCI at acquisition | 1,750 |
| Fair value of net assets at acquisition | (5,000) |
| | |
| Goodwill at acquisition | 2,750 |

(b) **Profit adjustments**

IAS 7 *Statement of Cash Flows* states that the indirect method of calculating cash generated from operations involves adjusting the profit (or loss) for the period for the effects of changes in working capital, non-cash items, and items which relate to investing or financing.

Finance costs in the statement of profit or loss are not a cash flow because they are accounted for on an accruals basis. Finance costs are therefore added back to profit to eliminate them. Any cash interest paid is separately presented in the statement of cash flows (normally below 'cash generated from operations').

A profit recorded on the disposal of PPE is not a cash item. The proceeds received should be reported in the statement of cash flows as an investing activity. The profit on disposal of PPE must be deducted from profit before tax to eliminate it from operating activities.

Depreciation and impairment losses are non-cash expenses. These are eliminated by adding them back to profit.

Businesses buy and sell goods on credit, but only cash receipts and cash payments should be reported in the statement of cash flows. Adjusting for the movement in working capital items eliminates the impact of accruals accounting. Some of the year-on-year movement in working capital relates to the acquisition of a subsidiary, rather than resulting from cash flows with customers and suppliers, and so the effect of this acquisition has been eliminated.

**Test your understanding 7 – Pearl**

**Consolidated statement of cash flows**

|  | $000 | $000 |
|---|---|---|
| **Cash flows from operating activities** |  |  |
| Profit before tax | 1,115 |  |
| Finance cost | 35 |  |
| Profit on sale of subsidiary | (100) |  |
| Income from associates | (115) |  |
| Depreciation | 385 |  |
| Impairment (W1) | 80 |  |
| Gain on disposal of PPE ($275 – $250) | (25) |  |
| Increase in inventories<br>($470 – $435 – $150 + $165) | (50) |  |
| Decrease in receivables<br>($390 – $330 – $240 + $120) | 60 |  |
| Decrease in payables<br>($800 – $725 – $220 + $80) | (65) |  |
|  | ——— |  |
|  | 1,320 |  |
| Interest paid | (35) |  |
| Tax paid (W4) | (180) |  |
|  | ——— |  |
|  |  | 1,105 |
| **Cash flows from investing activities** |  |  |
| Proceeds from sale of PPE | 275 |  |
| Purchases of PPE (W5) | (800) |  |
| Dividends received from associate (W6) | 85 |  |
| Acquisition of subsidiary ($1,500 – $80) | (1,420) |  |
| Disposal of subsidiary ($850 – $50) | 800 |  |
|  | ——— |  |
|  |  | (1,060) |
| **Cash flows from financing activities** |  |  |
| Proceeds from loans ($500 – $300) | 200 |  |
| Dividends paid to shareholders of the parent<br>(per CSOCIE) | (125) |  |
| Dividends paid to NCI (per CSOCIE) | (50) |  |
|  | ——— |  |
|  |  | 25 |
|  |  | ——— |
| Increase in cash and cash equivalents |  | 70 |
| Opening cash and cash equivalents |  | 140 |
|  |  | ——— |
| Closing cash and cash equivalents |  | 210 |
|  |  | ——— |

## Workings

### (W1) Goodwill

|  | $000 |
|---|---|
| Balance b/f | 1,850 |
| Acquisition of subsidiary (W2) | 350 |
| Disposal of subsidiary (W3) | (190) |
| Impairment (bal. fig.) | (80) |
| Balance c/f | 1,930 |

### (W2) Goodwill on acquisition of subsidiary

|  | $000 |
|---|---|
| Cost of investment | 1,500 |
| Fair value of NCI at acquisition | 340 |
| Fair value of net assets at acquisition | (1,490) |
|  | 350 |

### (W3) Goodwill at disposal date

|  | $000 |
|---|---|
| Cost of investment | 600 |
| Fair value of NCI at acquisition | 320 |
| Fair value of net assets at acquisition | (730) |
|  | 190 |

### (W4) Tax

|  | $000 |
|---|---|
| Balance b/f ($360 + $105) | 465 |
| Acquisition of subsidiary | 40 |
| Disposal of subsidiary | – |
| Profit or loss | 225 |
| Cash paid (bal. fig.) | (180) |
| Balance c/f ($400 + $150) | 550 |

**(W5) PPE**

|  | $000 |
|---|---|
| Balance b/f | 1,625 |
| Depreciation | (385) |
| Revaluation gain | 200 |
| Disposal of plant | (250) |
| Acquisition of subsidiary | 1,280 |
| Disposal of subsidiary | (725) |
| Cash paid (bal. fig.) | 800 |
|  | ——— |
| Balance c/f | 2,545 |
|  | ——— |

**(W6) Dividend from associate**

|  | $000 |
|---|---|
| Balance b/f | 540 |
| Share of profit of associate | 115 |
| OCI from associate | 50 |
| Dividend received (bal. fig.) | (85) |
|  | ——— |
| Balance c/f | 620 |
|  | ——— |

**Test your understanding 8 – Boardres**

| **Cash flows from investing activities** | $000 |
|---|---|
| Purchase of PPE (W1) | (3,038) |
| Proceeds from disposal of PPE | 854 |
| Dividend received from associate (W2) | 10 |
| Cash consideration paid on acquisition of subsidiary, net of cash acquired (1,268 (W3) – 232) | (1,036) |
|  | ——— |
|  | (3,210) |
|  | ——— |

Liberated was acquired during the year for cash consideration of $1,268,000 (see W3 below). This is a cash outflow that must be presented under investing activities. However, Liberated's cash and cash equivalents of $232,000 are also now controlled by the group and this represents a cash inflow. Therefore, in the consolidated statement of cash flows, Boardres must show the net cash impact of the subsidiary acquisition: a net cash outflow of $1,036,000.

**Workings**

**(W1) Property, plant and equipment**

| | $000 |
|---|---:|
| Bal b/fwd | 8,985 |
| Exchange gain | 138 |
| Acquisition of subsidiary | 208 |
| Depreciation | (907) |
| Disposal | (305) |
| Additions (bal. fig.) | 3,038 |
| Bal c/fwd | 11,157 |

**(W2) Dividends from associates**

| | $000 |
|---|---:|
| Bal b/fwd | 280 |
| Profit or loss | 30 |
| Dividend received (bal. fig.) | (10) |
| Bal c/fwd | 300 |

**(W3) Purchase consideration**

| | $000 |
|---|---:|
| Cash consideration (bal. fig.) | 1,268 |
| NCI at acquisition (18% × 833) | 150 |
| FV of net assets at acquisition | (833) |
| Goodwill at acquisition | 585 |

# Analysis and interpretation

## Chapter learning objectives

Upon completion of this chapter you will be able to:

- Discuss and apply relevant indicators of financial and non-financial performance including earnings per share and additional performance measure

- Discuss group statements of cash flows

- Discuss the increased demand for transparency in corporate reports, and the emergence of non-financial reporting standards

- Appraise the impact of environmental, social, and ethical factors on performance measurement

- Discuss the current framework for integrated reporting (IR) including the objectives, concepts, guiding principles and content of an Integrated Report.

**PER**

One of the PER performance objectives (PO8) is to analyse and interpret financial reports. You analyse financial statements to evaluate and assess the financial performance and position of an entity. Working through this chapter should help you understand how to demonstrate that objective.

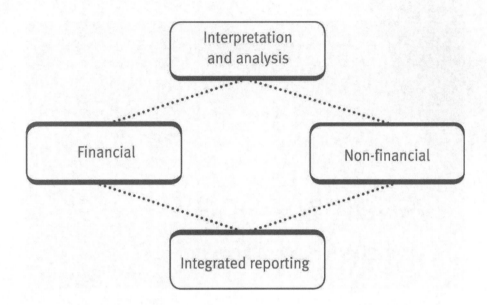

## 1 Analysis and interpretation

The SBR syllabus requires students to reflect on the usefulness of corporate reports to stakeholders and to discuss the nature of the information that would help stakeholders assess the future prospects of the entity.

Remember that, according to the *Conceptual Framework*, the purpose of financial reporting is to provide information to current and potential investors, lenders and other creditors that will enable them to make decisions about providing economic resources to an entity.

If investors, lenders and creditors are going to make these decisions then they require information that will help them to assess:

- an entity's potential future cash flows, and

- management's stewardship of the entity's economic resources.

Some of this information is found in financial statements. However, more and more companies are producing other types of reports, such as integrated reports. These shift the focus of reporting away from short-term financial measures and instead provide a more holistic and long-term representation of the entity's societal impact.

This chapter examines the different sources of information available, and a range of analysis techniques, that can enable key user groups to make informed investment decisions.

 **Progression**

Analysis was a key area of the Financial Reporting syllabus. SBR places much less emphasis on the calculation of ratios.

## 2 Assessing financial performance and position

In your previous studies, you will have learned a number of ratios that can be used to interpret an entity's financial statements.

A selection of the key ratios are provided below:

### Profitability

**Gross profit margin:**

$$\frac{\text{Gross profit}}{\text{Revenue}} \times 100\%$$

An increase in gross profit margin may be a result of:

- higher selling prices

- lower purchase prices (perhaps resulting from bulk-buy discounts)

- a change in the sales mix.

**Operating profit margin:**

$$\frac{\text{Operating profit}}{\text{Revenue}} \times 100\%$$

Operating profit margin is affected by more factors than gross profit margin. Many operating costs are fixed and therefore do not necessarily increase or decrease with revenue. This means that operating profit margin may be more volatile year-on-year than gross profit margin.

Be aware that many operating costs, such as depreciation and impairment losses, are heavily reliant on management judgement. This may hinder the ability to compare the operating profit margin of one company with another company.

**Return on capital employed (ROCE):**

$$\frac{\text{Operating profit}}{\text{Capital employed}} \times 100\%$$

Capital employed is equity plus interest bearing finance.

ROCE is a measure of how efficiently an entity is using its resources. It should be compared to:

- previous years' figures

- the target ROCE

- the ROCE of competitors

- the cost of borrowing.

### Liquidity and working capital

#### Current ratio:

$$\frac{\text{Current assets}}{\text{Current liabilities}} : 1$$

The current ratio measures whether an entity has sufficient current assets to meet its short-term obligations. The higher the ratio, the more financially secure the entity is. However, if the ratio is too high then it may suggest inefficiencies in working capital management.

#### Inventory turnover period:

$$\frac{\text{Inventories}}{\text{Cost of sales}} \times 365 \text{ days}$$

A high inventory turnover period may suggest:

- lack of demand for the entity's goods

- poor inventory control.

#### Receivables collection period:

$$\frac{\text{Trade receivables}}{\text{Credit sales}} \times 365 \text{ days}$$

An increase in the receivables collection period may suggest a lack of credit control, which could lead to irrecoverable debts.

#### Payables payment period:

$$\frac{\text{Trade payables}}{\text{Credit purchases}} \times 365 \text{ days}$$

This represents the credit period taken by the company from its suppliers. A long credit period can be a good sign because it is a free source of finance. However, if an entity is taking too long to pay its suppliers then there is a risk that credit facilities could be reduced or withdrawn.

### Long-term financial stability

#### Gearing:

$$\frac{\text{Debt}}{\text{Equity}} \quad \text{or} \quad \frac{\text{Debt}}{\text{Debt + equity}}$$

Gearing indicates the risk attached to the entity's finance. Highly geared entities have a greater risk of insolvency.

**Interest cover:**

Operating profit

Finance costs

Interest cover indicates the ability of an entity to pay interest out of the profits generated. A low interest cover suggests that an entity may have difficulty financing its debts if profits fall.

## Investor ratios

### P/E ratio:

Current share price

EPS

The P/E ratio represents the market's view of the future prospects of an entity's shares. A high P/E ratio suggests that growth is expected.

The calculation of EPS (earnings per share) is revised in the next section of this chapter.

**Test your understanding 1 – Starling**

Starling has issued B class shares and has recorded them as equity instruments in the statement of financial position. Under the terms of the shareholder agreement, Starling is obliged to redeem the shares in cash in three years' time.

**Required:**

**Discuss the impact on the financial statements of the above error. Your answer should make reference to financial statement ratios.**

## 3 IAS 33 *Earnings per Share*

### Scope

IAS 33 *Earnings per Share* applies to listed entities. If private entities choose to disclose earnings per share, it must be calculated in accordance with IAS 33.

**Investor perspective – EPS**

Cottage Group is a listed entity. It has a reporting period of 31 December 20X1. An extract from the 'earnings per share' disclosure note is provided below:

|  | 20X1 cents per share | 20X0 cents per share |
|---|---|---|
| Basic earnings | 17.4 | 23.8 |
| Diluted earnings | 16.3 | 22.4 |

Basic earnings per share must be calculated in accordance with IAS 33 *Earnings per Share*. This means that the EPS of one company can be easily compared to another company. A company with a higher EPS figure is likely to pay higher dividends per share (although not necessarily in the short-term). This helps investors to decide whether to buy, sell or hold the company's equities.

Many investors look to invest in companies with a steadily increasing 'earnings per share' figure. Cottage Group's year-on-year decline may cause concern. Further analysis of the financial statements is required to ascertain the reasons for this.

Of course, investors are often interested in future returns. For this reason, they may use earnings per share to calculate other ratios, such as the price/earnings ratio. A high price/earnings ratio suggests that the market is confident about the entity's future prospects. It is important to remember that the market can be wrong – as was the case with the dotcom collapse at the beginning of the twenty-first century.

### The basic calculation

The actual earnings per share (EPS) for the period is called the **basic EPS** and is calculated as:

$$\frac{\text{Profit or loss for the period attributable to equity shareholders}}{\text{Weighted average number of ordinary shares outstanding in the period}}$$

Profit for the period must be reduced (or a loss for the period must be increased) for any irredeemable preference dividends paid during the period.

If an entity prepares consolidated financial statements, then EPS will be based on the consolidated profit for the period attributable to the equity shareholders of the parent company (i.e. total consolidated profit less the profit attributable to the non-controlling interest).

The weighted average number of shares takes into account the timing of share issues during the year.

**Illustration 1 – Basic earnings per share**

An entity issued 200,000 shares at full market price on 1 July 20X8.

Relevant information is provided below:

|  | 20X8 | 20X7 |
| --- | --- | --- |
| Profit attributable to the ordinary shareholders for the year ending 31 Dec | $550,000 | $460,000 |
| Number of ordinary shares in issue at 31 Dec | 1,000,000 | 800,000 |

**Required:**

**Calculate basic EPS for the years ended 31 December 20X7 and 20X8.**

## Solution

**Calculation of earnings per share**

20X7 = $460,000/800,000 = 57.5c

20X8 = $550,000/900,000 (W1) = 61.1c

**(W1) Weighted average number of shares in 20X8**

| | |
|---|---:|
| 800,000 × 6/12 = | 400,000 |
| 1,000,000 × 6/12 = | 500,000 |
| | 900,000 |

Since the additional 200,000 shares were issued at full market price but have only contributed finance for half a year, a weighted average number of shares must be calculated. The earnings figure is not adjusted.

## Bonus issues

If an entity makes a bonus issue of shares then share capital increases. However, no cash has been received and therefore there is no impact on earnings. This means that a bonus issue reduces EPS.

For the purpose of calculating basic EPS, the bonus issue shares are treated as if they have always been in issue. The easiest way to do this is multiply the number of shares outstanding before the bonus issue by the bonus fraction.

The bonus fraction is calculated as follows:

$$\frac{\text{Number of shares after bonus issue}}{\text{Number of shares before bonus issue}}$$

EPS for the comparative period must be restated. The easiest way to achieve this is to multiply the EPS figure from the prior year's financial statements by the inverse of the bonus fraction.

### Illustration 2 – Bonus issues

An entity made a bonus issue of one new share for every five existing shares held on 1 July 20X8.

**Relevant information**

| | 20X8 | 20X7 |
|---|---|---|
| Profit attributable to the ordinary shareholders for the year ending 31 Dec | $550,000 | $460,000 |
| Number of ordinary shares in issue at 31 Dec | 1,200,000 | 1,000,000 |

> **Required:**
>
> (a) Calculate basic EPS for the year ended 31 December 20X8.
>
> (b) Calculate the prior year comparative EPS figure as it would appear in the financial statements for the year ended 31 December 20X8.

## Solution

(a) EPS = $550,000/1,200,000 (W1) = 45.8c

**(W1) Weighted average number of shares**

| | |
|---|---:|
| 1,000,000 × 6/12 × 6/5 (W2) | 600,000 |
| 1,200,000 × 6/12 | 600,000 |
| | ——— |
| Weighted average number of shares | 1,200,000 |
| | ——— |

**(W2) Bonus fraction**

It was a one for five bonus issue.

A shareholder who had five shares before the bonus issue would have six shares after the bonus issue.

The bonus fraction is therefore 6/5.

(b) EPS in the financial statements for the year ended 31 December 20X7 would have been 46.0c ($460,000/1,000,000).

This is re-stated in the financial statements for the year ended 31 December 20X8 by multiplying it by the inverse of the bonus fraction.

The restated comparative is therefore 38.3c (46.0c × 5/6).

## Rights issues

A rights issue of shares is normally made at less than the full market price. A rights issue therefore combines the characteristics of an issue at full market price with those of a bonus issue.

As already seen, the easiest way to deal with the bonus element is to calculate the bonus fraction and to apply this to all shares outstanding before the rights issue.

The bonus fraction for a rights issue is calculated as follows:

$$\frac{\text{Market price per share before rights issue}}{\text{Theoretical market price per share after the rights issue}}$$

EPS for the comparative period must be restated. The easiest way to achieve this is to multiply the EPS figure from the prior year's financial statements by the inverse of the bonus fraction.

**Illustration 3 – Rights issues**

An entity issued one new share for every two existing shares at $1.50 per share on 1 July 20X8. The pre-issue market price was $3.00 per share.

**Relevant information**

|  | 20X8 | 20X7 |
|---|---|---|
| Profit attributable to the ordinary shareholders for the year ending 31 Dec | $550,000 | $460,000 |
| Number of ordinary shares in issue at 31 Dec | 1,200,000 | 800,000 |

**Required:**

(a) Calculate basic EPS for the year ended 31 December 20X8.

(b) Calculate the prior year comparative EPS figure as it would appear in the financial statements for the year ended 31 December 20X8.

**Solution**

(a) EPS = $550,000/1,080,000 (W1) = 50.9c

(W1) **Weighted average number of shares**

| 800,000 × 6/12 × 3.00/2.50 (W2) | 480,000 |
|---|---|
| 1,200,000 × 6/12 | 600,000 |
| | |
| Weighted average number of shares | 1,080,000 |

(W2) **Bonus fraction**

The bonus fraction is calculated as:

$$\frac{\text{Market price per share before rights issue}}{\text{Theoretical market price per share after the rights issue}}$$

The bonus fraction is $3.00/$2.50 (W3).

(W3) **Theoretical share price after rights issue**

| | No. shares | Price per share $ | Market capitalisation $ |
|---|---|---|---|
| Before rights issue | 800,000 | 3.00 | 2,400,000 |
| Rights issue | 400,000 | 1.50 | 600,000 |
| | | | |
| | 1,200,000 | | 3,000,000 |

The theoretical price per share after the rights issue is $2.50 ($3,000,000/1,200,000).

> (b) EPS in the financial statements for the year ended 31 December 20X7 would have been 57.5c ($460,000/800,000).
>
> This is restated in the financial statements for the year ended 31 December 20X8 by multiplying it by the inverse of the bonus fraction.
>
> The restated comparative is therefore 47.9c (57.5c × 2.50/3.00).

## Diluted EPS

Many companies issue convertible instruments, options and warrants that entitle their holders to purchase shares in the future at below the market price. When these shares are eventually issued, the interests of the original shareholders will be diluted. The dilution occurs because these shares will have been issued at below market price.

The Examiner has indicated that diluted earnings per share will not be examined in detail. However, students should have awareness of the topic as summarised below:

- Shares and other instruments that may dilute the interests of the existing shareholders are called potential ordinary shares.

- Examples of potential ordinary shares include:

    - debt and other instruments, including preference shares, that are convertible into ordinary shares

    - share warrants and options (instruments that give the holder the right to purchase ordinary shares)

    - employee plans that allow employees to receive ordinary shares as part of their remuneration and other share purchase plans

    - contingently issuable shares (i.e. shares issuable if certain conditions are met).

- Where there are dilutive potential ordinary shares in issue, the diluted EPS must be disclosed as well as the basic EPS. This provides relevant information to current and potential investors.

- When calculating diluted EPS, the profit used in the basic EPS calculation is adjusted for any expenses that would no longer be paid if the convertible instrument were converted into shares, e.g. preference dividends, loan interest.

- When calculating diluted EPS, the weighted average number of shares used in the basic EPS calculation is adjusted for the conversion of the potential ordinary shares.

### Assessing EPS as a performance measure

The EPS figure is used to compute the major stock market indicator of performance, the Price/Earnings ratio (P/E ratio). The stock market places great emphasis on the earnings per share figure and the P/E ratio. IAS 33 sets out a standard method of calculating EPS, which enhances the comparability of the figure.

EPS also has limitations as a performance measure:

- An entity's earnings are affected by its choice of accounting policies. Therefore, it may not always be appropriate to compare the EPS of different companies.

- EPS does not take account of inflation. Apparent growth in earnings may not be true growth.

- EPS does not provide predictive value. High earnings may be achieved at the expense of investment, which would have generated increased earnings in the future.

- In theory, diluted EPS serves as a warning to equity shareholders that the return on their investment may fall in future periods. However, diluted EPS is based on current earnings rather than forecast earnings.

- EPS is a measure of profitability but profitability is only one aspect of performance. Concentration on earnings per share and 'the bottom line' arguably detracts from other important aspects of an entity's affairs, such as cash flow and stewardship of assets.

### Test your understanding 2 – Coe

Coe, a public limited company, is preparing its consolidated financial statements for the year ended 31 December 20X1. Coe has owned 75% of the equity shares of Crace for a number of years. The following accounting issues have yet to be finalised:

1. On 1 January 20X1, 1,000 of Coe's managers were granted 500 share options each. These will vest on 31 December 20X3 if the managers are still employed by Coe. The fair value of one share option at the grant date was $6. By 31 December 20X1, 50 of these managers had left the business and another 80 were expected to leave by the vesting date. The exercise price of the options is $3. The average price of one of Coe's equity shares over the year is $10. No entries have been posted in relation to this share option scheme.

2. Freehold land is accounted for using the revaluation model in IAS 16 *Property, Plant and Equipment*. A revaluation has taken place in the current year. However, one plot of land is still carried in Coe's financial statements at its purchase cost of $4 million. Similar plots of land have sold for $5 million.

3    On 31 December 20X1, Crace made an interest-free loan of $3 million to a charity and recognised this amount as a financial asset. The charity will repay the money on 31 December 20X4. Market rates of interest are 5%.

**Required:**

**(i)    Explain, with calculations, how the above events should be corrected in the consolidated financial statements for the year ended 31 December 20X1.**

**(ii)   Discuss the impact of these corrections on basic and diluted earnings per share. No calculations are required.**

# 4    Impact of policies and estimates

Accounting policies and estimates can significantly affect the view presented by financial statements, and the ratios computed by reference to them, without affecting an entity's cash generation.

This is a particularly important issue when:

- accounting standards permit a choice, such as between a cost model or a fair value model
- judgement is needed in making accounting estimates, such as with depreciation, allowances and provisions
- there is no relevant accounting standard (although this is extremely rare).

## Investor perspective – Accounting policy choices

Assume that two separate entities, A and B, both buy an identical building for $10m on 1 January 20X1 and classify them as investment properties. Each building is expected to have a useful life of 50 years. By 31 December 20X1, the fair value of each building is $11m.

Entity A measures investment properties using the cost model. Entity B measures investment properties at fair value.

Extracts from the financial statements of the two entities are provided below:

**Statement of financial position**

|  | Entity A $m | Entity B $m |
|---|---|---|
| Investment properties | 9.8 | 11.0 |

**Statement of profit or loss**

|  | Entity A $m | Entity B $m |
|---|---|---|
| Depreciation | (0.2) | – |
| Gain on investment properties | – | 1.0 |

Assuming no other differences between the two entities, entity B will report higher profits and therefore higher earnings per share than entity A. Entity B will also show higher equity in its statement of financial position, so its gearing will reduce.

As this example shows, the fact that IAS 40 permits a choice in accounting policy could be argued to reduce the comparability of financial information.

## Test your understanding 3 – Impact of policy choices

Entities A and B are identical in all respects, except for their application of IAS 16 *Property, Plant and Equipment*.

Entity A accounts for buildings using the cost model whereas Entity B uses the revaluation model. Property prices have risen recently and so Entity B recorded a revaluation gain at the beginning of the current reporting period.

Extracts from the financial statements of both entities are provided below:

**Statements of profit or loss (extracts)**

|  | A<br>$000 | B<br>$000 |
|---|---|---|
| Revenue | 220 | 220 |
| Operating costs (including depreciation) | (180) | (210) |
| | | |
| Profit from operations | 40 | 10 |

**Statements of financial position (extracts)**

|  | A<br>$000 | B<br>$000 |
|---|---|---|
| Share capital | 50 | 50 |
| Retained earnings | 90 | 60 |
| Other components of equity | – | 210 |
| | | |
| Total equity | 140 | 320 |
| Borrowings | 100 | 100 |
| | | |
| Total equity and liabilities | 240 | 420 |

**Required:**

**Using ratio analysis, compare the financial statements of Entity A and Entity B and explain how the differences may impact stakeholder perception.**

## 5 Statements of cash flows

### Usefulness of the statement of cash flows

A statement of cash flows provides information that is not available from the statement of financial position or the statement of profit or loss and other comprehensive income. There are a number of reasons why it is useful for stakeholder analysis:

- Profits can be manipulated through the use of judgement or choice of a particular accounting policy whereas cash flows are objective and verifiable.

- Cash generated from operations is a useful indication of the quality of the profits generated by a business. Good quality profits will generate cash.

- Statements of cash flows provide valuable information to stakeholders on the financial adaptability of an entity.

- Cash flow information has some predictive value. It may assist stakeholders in making judgements about the amount, timing and certainty of future cash flows.

---

**Test your understanding 4 – Tuyet**

Tuyet is a public limited company that prepares its financial statements in accordance with International Financial Reporting Standards and has a year end of 31 December 20X1. It manufactures furniture that is sold to a range of retail outlets. As at the year-end Tuyet has loans outstanding, with repayments of $7 million due annually in each of the next four years.

You are a potential investor in Tuyet. You are analysing its statement of cash flows for the year ended 31 December 20X1, which is presented below:

**Statement of cash flows for year ended 31 December 20X1**

|  | $m | $m |
|---|---|---|
| **Cash flows from operating activities** | | |
| Profit before tax | 35 | |
| Finance cost | 5 | |
| Depreciation | 12 | |
| Profit on disposal of PPE | (8) | |
| Reduction in provisions | (6) | |
| Increase in inventories | (19) | |
| Increase in receivables | (14) | |
| Increase in payables | 13 | |
| | ——— | |
| Cash generated from operations | 18 | |
| Interest paid | (5) | |
| Tax paid | (10) | |
| | ——— | |

3

**Cash flows from investing activities**

| | | |
|---|---|---|
| Proceeds from sale of PPE | 20 | |
| Purchases of PPE | (30) | |
| | ――― | |
| | | (10) |

**Cash flows from financing activities**

| | | |
|---|---|---|
| Proceeds from shares | 15 | |
| Repayment of loans | (7) | |
| Dividends paid | – | |
| | ――― | |
| | | 8 |
| | | ――― |
| Increase in cash and cash equivalents | | 1 |
| Opening cash and cash equivalents | | (5) |
| | | ――― |
| Closing cash and cash equivalents | | (4) |
| | | ――― |

**Required:**

**From analysis of the statement of cash flows, what conclusions would you draw about Tuyet?**

## 6 Additional performance measures

### Background

Users of financial statements are demanding more information. In response, many entities present additional performance measures (APMs) in their published many statements, such as:

- **EBIT** – earnings before interest and tax

- **EBITDA** – earnings before interest, tax, depreciation and amortisation

- **Net financial debt** – gross debt less cash and cash equivalents and other financial assets

- **Free cash flow** – cash flows from operating activities less capital expenditure.

### Benefits

APMs can have many benefits, such as:

- Helping users of financial statements to evaluate an entity through the eyes of management

- Enabling comparison between entities in the same sector or industry

- Stripping out elements that are not relevant to current or future year operating performance.

## Drawbacks

Presenting APMs in financial statements can create problems:

- An entity might calculate an APM in a different way year-on-year

- Two entities might calculate the same APM in a different way

- Entities often provide little information about how an APM is calculated or how it reconciles with the figures presented in the financial statements

- APMs might be selected and calculated so as to present an overly optimistic picture of an entity's performance

- Too much information can be confusing to users of the financial statements

- Giving an APM undue prominence may mislead users of the financial statements into believing it is a requirement of IFRS Standards.

### Investor perspective – underlying profit

Bug in a Rug Group, a public limited entity, reports 'underlying profit before tax' in its annual financial statements. In a disclosure note, 'underlying profit before tax' is reconciled to 'profit before tax'. Below is an extract from the financial statements:

*In order to provide shareholders with additional insight into the underlying performance of the business, items recognised in reported profit or loss before tax which, due to their size and or nature, do not reflect the Group's underlying performance are excluded from the Group's underlying results:*

|  | $m | $m |
|---|---|---|
| Underlying profit before tax |  | 600 |
| Profit on property disposals | 20 |  |
| Fair value movements on investment properties | (10) |  |
| Impairment of property | (17) |  |
| Transaction costs on subsidiary acquisition | (4) |  |
| IT write offs | (7) |  |
| Defined benefit expenses | (11) |  |
| Total adjustments |  | (29) |
| Profit before tax |  | 571 |

Some argue that the disclosure of additional performance measures makes it easier for stakeholders to assess the future profits and cash flows of an entity. However, as can be seen above, additional performance measures often present an entity's performance in a more favourable light than performance measures that are based solely on the application of IFRS Standards. This may mislead investors when they are assessing an entity's financial performance.

### Investor perspective – free cash flow

Below is an extract from the financial statement disclosure notes of Spotty Potty Group for the year ended 31 December 20X1:

*The Directors use the additional performance measure 'free cash flow' because it is critical to understanding the financial performance and financial health of the Group. As this is not defined by International Financial Reporting Standards, it may not be directly comparable with other companies who use similar measures.*

*Free cash flow is calculated as net cash generated from operations less cash capital expenditure excluding strategic capital expenditure. A calculation of this figure for the current period, and comparative period, is provided:*

|  | 20X1 $m | 20X0 $m |
|---|---|---|
| Cash generated from operations | 561 | 612 |
| Interest paid | (46) | (47) |
| Tax paid | (50) | (60) |
| Purchase of PPE | (243) | (230) |
| Strategic capital expenditure | 93 | – |
| Free cash flow | 315 | 275 |

Despite lower cash generated from operations in 20X1 compared to 20X0, the entity appears to have a higher free cash flow available to repay its debts and to pay dividends to investors. However, this increase year-on-year is a result of the exclusion of 'strategic capital expenditure'. No definition is provided as to what this relates to, making it difficult to assess the appropriateness of the adjustment. While this adjustment may be a legitimate attempt to present investors with like-for-like information, it could also be a conscious attempt to present the cash performance of the entity in a more favourable light.

## Exam focus

It is important that you refer to a real set of published financial statements. This will help you to appreciate the wide range of APMs that listed entities disclose. Think critically as you read through the financial statements: are the APMs useful, confusing or, even, misleading?

### Test your understanding 5 – Hutton

Hutton discloses an additional performance measure (APM) called 'underlying profit' in its financial statements. The following is an extract from one of Hutton's financial statement disclosure notes for the year ended 31 December 20X1:

|  | $m |
|---|---|
| Loss before tax | (8) |
| Finance cost | 4 |
| Depreciation | 10 |
| Amortisation | 8 |
| Impairment of brand | 7 |
| Foreign exchange loss on monetary items | 3 |
| Gains on FVPL financial assets | (5) |
| | ─── |
| Underlying profit | 19 |
| | ─── |

Hutton presents comparable information for the prior period.

**Required:**

**Discuss why this APM may not be useful to Hutton's stakeholders.**

## 7 Tech companies

According to the *Conceptual Framework*, the statement of financial position provides relevant information about a company's financial position and the statement of profit or loss provides relevant information about a company's financial performance.

However, there is growing concern that financial statements produced under IFRS Standards (as well as other national accounting standards) do not produce useful information with regards to tech companies (such as Amazon, Google, Facebook and Apple).

## Statement of financial position

The carrying amounts of net assets in the statement of financial position for a tech company tends to be significantly lower than its market capitalisation (share price multiplied by number of shares in issue). Tech company financial statements underreport a significant amount of 'value'.

One key reason is that tech companies have powerful and valuable brands. In accordance with IAS 38 *Intangible Assets*, internally generated brands are not recognised on the statement of financial position.

Another reason is that operating assets used by many tech companies are not owned or leased by the company itself (such as the music available on Spotify, or the cars available to ride through the Uber app). Tech companies benefit from these assets but they do not meet the criteria for recognition in the statement of financial position because they are controlled by other parties (such as record labels, or taxi drivers).

A further reason is that many intangible assets developed and used by tech companies appreciate in value as they are used even though accounting standards may require them to be depreciated or amortised. For example, each new user on a social media platform increases the benefits of the platform for existing users as well as increasing the advertising fees that the platform owner can charge. Although there will be some incremental operating costs associated with new users (in relation to help, support and regulation of online behaviour), the growth is mainly driven by the assets already in place.

## Statement of profit or loss

Many tech companies, such as Uber and Twitter, are valued at billions of dollars even though they have historically made losses. When assessing economic performance, it would seem that investors increasingly look beyond the statement of profit or loss.

Tech companies tend to incur high costs in the initial years after incorporation. However, once these costs are incurred, the further costs required to expand are lower in comparison (for example, companies that offer online services can expand by adding to server capacity, rather than by acquiring new premises). As such successful tech companies often report losses for many years but then high margins once established as a market-leader. Therefore, at all stages in the lifecycle of a tech company, the statement of profit or loss does not effectively match the revenues earned in the current period with the costs incurred to earn those revenues.

This is not to argue that the statement of profit or loss is worthless to the analysis of performance. Investors are certainly interested in the revenue generated by a tech company – after all, this is a good indicator or growth and market-share. Furthermore, the share price of many tech companies rises significantly in the first period when a profit is recorded, indicating that markets attach some importance to this performance measure. It may be that profit generation indicates that the business has moved into a different stage in its lifecycle – away from a high risk, capital demanding initial stage into a mature, less risky, cash generative stage.

## Remedies

Due to the weaknesses identified above, tech companies may need to report other types of information to investors and lenders. This might be done via:

- Integrated reporting (covered later in this chapter)
- Online real-time reporting of key performance indicators (such as membership numbers, monetary spend per user etc.).

## 8 Non-financial performance measures

Problems arise from an over-reliance on financial performance indicators:

- They are normally calculated from historical financial information and provide limited information about future performance.
- They do not provide information about key issues that impact long-term success, such as customer satisfaction
- There are concerns about whether traditional financial reporting adequately reports the financial position and performance of tech companies
- They can be manipulated through accounting estimates or policy choices.

Due to these limitations, analysis of non-financial performance measures is important. These measures are related to entity performance but are not expressed in monetary units.

Examples of non-financial performance measures include:

- Employee turnover
- Absentee rates
- Employee satisfaction
- Customer satisfaction
- Delivery times
- Brand awareness and brand loyalty.

Entities are not required to disclose non-financial performance measures. However, many choose to do so in their annual reports or as part of their integrated report.

**Test your understanding 6 – Lorenzo**

Lorenzo develops and manufactures desktop and laptop computers. Profit after tax for the year-ended 31 December 20X1 is 5% lower than the prior period. Lorenzo discloses the following non-financial performance measures in its Integrated Report for the year ended 31 December 20X1.

|  | 20X1 | 20X0 |
|---|---|---|
| Faults per 1,000 sales | 2.1 | 3.2 |
| Customer service helpline waiting time (minutes) | 1.5 | 4.2 |
| Staff turnover* (%) | 6.5 | 13.2 |

*(leavers/average number of employees × 100)

**Required:**

**Discuss how the above information might be interpreted by Lorenzo's current and potential investors.**

## 9 The impact of ethical, environmental and social factors

### Entity behaviour

Many investors will not financially support entities that they perceive to be unethical or harmful to the environment. Some will only invest in entities that meet the very highest ethical standards, even if this means achieving a low overall return.

Factors which may be of interest to investors include:

- **Animal welfare** – does the entity test its products on animals?

- **Arms** – does the entity, or any entities within its group, manufacture or supply weapons?

- **Emissions** – does the entity monitor and take steps to reduce harmful emissions, such as carbon dioxide?

- **Energy** – is the entity committed to using renewable energy?

- **Marketing** – does the entity use irresponsible or offensive marketing strategies?

- **Remuneration** – what is the gap between the highest and lowest paid employees?

- **Supply chain management** – are goods and services only purchased from entities that have high ethical standards?

- **Tax** – does the entity use tax avoidance schemes?

- **Transparency** – does the entity make enhanced disclosures about its social and environmental impact?

- **Treatment of workers** – are working conditions safe and humane?

Investors will prioritise these issues to different degrees.

## Reporting

Entities often provide this information in additional reports, such as:

- environmental reports
- social reports
- sustainability reports
- integrated reports.

A range of nonfinancial reporting standards have been published in recent years to guide preparers of such reports. Some of these are discussed later in the chapter.

## Ethical behaviour and profit

Entities that pay employees higher wages, or which reject tax avoidance schemes, are likely to have higher costs. Moreover, these entities may have to raise selling prices to compensate for higher costs, making their products and services less competitive. As a result, profit levels may fall.

However, a strong ethical stance might attract 'green' investors and customers. Some entities are the subject of boycotts as a result of their perceived unethical stance. Moreover, an ethical business model may be more sustainable than one which prioritises short-term profits.

As you can see, the relationship between ethics and profit is not straight forward.

## 10 Developments in sustainability reporting

### Background

Sustainable development consists of balancing local and global efforts to meet basic human needs without destroying or degrading the natural environment.

Sustainable Development Goals (SDGs) are a range of 17 goals agreed by UN member states that include no poverty, zero hunger, decent work, reduced inequalities, and responsible production and consumption. Some of these will only be achieved through the cooperation of industry.

There are lots of reasons why companies should set their own sustainable development goals:

- It is ethical
- Government funding will increasingly focus on sustainable businesses
- There will be a reduction in reputational and regulatory risk
- Sustainable products and services are a growth area
- Short-term, profit-based models are now less relevant for many investors.

Investors are increasingly interested in companies that make a credible contribution to some of the SDGs. Investors will see opportunities in companies that address the risks to people and the environment and those companies that develop new products and services which will have positive impacts on the achievement of SDGs. Conversely, when making investment decisions, some investors employ screening tactics, eliminating companies that exhibit specific characteristics, such as low pay or high levels of gender inequality.

## Reporting standards and initiatives

It is vital for companies to carefully consider how to communicate their commitment to, and progress towards, SDGs. There are many reporting initiatives that can be used:

- **The United Nations Global Compact** (UNGC) is an initiative to support UN goals. It encourages entities to produce an annual Communication in Progress (COP) report, in which they describe the practical actions taken to implement UN principles in respect of human rights, labour, the environment, and anti-corruption.

- **The Global Reporting Initiative** (GRI) publishes the most widely used standards on sustainability reporting and disclosure. Using the GRI standards should mean that entities produce balanced reports that represent their positive and negative economic, environmental and social impacts. GRI principles encourage stakeholder engagement in order to ensure that their information needs are met.

- **The International Integrated Reporting Council** has published the International Integrated Reporting Framework. This is discussed in more detail in the next section of this chapter.

## Legislation

Many countries are introducing legislation on sustainability reporting:

- The Singapore Stock Exchange has made sustainability reporting mandatory for listed companies, on a 'comply or explain' basis.

- The European Union requires certain large companies to disclose non-financial information on employee diversity.

Although these are positive moves, the lack of an agreed set of standards causes significant diversity in how entities report sustainability issues.

## 11 Integrated reporting

### What is the International Integrated Reporting Council?

The International Integrated Reporting Council (IIRC) was created to respond to the need for a concise, clear, comprehensive and comparable integrated reporting framework.

The IIRC define an integrated report (IR) as 'a concise communication about how an organisation's strategy, governance, performance and prospects, in the context of its external environment, lead to the creation of value in the short, medium and long term.'

The IIRC believe that integrated reporting will contribute towards a more stable economy and a more sustainable world.

### What is the role of the IIRC?

The role of the IIRC is to:

- develop an overarching integrated reporting framework setting out the scope of integrated reporting and its key components
- identify priority areas where additional work is needed and provide a plan for development
- consider whether standards in this area should be voluntary or mandatory and facilitate collaboration between standard-setters and convergence in the standards needed to underpin integrated reporting; and
- promote the adoption of integrated reporting by relevant regulators and report preparers.

### Objective of the Framework

The IR Framework establishes 'guiding principles' and 'content elements' that govern the overall content of an integrated report. This will help organisations to report their value creation in ways that are understandable and useful to the users.

The IR Framework is aimed at the private sector, although could be adapted for use by charities and the public sector.

The key users of an integrated report are deemed to be the providers of financial capital. However, the report will also benefit employees, suppliers, customers, local communities and policy makers.

The Framework is principles based and therefore does not prescribe specific KPIs that must be disclosed. Senior management need to use judgement to identify which issues are material. These decisions should be justified to the users of the report.

Those charged with governance are not required to acknowledge their responsibility for the integrated report. It was felt that such disclosures might increase legal liability in some jurisdictions and therefore deter some companies from applying the IR Framework.

## Fundamental concepts in the IR framework

An integrated report explains how an entity creates value over the short-, medium- and long-term. To this extent, a number of fundamental concepts underpin the IR framework. These are:

- The capitals

- The organisation's business model

- The creation of value over time.

The **capitals** are stocks of value that are inputs to an organisation's business model. The capitals identified by the IR Framework are financial, manufactured, intellectual, human, social and relationship, and natural.

The capitals will increase, decrease or be transformed through an organisation's business activities. For example:

- The use of natural resources will decrease natural capital, making a profit will increase financial capital.

- Employment could increase human capital through training, or reduce human capital through unsafe or exploitative working practices.

Central to integrated reporting is the overall impact that a business has on the full range of capitals through its business model.

The **business model** is a business' chosen system of inputs, business activities, outputs and outcomes that aims to create value over the short, medium and long term.

- An integrated report must identify key **inputs**, such as employees, or natural resources. It is important to explain how secure the availability, quality and affordability of components of natural capital are.

- At the centre of the **business model** is the conversion of inputs into outputs through business activities, such as planning, design, manufacturing and the provision of services.

- An integrated report must identify an organisation's key **outputs**, such as products and services. There may be other outputs, such as chemical by-products or waste. These need to be discussed within the business model disclosure if they are deemed to be material.

- **Outcomes** are defined as the consequences (positive and negative) for the capitals as a result of an organisation's business activities and outputs. Outcomes can be internal (such as profits or employee morale) or external (impacts on the local environment).

**Value** is created over time and for a range of stakeholders. IR is based on the belief that the increasing financial capital (e.g. profit) at the expense of human capital (e.g. staff exploitation) is unlikely to maximize value in the longer term. IR thus helps users to establish whether short-term value creation can be sustained into the medium- and long-term.

## Guiding principles

The following Guiding Principles underpin the preparation of an integrated report.

- **Strategic focus and future orientation** – An integrated report should provide insight into the organisation's strategy; how it enables the organisation to create value in the short, medium and long term; and its effects on the capitals.

- **Connectivity of information** – An integrated report should show a holistic picture of the factors that affect the organisation's ability to create value.

- **Stakeholder relationships** – An integrated report should provide insight into the nature and quality of the organisation's relationships with its stakeholders.

- **Materiality** – An integrated report should disclose information on matters that significantly affect the organisation's ability to create value.

- **Conciseness** – An integrated report should be concise.

- **Reliability and completeness** – An integrated report should be balanced and free from material error.

- **Consistency and comparability** – The information in an integrated report should be comparable over time, and comparable with other entities.

## The content of an integrated report

An integrated report should include all of the following content elements:

- **Organisational overview and external environment** – 'What does the organisation do and what are the circumstances under which it operates?'

- **Governance** – 'How does the organisation's governance structure support its ability to create value in the short, medium and long term?'

- **Opportunities and risks** – 'What are the specific opportunities and risks that affect the organisation's ability to create value over the short, medium and long term, and how is the organisation dealing with them?'

- **Strategy and resource allocation** – 'Where does the organisation want to go and how does it intend to get there?'

- **Business model** – 'What is the organisation's business model and to what extent is it resilient?'

- **Performance** – 'To what extent has the organisation achieved its strategic objectives and what are its outcomes in terms of effects on the capitals?'

- **Future outlook** – 'What challenges and uncertainties is the organisation likely to encounter in pursuing its strategy, and what are the potential implications for its business model and future performance?'

- **Basis of presentation** – 'How does the organisation determine what matters to include in the integrated report and how are such matters quantified or evaluated?'

Including this content will help companies shift the focus of their reporting from historical financial performance to longer-term value creation.

### Test your understanding 7 – AA

AA is a UK-based public limited company that purchases shoes directly from manufacturers and then sells them through its own UK-based shops. AA has been profitable for many years and has continued to expand, financing this through bank loans.

AA's shoes sell particularly well amongst lower income families and AA has therefore specifically targeted this demographic. AA offers a discount of 50% on school shoes if the child is entitled to free school meals. This discount is partly subsidised by a government grant.

AA maximises its profits by buying its inventory from overseas. In the past year there have been several press reports about poor working conditions and pay in factories where AA products are manufactured. AA is conscious that it needs to monitor its supplier's employment conditions more closely.

AA has also been criticised in the press for the quality of its products. Some customers have complained that the shoes are not well-made and that they must be regularly replaced. A major consumer magazine has strongly argued that AA products are a 'false economy' and that customers would save money in the long-term if they bought slightly more expensive but better quality shoes.

Staff who work in AA's shops are paid the national minimum wage. Training is minimal and staff turnover is extremely high.

AA does not fully engage with local or national recycling initiatives. The directors of the company believe these initiatives would increase operating costs, thus reducing the affordability of its products for its target demographic.

The success of the AA business model has led to an increased number of competitors. Although these competitors do not yet have the same high street presence as AA, some of them have invested more money into developing online stores. Although AA has a website, its products cannot be purchased online.

**Required:**

**Why would an integrated report provide useful information about AA?**

## 12 Not-for-profit entities

A **not-for-profit entity** is one that does not carry on its activities for the purposes of profit or gain to particular persons and does not distribute its profits or assets to particular persons.

The main types of not-for-profit entity are:

- clubs and societies

- charities

- public sector organisations (including central government, local government and National Health Service bodies).

### The objectives of a not-for-profit entity

The main objective of public sector organisations is to provide services to the general public. Their long-term aim is normally to break even, rather than to generate a surplus.

Most public sector organisations aim to provide value for money, which is usually analysed into the three Es – economy, efficiency and effectiveness.

Other not-for-profit entities include charities, clubs and societies whose objective is to carry out the activities for which they were created.

### Assessing performance in a not-for-profit entity

It can be difficult to monitor and evaluate the success of a not-for-profit organisation as the focus is not on a resultant profit as with a traditional business entity.

The success of the organisation should be measured against the key indicators that reflect the visions and values of the organisation. The strategic plan will identify the goals and the strategies that the organisation needs to adopt to achieve these goals.

The focus of analysis should be the measures of output, outcomes and their impact on what the charity is trying to achieve.

## 13 Chapter summary

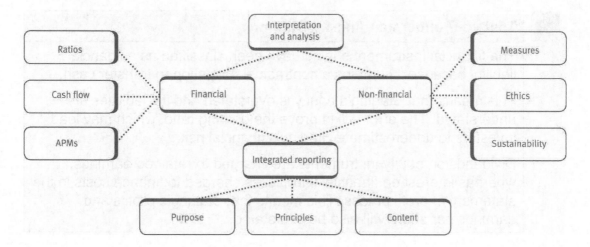

# Test your understanding answers

## Test your understanding 1 – Starling

The financial instrument should have been classified as a financial liability because it contains a contractual obligation to transfer cash.

This means that Starling's equity is overstated and its liabilities are understated. The error will improve the gearing ratio, which may lead investors to underestimate Starling's financial risk.

Dividends on equity instruments are charged to retained earnings, whereas interest on financial liabilities is charged to finance costs in the statement of profit or loss. This means that Starling's profits and earnings per share will also be overstated.

## Test your understanding 2 – Coe

### Share options

This is an equity-settled share-based payment. A remuneration expense should be recognised in profit or loss over the three year vesting period. This should be based on the fair value of the options at the grant date ($6) and the number of options expected to vest. The other side of the accounting entry is recognised in equity.

The expense is calculated as follows:

$(1,000 - 50 - 80) \times 500 \times \$6 \times 1/3 = \$0.9$ million.

The adjusting entry is:

| | |
|---|---|
| Dr Profit or loss | $0.9m |
| Cr Equity | $0.9m |

This adjustment reduces the profit attributable to the equity shareholders of the group by $0.9 million and so will reduce basic earnings per share and diluted earnings per share.

The share options represent a commitment to issue equity shares in the future at an amount that is below the average share price. These are therefore a dilutive instrument, which will cause a further reduction in diluted earnings per share.

### Land

In accordance with IFRS 13 *Fair Value Measurement*, the selling price of similar plots of land would constitute a level 2 input to the fair value hierarchy. It is unlikely that level 1 inputs exist. However, Coe should assess whether adjustments are required to the $5 million price to take into account the location and condition of its specific asset.

Assuming no adjustments are required to the valuation, the land should be revalued to its fair value of $5 million with a gain of $1 million recognised in other comprehensive income.

| | |
|---|---|
| Dr Property, plant and equipment | $1m |
| Cr Other comprehensive income | $1m |

In the statement of other comprehensive income, this gain will be presented as an item that will not be reclassified to profit or loss in the future.

This adjustment has no impact on profit. As such, it has no impact on basic and diluted earnings per share.

**Financial asset**

The loan is a financial asset because it gives Crace a contractual right to receive cash.

The financial asset should have been initially measured at fair value. Because the loan is interest-free, the $3 million price does not represent the asset's fair value. The fair value should be determined by discounting the future cash flows to present value using a market rate of interest:

$3m × 1/1.05^3 = $2.6 million.

The financial asset must be written down to $2.6 million. The $0.4 million loss is expensed to profit or loss:

| | |
|---|---|
| Dr Profit or loss | $0.4m |
| Cr Financial asset | $0.4m |

This adjustment reduces consolidated profit by $0.4 million. Of this, $0.3 million ($0.4m × 75%) is attributable to the equity shareholders of the group and the remaining $0.1 million is attributable to the non-controlling interest.

Basic and diluted earnings per share are calculated based on profit attributable to the equity shareholders of the group. As such, these ratios will deteriorate once the error is corrected.

**Test your understanding 3 – Impact of policy choices**

| | Entity A | Entity B |
|---|---|---|
| Operating profit margin | 18.2% | 4.5% |
| Return on capital employed | 16.7% | 2.4% |
| Gearing (debt/debt + equity) | 41.7% | 23.8% |

As a result of the upwards revaluation, Entity B has charged more depreciation to profit or loss than Entity A. This means that Entity B has lower profits and a lower operating profit margin.

Entity B's upwards revaluation has increased equity in the statement of financial position. This reduces its ROCE, making Entity B appear less efficient than entity A. However it also means that Entity B's gearing is lower than Entity A's, making it seem like a less risky investment.

### Test your understanding 4 – Tuyet

#### High level analysis

Tuyet has generated a cash surplus during the year. However, this is relatively small compared to the size of its outgoings. Moreover, Tuyet is in a negative overall cash position (i.e. it has overdrafts). This will lead to increased interest payments. There is also a risk that the overdraft could be withdrawn, placing Tuyet at considerable risk.

#### Operating cash flows

Tuyet has made an operating profit of $40 million ($35 + $5m) but it has only generated cash from operations of $18 million. This suggests that Tuyet's profits are relatively low quality and are not backed up by cash.

There have been substantial increases in the level of inventories year-onyear. This is having a negative impact on Tuyet's cash flows. This might be a response to bulk orders. Alternatively, it could be due to inefficient inventory management, exposing Tuyet to the risk of inventory obsolescence.

The increase in receivables suggests that customers are paying Tuyet more slowly. It would seem that Tuyet is compensating for this by taking longer to pay its own suppliers. This could cause Tuyet problems – particularly if its suppliers tighten or remove credit terms.

After making mandatory interest and tax payments, there is only a small cash surplus of $3 million from operating activities. Tuyet's trading operations are not generating enough cash to invest in PPE or to repay loans and so funds have been obtained from other less-sustainable sources.

#### Investing cash flows

Tuyet has invested in PPE during the year. This suggests that productive capacity can be maintained or improved.

However, it should be noted that substantial receipts have been generated by selling PPE – these cash flows will not recur year-after-year. Without these receipts, Tuyet would have recorded an overall decrease in cash and cash equivalents.

The high level of PPE disposals raises concerns: does Tuyet have idle assets (which may require impairment), or is it being forced into disposing of key assets in order to raise cash?

## Financing cash flows

Tuyet has repaid some of its loan this year. As a result interest payments should reduce in the future, freeing up operating cash flows.

However, the loan repayment was only possible as a result of a share issue. Tuyet cannot perform share issues indefinitely. Therefore, higher operating cash flows are required if Tuyet is to meet its future loan repayments.

Tuyet has not paid a dividend this year, no doubt due to its poor cash position. This may deter potential and current investors from providing further resources.

## Test your understanding 5 – Hutton

Depreciation and amortisation are judgemental, non-cash expenses. However, excluding them from underlying profit ignores the fact that the entity's non-current assets will need to be replaced or enhanced in the future.

The impairment of a brand suggests that the business outlook may be weaker than expected. It also indicates that management over-paid for the brand. Adding back this expense when calculating underlying profit diminishes its significance when assessing the past decisions of management and also when predicting Hutton's future performance.

Foreign exchange differences on monetary items can be volatile, and potentially distort an entity's performance profile. However, many monetary items, such as receivables and payables, are short-term in nature and so represent gains and losses that will be realised in the near future. It would seem that Hutton will be receiving less units of its functional currency (or paying more units) than originally expected when the overseas transactions are settled and so it seems odd to exclude these losses from underlying profit.

Fair value gains on financial assets measured at fair value through profit or loss are volatile and may make it difficult to compare an entity's performance year-on-year. However, these financial assets are likely to be sold in the short-term and so the gains (or losses) will be realised shortly. They are also unlikely to be one-off items – entities that trade material quantities of financial assets will probably enter into similar transactions on a regular basis.

Overall, it looks like Hutton is trying to disguise a weak performance – particularly as the APM has turned a loss before tax into a profit. This could be misleading, particularly if the APM is presented with prominence.

However, to Hutton's credit, it discloses the calculation behind the APM, thus allowing users to reconcile it to the figures in the financial statements. This will enable them to draw their own conclusions about the adequacy and usefulness of this APM.

## Test your understanding 6 – Lorenzo

### Profits

Lorenzo's profit decline year-on-year will be concerning to investors. However, the non-financial information presented in the integrated report paints a more optimistic picture of the entity's future prospects.

### Faults

A decline in the number of faults in Lorenzo's products will reduce future repair costs, increasing profits. Fewer faults will improve customer satisfaction. This may generate stronger brand loyalty, making it more likely that customers will make repeat purchases.

### Helpline

The reduction in helpline waiting times may be due to the reduction in the number of product faults or, potentially, to investment in the customer services department. Whatever the reason, this is likely to have a positive impact on customer perception which may, once again, improve brand loyalty.

### Staff turnover

Reduced staff turnover means that staff experience is being retained in the business. This might help to reduce recruitment and training costs in the future. Moreover, experienced staff will probably perform at a higher level than inexperienced staff. In fact, this may partly explain the improvement in fault levels and customer helpline waiting times. Reduced staff turnover could also have other benefits – more experienced staff might develop more innovative products.

### Summary and further information

In conclusion, the non-financial information in the Integrated Report provides an important insight into Lorenzo's future prospects. Nonetheless, it would be useful to compare these performance measures to other entities in the same sector. Furthermore, some investors may question the reliability of these disclosures unless assurance is provided by an assurance practitioner.

## Test your understanding 7 – AA

An integrated report might highlight a number of positive issues about AA:

- AA's financial capital has increased as a result of its profitable current business activities.

- Financial capital has increased due to the receipt of government grants and this will help AA to repay its debts in the short and also, potentially, the medium term.

- AA's has a positive impact on social capital by helping low income families to buy essential items of clothing. This is likely to foster brand loyalty from these customers, as well as generating good publicity. This may lead to a further increase in financial capital in the future.

However, it could be argued that the AA business model will not create value in the long-term. An integrated report might refer to the following issues:

- The government grants may not continue indefinitely. This could be due to government budget cuts, increasing competition or, perhaps, as a result of ongoing quality issues with AA products.

- AA does not invest highly in human capital. Unskilled and untrained staff are unlikely to foster brand loyalty and could lead to a loss of custom over time.

- AA uses cheap labour from overseas. Although this is likely to increase financial capital, it may lead to a net decrease in other capitals

  - AA may be criticised for not investing in local communities, or for exploiting overseas workers. By not investing in human capital there may also be a negative impact on social and relationship capital.

  - AA's recognition of the need to increasingly monitor its suppliers indicates that current economic benefits may not be sustainable in the longer-term.

- Purchasing goods from overseas will increase AA's carbon footprint. Moreover, AA does not widely recycle. Its activities thus place an overall drain on natural capital and this may deter some investors and consumers.

- A focus on high street expansion may leave AA vulnerable to online competitors, who will be able to offer the same products more cheaply. AA's lack of investment in staff may compound this because the retail stores are unlikely to offer a greater experience or level of service than can be obtained online. The current business model may therefore not be resilient in the medium or long term.

**Summary**

AA's business model is currently profitable. Such information could be obtained from the historical financial statements. However, an integrated report that looks at value creation and stability in the medium and longer term may offer a more pessimistic outlook. Banks are more likely to invest in companies who have sustainable business models and therefore integrated reports will help them to make stronger investment decisions. Other investors, such as potential or current shareholders, would also be able to make more informed decisions.

Producing an Integrated report is not mandatory. Businesses which have a detrimental net impact on capitals (particularly non-financial capitals) are unlikely to voluntarily produce an integrated report. In contrast, companies who create value in sustainable ways are more likely to want to disclose this to users. However, if the production of an integrated report was mandatory, then it might motivate a company like AA to shift its focus from increasing short term financial capital to the generation of an array of capitals over the medium and long-term.

# Current issues

## Chapter learning objectives

Upon completion of this chapter you will be able to:

- Identify issues and deficiencies which have led to proposed changes to an accounting standard

- Discuss the impact of current issues in corporate reporting:
    - accounting in the current business environment
    - accounting policy changes
    - materiality in the context of financial reporting
    - disclosure of accounting policies
    - defined benefit plan amendments, curtailments and settlements
    - management commentary
    - developments in sustainability reporting
    - debt and equity
    - deferred tax

- Discuss developments in devising a structure for corporate reporting that addresses the needs of stakeholders.

**PER**

One of the PER performance objectives (PO2) is stakeholder relationship management. You manage stakeholder expectations and needs, developing and maintaining productive business relationships. You listen to and engage stakeholders effectively and communicate the right information to them when they need it. Working through this chapter should help you understand how to demonstrate that objective.

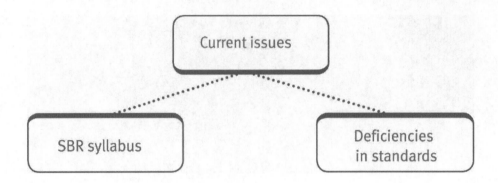

## 1 Key current issues

### Current syllabus

The SBR syllabus and list of examinable documents identifies the following current issues:

- accounting in the current business environment
- accounting policy changes
- materiality
- disclosure of accounting policies
- defined benefit plan amendments, curtailments and settlements
- management commentary
- developments in sustainability reporting
- debt and equity
- deferred tax.

> **Progression**
>
> You will not have studied this topic before. It is a core area of the SBR syllabus.

## 2 Accounting in the current business environment

SBR exam questions are likely to be set in a contemporary context. Current issues in the accounting profession include the application of IFRS Standards to current business transactions and scenarios. Thus the business environment in which questions are framed can constitute a current issue.

This section discusses the accounting treatment and accounting dilemmas raised by two contemporary issues: cryptocurrency and natural disasters.

## Cryptocurrency

Cryptocurrencies are virtual currencies that provide the holder with various rights. They are not issued by a central authority and so exist outside of governmental control. Cryptocurrencies, such as the Bitcoin, can be used to purchase some goods and services although they are not yet widely accepted. The market value is extremely volatile and some investors make high returns through short-term trade.

The accounting treatment of cryptocurrency is not clear cut.

Cryptocurrencies do not constitute 'cash' because they cannot be readily exchanged for goods and services. Moreover, they do not qualify as a 'cash equivalent' (in accordance with IAS 7 *Statement of Cash Flows*) because they are subject to a significant risk of a change in value.

An investment in cryptocurrency does not represent an investment in the equity of another entity or a contractual right to receive cash, and so does not meet the definition of a financial asset as per IAS 32 *Financial Instruments: Presentation*.

The most applicable accounting standard would appear to be IAS 38 *Intangible Assets* because cryptocurrency is an identifiable non-monetary asset without physical substance.

Although cryptocurrencies most likely fall within the scope of IAS 38, the measurement models in that standard do not seem appropriate. The fair value of cryptocurrency is volatile so a cost based measure is unlikely to provide relevant information. The revaluation model in IAS 38 initially seems more appropriate, but this requires gains on remeasurement to fair value to be presented in other comprehensive income. Many entities invest in cryptocurrencies to benefit from short-term changes in fair value and gains or losses on short-term investments are normally recorded in profit or loss (e.g. assets inside the scope of IFRS 9 *Financial Instruments*).

As can be seen, the accounting treatment of cryptocurrencies is not straight-forward. In the absence of an appropriate accounting standard, preparers of financial statements should refer to the principles in existing IFRS Standards as well as the *Conceptual Framework* in order to develop an accounting policy.

## Natural disasters

Natural disasters include volcanic eruptions, earthquakes, droughts, tsunamis, floods and hurricanes. Many of these have become more prevalent, most likely as a result of climate change. Natural disasters devastate communities, and the process of recovery can last for years. Companies that operate in areas effected by natural disasters will also have to consider the financial reporting consequences. Some of these are considered below.

## Impairments

A natural disaster is likely to trigger an impairment review – particularly in relation to property, plant and equipment (PPE). This is because, in accordance with IAS 36 *Impairment of Assets*, there are likely to be indicators of impairment. This may be because individual assets are damaged, or it may be because the economic consequences of the disaster trigger a decline in customer demand. If PPE is destroyed, then it should be derecognised rather than impaired.

In line with IFRS 9 *Financial Instruments,* entities that lend money will need to assess whether credit risk associated with the financial asset has increased significantly. A natural disaster is likely to lead to a higher default rate, so some financial assets will become credit-impaired.

Natural disasters may lead to inventory damage. Alternatively, the economic consequences of the disaster may mean that inventory must be sold at a reduced price. As per IAS 2 *Inventories*, some inventory may need to be remeasured from its cost to its net realisable value.

## Insurance

It is likely that entities affected by natural disasters will need to account for insurance claims. This can be a difficult area because of uncertainty regarding the nature of the claim, the type of coverage provided by the insurance, and the timing and amount of any proceeds recoverable.

IAS 37 *Provisions, Contingent Liabilities and Contingent Assets* only allows the recognition of an asset from an insurance claim if receipt is virtually certain. This is a high threshold of probability and so recognition is unlikely. However, if an insurance pay-out is deemed probable then a contingent asset can be disclosed.

## Additional liabilities

As a result of a natural disaster, an entity may decide sell or terminate a line of business, or to save costs by reducing employee headcount. In accordance with IAS 37, a provision will be recognised if there is a present obligation from a past event and an outflow of economic benefits is probable. An obligation only exists if a restructuring plan has been implemented or if a detailed plan has been publicly announced. When measuring the provision, only the direct costs from the restructuring, such as employee redundancies, should be included.

Provisions may be required if there is an obligation to repair environmental damage. Moreover, decommissioning provisions (when an entity is obliged to decommission an asset at the end of its life and restore the land) will require review because the natural disaster may alter the timing or amount of the required cash flows.

## Going concern

Natural disasters will lead to changes in the economic environment, as well as business interruption and additional costs. If there are material uncertainties relating to going concern, then these must be disclosed in accordance with IAS 1 *Presentation of Financial Statements*. If the going concern assumption is not appropriate then the financial statements must be prepared on an alternative basis and this fact must be disclosed.

## 3    Accounting policies

### The accounting treatment

In accordance with IAS 8 *Accounting Policies, Changes in Accounting Estimates and Errors*, an entity should only change an accounting policy if:

* required by an IFRS Standard, or

* results in more reliable and relevant information for financial statement users.

When a change is required by an IFRS Standard, then the standard normally specifies transitional provisions. When the change is not required by an IFRS Standard then it is implemented retrospectively, unless it is impractical to do so.

In contrast, a change in accounting estimate is dealt with prospectively. Unlike with a change in policy, this will impact the statement of profit or loss in the current year only.

### The problem

Calculating the prior year impact of accounting policy changes is a costly and time consuming process. The Board is concerned that retrospective application dissuades entities from voluntarily changing accounting policies, even though the change would benefit financial statement users.

The Board is particularly concerned about changes in policy that arise as a result of **agenda decisions** made by the **IFRS Interpretations Committee**.

**Agenda decisions**

> The IFRS Interpretations Committee's role is to respond to questions about the application of IFRS Standards that are submitted by stakeholders. If the Committee concludes that the existing IFRS Standard is adequate then they publish an agenda decision. This details the reasons why the IFRS Standard does not require revision, but also explains how best to apply that standard. Agenda decisions therefore provide helpful guidance and best-practice.

As a result of an agenda decision, an entity may wish to change an accounting policy but be deterred by the time and cost involved in retrospective application.

## The proposal

The Board has issued an Exposure Draft ED/2018/1 *Accounting Policy Changes.* In this the Board proposes that an accounting policy change resulting from an agenda decision should be implemented retrospectively **unless**:

- it is impracticable to do so (due to a lack of data), or

- the cost of working out the effect of the change exceeds the benefits to the users of the financial statements.

When considering the benefits to users of retrospective application, the Board proposes that entities consider:

- the magnitude of the change

- the pervasiveness of the change across the financial statements

- the effect on trend information.

## 4 Materiality

### Background

Materiality as a concept is used widely in financial reporting. However, the Board accepts that further guidance is needed on how to apply it to the preparation and interpretation of financial statements.

### The Practice Statement

The Board have issued a Practice Statement called *Making Materiality Judgements.* This provides non-mandatory guidance that may help preparers of financial statements when applying IFRS Standards.

The key contents of the Practice Statement are summarised below.

### Definitions and objectives

The current definition of materiality is that an item is material if its omission or misstatement would influence the economic decisions of financial statement users.

The Board are proposing to expand this definition to say that an item is also material if obscuring it would influence the economic decisions of financial statement users.

The objective of financial statements is to provide useful information about the reporting entity to existing and potential investors, lenders and other creditors to help them make decisions about providing resources to that entity. This requires that the preparers of the financial information make materiality judgements.

When assessing whether information is material, an entity should consider:

- Quantitative factors – measures of revenue, profit, assets, and cash flows

- Qualitative factors – related party transactions, unusual transactions, geography, and wider economic uncertainty.

Materiality judgements are relevant to recognition, measurement, presentation and disclosure decisions.

**Recognition and measurement**

An entity only needs to apply the recognition and measurement criteria in an IFRS Standard when the effects are material.

 **Recognition criteria**

An entity buys fixtures and fittings that are in the scope of IAS 16 *Property, Plant and Equipment* (PPE). IAS 16 stipulates that the cost of an item of PPE should be recognised as an asset. However, to save time, the entity decides that expenditure on fixtures and fittings costing below $1,000 should be written off to profit or loss. As long as the impact of this policy is not material, the entity's financial statements will still comply with IAS 16.

**Presentation and disclosure**

An entity only needs to apply the disclosure requirements in an IFRS Standard if the resulting information is material.

The entity may need to provide additional information, not required by an IFRS Standard, if necessary to help financial statement users understand the financial impact of its transactions during the period.

 **Disclosure requirements**

IAS 16 requires disclosure of an entity's contractual commitments to purchase PPE.

If such commitments are immaterial, then the disclosure is not required.

When organising information, entities should:

- Emphasise material matters

- Ensure material information is not obscured by immaterial information

- Ensure information is entity-specific

- Aim for simplicity and conciseness without omitting material detail

- Ensure formats are appropriate and understandable (e.g. tables, lists, narrative)

- Provide comparable information

- Avoid duplication.

## Users

Materiality judgements must be based on the needs of the primary users of financial statements.

The primary users are **current and potential** investors, lenders and creditors.

Financial statements cannot meet all of the information needs of the primary users.7 However, preparers of financial statements should aim to meet common information needs for each group of primary users (e.g. investors, lenders, other creditors).

### Users

Fifty investors each hold 2 per cent of an entity's ordinary shares. One of these investors is interested in information about the entity's expenditure in France because that investor operates other businesses in that country.

In making materiality judgements, the entity does not consider the specific information needs of that single investor if expenditure in France is immaterial information for its primary users as a group.

## Process

The Board recommends a systematic process when making materiality judgements:

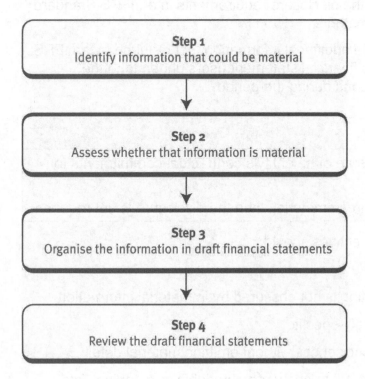

**Step 1**
Identify information that could be material

**Step 2**
Assess whether that information is material

**Step 3**
Organise the information in draft financial statements

**Step 4**
Review the draft financial statements

## 5 Disclosure of accounting policies

### Background

IAS 1 *Presentation of Financial Statements* requires entities to disclose 'significant accounting policies'. Below is an extract from an entity's 'accounting policies' disclosure note:

**Accounting policy disclosure**

Assets are classified as held for sale when their carrying amount is to be recovered principally through a sale transaction and a sale is considered highly probable. On classification as held for sale, assets are stated at the lower of carrying amount and fair value less costs to sell.

The above disclosure is full of standardised (rather than entity-specific) information and does little more than summarise or duplicate the content of IFRS Standards. As such, it is not useful. In fact, it arguably adds clutter to the financial statements, obscuring information that is useful.

In the Exposure Draft ED 2019/6 *Disclosure of Accounting Policies*, the Board has proposed amendments to IAS 1 *Presentation of Financial Statements* and the Practice Statement *Making Materiality Judgements* in order to help preparers of financial statements apply the concept of materiality to accounting policy disclosures.

### Terminology

IAS 1 currently requires entities to disclose 'significant accounting policies'. The Board propose to amend this to 'material accounting policies'.

The Board wish to clarify that a disclosure of an accounting policy is material if, when taken with the information in the rest of the financial statements, it could influence the economic decisions of the financial statement users.

Accounting policies relating to immaterial transactions do not need to be disclosed.

### Guidance

Not all accounting policies relating to material transactions are, in themselves, material.

The Board note that an accounting policy is likely to be material to the financial statements if it relates to a material transaction and:

- was changed during the period
- was chosen from one or more alternatives
- was developed in the absence of an IFRS Standard that explicitly applies

- relates to an area where the entity has to make significant judgements or assumptions

- applies the requirements of an IFRS Standard in a way that is entity specific.

## Accounting policy disclosure

Distinction is an accountancy tuition provider. It enters into contracts with customers that, in accordance with IFRS 15 *Revenue from Contracts with Customers*, contain two performance obligations as detailed below:

- to provide the customer with a textbook – revenue is recognised at a point in time, when the textbook is provided to the customer

- to provide the customer with five days of lectures – revenue is recognised over-time, as the entity provides the lectures.

Revenue from these contracts is material.

Distinction must decide whether to disclose the above accounting policies. The following factors suggest that disclosure is not required:

- the revenue recognition policy was not changed during the period

- the policies were not chosen from alternatives

- the transactions in question were covered by an IFRS Standard.

However, Distinction's revenue recognition policies:

- relate to an area where judgement is required, such as the allocation of the transaction price to each performance obligation, and the determination of when control of the textbooks transfers to the customer

- were applied in entity-specific ways.

Distinction concludes that disclosing the accounting policies for revenue recognition is necessary for the primary users of its financial statements to understand information in the financial statements. For example, understanding that some revenue is recognised at a point in time and some is recognised over time will help users understand how reported revenue relates to historical and future cash flows. This will help users to assess the entity's future cash flows and thus aid them when making investment decisions.

## Test your understanding 1 – Heron

During the current period, Heron, a listed company, has made a material investment in a cryptocurrency. It has never invested in cryptocurrency before. In the absence of an IFRS Standard covering cryptocurrency, Heron has used the *Conceptual Framework* to derive an accounting policy.

**Required:**

**In accordance with Exposure Draft ED 2019/6 *Disclosure of Accounting Policies*, should the accounting policy for cryptocurrency be disclosed in Heron's financial statements?**

## 6 Defined benefit plan amendments, curtailments and settlements

### The problem

If there is a plan amendment, settlement or curtailment (PASC) then the effect of this is calculated by comparing the net defined benefit deficit before and after the event.

Even though the reporting entity remeasures the defined benefit deficit in the event of a PASC, IAS 19 did not previously require the use of updated assumptions to determine current service cost and net interest for the period after the PASC.

The Board argued that ignoring updated assumptions is inappropriate, because these are likely to provide a more faithful representation of the impact of the entity's defined benefit pension plan during the reporting period.

### Amendments

The Board amended IAS 19 to clarify that the reporting entity must determine:

- the current service cost for the remainder of the reporting period after the PASC using the actuarial assumptions used to remeasure the net defined benefit liability

- net interest for the remainder of the reporting period after the PASC using the remeasured defined benefit deficit and the discount rate used to remeasure the defined benefit deficit.

## 7 Management commentary

### Purpose of Management Commentary

The IFRS Practice Statement *Management Commentary* provides a framework for the preparation and presentation of management commentary on a set of financial statements.

Management commentary provides users with more context through which to interpret the financial position, financial performance and cash flows of an entity.

It is not mandatory for entities to produce a management commentary.

## Framework for presentation of management commentary

The purpose of a management commentary is:

* to provide management's assessment of the entity's performance, position and progress

* to supplement information presented in the financial statements, and

* to explain the factors that might impact performance and position in the future.

This means that the management commentary should include information which is forward-looking.

Information included in management commentary should possess the qualitative characteristics of useful information (as outlined in the *Conceptual Framework*). In other words, the information should be relevant, faithfully represented, comparable, timely, verifiable and understandable.

## Elements of management commentary

Management commentary should include information that is essential to an understanding of:

* the nature of the business

* management's objectives and strategies

* the entity's resources, risks and relationships

* the key performance measures that management use to evaluate the entity's performance.

Historical financial statements are often criticised for lacking adequate discussion about risk. The inclusion of management commentary would therefore be extremely beneficial to the primary users of the financial statements – current and potential investors as well as lenders and other creditors. This should help them to make more informed economic decisions.

Performance measures should be reported in a consistent manner to enable comparability of the management commentary over time. Comparability with other entities is enhanced if the entity discloses performance measures widely used by the industry it operates in. Entities are encouraged to present non-financial performance measures because these are typically absent from traditional financial reporting.

Management commentary should not be generic. This additional clutter makes it harder for investors to locate relevant information within the report.

**Test your understanding 2 – Management commentary**

The directors of Carsoon are committed to producing high quality reports that enable its investors to assess the performance and position of the business. They have heard that the Board has published a Practice Statement on management commentary. However, they are unsure what is meant by management commentary, and the extent to which it provides useful information.

**Required:**

**Discuss the nature of management commentary and the extent to which it embodies the qualitative characteristics of useful financial information (as outlined in the *Conceptual Framework*).**

## 8 Sustainability

This topic was covered in the previous chapter.

## 9 Debt and equity

### The problem with debt and equity

The distinction between financial liabilities and equity, as outlined in IAS 32 *Financial Instruments: Presentation* is important. Not only are liabilities perceived as riskier than equity, but changes in the carrying amount of a liability impact profit or loss. However, the application of IAS 32 has posed problems.

In accordance with IAS 32, a contract that obliges an entity to deliver a variable number of its own shares is classified as a financial liability. However, there is no clear rationale for why this is the case. Moreover, a contract that obliges an entity to deliver a variable number of its own shares does not appear to meet the definition of a liability in the *Conceptual Framework*.

The lack of rationale has resulted in diversity in practice when entities account for instruments that are not explicitly covered by IAS 32 – such as put options on a non-controlling interest.

The Board have published a discussion paper on the topic of debt and equity. In this, the Board outlines its initial proposals for accounting standard amendments and requests comments from interested parties.

### Proposals

The Board propose that a financial instrument should be classified as a liability if it exhibits **one** of the following characteristics:

- **'An unavoidable contractual obligation to transfer cash or another financial asset at a specified time other than liquidation**

- **An unavoidable contractual obligation for an amount independent of the entity's available economic resources'** (DP/2018/1: IN10)

## Impact of proposals

For many financial instruments, these proposals would not impact their classification or measurement.

### A bond that pays 5% interest per year

There is a contractual obligation to transfer cash each year.

Moreover, the amount payable is independent of the entity's available resources, because the entity may not have sufficient liquid assets to settle.

Under the proposals, the accounting treatment of the bond would not change. It would be classified as a financial liability.

### Ordinary shares

There is no contractual obligation to transfer cash other than at liquidation (because dividends and redemption are at the entity's discretion)

At liquidation, any amounts transferred to shareholders are restricted to the entity's remaining resources.

As such, under the proposals, ordinary shares would still be classified as equity.

### An obligation to issue shares worth $30 million in 5 years' time.

There is no contractual obligation to transfer cash or another financial asset

However, there is an unavoidable obligation to transfer an amount independent of the entity's available resources. Although the entity's shares may have minimal value in 5 years' time, the obligation to transfer shares worth $30 million remains and the entity must fulfil it.

As such, under the proposals, this type of contract would still be classified as a financial liability.

### Irredeemable fixed-rate cumulative preference shares

Assume that the terms of these shares state that unpaid dividends accumulate. Unpaid dividends are payable at the entity's discretion or on liquidation.

There is no contractual obligation to transfer cash except at liquidation.

However, the amount payable on liquidation is independent of the entity's available resources. This is because the dividends accumulate over-time. At liquidation, the entity may have insufficient resources to pay these accumulated dividends.

In accordance with IAS 32, this financial instrument is classified as equity. However, under the new proposals, it would be classified as a financial liability.

### Convertible bonds

Under the Board's proposals, the accounting treatment of a convertible bond where the holder can choose redemption in the form of cash or a fixed number of the entity's own equity shares would not change. In other words, the issuer of the bond would continue to split the instrument into a liability component and an equity component.

## Test your understanding 3 – Wellington

Wellington, a public limited entity, issues shares. The annual dividend payable is 5% of the share's nominal value. The dividend rate resets to a higher rate each year in which the dividend is not paid, until the dividend is paid at the option of Wellington or at liquidation.

**Required:**

**In accordance with the Board's recent discussion paper, discuss whether the shares would be classified as equity or a financial liability in Wellington's financial statements.**

## 10 Deferred tax

### The recognition exemption

As noted in Chapter 13, IAS 12 *Income Taxes* prohibits the recognition of deferred tax if the temporary difference arises from a transaction that is not a business combination and affects neither accounting profit nor taxable profit.

## Recognition exemption – an example

On the reporting date, Enchilada purchases a factory building for $1 million and recognises this as property, plant and equipment. In Enchilada's jurisdiction, the building is not deductible for tax. The tax rate is 20%.

The carrying amount of the asset is $1 million. The tax base is nil because no tax deductions are permitted. As such, a taxable temporary difference of $1 million arises.

Despite the fact that the factory building will generate taxable income of at least $1 million (otherwise the asset's carrying amount is over-stated) and thus a tax charge of at least $0.2 million over its useful life, no deferred tax liability is recognised. This is because the temporary difference arises from the initial recognition of an item that has not affected accounting profit (the asset was capitalised) or taxable profit (the asset is unrecognised for tax purposes).

The logic behind this exemption is that recognition would not provide useful information. Think about the double entry:

Dr ??? $0.2m

Cr Deferred tax liability $0.2m

The debit cannot be posted to profit or loss or OCI because the transaction itself has not affected those statements. To-date the transaction been recorded in PPE, but debiting PPE with a further $0.2 million would make little sense and would reduce the understandability of financial statements.

### Leases and the recognition exemption

IFRS 16 *Leases* requires lessees to recognise a right-of-use asset and a lease liability for all leases, unless the lease is short-term or of minimal value.

Assume that an entity enters into a lease agreement and that the present value of the payments to be made is $4 million. It would post the following double entry:

Dr Right-of-use asset $4m

Cr Lease Liability $4m

The tax base of the right-of-use asset and lease liability depend on tax law within the jurisdiction:

If the tax deduction received is in respect of the leased asset then:

- the right-of use asset has a tax base of $4 million (the future allowable tax deduction)

- the lease liability has a tax base of $4 million (carrying amount less any amount that will be deductible for tax purposes in future periods - i.e. $4m – nil).

No temporary difference arises on initial recognition of the transaction and so no deferred tax is accounted for. Deferred tax will be recognised subsequently if temporary differences arise.

If the tax deduction received is in respect of the lease liability then:

- the right-of use asset has a tax base of nil (the future allowable tax deduction)

- the lease liability has a tax base of nil (carrying amount less any amount that will be deductible for tax purposes in future periods - i.e. $4m – $4m).

Temporary differences arise because the right-of-use asset and lease liability are both initially carried at $4 million. However, in accordance with IAS 12 *Income Taxes*, no deferred tax is recognised on this transaction either initially or subsequently because the transaction affects neither accounting profit nor taxable profit at initial recognition. This means that the entity's financial statements would show the tax impact of the lease as tax deductions are made available (potentially based on lease payments) rather than as the leased asset and liability are recovered and settled. This would lead to a difference between the entity's effective tax rate and the tax rate for the transaction in its jurisdiction.

### Proposals

As a result of the above, the Board wish to revise IAS 12 and have published Exposure Draft ED/2019/5 *Deferred Tax related to Assets and Liabilities arising from a Single Transaction*.

If a transaction is not a business combination and affects neither accounting nor taxable profit **but** equal amounts of deductible and taxable differences are created, then the Board are proposing that:

*   A deferred tax asset is recognised in relation to the deductible temporary differences to the extent that future profits will be available against which the difference can be utilised

*   A deferred tax liability is recognised for the taxable temporary difference but must not exceed the amount of deferred tax asset recognised above.

### Test your understanding 4 – Bittern

Bittern has a reporting date of 31 December 20X1. On the reporting date, it enters into a lease agreement to hire a machine. The present value of the lease payments to be made is $10 million. In Bittern's tax jurisdiction, tax relief on leases is given in respect of the lease liability as payments are made. The tax rate is 30%.

**Required:**

**In accordance with ED/2019/5 *Deferred Tax related to assets and liabilities arising from a single transaction*, discuss the deferred tax implications of the above in the year ended 31 December 20X1.**

### Additional lease payments

Lease payments made in advance or initial direct costs incurred by the lessee are added to the carrying amount of the right-of-use asset. This would mean that taxable and deductible temporary differences associated with the lease do not offset. The Board have therefore clarified that temporary differences arising from payments in advance or initial direct costs are assessed separately from any equal and offsetting temporary differences arising from the underlying lease transaction.

### Leases and fees – an example

The present value of the lease payments due is $3 million. In addition, the lessee incurred fees of $1 million on the lease. The lessee posts the following entry:

Dr Right-of-use asset $4m

Cr Lease liability $3m

Cr Cash $1m

Assume that tax relief is given on the fees when they are paid and the tax rate is 20%.

> For deferred tax purposes, the fees are dealt with separately. The carrying amount of the right-of-use asset relating to the fees is $1 million and the tax base in nil and so a taxable temporary difference of $1 million arises. A deferred tax liability of $0.2 million ($1m × 20%) must be recognised, with a corresponding tax expense recorded in the statement of profit or loss.
>
> The remaining $3 million carrying amount of the right-of-use asset and lease liability are assessed for deferred tax separately from the initial fees. In accordance with IAS 12 *Income Taxes*, no deferred tax will be recognised on any temporary differences arising because the transaction is not a business combination and, excluding the fees, affects neither accounting nor taxable profit. However, under the Board's proposed changes to IAS 12, deferred tax would be recognised if equal amounts of deductible and taxable differences are created.

## 11 Extant standards

Although developments in the accountancy profession and forthcoming standards are central parts of the SBR syllabus, it is also important to be able to critique existing accounting standards. Critiques of existing standards can be found within the relevant chapters in this text. For example:

- IAS 1 *Presentation of Financial Statements* – Chapter 3

- IFRS 15 *Revenue from Contracts with Customers* – Chapter 4

- IFRS 2 *Share-based payments* – Chapter 10

- IAS 37 *Provisions, Contingent Liabilities and Contingent Assets* – Chapter 11

- IFRS 8 *Operating Segments* – Chapter 14

- IFRS 3 *Business Combinations* – Chapter 18

- IAS 7 *Statement of Cash Flows* – Chapter 21

**Test your understanding 5 – Mineral**

Mineral owns a machine that is central to its production process. At the reporting date, the machine's carrying amount exceeds its tax base. This difference is due to the revaluation of the asset to fair value in the financial statements. Due to its importance, it is extremely unlikely that the machine will be sold.

At the year-end, Mineral received $10 million. In return, Mineral must issue ordinary shares in 12 months' time. The number of shares to be issued will be determined based on the quoted price of Mineral's shares at the issue date.

**Required:**

**For each of the transactions above:**

(i) **Briefly explain how it should be accounted for in accordance with International Financial Reporting Standards**

(ii) **Discuss why the accounting treatment could be argued to contradict the definition of the elements given by the *Conceptual Framework*.**

## 12 Chapter summary

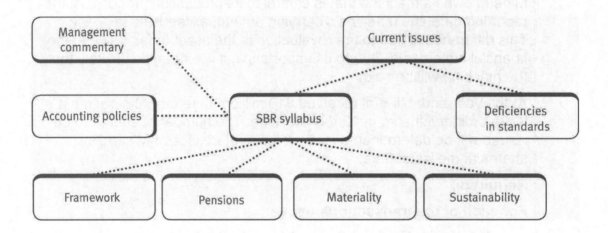

# Test your understanding answers

## Test your understanding 1 – Heron

The policy should be disclosed. Firstly, the transaction is material. Moreover, the accounting policy itself is material. This is the first time that Heron has engaged in this particular type of transaction and so users need to be informed about recognition and measurement issues. Moreover, the accounting policy was developed by management due to the absence of an applicable IFRS Standard and this would have required significant judgement. Users need to be able to assess these judgements and to be able to understand how the balances recognised in the financial statements will impact future profits and future cash flows.

## Test your understanding 2 – Management commentary

**Management commentary**

Management commentary is a narrative report in which management provide context and background against which stakeholders can assess the financial position and performance of a company. It is not mandatory to produce a management commentary. However, if entities produce a management commentary then it should include information that is essential to an understanding of:

- the nature of the business

- management's objectives and its strategies for meeting those objectives

- the entity's resources, risks and relationships

- the results of operations and prospects, and

- the key performance measures that management use to evaluate the entity's performance.

Management commentary should include forward-looking information. The commentary should be entity-specific, rather than generic.

**Link to *Conceptual Framework***

The Practice Statement states that management commentary should include information that possesses the qualitative characteristics of useful financial information. The fundamental qualitative characteristics are relevance and faithful representation. The enhancing qualitative characteristics are understandability, verifiability, comparability and timeliness.

Management commentary provides users with information about risk management, as well as the extent to which current performance may be indicative of future performance. This forward-looking information is relevant because it helps users to make decisions about whether to hold or sell investments in an entity.

To enhance relevance, management commentary should include material information and should focus on the most important information. Generic information is not relevant and should be avoided.

To maximise understandability, management commentary should be presented in a clear and straightforward manner.

When selecting key performance measures, management should use those that are accepted and used widely within the industry. This will enable users to draw comparisons between entities. Management should calculate and report performance measures consistently over time, thus enabling users to compare the performance of the entity year-on-year.

If information from the financial statements is adjusted for inclusion in management commentary then this fact should be disclosed. Financial performance measures should be reconciled to the figures in the financial statements. Users are therefore able to verify the nature of the calculations. They can also assess whether the performance measures included offer a faithful presentation of the entity's financial performance and position.

### Test your understanding 3 – Wellington

Wellington can defer dividend payments until liquidation. Therefore, there is no contractual obligation to transfer cash at a time other than liquidation.

However, there is an unavoidable obligation to transfer an amount that is independent of the entity's available resources. If dividends are not paid then the amount payable, either at a discretionary date or on liquidation, increases. The entity's available resources may not increase at the same rate.

As such, in accordance with the Discussion Paper, the shares would be classified as a financial liability.

### Test your understanding 4 – Bittern

In accordance with IFRS 16 *Leases*, a right-of-use asset and a lease liability are recognised for $10 million.

The tax relief granted relates to the lease liability rather than the right-of-use asset. The tax base of the right-of-use asset is nil (no future tax relief is granted). Its carrying amount is $10 million and so a taxable temporary difference of $10 million arises.

The tax base of the lease liability is nil ($10m carrying amount less $10m future tax relief). The carrying amount of the lease liability is $10 million so a deductible temporary difference of $10 million arises.

This transaction is not a business combination and it affects neither accounting profit nor taxable profit. However, equal amounts of deductible and taxable temporary differences are created.

In accordance with the Board's proposed revisions to IAS 12 *Income Taxes*, a deferred tax asset would be recognised for $3 million ($10m × 30%), assuming that sufficient future profits are expected against which the difference can be utilised. A deferred tax liability would also be recognised for $3 million. The entry required is:

Dr Deferred tax assets $3m

Cr Deferred tax liabilities $3m

## Test your understanding 5 – Mineral

### Deferred tax

The carrying amount of the asset exceeds the tax base. Per IAS 12 *Income Taxes* a deferred tax liability must be recognised. This is measured by multiplying the temporary difference by the tax rate. The tax charge will be recognised in other comprehensive income.

Deferred tax is an application of the accruals concept in that it recognises the tax effects of a transaction in the period when the transaction occurs. Mineral has no plans to sell this asset so there is no present obligation to pay tax that arises on its disposal. The *Conceptual Framework* defines a liability as '**a present obligation of the entity to transfer an economic resource as a result of a past event**' (para 4.26).The deferred tax liability does not appear to meet the definition of a liability in the *Conceptual Framework*.

However, the Board rejects this position. They argue that increases in the carrying amount of an asset must result in future economic benefits for the reporting entity (otherwise the carrying amount is overstated) and that these inflows of economic benefits will be subject to tax. For example, the machine's fair value gain may be due to higher selling prices for its output, which will therefore increase taxable profits. The Board argue that tax is payable on the revaluation irrespective of how the asset is used.

### Financial instruments

IAS 32 *Financial Instruments: Presentation* states that a financial liability is a contract to deliver cash, another financial asset, or a variable number of the entity's own shares.

The contract requires that Mineral delivers as many of its own equity instruments as are equal in value to a certain amount. Per IAS 32, this contract should be classified as a financial liability.

An equity instrument is not a resource of an entity and so this contract does not represent an obligation to transfer an economic resource. This means that the financial liability does not meet the definition of a liability in the *Conceptual Framework*.

# UK GAAP

## Chapter learning objectives

This chapter contains the additional syllabus content required for those sitting the SBR UK exam. If you are sitting the SBR INT exam then you **do not** need to study this chapter.

Upon completion of this chapter you will be able to:

*   Discuss the financial reporting requirements for UK and Republic of Ireland entities (UK GAAP) and their interaction with the Companies Act requirements

*   Discuss the reasons why an entity might choose to adopt FRS 101 or FRS 102

*   Discuss the scope and basis of preparation of financial statements under UK GAAP

*   Discuss the concepts and pervasive principles set out in FRS 102

*   Discuss and apply the principal differences between UK GAAP and IFRS.

**PER**

One of the PER performance objectives (PO7) is to prepare external financial reports. You take part in preparing and reviewing financial statements – and all accompanying information – and you do it in accordance with legal and regulatory requirements. Working through this chapter should help you understand how to demonstrate that objective.

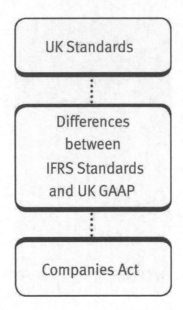

## 1 Purpose of chapter

This chapter contains the additional syllabus content required for those sitting the SBR UK exam.

If you are sitting the SBR INT exam then you **do not** need to study this chapter.

## 2 UK GAAP

### The accounting standards

Guidance about the accounting standards that UK companies should apply is found within FRS 100 *Application of Financial Reporting Requirements*. The rules are as follows:

- Listed groups must prepare their accounts under IFRS Standards.
  - However, the companies within the group can take advantage of disclosure exemptions outlined in FRS 101 when preparing their individual (non-consolidated) financial statements.

- Other UK companies will apply FRS 102 *The Financial Reporting Standard Applicable in the UK and the Republic of Ireland* unless:
  - they voluntarily choose to apply IFRS, or
  - they are a micro-entity and choose to apply FRS 105 *The Financial Reporting Standard Applicable to the Micro-Entities Regime*.

- A small entity that applies FRS 102:
  - does not have to show other comprehensive income
  - does not have to produce a statement of cash flows
  - is exempt from many of the disclosure requirements of FRS 102.

## FRS 101 *Reduced Disclosure Framework*

FRS 101 permits exemptions from many of the disclosure requirements found in International Financial Reporting Standards. FRS 101 can only be applied in the individual financial statements of subsidiaries and parent companies that otherwise fully apply International Financial Reporting Standards.

Some public interest entities, such as banks, cannot take advantage of all of the exemptions outlined in FRS 101. These entities must still make disclosures with regards to financial instruments and fair value.

The application of FRS 101 results in cost-savings and time-savings for entities without severely impacting the quality of financial reporting. Moreover full disclosures on a group level can be found in the consolidated financial statements, and these are likely to be of greater use for investors and lenders.

## FRS 105 *The Financial Reporting Standard Applicable to the Micro-entities Regime*

Micro-entities can choose to prepare their financial statements in accordance with FRS 105.

An entity qualifies as a micro-entity if it satisfies two of the following three requirements:

- Turnover of not more than £632,000 a year

- Gross assets of not more than £316,000

- An average number of employees of 10 or less.

FRS 105 is based on FRS 102 but with some amendments to satisfy legal requirements and to reflect the simpler nature of micro-entities. For example, FRS 105:

- Prohibits accounting for deferred tax

- Prohibits accounting for equity-settled share-based payments prior to the issue of the shares

- Prohibits the revaluation model for property, plant and equipment, intangible assets and investment properties

- Prohibits the capitalisation of borrowing costs

- Prohibits the capitalisation of development expenditure as an intangible asset

- Simplifies the rules around classifying a financial instrument as debt or equity

- Removes the distinction between functional and presentation currencies.

There are very few disclosure requirements in FRS 105.

## FRS 102 *The Financial Reporting Standard Applicable in the UK and the Republic of Ireland*

FRS 102 is a single standard that is organised by topic. It is based on IFRS for Small and Medium Entities (the SMEs Standard), although there are some differences.

The UK syllabus requires students to be able to discuss the concepts and pervasive principles set out in FRS 102 (the equivalent of the Conceptual Framework for Financial Reporting). These are outlined below.

### Objective of financial statements

FRS 102 says that the objective of financial statements is to provide information about an entity's financial position, performance and cash flows, as well as the results of the stewardship of management. This information should be useful to a range of users.

### Qualitative characteristics of information

- **Understandability** – information should be understandable to users with a reasonable knowledge of business and accounting.

- **Relevance** – information should be capable of influencing the economic decisions of users.

- **Materiality** – information is material, and is therefore relevant, if its omission or misstatement could influence the economic decisions of users.

- **Reliability** – information is reliable if it is free from material error, bias, and offers a faithful representation of the transactions an entity has entered into.

- **Substance over form** – transactions should be accounted for in accordance with their economic substance rather than their legal form.

- **Prudence** – caution should be exercised when making judgements.

- **Completeness** – the information included in financial statements should be complete, within the bounds of cost and materiality.

- **Comparability** – users should be able to compare the financial statements of an entity through time, and they should also be able to compare the financial statements of different entities.

- **Timeliness** – information is more relevant if it is provided without undue delay.

- **Balance between benefit and cost** – the benefits that information provides to users should exceed the cost of providing it.

## Elements and recognition

The definitions of the elements are as follows:

- **Assets** – a resource controlled by an entity from a past event from which future economic benefits are expected to flow to the entity.

- **Liabilities** – a present obligation of an entity from a past event, the settlement of which is expected to result in an outflow of economic benefits.

- **Equity** – the residual interest in the assets of the entity after deducting all its liabilities.

- **Income** – increases in economic benefits in the reporting period that result in an increase in equity (other than contributions from equity investors).

- **Expenses** – decreases in economic benefits in the reporting period that result in a decrease in equity (other than distributions to equity investors).

An element should be recognised in the financial statements if:

- It is probable that economic benefits will flow to or from the entity

- Its cost or fair value can be measured reliably.

The above definitions and recognition criteria are based on the 2010 *Conceptual Framework*. As such, the definitions of assets and liabilities and the recognition criteria outlined in FRS 102 differ from those in the 2018 *Conceptual Framework*.

## Measurement

FRS 102 says that there are two common measurement bases:

- **Historical cost** – the amount of cash and cash equivalents paid to acquire an asset, or the amount of cash and cash equivalents received in exchange for an obligation.

- **Fair value** – the amount for which an asset could be exchanged, or a liability settled, between knowledgeable parties in an arm's length transaction.

## Accruals basis

FRS 102 emphasises that financial statements, other than statements of cash flow, are prepared using the accruals basis.

## Offsetting

An entity should not offset assets and liabilities unless required to or permitted by FRS 102.

> ### Test your understanding 1 – FRS 105
>
> You advise a client who is in the process of incorporating a new UK-based company. The company would qualify as a micro-entity and, as such, could apply FRS 105 *The Financial Reporting Standard applicable to the Micro-entities Regime*. Alternatively, it could apply FRS 102 *The Financial Reporting Standard applicable in the UK and Republic of Ireland*.
>
> **Required:**
>
> **What factors should be considered when establishing whether the client should use FRS 105?**

## 3 Examinable differences between International and UK standards

Students sitting the UK paper are required to know the key differences between FRS 102 and International Financial Reporting Standards. These are outlined below:

### Concepts and principles

FRS 102 notes that there are two commonly used measurement bases. These are:

- Historical cost, and
- Fair value.

In contrast, the *Conceptual Framework for Financial Reporting* outlines:

- Historical cost, and
- Current value.

### Financial statement presentation

### True and fair override

To comply with Companies Act, FRS 102 allows a 'true and fair override'. If compliance with FRS 102 is inconsistent with the requirement to give a true and fair view, the directors must depart from FRS 102 to the extent necessary to give a true and fair view. Particulars of any such departure, the reasons for it and its effect are disclosed.

### Statement of financial position

In the UK, Companies Act requirements dictate the format of the statement of financial position. It is set out as follows:

Assets – Liabilities = Equity

## Income statement

FRS 102 refers to the statement of financial performance as the 'income statement' (as opposed to 'the statement of profit or loss'). Its format is dictated by Companies Act.

If activities are discontinued during the year, FRS 102 requires that a line-by-line analysis is provided on the face of the income statement in a column called 'discontinued operations'. In contrast IFRS 5 Non-current Assets Held for Sale and Discontinued Operations allows a single figure to be presented on the face of the statement of profit or loss (with more detailed analysis provided in the disclosure notes).

## Statement of cash flows

Under FRS 102, small entities, mutual life assurance companies, pension funds and certain investment funds are not required to produce a statement of cash flows. This exemption does not exist in IAS 7 Statement of Cash Flows.

## Inventories

FRS 102 provides more guidance than IAS 2 Inventories about what costs should be included in production overheads. For example, it says that production overheads should include the costs of any obligation to restore a site on which an item of property, plant and equipment is located that are incurred during the reporting period as a consequence of having used that item of property, plant and equipment to produce inventory.

FRS 102 permits the reversal of inventory impairments, whereas IAS 2 does not.

## Changes in accounting policy

FRS 102 states that the change to a cost model when a reliable estimate of fair value in unavailable is not a change in accounting policy. This exemption is not mentioned in IAS 8 Accounting Policies, Changes in Accounting Estimates and Errors.

## Financial instruments

### Measurement

FRS 102 adopts a simplified approach to financial instruments:

- Investments in shares are measured at fair value through profit or loss if their fair value can be reliably measured. Otherwise, they are measured at cost less impairment.

- Simple debt instruments (whether receivable or payable) are measured at amortised cost.

- Commitments to make or receive a loan are measured at cost (if any) less impairment.

- More complicated debt instruments (whether receivable or payable) are measured at fair value through profit or loss.

## Impairment

FRS 102 adopts an incurred loss model. This means that an impairment loss is only recognised in respect of financial assets if objective evidence of impairment has occurred – such as the bankruptcy of a credit customer.

For an asset measured at amortised cost, FRS 102 says that the impairment loss is calculated as the difference between its carrying amount and the present value of the expected future cash flows (discounted at the original effective rate of interest).

In contrast, IFRS 9 *Financial Instruments* adopts an 'expected loss' model for financial asset impairments. This involves recognising a loss allowance for all financial assets measured at amortised cost or fair value through other comprehensive income (except equity instruments) based on the level of credit risk.

## Derecognition

FRS 102 contains simpler rules than IFRS 9 for deciding whether or not to derecognise a financial instrument.

### Test your understanding 2 – Cocoa

Cocoa purchased a debt instrument in the current reporting period that is measured at amortised cost. By the reporting date no actual defaults had occurred. However, due to a general economic decline, the directors of Cocoa concluded that credit risk associated with the remaining loan period had increased significantly.

The following credit losses have been calculated:

12 month expected credit losses: $0.3 million

Lifetime expected credit losses: $1.0 million

**Required:**

**Explain how the above should be dealt with under International Financial Reporting Standards and FRS 102.**

## Joint ventures

FRS 102 uses the term 'joint venture' with regards to any arrangement whereby an economic activity is subject to joint control. FRS 102 says that there are three types of joint ventures:

- Jointly controlled operations – this is where each venturer contributes their own assets for use by the joint venture.

- Jointly controlled assets – this is where the venturers jointly control or jointly own the assets used by the joint venture.

- Jointly controlled entities – this involves the establishment of a separate entity that is under joint control. In the consolidated financial statements, such investments are accounted for using the equity method.

IFRS 11 *Joint Arrangements* classifies activities subject to joint control in one of two ways:

- joint operations – where the venturers have rights to the assets, and obligations for the liabilities, of the operation.

- joint ventures – where the venturers have rights to the net assets of the arrangement, usually as a result of a separate entity being established.

### Investment property

FRS 102 requires the use of the fair value model unless the fair value cannot be determined reliably. In contrast, IAS 40 *Investment Property* allows entities to measure investment property using either the cost model or the fair value model.

FRS 102 allows an entity that rents investment property to another company in the same group to account for it as property, plant and equipment in its separate financial statements. If so, it is measured at cost less depreciation. IAS 40 does not permit this treatment.

IAS 40 states that a property which is held to earn rental income should be treated as property, plant and equipment if ancillary services are provided that are significant to the arrangement e.g. the services provided to hotel guests. FRS 102 does not cover this situation.

### Intangible assets

#### Development

FRS 102 says that the capitalisation of development expenditure is **optional**. In contrast IAS 38 *Intangible Assets* **requires** that development expenditure is capitalised if certain criteria are met.

#### Grants

FRS 102 specifies that an intangible asset acquired by way of a grant shall be recognised at its fair value on the date that the grant is received or receivable.

#### Useful life

FRS 102 specifies that intangible assets should be considered to have a definite useful economic life. FRS 102 says that if the useful life of an intangible asset cannot be measured reliably then it must be estimated. The estimate used should not exceed ten years.

IAS 38 allows entities to regard an intangible asset as having an indefinite useful economic life if it cannot foresee an end to the period over which the asset will generate economic benefits.

## Non-current assets

### Held for sale

FRS 102 does not contain the concept of 'held for sale'. As such, assets are depreciated or amortised up to the date of disposal. However, FRS 102 identifies the decision to sell an asset as a potential indicator of impairment, meaning that an impairment review should be performed.

### Borrowing costs

Under FRS 102, an entity **may** adopt a policy of capitalising borrowing costs. IAS 23 Borrowing Costs **requires** that borrowing costs attributable to a qualifying asset are capitalised.

FRS 102 is more specific than IAS 23 about the capitalisation rate to be used.

### Estimate reviews

FRS 102 only requires entities to review the useful economic life of assets if evidence exists that they have changed. IAS 16 Property, Plant and Equipment and IAS 38 Intangible Assets require that an entity reviews residual values and useful lives annually.

> ### Test your understanding 3 – Jelly Roll
>
> Jelly Roll has a year end of 31 December 20X1. On 30 June 20X1 the directors made the decision to sell a building. On this date the building – classified as property, plant and equipment – had a carrying amount of $2 million, a remaining useful life of 20 years, and nil residual value. The building was immediately advertised for sale at its fair value of $5 million and a sale within 12 months was deemed to be highly probable.
>
> Costs to sell are negligible and can be ignored.
>
> **Required:**
>
> **How should the above be treated in accordance with International Financial Reporting Standards and FRS 102?**

### Leases

FRS 102 requires lessees to classify leases as operating leases or finance leases and account for them as follows:

- Finance leases – an asset and liability is recognised at the lower of the asset's fair value and the present value of the minimum lease payments. Depreciation on the asset and interest on the liability is charged to profit or loss.

- Operating leases – lease payments are recognised as an expense in profit or loss on a straight line basis.

This means that no liability is recognised in respect of operating leases in the financial statements of a lessee, even though it meets the definition of a liability as outlined in FRS 102.

IFRS 16 *Leases* requires lessees to recognise a lease liability and right-of-use asset in respect of all leases, unless short-term or of low value.

## Provisions

IAS 37 *Provisions, Contingent Liabilities and Contingent Assets* provides detailed guidance on restructuring provisions – such as when a constructive obligation arises, and the amounts that can be included in the provision. FRS 102 simply states that a provision for restructuring costs should be recognised when a legal or constructive obligation exists.

In accordance with FRS 102, financial guarantee contracts (such as when one company guarantees the overdraft or loan of another company) may be classified as provisions or contingent liabilities (depending on the probability of payment). Under International Financial Reporting Standards, financial guarantee contracts are accounted for using IFRS 9 *Financial Instruments*.

## Revenue

FRS 102 splits revenue accounting into three main areas:

- Revenue from goods – recognised when the risks and rewards of ownership transfer from the buyer to the seller.

- Revenue from services – recognised according to the stage of completion.

- Revenue from construction contracts – recognised according to the stage of completion.

IFRS 15 *Revenue from Contracts with Customers* adopts a five step model for revenue recognition.

## Government grants

### Recognition

Under FRS 102, two methods of recognising government grants are allowed:

**The performance model** – If no conditions are attached to the grant, it is recognised as income immediately. If conditions are attached to the grant, it is only recognised as income when all conditions have been met.

**The accruals model** – Grants are recognised as income on a systematic basis, either as costs are incurred (revenue grants) or over the asset's useful life (capital grants).

IAS 20 *Accounting for Government Grants and the Disclosure of Government Assistance* adopts an accruals model for government grant recognition.

## Repayment

A government grant may need to be repaid if its conditions are not complied with. IAS 20 provides detailed guidance on how to deal with the repayment of a government grant. FRS 102 simply says that a liability should be recognised when the repayment meets the definition of a liability.

## Share-based payment

### Valuation

When measuring the fair value of equity instruments granted, FRS 102 requires the use of a three tier hierarchy:

1    Observable market prices

2    The use of entity specific market data, such as recent transactions in the instrument

3    A valuation method that uses, wherever possible, market data.

### Recognition

FRS 102 provides simpler recognition rules than IFRS 2 *Share-based Payment*. For example, under FRS 102, schemes which offer a choice of settlement are not split into an equity component and a liability component. Instead FRS 102 provides rules to determine whether to account for them as a wholly cash-settled transaction or a wholly equity-settled transaction.

## Impairment of assets

FRS 102 specifies that a recoverable amount need not be determined unless there are indicators of impairment. In contrast IAS 36 *Impairment of Assets* requires that some assets are subject to annual impairment review (such as goodwill acquired in a business combination).

FRS 102 is much less detailed with regards to impairments than IAS 36.

## Employee benefits

Under FRS 102 an entity only accounts for termination benefits when it has a detailed formal plan for the restructuring and has no realistic possibility of withdrawal. In contrast IAS 19 *Employee Benefits* says that termination benefits are recognised at the earlier of:

- the date when the entity can no longer withdraw the offer, and

- the date when costs associated with a restructuring are recognised under IAS 37 *Provisions, Contingent Liabilities and Contingent Assets*.

## Income tax

The income tax section of FRS 102 differs significantly from IAS 12 *Income Taxes*.

### Profit or loss/statement of financial position

FRS 102 adopts a profit or loss approach to the recognition of deferred tax. Timing differences are defined as differences between taxable profits and total comprehensive income as stated in the financial statements that arise from the inclusion of income and expenses in tax assessments in periods different from those in which they are recognised in financial statements.

FRS 102 makes an exception to this rule. It states that deferred tax should also be recognised based on the differences between the tax value and fair value of assets and liabilities acquired in a business combination.

In contrast, IAS 12 conceptualises deferred tax through the statement of financial position. The standard states that deferred tax should be accounted for based on differences between the amounts recognised for the entity's assets and liabilities in the statement of financial position and the recognition of those assets and liabilities by the tax authorities.

### Permanent differences

FRS 102 uses the concept of permanent differences. Permanent differences arise because certain types of income and expenses are non-taxable or disallowable, or because certain tax charges or allowances are greater or smaller than the corresponding income or expense in the financial statements. Deferred tax is not recognised on permanent differences.

IAS 12 does not use the terminology 'permanent difference'. Instead, it says that deferred tax assets and liabilities are recognised for 'temporary differences'.

## Foreign currency translation

Unlike IAS 21 *The Effects of Changes in Foreign Exchange Rates*, FRS 102 does not require the presentation of a separate translation reserve for foreign exchange differences arising on the translation of a subsidiary.

Under FRS 102, foreign exchange differences are **not** reclassified from other comprehensive income to profit or loss on the disposal of the overseas subsidiary (whereas they are reclassified under IAS 21).

## Events after the reporting period

Under both FRS 102 and IAS 10 *Events after the Reporting Period*, no liability is recognised for dividends declared after the reporting date. However, FRS 102 says that the dividend can be presented as a separate component of retained earnings.

### Related parties

FRS 102 has additional disclosure exemptions. It states that disclosures need not be given of transactions entered into between two or more members of a group, provided that any subsidiary which is a party to the transaction is wholly owned by such a member.

FRS 102 only requires disclosure of key management personnel compensation in total. In contrast, IAS 24 *Related Party Disclosures* requires that disclosure of key management personnel compensation is broken down into:

- short-term benefits
- post-employment benefits
- other long-term benefits
- termination benefits
- share-based payments.

### Agriculture

FRS 102 says that, for each class of biological assets, an entity can choose to use the cost model or the fair value model. Under the cost model, the asset is measured at cost less accumulated depreciation and accumulated impairment losses. The fair value model is consistent with IAS 41 Agriculture (below).

IAS 41 *Agriculture* requires biological assets to be measured using a fair value model. This means that they are initially recorded at fair value less costs to sell. They are then remeasured to fair value less costs to sell at each reporting date with gains and losses recorded in profit or loss.

### Consolidated and separate financial statements

### Control

The definition of control in FRS 102 is different from the definition in IFRS 10 *Consolidated Financial Statements*. FRS 102 says that control is the power to govern the financial and operating policies of an entity so as to obtain benefits from its activities. FRS 102 says that control is presumed to exist if an entity owns more than half of the voting rights of another entity, although this assumption can be rebutted in exceptional circumstances.

IFRS 10 *Consolidated Financial Statements* says that an investor controls an investee if it:

- has power over the investee
- has rights or exposure to variable returns
- can affect these returns through its power over the investee.

### Individual financial statements of a parent

If a parent applies FRS 102 and is required to produce individual financial statements, the parent must measure its investments in subsidiaries using one of the following methods:

- cost less impairment

- fair value with gains and losses in other comprehensive income

- fair value with gains and losses in profit or loss.

IAS 27 *Separate Financial Statements* also allows investments in subsidiaries to be accounted for in the parent's financial statements using the equity method.

### Exclusions

FRS 102 says that a subsidiary is excluded from consolidation if severe long-term restrictions hamper the ability of the parent to exercise control. This exemption does not exist in full IFRS Standards.

## Business Combinations and goodwill

### Consideration

With regards to contingent consideration, FRS 102 states that the estimated amount payable is only included in the calculation of goodwill if it is probable that it will be incurred. Costs directly attributable to the acquisition are also included in the calculation of goodwill (such as legal and professional fees).

Under IFRS 3 *Business Combinations*, contingent consideration is measured at its fair value and included in the calculation of goodwill. The fair value of the contingent consideration will incorporate the probability that the payment will be made. Any transaction costs related to the acquisition are expensed to profit or loss.

### Control in stages

If control in a subsidiary is achieved in stages (e.g. from a 10% holding to a 60%) then IFRS 3 *Business Combinations* requires earlier investments to be remeasured to fair value at the date control is achieved. In contrast FRS 102 says that the earlier share purchases are not remeasured.

### Net assets of acquiree

IFRS 3 *Business Combinations* says that intangible assets other than goodwill arising from a business combination are recognised at fair value if they are separable or if they arise from legal or contractual rights.

FRS 102 only **requires** recognition of intangible assets other than goodwill arising on a business combination if they are separable **and** arise from legal or contractual rights. However, FRS 102 permits entities to recognise additional intangibles if they are separable **or** if they arise from legal or contractual rights.

### Negative goodwill

According to FRS 102, negative goodwill (where the fair value of the net assets acquired exceeds the consideration) is recognised on the statement of financial position immediately below goodwill. It should be followed by a subtotal of the net amount of goodwill and the negative goodwill, i.e. it is presented as a negative asset.

The subsequent treatment of negative goodwill is that any amount up to the fair value of non-monetary assets acquired is recognised in profit or loss in the periods in which the non-monetary assets are recovered. Any amount exceeding the fair value of non-monetary assets acquired must be recognised in profit or loss in the periods expected to be benefited.

IFRS 3 *Business Combinations* refers to negative goodwill as a 'gain on bargain purchase'. This is recognised immediately in profit or loss.

### Amortisation

FRS 102 requires that goodwill is amortised over its useful economic life. If this cannot be reliably measured then the useful life should not exceed ten years.

Under International Financial Reporting Standards, goodwill is not amortised but is instead subject to an annual impairment review.

### Non-controlling interest (NCI)

FRS 102 requires that the NCI at acquisition is only measured using the proportionate method.

IFRS 3 *Business Combinations* allows the NCI at acquisition to be measured at either:

- Fair value, or
- Its proportionate share of the subsidiary's identifiable net assets.

### Fair value

IFRS 3 *Fair Value Measurement* includes more detailed information on fair values than FRS 102.

### Subsidiaries held exclusively with view to resale

In the consolidated financial statements, FRS 102 requires that an election is made to measure such investments at either:

- cost less impairment, or
- fair value with gains and losses in other comprehensive income, or
- fair value with gains and losses in profit or loss.

If the subsidiary is held as part of an investment portfolio, then it must be measured at fair value with gains and losses in profit or loss.

In contrast, IFRS 5 *Assets Held for Sale and Discontinued Operations* requires that a subsidiary acquired for resale is classified as 'held for sale'. This means that all of its assets will be amalgamated into one line in the statement of financial position, and all of its liabilities will be amalgamated into another line.

## Associates

FRS 102 specifies that any transactions costs are added onto the initial carrying amount of an associate. Under International Financial Reporting Standards, these costs are expensed to profit or loss.

FRS 102 specifies that any difference between the consideration paid to acquire an associate and the investor's share of the fair value of the associate's net assets is implicit goodwill. This goodwill should be amortised over its useful economic life.

### Test your understanding 4 – Peanut

On 1 January 20X1, Peanut acquired 30% of the ordinary shares of Almond for $4 million.

At this date, Almond's identifiable net assets were carried at $10 million. This was the same as their fair value. The useful economic life of any goodwill acquired cannot be measured reliably, but Peanut used the largest estimate permitted.

In the year ended 31 December 20X1, Almond made a profit after tax of $2 million.

**Required:**

**In accordance with FRS 102, explain how the investment in the associate should be accounted for in the consolidated financial statements for the year ended 31 December 20X1.**

### Test your understanding 5 – Pizza

On 31 December 20X1, Pizza acquires 80% of Spaghetti. Pizza pays $3 million cash and will pay further cash consideration in one year's time if Spaghetti exceeds profit targets. The present value of this arrangement is $2 million and the fair value is $1.3 million. The directors believe that there is a 60% chance that the profit target will be met. Legal fees of $0.1 million were also incurred and are directly attributable to the purchase of the shares.

The fair value of Spaghetti's net assets at the acquisition date is $7 million. The fair value of the non-controlling interest at acquisition is $1.2 million.

**Required:**

**In accordance with FRS 102, explain how the above will be dealt with in the consolidated financial statements for the year ended 31 December 20X1.**

## 4 Companies Act

The UK syllabus specifies that candidates must know the following basic Companies Act requirements relating to single and group entity financial statements.

### Single entity financial statements

A company is exempt from the requirement to prepare individual accounts for a financial year if:

- it is itself a subsidiary undertaking
- it has been dormant throughout the whole of that year, and
- its parent undertaking is established under the law of an EEA State.

### Group financial statements

A company subject to the small companies regime **may** prepare group accounts for the year.

If not subject to the small companies regime, a parent company **must** prepare group accounts for the year unless one of the following applies:

- A company is exempt from the requirement to prepare group accounts if it is itself a wholly-owned subsidiary of a parent undertaking.
- A parent company is exempt from the requirement to prepare group accounts if, under section 405 of Companies Act, all of its subsidiary undertakings could be excluded from consolidation.

### Exclusion of a subsidiary from consolidation

Where a parent company prepares Companies Act group accounts, all the subsidiary undertakings of the company must be included in the consolidation, subject to the following exceptions:

- A subsidiary undertaking may be excluded from consolidation if its inclusion is not material for the purpose of giving a true and fair view (but two or more undertakings may be excluded only if they are not material taken together).
- A subsidiary undertaking may be excluded from consolidation where:
  - severe long-term restrictions substantially hinder the exercise of the rights of the parent company over the assets or management of that undertaking
  - the information necessary for the preparation of group accounts cannot be obtained without disproportionate expense or undue delay
  - the interest of the parent company is held exclusively with a view to subsequent resale.

## 5 Chapter summary

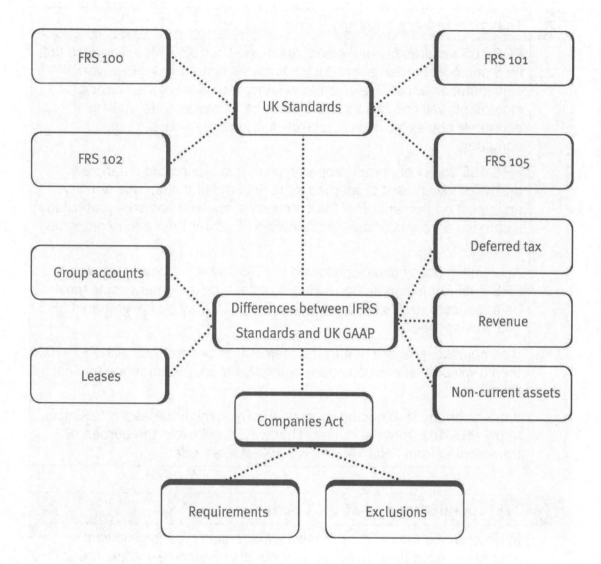

# Test your understanding answers

### Test your understanding 1 – FRS 105

FRS 105 requires fewer disclosures than FRS 102. This will reduce the time and cost burden of producing financial statements. However, consideration should be given to whether the users of the financial statements will find this lack of disclosure a hindrance to making economic decisions. This is unlikely in the case of such a small company.

FRS 105 does not permit property, plant and equipment, intangible assets or investment properties to be held at fair value. This will have an impact on perception of the company's financial position, particularly if carrying amounts of assets are materially lower than other companies as a result.

Accounting policy choices allowed in FRS 102 have been removed in FRS 105. For instance, borrowing costs and development costs must be expensed. Profits reported under FRS 105 may be lower than if FRS 102 was applied.

If competitors prepare financial statements in accordance with FRS 105 then it will be easier to compare and benchmark performance against them.

If the company is expected to grow quickly, it might be easier to simply apply FRS 102 from the outset. That way, it will avoid the burden of transitioning from FRS 105 to FRS 102 at a later date.

### Test your understanding 2 – Cocoa

In accordance with IFRS 9 *Financial Instruments*, a loss allowance should be recognised at an amount equal to lifetime expected credit losses if credit risk has increased significantly since inception. As such an allowance for $1 million, and a corresponding charge to profit or loss, should be recognised.

In accordance with FRS 102, financial asset impairments are calculated if there is objective evidence that impairment has occurred. No objective evidence exists about the particular borrower involved, and no default of payments has occurred. Therefore no impairment loss is recognised.

**Test your understanding 3 – Jelly Roll**

In accordance with IFRS 5 *Non-current Assets Held for Sale and Discontinued Operations*, the building will be classified as held for sale because its carrying amount will be mainly recovered through a sale. The building will continue to be held at $2 million as this is the lower of its carrying amount and its fair value less costs to sell. No more depreciation will be charged. The building will be reclassified as a current asset.

In accordance with FRS 102, an impairment review should be conducted. However, the asset is not impaired because its fair value is significantly higher than its carrying amount. The building will continue to be classified as property, plant and equipment and will be depreciated. It will have a carrying amount at 31 December 20X1 of $1.95 million ($2m × 19.5/20).

**Test your understanding 4 – Peanut**

The associate is initially measured at its cost of $4 million.

The carrying amount of associate will be increased by Peanut's share of the profit after tax, which amounts to $0.6 million ($2m × 30%). This will also be recorded in profit or loss.

On the purchase of the associate, implicit goodwill of $1 million ($4m – (30% × $10m)) arose. If the useful life of goodwill cannot be estimated reliably then the maximum permitted estimate is 10 years. The amortisation charge of $0.1 million ($1m/10 years) will reduce the carrying amount of the investment and will also be charged against profit or loss.

The total carrying amount of the investment in the associate in the consolidated statement of financial position will be $4.5 million ($4m + $0.6m – $0.1m).

The share of the profits of the associate reported in the income statement is $0.5 million ($0.6m – $0.1m).

## Test your understanding 5 – Pizza

The present value of the contingent consideration will be included in the goodwill calculation because it is probable that it will be paid. FRS 102 requires that costs related to the acquisition are also included in the goodwill calculation.

FRS 102 does not permit the NCI at acquisition to be measured at fair value. Only the proportionate method can be used.

|  | $m |
|---|---|
| Cash consideration | 3.0 |
| Contingent consideration | 2.0 |
| Fees | 0.1 |
| NCI at acquisition ($7m × 20%) | 1.4 |
| FV of identifiable net assets at acquisition | (7.0) |
| Negative goodwill | (0.5) |

The negative goodwill is not recognised as a gain in profit or loss but instead as a negative asset on the statement of financial position.

KAPLAN PUBLISHING

# Questions & Answers

## Test your understanding 1 – Cookie

Cookie, a company, prepares its financial statements in accordance with International Financial Reporting Standards. It has investments in several subsidiaries. The Cookie group has a year end of 30 April 20X4.

### Biscuit

On 1 May 20X3, Cookie acquired 60% of Biscuit's 10 million $1 ordinary shares. A gain on a bargain purchase arising on the acquisition of Biscuit was calculated using the following data:

|  | $m |
| --- | --- |
| Cash consideration | 30 |
| Fair value of NCI at acquisition | 45 |
| Carrying amount of net assets at acquisition | 80 |

The gain on bargain purchase was recognised in profit or loss. No entries have been posted in the consolidated financial statements in respect of the following issues:

- As part of the purchase consideration, Cookie issued 5 million of its own $1 ordinary shares. These had a fair value of $4.50 each on 1 May 20X3.

- At the acquisition date Biscuit owned an internally generated brand that was unrecognised in its separate financial statements. The fair value of the brand at this date was $15 million. It was estimated to have a remaining useful economic life of 5 years.

- The recoverable amount of the net assets of Biscuit, including goodwill, was $107 million as at the reporting date. No impairment review has yet been performed.

At the reporting date, Biscuit's retained earnings balance was $84 million in its separate financial statements.

**Specialised plant**

Included in Cookie's property, plant and equipment is an item of specialised plant. This was internally constructed. Construction began on 1 May 20X3 and was completed on 31 October 20X3. The asset was initially recorded at a cost of $15 million and depreciated based on a useful economic life of five years. A breakdown of the cost is as follows:

|  | $m |
|---|---|
| Materials for construction | 7.3 |
| Directly attributable labour | 2.9 |
| Testing of machine | 0.6 |
| Training staff to use machine | 0.5 |
| Allocated general overheads | 3.7 |
|  | ——— |
|  | 15.0 |
|  | ——— |

**Required:**

(a)  **Discuss, with calculations, how to correct the accounting errors made in respect of the investment in Biscuit in the consolidated financial statements for the year ended 30 April 20X4. Provide the adjustments required.**

(b)  **Discuss how to correct the treatment of specialised plant in the consolidated financial statements for the year ended 30 April 20X4.**

---

### Test your understanding 2 – Pineapple

Pineapple is a public limited company which has investments in a number of subsidiary companies. It has a reporting date of 30 September 20X3 and prepares financial statements in accordance with IFRS Standards.

**Sale of shares in Satsuma**

Pineapple acquired 70% of Satsuma's 2 million $1 ordinary shares several years ago for cash consideration of $4,900,000. At the acquisition date, retained earnings of Satsuma were $2,045,000 and the fair value of the non-controlling interest was $1,600,000.

On 1 October 20X2, Satsuma had retained earnings of $2,342,000. It made a profit of $568,000 in the year ended 30 September 20X3. Profits accrued evenly.

On 31 March 20X3, Pineapple sold its entire shareholding in Satsuma for $5,600,000. Goodwill arising on the acquisition of Satsuma was impaired by 40% in the year ended 30 September 20X2. Satsuma is geographically and operationally distinct from the rest of the Pineapple group.

## Interest-free loan

On 1 October 20X2, Pineapple made an interest-free loan of $1,500,000 to Blueberry, a key supplier that was in financial difficulties. This loan is repayable on 30 September 20X6. If the supplier had borrowed the money from a bank, they would have been charged annual interest of 12%. Pineapple recorded the cash outflow and a corresponding financial asset at $1,500,000. No other accounting entries have been made, except to correctly record the required loss allowance.

### Required:

(a) **Discuss how the sale of the shares in Satsuma should be accounted for in the consolidated financial statements of the Pineapple group for the year ended 30 September 20X3.**

(b) **Discuss how to correct the treatment of the interest-free loan in the consolidated financial statements of the Pineapple group for the year ended 30 September 20X3. Provide the adjustments required.**

## Test your understanding 3 – Vinyl

Vinyl has investments in many subsidiaries. One of these, CD, is located overseas and prepares its individual statements using the Mark (MK). The presentation currency of the Vinyl group is the dollar ($). An extract from CD's statement of financial position as at 30 September 20X4 is presented below:

| Equity | MK(m) |
|---|---|
| Equity capital MK1 shares) | 76 |
| Retained earnings | 275 |
| Other components of equity | – |
| | 351 |

The following information is relevant to the preparation of the consolidated financial statements.

### Purchase of CD shares

Vinyl acquired 75% of the ordinary shares in CD on 1 October 20X3 for MK360 million. The fair value of the non-controlling interest at the acquisition date was MK90 million and the retained earnings of CD were MK210 million. There were no other components of equity. The fair value of the net assets of CD approximated their carrying amounts with the exception of a brand. This brand was not recognised by CD but Vinyl estimates that it had a fair value of MK10 million at the acquisition date. The brand was deemed to have an indefinite useful economic life.

CD did not pay any dividends during the reporting period.

The following exchange rates are relevant:

|  | MK to $1 |
|---|---|
| 1 October 20X3 | 1.2 |
| 30 September 20X4 | 1.7 |
| Average rate for the year to 30 September 20X4 | 1.4 |

**Convertible bonds**

Included within Vinyl's non-current liabilities are the proceeds from the issue of convertible bonds on 30 September 20X4. On this date, Vinyl issued 500,000 $100 4% convertible bonds at par. Interest is payable annually in arrears. These bonds will be redeemed at par for cash on 30 September 20X7, or are convertible into 75,000 ordinary shares. The interest rate on similar debt without a conversion option is 9%.

**Required:**

(a) **With respect to the translation and consolidation of CD, discuss how to calculate and account for the foreign exchange differences in the consolidated financial statements of the Vinyl group for the year ended 30 September 20X4.**

(b) **Discuss how to correct the treatment of the convertible bond in the consolidated financial statements of the Vinyl group for the year ended 30 September 20X4. Provide the adjustments required.**

**Test your understanding 4 – Frank**

The following financial statement extracts relate to the Frank Group:

**Extracts from consolidated statement of financial position as at 30 September 20X4 (with comparatives)**

|  | 20X4 $m | 20X3 $m |
|---|---|---|
| **Non-current assets** |  |  |
| Property, plant and equipment (PPE) | 221 | 263 |
| Goodwill | 75 | 142 |
| Investment properties | 82 | 60 |
| **Current assets** |  |  |
| Inventories | 256 | 201 |
| Trade and other receivables | 219 | 263 |
| **Current liabilities** |  |  |
| Trade and other payables | 524 | 486 |

---

**Extracts from consolidated statement of profit or loss and other comprehensive income for the year ended 30 September 20X4**

|  | $m |
|---|---|
| Profit from operations | 79 |
| Share of profit of associate | 21 |
| Finance cost | (12) |
| | ——— |
| Profit before tax | 88 |
| | ——— |

Other comprehensive income
Items that will not be reclassified to profit or loss

| | |
|---|---|
| Gain on revaluation of PPE | 50 |

**Notes**

The following information is relevant to the Frank group:

1   PPE with a carrying amount of $12m was disposed of for cash proceeds of $10m. PPE costing $53m was purchased during the period.

2   Investment properties are accounted for at fair value. Gains and losses are recorded within operating income. New investment properties were purchased during the period for $14m in cash.

3   During the reporting period, the Frank Group sold some ordinary shares in Chip, one of its subsidiaries, for $41m cash. Frank held 90% of the ordinary shares in Chip before the sale and 40% of the shares after the sale (leaving it with significant influence). A profit on disposal has been correctly calculated and credited to operating income in the statement of profit or loss. The interest in Chip retained by Frank after the share sale had a fair value of $32m. Goodwill and the non-controlling interest at the disposal date were $40m and $4m respectively.

A breakdown of the carrying amount of Chip's net assets at the date of the share sale is provided below:

|  | $m |
|---|---|
| Property, plant and equipment | 81 |
| Trade and other receivables | 32 |
| Cash and cash equivalents | 6 |
| Loans | (30) |
| Trade and other payables | (55) |
| | ——— |
| Net assets at disposal date | 34 |
| | ——— |

**Required:**

**In accordance with IAS 7 *Statement of Cash Flows,* prepare 'cash generated from operations' for the year ended 30 September 20X4 using the indirect method.**

**Test your understanding 5 – Sunny Days**

Sunny Days is an entity that breeds and matures beef cattle for sale. It prepares its financial statements in accordance with International Financial Reporting Standards and has a year end of 30 September 20X4. The directors need help with a number of unresolved accounting issues that are detailed below.

(a) In the financial statements for the year ended 30 September 20X3 Sunny Days reported biological assets of $1.8 million. Cattle with a carrying amount of $0.1 million died during the year ended 30 September 20X4 and Sunny Days sold cattle with a carrying amount of $0.4 million. During the current year, the company purchased new cattle and correctly recognised it at a value of $0.8 million. This was partly funded by an unconditional grant of $0.2 million from a local government agency.

Sunny Days does not have the information available to identify the principal market for its cattle. Details of the prices that Sunny Days could obtain for its entire herd at the two markets available to it at the reporting date are provided below:

|  | Market 1 | Market 2 |
| --- | --- | --- |
| Estimated selling price ($m) | 2.6 | 2.8 |
| Cost of transporting cattle to market ($m) | 0.1 | 0.4 |
| Costs to sell (as % of selling price) | 0.5% | 0.5% |

The farmland used by Sunny Days to rear its cattle was purchased for $3 million on 1 October 20X2 but was revalued to $3.2 million on 30 September 20X3. Due to declining property prices in the area, the land was deemed to have a fair value of $2.7 million as at 30 September 20X4.

**(12 marks)**

(b)　On 1 January 20X4, the government announced new legislation which made some of Sunny Days' farming methods illegal. These laws became effective on 1 September 20X4. Due to short term cash flow difficulties, Sunny Days has not yet started to comply with the new legislation. It is estimated that the cost of compliance will be approximately $0.8 million. The government has said that fines for non-compliance are $0.1 million per month and will be strictly enforced.

The directors of Sunny Days wish to know how to account for the above costs as well as any resulting deferred tax impact. Fines are not a tax allowable expense. Sunny Days pays tax at a rate of 20%.

**(6 marks)**

(c)　Sunny Days enters into a contract with a supplier to use a specific retail unit (Unit 5A) for a period of five years. Unit 5A is part of a larger retail space owned by the supplier. Sunny Days will use the retail unit to sell farm produce to the general public.

During the five year period, the supplier can force Sunny Days to relocate to one of the other retail units. The terms of the contract state that the supplier would have to pay all of Sunny Day's relocation costs, and make a payment to compensate for the inconvenience. The supplier would only benefit from moving Sunny Days if a larger retailer wished to move into Unit 5A and if they were willing to commit to using this space for more than five years. This is thought to be possible, but unlikely.

Sunny Days must open and operate Unit 5A during the hours when the larger retail space is open. However, Sunny Days can sell whatever products it wishes, at whatever prices it determines. The supplier will provide cleaning and security services.

Sunny Days will make fixed quarterly payments to the supplier. Sunny Days must also make an annual variable payment, calculated as a percentage of the revenue generated by Unit 5A.

The directors of Sunny Days require advice on whether this contract contains a lease.

**(7 marks)**

**Required:**

**Discuss the accounting treatment of the above transactions in the financial statements of Sunny Days for the year ended 30 September 20X4.**

**Note: the mark allocation is shown against each of the three events above.**

**(Total: 25 marks)**

## Test your understanding 6 – Coffee

Coffee is a company with a reporting date of 30 September 20X4. Its financial statements are prepared in accordance with International Financial Reporting Standards. There are a number of unresolved accounting issues, which are detailed below.

(a) The financial controller of Coffee was appointed during the current reporting period. She is concerned that some of the payments made this year are significantly larger than the amounts that were provided and accrued for. The two largest discrepancies are detailed below:

– Legal experts had previously advised Coffee that it would probably be found not liable in a court case concerning breaches in employee health and safety legislation. As such, a contingent liability was disclosed in the financial statements for the period ended 30 September 20X3. However, on 1 July 20X4, Coffee was found liable and was ordered to pay damages of $2 million.

– In its financial statements for the year ended 30 September 20X3, Coffee provided for income tax payable of $3 million. However, in January 20X4, Coffee's records were inspected by the tax authorities and a number of errors were discovered. The tax authorities recommended that Coffee improve its controls and training to prevent such mistakes from happening again. Coffee was not levied with any fines but the authorities deemed that the correct amount of tax payable on profits earned in the period ended 30 September 20X3 was $4 million. Coffee paid this in July 20X4.

Coffee requires advice as to the correct accounting treatment of these two events.

**(7 marks)**

(b) Coffee makes a number of loans to its customers. The interest rate on these loans is at a market rate. Within the first 12 months, Coffee sells these loan assets to another company called Tea. Tea, which is a subsidiary of Coffee, holds the loans until maturity.

At the period end, Coffee holds loan assets that it has yet to sell to Tea. Coffee wishes to know the accounting treatment of these loan assets in both its individual and group financial statements.

**(8 marks)**

(c) At the end of the reporting period, Coffee bought 200 kg of gold bullion for $4 million in cash. Gold bullion is traded on an active market and can be bought and sold instantly. The fair value of gold bullion changes erratically, and Coffee made the investment with the intention of trading it at a profit in the short-term.

Coffee is unsure whether the $4 million holding of gold bullion should be classified as cash and cash equivalents in its statement of cash flows.

**(5 marks)**

(d) On 1 October 20X3, Coffee spent $2 million on acquiring a customer list that would provide benefits to the business for 18 months. Coffee has used its own knowledge and expertise to enhance the customer list, and believes that this enhanced list will bring it benefits indefinitely. The directors estimate that, at the reporting date, the original list has a fair value of approximately $1.5 million and that the enhanced list has a fair value of approximately $5 million.

Coffee requires advice as to the correct accounting treatment of the customer list.

**(5 marks)**

**Required:**

**Discuss the correct accounting treatment of the above transactions for the year ended 30 September 20X4.**

**Note: the mark allocation is shown against each of the four events above.**

**(Total: 25 marks)**

KAPLAN PUBLISHING

### Test your understanding 7 – Bath

Bath is a public limited company with a reporting date of 30 September 20X4. Its financial statements are prepared in accordance with International Financial Reporting Standards. There are a number of unresolved accounting issues, which are detailed below.

(a) The directors of Bath have identified a number of operating segments. Details of these are provided below:

| | Total revenue $m | External revenue $m | Total assets $m | Profit/ (loss) $m |
|---|---|---|---|---|
| Delivery services | 304 | 281 | 215 | (10) |
| Vehicle hire | 217 | 96 | 94 | 62 |
| Removal services | 51 | 46 | 173 | 14 |
| Vehicle repairs | 22 | 14 | 6 | 8 |
| Road rescue | 15 | 15 | 8 | 3 |
| | 609 | 452 | 496 | 77 |

The segments all earn different gross profit margins and, accordingly, Bath has concluded that they exhibit different economic characteristics.

Bath requires advice as to which of the segments are reportable in its operating segments disclosure note. For this purpose, information provided in parts (b), (c) and (d) should be ignored.

**(7 marks)**

(b) Bath's road rescue division was launched in the current financial year. Customers are charged an annual upfront fee. If the customer's vehicle breaks down during the following 12 months, Bath will send one of its mechanics out to fix or recover it.

The finance director of Bath has noticed that the vast majority of the road rescue customers did not require any breakdown assistance during the year. As such, he is proposing to recognise revenue upon receipt of the annual fee.

**(5 marks)**

(c)   Bath purchased a new office building on 1 October 20W4 for $20 million and this was attributed a useful economic life of 50 years. On 30 September 20X4, the decision was made to sell the office building. At this date, the fair value was $17 million and costs to sell were estimated to be $0.1 million. The building was immediately marketed for sale at $17 million and it was expected that the sale would occur within 12 months.

In October 20X4, interest rates rose dramatically leading to a sharp decline in the property market. At 31 October 20X4, it was estimated that the fair value of the building was $13 million but Bath has not reduced the advertised sales price of the building.

Bath wishes to know the correct accounting treatment of the office building in the period ended 30 September 20X4.

**(6 marks)**

(d)   During the reporting period, Bath purchased an investment in the shares of Bristol for $16 million and made a designation to measure them at fair value through other comprehensive income. Bath received dividends of $3 million during the reporting period. At the reporting date, the quoted price of the shares was $20 million and the present value of the estimated dividends that Bath will receive over the next 5 years was $18 million.

Bath pays income tax at a rate of 25%. The tax base of the investment in shares is based on historical cost. Since there are no plans to sell the shares, Bath believes that it would be misleading to account for any related deferred tax effects.

Bath requires advice about the accounting treatment of the investment in the shares of Bristol for the period ended 30 September 20X4.

**(7 marks)**

**Required:**

**Discuss the correct accounting treatment of the above transactions for the year ended 30 September 20X4.**

**Note: the mark allocation is shown against each of the four events above.**

**(Total: 25 marks)**

## Test your understanding 8 – Integrated Reporting

(a)   It is sometimes claimed that the primary financial statements and disclosure notes do not satisfy the information needs of user groups, particularly shareholders and other providers of financial capital. As a result, many entities now produce an array of non-financial reports. Integrated Reporting <IR>, in particular, has received increased international recognition. The International Integrated Reporting Framework outlines the purpose and proposed content of an Integrated Report. Although optional, it is hoped that the preparation of Integrated Reports by companies will address some of the problems associated with traditional financial reporting.

**Required:**

(i)   **Discuss the limitations of financial reporting.**

(6 marks)

(ii)   **Discuss the purpose and suggested content of an Integrated Report.**

(6 marks)

(iii)   **Discuss the extent to which Integrated Reporting addresses the limitations of traditional financial reporting.**

(5 marks)

(b)   TinCan is a company involved in developing and manufacturing scientific instruments. Its financial statements are prepared in accordance with International Financial Reporting Standards and it has a reporting date of 30 November 20X4. TinCan has a large team of highly qualified research scientists. Employing these motivated and skilled members of staff enables TinCan to produce the most innovative and desirable products on the market, which are sold at high margins. Employee turnover is very low, with few employees leaving to work for its competitors. This is a result of TinCan's flexible working conditions, commitment to staff training, and high rates of pay.

**Required:**

**In relation to the above issue, explain the likely benefits of TinCan producing an Integrated Report.**

(8 marks)

(Total: 25 marks)

## Test your understanding answers

### Test your understanding 1 – Cookie

(a) **Biscuit**

Cookie has recognised a gain on bargain purchase of $5 million ($30m + $45m – $80m) in profit or loss. However, errors have been made.

**Consideration**

IFRS 3 *Business Combinations* states that purchase consideration should be measured at its fair value at the acquisition date. As such, the shares issued by Cookie should have been included in the goodwill calculation at $22.5 million (5m × $4.50). This will increase goodwill and equity. The adjustment is as follows:

| | |
|---|---|
| Dr Profit or loss (to remove gain on bargain purchase) | $5.0m |
| Dr Goodwill | $17.5m |
| Cr Share capital | $5.0m |
| Cr Other components of equity/share premium | $17.5m |

**Brand**

On the acquisition date, Biscuit's identifiable net assets should have been recognised in the consolidated financial statements at fair value. This means that the internally generated brand should have been recognised at $15 million at the acquisition date, reducing goodwill by the same amount. The adjustment required is:

| | |
|---|---|
| Dr Intangible assets | $15m |
| Cr Goodwill | $15m |

The amortisation charge on the intangible asset should be based on its carrying amount in the consolidated financial statements. As such, amortisation must be charged on the fair value uplift of $15 million. This amounts to $3 million ($15/5 years). The adjustment required is:

| | |
|---|---|
| Dr Amortisation expense | $3m |
| Cr Intangible assets | $3m |

Of the $3 million expense, $1.8 million ($3m × 60%) is attributable to the equity owners of Cookie and the remaining $1.2 million is attributable to the non-controlling interest.

The brand has a carrying amount at the reporting date of $12 million ($15m – $3m).

## Impairment

After adjusting for the above, goodwill arising on the acquisition of Biscuit is $2.5 million ($17.5m – $15m). According to IAS 36 *Impairment of Assets*, goodwill must be subject to annual impairment review. An asset is impaired if its carrying amount exceeds its recoverable amount.

Goodwill does not generate independent cash flows so an impairment review is performed on the cash generating unit that it forms a part of. Goodwill arising on the acquisition of Biscuit does not require grossing up for this review because the full goodwill method was used. The impairment calculation is provided below:

|  | $m | $m |
|---|---|---|
| Year-end net assets: | | |
| Share capital | 10 | |
| Retained earnings | 84 | |
| Brand uplift | 15 | |
| Brand amortisation | (3) | |
| | ——— | |
| | | 106.0 |
| Goodwill | | 2.5 |
| | | ——— |
| | | 108.5 |
| Recoverable amount | | (107.0) |
| | | ——— |
| Impairment | | 1.5 |
| | | ——— |

The goodwill impairment of $1.5 million is charged to the statement of profit or loss. The adjustment required is:

| | |
|---|---|
| Dr Profit or loss | $1.5m |
| Cr Goodwill | $1.5m |

Under the full goodwill method, the impairment must be allocated between the group and the NCI based on their shareholdings.

Group share: 60% × $1.5m = $0.9m

NCI share: 40% × $1.5m = $0.6m

Goodwill as at the reporting date is $1 million.

(b) **Specialised plant**

Per IAS 16 *Property, Plant and Equipment* (PPE), items of PPE should be initially recognised at cost. This includes costs directly attributable to getting the asset ready for use. General overheads and training cannot be capitalised and must be written off to profit or loss as incurred. Therefore $4.2m ($3.7m + $0.5m) should be written off to profit or loss.

| | |
|---|---|
| Dr Profit or loss | $4.2m |
| Cr PPE | $4.2m |

Depreciation should start when the PPE is available for use. As a result of the error above, depreciation for the year will be incorrect.

Depreciation charged on this asset is $1.5m ($15m/5 years × 6/12). Depreciation of $1.1 m (($15m – $4.2m)/5 years × 6/12) should have been charged. This means that depreciation in profit or loss must be reduced by $0.4m. The correcting entry is:

| | |
|---|---|
| Dr PPE | $0.4m |
| Cr Profit or loss | $0.4m |

## Test your understanding 2 – Pineapple

(a) **Sale of shares in Satsuma**

Pineapple controlled Satsuma for the first six months of the reporting period. This means that Pineapple should consolidate Satsuma's results for these six months.

The sale of shares results in Pineapple losing control over Satsuma. The net assets, goodwill and non-controlling interest of Satsuma should therefore be derecognised from the consolidated financial statements. A profit on disposal arises for the difference between these amounts and the consideration received from the disposal.

The profit on disposal is calculated as follows:

|  | $000 | $000 | $000 |
|---|---|---|---|
| Proceeds from disposal | | | 5,600 |
| Goodwill at disposal: | | | |
| Consideration | 4,900 | | |
| NCI at acquisition | 1,600 | | |
| FV of net assets at acquisition ($2,000 + $2,045) | (4,045) | | |
| | ——— | | |
| Goodwill at acquisition | 2,455 | | |
| Impairment (40%) | (982) | | |
| | ——— | | |
| | | 1,473 | |
| Net assets at disposal: | | | |
| Share capital | 2,000 | | |
| Retained earnings b/fwd | 2,342 | | |
| Profit to disposal date | 284 | | |
| ($568 × 6/12) | ——— | | |
| | | 4,626 | |
| NCI at disposal: | | | |
| NCI at acquisition | 1,600 | | |
| NCI share of post-acquisition net assets (30% × ($4,626 – $4,045)) | 174 | | |
| NCI share of impairment (30% × $982) | (295) | | |
| | ——— | | |
| | | (1,479) | |
| | | ——— | |
| Carrying amount of sub at disposal | | | (4,620) |
| | | | ——— |
| Profit on disposal | | | 980 |
| | | | ——— |

Satsuma is a discontinued operation in accordance with IFRS 5 *Non-current Assets Held for Sale and Discontinued Operations* because it is an operationally and geographically distinct part of the business that has been sold during the period. As such, a single figure is presented on the face of the statement of profit or loss in respect of Satsuma, which comprises its profit up to the disposal date and the profit on disposal. This 'profit from discontinued operations' is calculated as follows:

|  | $000 |
|---|---|
| Profit to disposal date ($568 × 6/12) | 284 |
| Profit on disposal | 980 |
|  | ———— |
| Profit from discontinued operations | 1,264 |
|  | ———— |

(b) **Financial assets**

According to IAS 32 *Financial Instruments: Presentation*, the loan is a financial asset because Pineapple has a contractual right to receive cash. Pineapple will hold the financial asset to collect the contractual cash flows and so, according to IFRS 9 Financial Instruments, it should be measured at amortised cost.

The financial asset should have been initially recognised at fair value. IFRS 13 *Fair Value Measurement* defines fair value as the price at which an asset would be sold in an orderly transaction between market participants at the measurement date. The price paid of $1,500,000 does not represent the fair value of the asset because market participants (i.e. banks) do not lend money interest-free. The fair value should be calculated as the present value of the future cash flows, discounted using the market rate of interest This amounts to $953,000 ($1,500,000 × (1/1.12$^4$)).

The asset must be written down by $547,000 ($1,500,000 – $953,000), and the loss charged to profit or loss.

| | |
|---|---|
| Dr Profit or loss | $547,000 |
| Cr Financial asset | $547,000 |

For financial assets measured at amortised cost, interest income is calculated using the effective rate. This amounts to $114,000 ($953,000 × 12%). It is recognised in profit or loss and increases the carrying amount of the financial asset.

| | |
|---|---|
| Dr Financial asset | $114,000 |
| Cr Profit or loss | $114,000 |

At the reporting date the financial asset will have a carrying amount of $1,067,000 ($953,000 + $114,000).

## Test your understanding 3 – Vinyl

(a) **Investment in CD**

Goodwill arising on the acquisition of CD is calculated in Marks. IAS 21 *The Effects of Changes in Foreign Exchange Rates* states that it should be treated as an asset of the foreign operation and translated at each reporting date using the closing rate of exchange. Foreign exchange gains or losses arise, which are recorded in other comprehensive income.

The goodwill arising on the acquisition of CD is calculated as follows:

|                                   | MKm   | MKm     |
| --------------------------------- | ----- | ------- |
| Consideration                     |       | 360.0   |
| FV of NCI at acquisition          |       | 90.0    |
| FV of net assets at acquisition:  |       |         |
| Share capital                     | 76    |         |
| Retained earnings                 | 210   |         |
| Brand                             | 10    |         |
|                                   |       | (296.0) |
| Goodwill                          |       | 154.0   |

When translated at the closing rate, goodwill at the reporting date on the consolidated statement of financial position is $90.6 million (MK154/1.7). At the acquisition date it would have been $128.3 million (MK154/1.2). As such an exchange loss of $37.7 million ($128.3 – $90.6m) is recorded in other comprehensive income. This must be split between the group and the non-controlling interest because full goodwill was calculated. The group's share of $28.3 million (75% × $37.7m) is held in a translation reserve in equity. The NCI's share of $9.4 million (25% × $37.7m) is held in the NCI reserve in equity.

A foreign exchange loss also arises on the translation of the opening net assets and profits of CD. This is calculated as follows:

|                        | MKm   | Exchange Rate | $m      |
| ---------------------- | ----- | ------------- | ------- |
| Opening net assets     | 296.0 | 1.2           | 246.7   |
| Profit (275 – 210)     | 65.0  | 1.4           | 46.4    |
| Exchange loss          | –     | Bal. fig.     | (80.7)  |
| Closing net assets     | 361.0 | 1.7           | 212.4   |

The $80.7 million loss is recorded in other comprehensive income. It is split between the group and the NCI based on their respective shareholdings. The group's share of $60.5 million (75% × $80.7m) is held in the translation reserve in equity. The NCI's share of $20.2 million (25% × $80.7m) is recorded in the NCI reserve in equity.

(b) **Convertible bond**

In accordance with IAS 32 *Financial Instruments: Presentation*, the convertible bond should have been split into a liability component and an equity component. The liability component is calculated as the present value of the repayments, discounted using the interest rate on a similar debt instrument without a conversion option. The equity component is the balance of the proceeds.

The repayments are interest of $2m (500,000 × $100 × 4%) per year, plus the repayment of $50m (500,000 × $100) on 30 September 20X7.

| Date | Cash flow | Discount rate | Present value |
|------|-----------|---------------|---------------|
| | $m | | $m |
| 30/9/X5 | 2.0 | $1/1.09$ | 1.8 |
| 30/9/X6 | 2.0 | $1/1.09^2$ | 1.7 |
| 30/9/X7 | 52.0 | $1/1.09^3$ | 40.2 |
| | | | ___ |
| Liability | | | 43.7 |
| | | | ___ |

The liability component should have been initially recognised at $43.7m and the equity component should have been recognised at $6.3m ($50m – $43.7). The following adjustment is therefore required:

| | |
|---|---|
| Dr Non-current liabilities | $6.3m |
| Cr Other components of equity | $6.3m |

## Test your understanding 4 – Frank

### Cash generated from operations

|  | $m |
|---|---|
| Profit before tax | 88 |
| Finance cost | 12 |
| Share of profit of associates | (21) |
| Loss on disposal of PPE ($10 – $12) | 2 |
| Depreciation (W1) | 52 |
| Gain on investment properties (W2) | (8) |
| Impairment of goodwill (W3) | 27 |
| Profit on disposal of subsidiary (W4) | (3) |
| Increase in inventories ($256 – $201) | (55) |
| Reduction in receivables ($219 – $263 + $32) | 12 |
| Increase in payables ($524 – $486 + $55) | 93 |
| | ——— |
| Cash generated from operations | 199 |
| | ——— |

### Workings

#### (W1) Property, plant and equipment

|  | $m |
|---|---|
| Bal b/fwd | 263 |
| Additions | 53 |
| Disposal of PPE | (12) |
| Revaluation of PPE (OCI) | 50 |
| Disposal of subsidiary | (81) |
| Depreciation (bal. fig.) | (52) |
| | ——— |
| Bal c/fwd | 221 |
| | ——— |

#### (W2) Investment properties

|  | $m |
|---|---|
| Bal b/fwd | 60 |
| Additions | 14 |
| Gain in P/L (bal. fig.) | 8 |
| | ——— |
| Bal c/fwd | 82 |
| | ——— |

**(W3) Goodwill**

| | $m |
|---|---:|
| Bal b/fwd | 142 |
| Disposal of subsidiary | (40) |
| Impairment (bal. fig.) | (27) |
| Bal c/fwd | 75 |

**(W4) Disposal of subsidiary**

| | $m | $m |
|---|---:|---:|
| Cash proceeds | | 41 |
| FV of interest retained | | 32 |
| Goodwill at disposal | 40 | |
| Net assets at disposal | 34 | |
| NCI at disposal | (4) | |
| CA of subsidiary at disposal | | (70) |
| Profit on disposal | | 3 |

## Test your understanding 5 – Sunny Days

**(a) Biological assets**

IAS 41 *Agriculture* states that unconditional government grants related to biological assets are recognised in profit or loss when they become receivable. The government grant of $0.2 million will be recognised immediately in profit or loss because it was unconditional.

At the reporting date, biological assets are remeasured to fair value less costs to sell with gains or losses reported in profit or loss. Fair value is defined as the price that would be received from selling an asset in an orderly transaction amongst market participants at the measurement date. Fair value is determined by reference to the principal market or, in the absence of a principal market, the most advantageous market. The most advantageous market is the market which maximizes the net selling price that an entity will receive.

The principal market cannot be determined so the fair value of the biological assets at year end must be determined with reference to the most advantageous market. The net price received in market 1 is $2.49 million ($2.6m – $0.1m – ($2.6m × 0.5%)). The net price received in market 2 is $2.39 million ($2.8m – $0.4m – ($2.8m × 0.5%)). Market 1 is the most advantageous market and should be used to determine fair value.

The fair value of the herd is therefore $2.5 million ($2.6m – $0.1m) and the fair value less costs to sell is $2.49 million (see calculation above). The herd should be recognized at $2.49 million at the reporting date and a gain of $0.39 million (W1) will be recorded in profit or loss.

**Land**

The land is an item of property, plant and equipment. Revaluation losses on property, plant and equipment are recorded in profit or loss unless a revaluation surplus exists for that specific asset.

The revaluation on 30 September 20X3 of $0.2 million ($3.2m – $3.0m) would have been recorded in other comprehensive income and held within a revaluation reserve in equity. The downwards revaluation in the current reporting period is $0.5 million ($3.2m – $2.7m). Of this, $0.2 million will be charged to other comprehensive income and the remaining $0.3 million will be charged to profit or loss.

(W1) **Gain on revaluation of biological assets**

|  | $m |
|---|---|
| Bfd | 1.8 |
| Additions | 0.8 |
| Death and disposal | (0.5) |
| Gain | 0.39 |
| Cfd | 2.49 |

(b) To recognise a provision, IAS 37 *Provisions, Contingent Liabilities and Contingent Assets* says that the following criteria must be satisfied:

– There must be a present obligation from a past event

– There must be a probable outflow of economic benefits

– The costs to settle the obligation must be capable of being estimated reliably.

No provision should be recognised for the $0.8 million costs of compliance because there is no obligation to pay (Sunny Days could simply change the nature of its business activities).

A provision should be made for the $0.1 million fine because there will be a probable outflow of resources from a past obligating event (breaking the law).

The fine is not an allowable expense for tax purposes and so the difference between accounting and tax treatments is not temporary. This means that no deferred tax balance is recognised.

(c) A contract contains a lease if it **'conveys the right to control the use of an identified asset for a period of time in exchange for consideration'** (IFRS 16, para 9).

To assess whether this is the case, IFRS 16 *Leases* requires entities to consider whether the customer has:

- the right to substantially all of the identified asset's economic benefits, and

- the right to direct the identified asset's use.

An asset – Unit 5A – is explicitly identified in the contract. Although Sunny Days can be relocated to a different unit, the supplier is unlikely to benefit from this. Therefore Sunny Days has the right to use an identified asset over the contract term.

Sunny Days has the right to substantially all of the economic benefits resulting from the use of the unit. This is because it has exclusive use of Unit 5A for five years, enabling it to make sales and to generate profits. The payments made to the supplier based on the revenue generated are a form of consideration that is transferred in exchange for the right to use the unit.

Sunny Days has the right to direct the use of the unit because it decides what products are sold, and the price at which they are sold. The restrictions on opening times outlined in the contract define the scope of a Sunny Day's right of use, rather than preventing Sunny Days from directing use. The supplier's provision of security and maintenance services has no impact on how Unit 5A is used.

Based on the above, it would seem that the contract between Sunny Days and its supplier contains a lease.

**Test your understanding 6 – Coffee**

(a) IAS 8 *Accounting Policies, Changes in Accounting Estimates and Errors* says that a prior period error is a misstatement in prior year financial statements resulting from the misuse of information which should have been taken into account. Prior period errors are adjusted for retrospectively, by restating comparative amounts. Changes in accounting estimates are accounted for prospectively by including the impact in profit or loss in the current period and, where relevant, future periods.

**The court case**

This is not a prior period error because Coffee had based its accounting treatment on the best information available. The payment of $2 million will be expensed to profit or loss in the year ended 30 September 20X4.

**Tax**

The mistakes made in the financial statements for the year ended 30 September 20X3 should not have been made based on the information available to Coffee. This therefore satisfies the definition of a prior period error. In the financial statements for the year ended 30 September 20X3 the current tax expense and the income tax payable should both be increased by $1 million.

(b) According to IFRS 9 *Financial Instruments*, an investment in debt should be held at amortised cost if it passes the 'contractual cash flows characteristics' test and if an entity's business model is to hold the asset until maturity. The contractual cash flows characteristics test is passed if the contractual terms of the financial asset give rise on specified dates to cash flows that are solely payments of principal and interest on the principal amount outstanding.

If an entity's business model is to both hold the assets to maturity and to sell the assets, and the asset passes the contractual cash flows characteristics test, then the debt instrument should be measured at fair value through other comprehensive income. All other investments in debt instruments should be measured at fair value through profit or loss.

**Coffee's individual financial statements**

Coffee regularly sells the financial assets, and therefore does not hold them in order to collect the contractual cash flows. In Coffee's individual financial statements, the financial assets should be measured at fair value at the reporting date with any gains or losses reported in profit or loss.